55 YEARS RUNNING

EDWIN OXLADE

ON THE SPORT OF LONG DISTANCE RUNNING

CW01560629

Published in 2013 by Edwin Oxlade
©2013 Edwin Oxlade

ISBN 978-0-9927684-0-9

First Edition
First Impression

Designed by April Sky Design, Newtownards
www.aprilsky.co.uk
Cover artwork by Edwin Oxlade with permission
of Ordnance Survey of Northern Ireland

The author has asserted his right under the Copyright,
Designs and Patents Act, 1988, to be identified as author of this work.

A catalogue record for this book is available from the British Library.

CONTENTS

PREFACE

Most books on running are either biographies or autobiographies of famous runners, or are primarily instructional. This book is neither of those. It's a mixture of things. There is a strong autobiographical theme, of course. No writer picks up a pen without an element of autobiography colouring the ink. I like to think of the book as a personal view of the history of distance running, in particular British distance running, during the course of my lifetime. For most of that time I have been a runner myself; hence the title, 'Fifty five years running'. I still run, although I'm well into my seventh decade. I'm not sure why. I suppose it's just a habit I can't break – that, and because running is the best way I know of raising the twin after-delights of a good shower and a cold beer into the realms of the sublime.

Edwin Oxlade
2013

ACKNOWLEDGEMENTS

I would like to thank all my sources of information and quotes. In particular I am grateful to the editor of Athletics Weekly for permission to reprint passages from the magazine and to the editor of Running Fitness and to his columnist, John Brewer for permission to quote from the Home Brew column. Wherever I have used material in this way I have identified the source in the text.

I owe a huge debt of gratitude to all the runners I have ever run with or competed against, or with whom I have merely shared the running scene over the years. They have been my constant support and inspiration and I dedicate this book to them, making no distinction between those who reached the very top and those who achieved even less than I did. I also thank all those who either never ran themselves or were retired from running but who voluntarily and enthusiastically made the sport possible: the organisers of races, the club officials, the timekeepers, recorders and markers, tea and sandwich makers, sponsors and facilitators. Only now do I appreciate the work done by so many people in the days before running became a multi-million pound business, for no more reward than a delight in the sport of distance running. Everyone who ever ran competitively owes them a lot.

I especially thank my wife, who has put up with my running habit for nearly fifty years, supporting me in hundreds of races and listening, to the point of total saturation, to my geekish views on all aspects of running and my every new training theory. She deserves a rest.

INTRODUCTION

'I shall say, are you ready? And then
– very short and very sharp – Go!'

Somewhat old fashioned and eccentric schoolmaster just about
to start a cross country race between two school teams in rural
Somerset in the seventies.

Where shall I begin? At the end, I think. I am running along the towpath. It is more than fifty years since I first ran in a long distance race. With every stride there is a sharp pain in my knee when my foot strikes the ground. It is the same for both knees. There is a dull ache in my back where the vertebrae fuse with the pelvis. It is worse on one side than the other. I am warmed up now, twenty minutes since I started, but for the first mile of my run I felt as if it would be my last. I am running about three minutes per mile slower than I would have been at my best. Age does that to you.

It occurs to me that my running career, my fifty five years or so as a competitive long distance runner, has mirrored almost exactly the history of distance running in Britain during the same period: a steady improvement in standard, a peak spanning the nineteen sixties and seventies and continuing hesitantly into the eighties, followed by an ever more hastening decline. Such has that decline been in recent years that both I and British distance running as a whole are now at a catastrophic low point.

I have an excuse. I have succumbed to the inevitable effects of advancing years. But what of the sport itself, the tradition of distance running that brought Britain to the top of the world scene on the road, over the country, and on the track for nearly forty years following the end of the second world-war?

If the best fifty or one hundred British distance runners of any year between 1960 and 1980 could miraculously appear, as if time had stood still, and line up against the same number of the best British runners of today, it would be surprising if more than a handful of the latter beat any of the former. This is a strange phenomenon in a sport where, just as in all other sports, standards should be expected always to get better with time. World records have progressed in the manner that records do, like a juggernaut on a downhill gradient, but not so British top-ranked times. There are many runners in the world today who are running faster than anyone did fifty, forty or thirty years ago, but hardly any of them are British. Of the twenty five fastest marathon times ever recorded by British men, sixteen were run prior to 1990 and only one later than 2000 (2:09:17, by Mark Steinle in 2002). The fastest of the lot, the current British record of 2:07:13 by Steve Jones, was run in 1985, and two of those fastest times (Ian Thompson's 2:09:12 and Ron Hill's 2:09:28) have stood since the early seventies.

Performance at the very top is only one measure of the health of a sport, and not a particularly good one at that. Of far more note is the decline in the body of British distance running, the demise of what is referred to as the 'good club runner', and the general lowering of overall standards. So noticeable has this decline become, so undeniably nearly terminal, that it is a phenomenon just begging for some explanation.

I try to understand it myself. My puzzlement over why the running scene in this country was so very different forty or so years ago has been the main stimulus for this book. The real answer probably has very little to do with running; it is more to do with social, commercial and historical factors. So, to make this book a book about running, I have chosen to take a personal view of the running scene I knew and was part of, and to compare it with what I know about the running scene of today.

In case there is any doubt as to what I am talking about, here is one example to help set the scene. Between 1970 and 1985 I competed in the Finchley 20 mile road race on ten occasions. The Finchley 20 is a long-standing road race held each year on the suburban and semi-rural roads of North West London. First run in 1933, it became, like many road races throughout the country, a habitual part of many a serious road runner's calendar, being one of the few twenty milers available and incorporating several county championships. Recently it has become a popular warm up event for runners intending to run in the London Marathon and, perhaps for that reason, it still attracts a large entry. The field is invariably filled to the maximum permitted entry of six hundred (which it was in 2011, when I last ran the race) before the closing date. Superficially, therefore, little about the Finchley 20 has changed since I first ran it: the same popularity, the same course, the same physical activity.

But look at the results of the race year by year and big differences appear. In 1971 I ran my best time, 1:46:41, a time that would have won the race every year, bar one, from 1985 to 2011. But in 1971 it brought me home in only thirteenth place. Twenty seven runners that year completed the course in under 1:50:00 and no less than seventy eight under 2:00:00. Make no mistake, two hours for running a twenty mile road race is a highly respectable time, the sporting equivalent, perhaps, of playing for a premier league football team or for a county cricket team or competing in the Tour de France. No one runs twenty miles in under two hours without a lot of effort, both during the race itself and in the months and years leading up to it. It cannot be done without dedication, lots of training and a degree of adaptation of life style which points to a high level of motivation.

From the sixties up to the early eighties each year something like fifty or more runners always completed the Finchley 20 in under two hours and, usually, at least ten (an amazing forty three in 1972) in under 1:50. In 1983, when I ran the race for the penultimate time as a seriously competitive runner, the first signs of a decline had become noticeable. Over thirty runners still managed to break two hours but only four were under 1:50. Things looked up the following year, mainly because the race incorporated the Inter-Counties Championship. I ran in that race and it was like old times. A respectable 1:48:32 could only bring me home in sixteenth position and, behind me a further sixty three runners broke the two hour barrier. But it was a false dawn, and the decline from then on proceeded apace. 1991 became the first year since 1954 that the race was won in a time slower than 1:50, and, in the subsequent years, there have been more winning times outside this bench-mark than there have been quicker ones. By 2006 the number of finishers under two hours was down to a measly four, a circumstance which, as if to confirm the abject deterioration of the sport, was repeated the following year.

All road races with a long history tell the same story. The parallel in football, for example, would be if only one team in the country was any longer of premiership standard and the rest were all just amateur league. The stuffing has simply gone from the sport of distance running in the UK.

Strangely I do not regret this fact as much as perhaps I should, and I have no urge to be part of any attempt to revive the sport amongst the present and future generations. I do not look for things or persons to blame for the changes in the running scene during my lifetime. Of course I am nostalgic, but my nostalgia is not based on a comparison, however damning it might be, between what has gone and what remains. Even if the depth and standard of running had kept going from strength to strength and were still improving today, my small part in the running scene would still have shrunk into decrepitude and, eventually, vanished altogether. That would be reason enough for any amount of nostalgia.

I don't think an in depth analysis of the causes of the decline in the sport would do anything other than stimulate debate and satisfy idle curiosity. Even if definitive answers could be found it would change little. Knowing the reasons for the decline would not necessarily be a recipe for reversing it.

The sport of distance running has changed drastically in the last thirty years. That is a fact, not a value judgement. Rather than disparage the state of things today and find fault with the present generation of runners, I prefer to remember what it was like when I was young and fit. The world of running in Britain during the glory days of the sixties, seventies and eighties was a phenomenon worth recalling and celebrating, regardless of what became of it. I know. I was there.

Running is, or should be, the simplest sport of all. It may be the oldest. All it took was for one ancient man to invent the concept of a race and, all at once, he turned an activity as natural as eating and sleeping into a sport. This book is not about running *per se*. It is about the sport of running. People will always run; they will run for the sheer joy of it, to get somewhere quickly, to escape something unpleasant or dangerous, as part of some other sport, as healthy exercise or to keep warm on a cold day, but will they continue to engage in running as a sport? Already there are signs that, in this country, and others as well, fewer and fewer young people are participating wholeheartedly in running as sport.

That may seem a ridiculous thing to say in the light of the clamour of thousands of runners for places on the starting line of any big city road race held today. Over one hundred thousand names go into the hat for the London marathon each year alone. To suggest that the sport of running is dying is surely, at the very least, the ranting of someone in severe denial. Not so. I can see, of course, and do not deny, that running has never been more popular, but I also see its sporting context being continuously and rapidly diluted. I do not believe that distance running in this country will ever again reach the heights that it attained as a sport on the world scene during my lifetime, and if I were pushed to predict the future of the sport, I would suggest that in the not too distant future it will be all but extinct as I knew it.

The key to my interpretation of the state of British distance running lies in the very different reasons that there are for running, and in the meaning of the word 'sport'. I may, throughout this book, use the term 'serious' running synonymously with running as a form of sport. Until the end of the seventies that was the only type of organised running that existed. All participants in races, whether road, cross country or track, were serious runners, running for reasons of sport alone. People may also have run for recreation, and for other reasons, but they didn't enter races. So what do I mean by serious running? Why, when I ran races as a twenty, thirty or forty year old was I doing so seriously, while someone today who decides to enter a running event, perhaps to raise funds for charity, and whose aim is no more than to complete the distance and, at most, to meet an easily achieved target is not? The distinction is not one of merit or effort. It hinges on the simple issue of what defines a sport.

The definition of sport has been argued about in relation to numerous activities. Should synchronised swimming, for example, be an Olympic sport, and if so, then why not darts, or snooker, or even chess? When is a sport not a sport but just a game? And when is it recreation, or an art form? And, of crucial relevance here, what makes one person's running sport and another's not?

I believe the answer is quite simple. A sport has to include two vital ingredients. It has to be, rather obviously, competitive, and, secondly, and more importantly, it has to involve extremes of physical activity. Physical activity by itself is not enough. A sport has to test all or some of the body's physical powers to their limits, and the sportsman or woman has to be willing, indeed it has to be his or her paramount purpose, always to strive to extend those limits. Demonstrating acquired physical prowess in competition is the essence of any sport. If you run to your limit in competition, that is sport. If you run in any other way, it probably isn't.

During the last thirty or forty years, the truly serious runners who form the basis of the sport, those who are motivated solely by the philosophy of being prepared to go to almost any lengths to run as fast as they possibly can, have gradually been submerged in a sea of runners of other persuasions. In big road races today, for every serious runner there are now dozens or hundreds who are not participating in the context of running as a sport. Is it any wonder that the real sport is suffering?

As I have got older I have discovered a purpose in running that I share with runners whom I would describe as 'less than serious'. I no longer get much satisfaction from competitive running – from the sport of running – because I am no longer any good at it. So that part of my running has gone. What remains is the ambition to run well. I do not mean to run fast; I've already said that I can't do that. I mean to run fluently, enjoyably, with an almost effortless rhythm and with a sense of perpetual motion. I want to recapture the runner's high to which I was addicted for so many years. To achieve that goal I still have to train, knowing that I cannot aspire to any success in races, but thinking it worthwhile nevertheless. I still enter the occasional marathon and half marathon and am pleased if I can finish without too much discomfort, having run at least parts of it well. I accept that I am likely to be well beaten, even by runners of my own age, and it doesn't bother me. I run as if in a vacuum, and if I feel good, however slowly I'm going, I'm happy.

In a way it's a relief to be rid of the competitive drive of my younger days. Now that it's gone I understand the present day popularity of running. I empathise with the large numbers of new generation runners who enter road races in their thousands and who keep the jogging craze snowballing along. I do more than that. I understand them and I admire them. They are not like the runners I knew in the seventies, but they are no less justifiable. They enjoy their running. They have their own goals and put a lot of time and effort into achieving them. In some ways they are more admirable than serious runners because the majority of them will never achieve as much in competitive terms. What they don't do, anymore than I do now, is contribute anything to the strength of the sport of running.

Perhaps it's not possible for recreational running, the sort that I'm now content with, and serious competitive running to thrive side by side. Each feeds off the same sources as the other. I know for sure that they can't both be catered for by the same big races. If one is going to win out over the other in this country, it looks as if it will be the less serious of the two. I don't mind. In a way it's nice to look back at something that will probably never come again. As to what that was, I'll try to recount it in the following chapters.

CHAPTER 1
The start

'I always loved running – it was something you could do by yourself and under your own power. You could go in any direction, fast or slow as you wanted, fighting the wind if you felt like it, seeking out new sights just on the strength of your feet and the courage of your lungs.'

Jesse Owens

For me it started in 1952 by the side of a suburban tree lined road in Ruislip, Middlesex. Coincidentally it could be said that the glory days of British distance running started at more or less the same time.

My family lived in Eastcote, just one stop on the London Metropolitan underground line from Ruislip Manor, where I was born, two stops from Ruislip itself. My father took me to see the Finchley 20 road race, in which the famous Jim Peters was running. I was still only five years of age, not old enough to understand the significance of the event, nor really what it was at all. But from how my father behaved and from what he told me and from the tone of his voice and his obvious enthusiasm, subdued though it was, I knew that something important was up. I knew, even before we left the house, in the same way that today my dogs know when I put on a coat and wellington boots that they are going to enjoy themselves, exciting things were about to happen .

We walked, of course. Very few families had a car in 1952 and we were certainly not one of them. The nearest part of the course, along Bury Street on the outskirts of Ruislip, was just over two miles from our home and it was a dry day. I know that, because I don't remember getting wet but, as to the rest of the weather, I have no idea. I think, or like to think, that it was a pleasant warm day. Just as I don't remember getting wet I don't remember getting cold or having to put on anything more than my normal outdoor clothing. The Finchley 20 is held in the spring. In those days it was usually in April though now it has been brought forward to March in order to make it a good warm up race for people running the London marathon. No one wants to run a twenty miler followed by a marathon without a good few weeks in between.

I associate the Finchley 20 with the peak of the cherry blossom. The roads of that area of London are lined with trees and a large number of them are flowering cherries. As my father and I walked up Abbotsbury Gardens, where we lived, towards Eastcote shops and on down to old Eastcote village we would have passed masses of trees in blossom, both pink and white flowered. Some of those same trees are still there. Even now, when I travel along tree-lined suburban roads of any major town or city, flanked by pavements and grass verges, hedges and front gardens, I want to be running along them, through a scattering of flower petals in the spring or dead leaves in the autumn. In over fifty years of running I must have covered thousands of miles of such roads, mainly in training, usually after dark, my way lit by a street light every fifty yards or so. I often did measured interval runs using the street lamps as markers. In 1952 some of those street lamps in the London suburbs were still lit by gas.

When the Olympics were held in London in 1948, the marathon course came through Eastcote village, very close to where the Finchley 20 is still run. Today there is a small glass-fronted display board sited on a patch of grass between the road along which the Olympic marathon came and the river Pinn, where I used to catch sticklebacks as a child. It gives details of the race and marks the fact that it came that way. The event was won by the Argentinian Delfo Cabrera in 2:34:52, with Tom Richards of Great Britain second in 2:35:08. Tom Richards won the Finchley 20 on eight occasions between 1941 and 1949 (he missed out to Jack Holden in 1947) and it could be argued that he, or Holden, who won the AAA championship marathon four years running between 1947 and 1950, rather than Jim Peters, led the post war charge in British long distance running. When you consider, however, the leap that Jim Peters made between the year of the London Olympics (which he didn't himself run) and the year that my father took me to see him running in Ruislip, and the even more colossal leap he made in the following few years, he becomes, without a doubt in my mind, the pre-eminent, ground-breaking figure who initiated nearly thirty years of British dominance in distance running. By 1952, a mere four years after the Olympic marathon, Peters had set a world best for the marathon distance of more than ten minutes quicker than Cabrera's winning Olympic time. In the space of two years between June 1952 and June 1954 he improved the British marathon best by over thirteen minutes and the world best by nearly eight minutes. No one, before or since, has made such an impact on marathon running.

Peters won the Finchley 20 the day my father took me to see him running. I remember standing at the kerbside as he came by, appearing to be leaning slightly in my direction, and so close I could have reached out and touched him. Then, I suppose, other runners passed me, and then again on the second, third and fourth laps of the race. But it was Jim Peters I remember, going by for the first time. He had striking dark hair, cut in the obligatory short back and sides of the time, leaving a mop of straight hair on top to bounce slightly as he ran. So this was what I had come to see. It must have left an impression. Why else would I remember it after over sixty years, when so little of my life at that time, even of that particular day, still remains clear in my memory?

It would be fanciful to suggest that seeing Jim Peters running the Finchley 20 ignited my future interest in running. Even without that experience I have no doubt I would have become a runner. Two things made my future participation in the sport practically inevitable. Firstly, I enjoyed running and, secondly, I was quite good at it. When I say I enjoyed it, I mean that to me it was the most natural, the most exhilarating, most satisfying mode of progression. It was enjoyable for its own sake, with the same rewards, both physical and mental, as dancing, or gymnastics, or swimming, or any other physical activity in which the body moves smoothly, rhythmically and efficiently, with all the life enhancing feedback of a finely evolved biomechanical system.

I didn't need anyone to run with or against. I just ran, and I loved it. Running was quick (I am an impatient person) and felt good. Why would I walk when I could run? I ran to school and I ran home. I ran in the school playground at break time. I ran in the school corridors and was shouted at for doing so. In the summer I ran to the park to play football with my friends and stayed until nearly bedtime. Then I ran home.

I was not unusual in this. Most children when I was growing up did a lot of running about. We were skinny, independent, over-excited, always hungry, but always full of energy. We were by preference outdoor people. If running as a sport has changed in the last thirty years or so, maybe it has something to do with the evolving lifestyle of children of primary school age. It never occurred to us that running could be a serious sporting activity, nor, not for one fraction of a second, that it might ever be hard. It was just the way we moved when we wanted to get from one place to another as quickly as possible, and it was as natural as breathing.

I first came to the conclusion that I was quite good at running when I was about nine or ten. At that age the longest distance which we were officially allowed to run in any way competitively was seventy five yards. At the primary school there were standards for four athletic events: long jump, high jump, throwing the cricket ball and seventy five yard run. I always managed to achieve the standard for my age for the run, though I was never one of the fastest boys. At the same time I instinctively knew that had there been a longer run I would have done relatively better. The further I ran the easier it seemed to get.

The seventy five yard event was a sprint. We ran it as fast as we possibly could, to the point where the muscles and the joints and the nerves to the legs couldn't keep up with the brain, and co-ordination was in danger of being lost. And, since co-ordination is so much a part of running, you could say that running fast, i.e. sprinting, is the true test of a runner, even a distance runner. In a perverse way, if you can't run fast then you can't run slowly. And, because I could run seventy five yards fast for my age, that, together with my natural inclination, pointed to my being able to become a good distance runner.

Then I had my first taste of competition over a long distance. It was a very informal affair, not a race nor a time trial but, nevertheless, a chance to run against other boys. A colleague of my father ran a club for boys from the more deprived areas of London and regularly took them on camping trips. They stayed in an old bus that had long since lost all power of movement. Fixed permanently on a riverside site it had been converted into caravan type accommodation with sleeping space for about eight people. The river was the Thame in Buckinghamshire.

I was on a day visit, a day that coincided with the boys catching crayfish in the morning and taking part in a paper chase in the afternoon. I must have been the youngest there, still in short trousers, my standard school wear. Short trousers on any boy might look ridiculous today, but they were perfectly normal for a pre-teenage boy in the nineteen fifties. I wore sandals, short socks, a vest and a white shirt. I may have been wearing braces. I forget.

It was the paper chase that gave me my first taste of running for a long way in a competitive context. Running as a sport is nothing if it is not competitive. I would never have taken it up seriously and devoted hours of my life to pursuing improvement if I had not been competitive. All runners would say the same thing, assuming that they used the term competitive in the way that I am using it here.

As to what the meaning of the word is, I discovered it during that scramble across fields, gates and hedges, along footpaths and short stretches of country lanes, pursuing an unseen hare who had left a trail of torn-up paper to follow. I soon parted company with the rest of the hounds, some in front of me and some behind, and when I stopped to get my bearings, alone in the middle of the English countryside, hot and breathing deeply, nettle-stung and bramble-scratched, my shirt sticking to me with sweat and my socks stuck through with irritating pieces of grass, I understood that running could be more than a way of getting somewhere and more than an enjoyable physical experience.

Running could be a way of feeling good about myself in the presence of others. In short, running could be competitive. Here I was, ahead of boys two or three years older than me, behind others admittedly, but not disgracefully nor irretrievably so, and seeming to run better and better the further we went.

I suppose at that moment, as I took a breather in a Buckinghamshire field I knew what it was to be motivated, not just by the feel-good factor that comes with running, but with the satisfaction of doing well. And the fact that one is doing well can only be realised by comparison with the performance of others. For years I had enjoyed running, felt that, for me, it was easy, and wanted to do more of it, but here, for the first time, I had some measure of how well I could run. It was the achievement of doing well that became my motivation, then and for years afterwards, as it still is today.

Nearly sixty years after that day, as if in a long delayed echo of the sentiments I experienced during and after my first competitive cross country run, I read more or less the same idea advanced by one of the greatest distance runners of modern times. Talking of his first race, a 1,500m race, which he ran in 1980 at the age of seven, Haile Gebrselassie, Ethiopian running super-star and one time world marathon record holder, recounts that, after he had won the race, *'The head teacher called me up on stage for prize-giving and I became very famous locally. One moral I understand about sport is that finding a talent you can earn respect for is worth more than anything. It encouraged me, it brought me up from zero.'*

I am trying in this chapter to understand the reasons that throughout my life I devoted so much of my time and energy to the sport of distance running, and, by implication, the reasons why anyone else might also do so. It is, after all, a sport which is not obviously very exciting nor, to the casual observer, very enjoyable, either for spectator or participant. The men's English National Cross Country Championship was once described by a journalist reporting on the race for a major Sunday paper as *'the greatest sporting bore'*. He should have known better. It was an extremely ignorant (in the Northern Irish sense of the word) thing to say about a sport to anyone who didn't share his opinion, and, presumably, most of those who wished to read a report of a cross country running event were not of the same mind. I wondered at the time whether that same Sunday newspaper would have given me a job as an opera or ballet correspondent if I had first admitted that neither art form did anything for me. I don't think so. But they allowed a man who found cross country running boring to write about it.

I have always loved running as a sport and watching running events, and found running, not just interesting, but addictively compelling. Even at primary school I was instantly excited by the story of Guto Nyth Bran, the legendary Welsh runner from the eighteenth century, whose life is now commemorated by the Nos Galan road race held each year in Mountain Ash on New Year's eve. After a lifetime of being actively involved in the sport I find no better explanation for my devotion to it than the three things I've already mentioned. I enjoyed running; I was good at it; and now, during a paper chase in the Buckingham countryside, I found that it fulfilled a need, that some might even say amounted to a personality defect, for achievement and approbation.

Doing well at anything, including running, is not the same as being better than other people, and competition, in the sense I am using the word, is not simply about beating or trying to beat others. I always knew that. If you can find someone who's bad enough it's very easy to beat them. If you want to beat a slow runner you don't have to run fast or hard to do so. Conversely, if you run against someone who is considerably better than you, you will be beaten. It doesn't follow that you have not run well. Doing well is relative only to one's own performance. In a sense, in any race there is only one competitor that matters and that is oneself. That is why I have never gone along with the adage 'winning is everything'. Winning is nothing compared with doing as well as you possibly can, striving to achieve higher and higher standards and sometimes surprising yourself with how well you have done. That is what competition is. It's a highly individual and introverted thing. It relates to your own performance and to no one else's.

The irony is that although, at least in my view, competition need only involve one runner, there have to be others for it to be recognised. How well you can run will always be a secret to yourself, and to everyone else as well, until you run against others. For all I knew, the ease with which I ran was common to all boys of my age and, while, of course, I had some inkling that some children could run better than others, I had never put it to the test over anything more than a very short distance. It was a revelation, therefore, to discover that my enjoyment of running and the way running came easily to me were things that I didn't necessarily share, and were even things that could enable me to stand out from the crowd.

That is one aspect of competitiveness, the urge to be as good as possible at something, measured by comparison with your peers. But it is not the whole story. There is a related but less compelling and less savoury side to competition that I was aware of from a very early age. It has something to do with wanting to get the better of other people, an instinct we are all born with. It is what makes us love challenges and games of chance. It is also what motivates people to cheat. When any of my friends and I started the long walk down to the corner shop to buy some sweets or a comic it was just a matter of who would be the first to lose patience and set off at a run with the cry, 'Race you!' But this was never a serious attempt to get to the shop first. The outcome of the race was not important and the one who was ahead as the shop approached usually gave in anyway and let the others catch up. I don't think we were ever really competing against each other, just playing out the idea of competing, just as we had mock fights and regularly shot each other dead with toy guns. The main thing was to steal a march on the others, not to run as fast as we possibly could in a serious attempt to beat them.

I was one of those who learned to channel his natural, childlike competitiveness into the pursuit of achievement. In my case it was running. Other people choose other sports, or music, or art, or business or whatever, but, without that determination to become good at something, no one would bother. Inevitably, as one person strives to be better and better at something, others become relatively worse. That is the politically incorrect aspect of competition. It seems so unfair. But, if you want progress you can't do without competition. Or, if, on the other hand, you believe in the socialist ideal of unadulterated equality, competition simply cannot be allowed, and the result will be stagnation.

Thankfully, when I was at school, children were encouraged to compete. Elitism thrived. It was recognised that no system could get better unless individuals within it got better, and were allowed to do so in competition with others, just as a wall cannot get higher unless some bricks are placed on top of others. I can't help feeling that the decline in British distance running as a highly competitive individual sport had something to do with the left wing philosophy of equality that came to prominence in this country in the late twentieth century and with it the vilification of the concept of anyone being better than anyone else at anything. At the height of equality madness in some cases school children were not allowed to compete in races in case they were beaten. Competitive school sports were stopped and the results of football matches were omitted from newspapers if the score was too one-sided. For all I know this nonsense still goes on. Perhaps one day we'll realise again that it's no good pretending that everyone wins prizes.

In any case, the thinking behind protecting children from being shown up as slower or weaker or less able is highly dubious. Much of my motivation as a child came from the fact that I was the youngest of four children and small for my age and was therefore usually the slowest and weakest of any group I played in. Far from being permanently traumatised by a succession of beatings in games and competitions I became even more determined to succeed. I would go as far as to say that lack of accomplishment in my early years, rather than the opposite, was the making of me. Failure can often be as great a spur as success; ask Robert the Bruce.

Given an amount of natural ability, competitive distance running is all about motivation, about wanting to improve and reach some sort of ultimate attainable level of performance, and having the will power to stick to the task of getting there. I think I realised as a ten year old that I was highly motivated. Later I discovered that other runners were equally highly motivated and others still, judging by their determination and willingness to stick to immensely rigorous training regimes, were far more so. This shared motivation was what held the running fraternity so closely together in the peak years of British distance running and what has been so sadly diluted in recent times.

There are two types of motivation, extrinsic and intrinsic. People can do dead-end jobs purely out of necessity, their only motivation being the extrinsic type, their pay packet at the end of the week. I suppose a good runner could come from the same sort of approach, training done as a job of work, unwillingly and with no sense of enjoyment but, certainly in the nineteen fifties, and for many years afterwards, there was no prospect of any payment for running. The closest that some runners might have got to being primarily extrinsically motivated was through having a strong minded coach who took on the dual role of both motivator and enforcer. There was always the suspicion that in some less liberal countries the state took on the task of producing good runners, supporting them and giving them all the motivation they needed, even if that should be the worst sort of coercion. Vladimir Kutz, the Russian hero of the 1956 Melbourne Olympic Games, was a perfect example of a runner who was suspected, simply because of his country of origin, of being made rather than self motivated. At the height of the cold war he emerged in Melbourne to win both the 5,000m and the 10,000m with a metronomic display of front running that seemed to reflect his military background (he was in the Russian navy) and the ethos of the state that produced him.

But here in Britain we relied almost entirely on intrinsic motivation. When Chris Chataway, in 1954, beat Kutz by a chest, at the White City, setting a world record of 13:56 for 5,000m in the process, it was much more than a middle distance running race. It was a clash of two cultures and a triumph of intrinsic, unpaid, unsupported, individualistic endeavour over state manufacture and sponsorship; the true amateur from the free world conquering the communist professional. That was how it was seen, anyway. The truth, of course, was probably somewhere in between and, most likely, there was very little difference in the motivation that created Kutz on the one hand and Chataway on the other, or Kutz's other famous British rival, Gordon Pirie. A man can be made to run and train hard day after day but he cannot be forced to give every last drop of energy and resolve or, in vulgar terms, to spill his guts in competition. When he is alone, out on the track or on the road or in a cross country race, it has to come from within.

My motivation was always solely intrinsic, a driving desire to be as good as I could, by myself and purely for my own satisfaction. I suspect that in that respect I was like most of my contemporaries. If I have any regrets about my running career, one is that I never had any motivation other than what could be summoned up from my own psychological reserves. Like most of the runners of my generation I had no coach to exhort me. There were no prizes of any significance to make material gain a realistic source of motivation. I had no pushy parent, pushy brother or sister or pushy friend. At school no teacher took any active role in either cross country running or athletics. We, the boys who took part in running events, managed entirely by ourselves, progressing on our own initiative from a very unpromising foundation of ignorance and trial and error. It's a wonder we got where we did. There was another boy from my school, running in the same races as me, who eventually ran internationally. He was tall, with sandy hair, a year younger than me. I usually, but not always, beat him at that time, but he went on to become a much better runner than I ever was. He ran cross country for Scotland and once finished third in the senior English National Cross Country Championship. As far as I know he had no more help with his running at school than I or any of the other boys did.

Perhaps that's exactly how I liked it. If you achieve something entirely alone it not only gives you a greater sense of fulfilment but it satisfies the selfish need not to have to share. Achievement is what it's all about. The quest for achievement and the recognition of that achievement is at the root of a runner's motivation. Psychologists call it simply, 'need for achievement'.

You might think that at least some of my motivation came from hero worship and the desire to imitate inspiring role models. I have already mentioned seeing Jim Peters, a runner whom I still regard as the seminal figure in the history of marathon running, when I was five years old. On Thursday 6th May 1954, when I was seven, Roger Bannister became the first man to break the four minute mile barrier for one mile. Three months later, at the Vancouver Empire Games, he won what became known, somewhat prematurely perhaps, with another forty six years still to go, as the 'mile of the century', beating John Landy of Australia, the second man to break the four minute mile barrier. This was the same year that Chris Chataway became the first BBC Sportsview Personality of the Year. A year later it was Gordon Pirie's turn to win the same award. Chris Brasher won the Olympic gold medal in the 3,000m steeplechase in Melbourne in 1956 and, at the same games, Derek Ibbotson won a bronze medal in the 5,000m. The following year Ibbotson set a new world record for the mile of 3:57.2.

In international cross country running during the decade of the 1950s England was consistently dominant, winning the team title six times and never out of the top three team places. The outstanding English runner was Frank Sando, who was individual winner of the international event in 1955 and 1957, and a silver or bronze medal winner in 1953, 56, 58 and 59. Sando also ran in the 10,000m at both the 1952 Helsinki and the 1956 Melbourne Olympics, finishing fifth and tenth respectively. England provided three other individual winners of the international cross country event in the fifties: G. B. Saunders in 1951, Stan Eldon in 1958 and Fred Norris in 1959.

All this goes to show that these were heady years for British middle and long distance running. I should not have had to look hard, nor far, for motivation and for idols to worship. I entered the fifties as a three year old and exited as a first year teenager. Surely some of the glamour of British distance running at this time must have attached itself to me, even if only by an imperceptible form of osmosis. The fact that the first two BBC Sportsview personalities were runners was a measure of the status that running achieved in the public eye at the time.

The truth is, however, that I was aware of virtually none of it. When my father took me to see the Finchley 20 in 1954 I was too young for it to mean anything more than being an event of reflected significance. I knew it was exciting and important, but I didn't know why. When Chris Chataway was voted the first BBC Sportsview personality in 1954, and Gordon Pirie the next, my only experience of television was a rare visit to a friend's house to watch the Cisco Kid and his partner Pancho on a tiny screen that quivered and sparkled like a snow storm. There was no television in our house until 1963. If I had any source of motivation for running before I became a teenager, other than my congenital inclination, it didn't come from anywhere outside my own limited experience. I only learned of the great British running feats and personalities of the nineteen fifties when the decade was well and truly over.

Perhaps I had one running hero as a child, my eldest brother Colin, ten years older than me and the only person I knew who ran competitively. I remember seeing him run the so called 'field race' at his school sports day. As with my experience of watching Jim Peters, despite my very young age, seven at most, I knew I liked what I saw. It gave me a buzz, and an urge, one day, to do it myself. At one point in the race the boys crossed the River Colne, a not insignificant stretch of water, waist-deep and at least ten feet wide. That was particularly exciting for me, standing with my mother in the long grass on the river bank, waiting for Colin's turn to plunge into the water and wade his way to the other side. Today, of course, no school would dare let its pupils do anything quite so dangerous. By the time I joined the school the field race was a thing of the past.

I am leading to the view that my lifetime indulgence in running was inevitable. It was inborn. This is not such a fanciful idea. The tendency to run and the enjoyment of running must be in our genes, just as the inclination to chase and to hunt is in a dog's genes and the desire to soar through the air and stoop on its prey is in a falcon's genes. My love of running was as natural as every other part of me. All it needed was its combination with my exaggeratedly competitive nature and desperate need for success and recognition, and my future as a competitive runner became set in stone.

I have found it hard to separate the factors that contributed to the motivation that set me on a career as a runner. I find it even harder to detect any change in those factors over the course of my running lifetime. Yet there has been some change. As I mentioned in the introduction, I do not run now, in my sixties, for quite the same reasons as when I was much younger. That's probably because I don't get the same things out of running. I have running friends who, having retired from a successful running career, full of achievement at the highest level, continue to train but not to race. At first I couldn't understand what seemed to me to be a pointless waste of effort. Note that I said train rather than run. To continue to run is eminently sensible for enjoyment, for health benefits and for general well being, but training is something else. It can be hard. It requires some commitment and a lot more effort than just going for a run, and it involves more time than just running.

Then, when I became too old for serious competition, I understood. I still needed the challenge of a goal in the form of a race, maybe just one a year, to use as a yardstick and to force me to train, but I learned that the sort of fitness that can only come from serious training can become a goal in itself. No one else need know about it. It is intrinsic motivation in its purest form. If you can sit in front of the TV feeling as totally relaxed as anyone possibly can, with your heart ticking over at a phenomenally low rate and your limbs feeling empty of anything but incipient power, your brain alert and your breathing almost nonexistent, knowing that only proper training can have brought you to that condition, then you too will understand. Running can keep you fit but only training that involves both long runs and hard runs can bring you to such a state of physical nirvana.

Nevertheless, motivation for me, at the start, depended on dreams of competitive success. My paper chase through the Thame valley was my first taste of success at running in any form. I had run further, possibly, than ever before. It had felt good and it still felt good afterwards. I had held my own against other boys, mostly older than me, and, best of all it had been noticed. I don't remember what, if anything was said to me. It didn't matter. It was enough to know that my running well must have been evident. I had become, in an afternoon, an addict to running success, willing to go to great lengths in future years for my regular fix, always looking for a larger and sweeter dose.

In 1957 I took the eleven plus exam and left primary education. My move to secondary school saw the allowed distances for races increase to a maximum of 440 yards for my age group, the under-thirteens. Because I was young for my year I had two chances at the under thirteen races. Like the standards we had had at primary school we had four events to compete in: high jump, long jump, 100 yards and 440 yards. In my first year a boy called Paul Thomas won all four events. His initials were P.A.P. so, naturally, he was called Pap Thomas. He was a gifted sportsman but, more to the point, he was advanced for his age and I had my first lesson on the unfairness of sport, especially in the younger age groups. I was reminded of this many years later when I went to Gateshead to run in a big cross country event and, with a friend from my club, was watching the youths' race. A line of boys of all stages of development passed by, some no more than scrawny children, like new born foals, with less flesh on them than they seemed to need simply to stand up, others twice as tall and well built. Then along came a 'boy' who had more hair on his legs than I had on my whole body. And what legs! More like a weightlifter's than a runner's. 'There's always a honey monster', said my friend.

The fact is that performance at a young age is more or less meaningless and an aspiring runner has to live through this period of imbalance and emerge with his or her motivation and ambition intact. It is probably more difficult for the 'advanced for their age' runners than for the likes of me, the late developers. At least we find ourselves getting relatively better with increasing age.

Development was on my side in my second year as an under-thirteen year old since I was, by then, very nearly thirteen and, therefore, one of the oldest in the age group. I managed to win both the 100 yards (13.8s) and the 440 yards (73s). The father of the boy who came second in the 100 yards took a picture of the finish of the race. That, in itself was unusual at the time as cameras were like so many things we now take for granted, by no means the automatic possession of everyone. That photo had a profound effect on me. There I was, mouth full open, one arm flung wildly to the side as if catching a ball over my shoulder, the other still roughly in a running position, both feet well off the ground and my crop of straight hair, above the short back and sides, (reminiscent of Jim Peters) flying like a small dark flag. I had never before been caught in the act of doing anything remotely impressive, only posing for a school photograph, playing on the beach with my brother, sitting glumly at my sister's wedding, but never in action. The picture was special because it was a recording of something that I had done that meant a lot to me and, just as people say of a gold medal, 'you can't take it away', neither can you take away a recording, not even a small, faded, black and white photograph.

Nor can you take away a name engraved on a cup or printed in the school magazine. My name is still there, in both those places. I can show you the relevant report of the school sports day in the July 1959, edition of the school magazine and somewhere, in one of the cupboards, display cases or storerooms of my old school are the two cups that I won and, on them, amongst all the other winners of the events over the years, my name, engraved in the worn silver plate.

One of my great regrets, looking back on a life of running, is that I have never seen myself running. I have plenty of still photographs and I believe there is some film footage of races that I competed in, hidden away somewhere in other people's archives, but I have never seen it. The age of the instant movie, of YouTube and pocket sized digital film recorders had not arrived when I was active. Sometimes, when I am watching a race on television, especially an élite women's race, and being impressed by how good the runners look and how fast they seem to be going, I suddenly realise that they are running no better and travelling no faster than I would have been at the high points of my career. It sounds pathetically self indulgent and narcissistic, but I long with a pang of real remorse for some such recording of my own running. It would be more valuable to me than any amount of money prizes.

The remarkable thing is that all these and other similar, seemingly rather trifling tokens of success at running, or any sport, or any other field of endeavour for that matter: a name or a report in a newspaper, a result, written down or announced, a cup or a medal or a prize, a photo or piece of film, just a mention in a conversation, are the be-all and end-all of what motivates a runner. It all boils down to evidence of success, and praise for something you have done. What else is there? I think I learned as much in 1959, when I won my first two running races. I instinctively knew that I could expect no more reward, however good I might one day be. At the same time I couldn't deny the motivating power of such insignificant symbols of achievement. They were quite enough by themselves to set me on a life of striving to become a better runner. They amounted to the one thing we all crave – recognition; and recognition is the first step towards fame, another thing that has absolutely no value but which can motivate people to go to the ends of the earth, do the most extraordinary things or suffer the worst pain and indignities.

You may think that it cannot be true that such small things can be sufficient reward to initiate the years of hard work and dedication needed to be a good runner. In a way you would be right but, then again, you would be wrong. It is not the things themselves that motivate, it is the fact that they are an indication that your achievement has been noted. These small things are evidence of an audience.

I often ask myself why I did it. Why did I do the running that I did, running that at my peak occupied me for at least ten hours every week, that was often hard and could at times and in some ways be unpleasant, that moved me over hundreds of miles without getting me any further than where I started, that cost me I dread to think how much money, that gave me guilt complexes, physical injuries and periods of self doubt, depression and anguish, and left me ultimately questioning whether I did myself justice? Then I think of all the other runners I have known and how much more dedicated many of them were compared with me and I have to ask why they did what they did. There is only one answer. We were all motivated by an obsessive craving for achievement and for the recognition of that achievement.

None of us would have strived as we did, I am quite sure, had we lived on a desert island, cut off from the running scene, indeed from anyone who could witness our running. Motivation needs to feed off something and, in my peak years as a runner, when competitive British distance running was buzzing like it has never buzzed since, there was an air of shared motivation which fed off itself. Each of us was highly motivated because we were all highly motivated. Every runner was part of a shared environment of competitions and performances and results and tales of successes, training and feats of endurance. Every individual performance motivated every other runner to try that little bit harder. In that sort of climate it was easy to convince oneself that what to any normal person might have seemed a form of madness – such hard work for such little reward – was worth every moment.

At the age of thirteen I didn't know that I would one day embrace this philosophy completely but I had learned what it was that was to motivate me from then on and I had already made an irreversible if latent commitment to the running habit.

CHAPTER 2
The teenage years. 1959 - 1966

'Growth is a greater mystery than death....not even the successful man can begin to describe the impalpable elations and apprehensions of growth.'

Norman Mailer

Sometime in the last days of the nineteen fifties my genitalia expanded, my voice broke (so I'm told), hair started to sprout from various parts of my body and my running went to pot. It was touch and go whether I would keep any attachment to the sport at all. The main reason for this, apart from the effects of the physical changes, the tiredness, the inability of some of my bodily systems to keep up with the growth of others, and the loss of my previous youthful enthusiasm was that the school I attended did its very best to kill any enjoyment I may have had in running.

As a new recruit to the teenage years there were only two sports that I was allowed to participate in on games afternoons, rugby in the winter and cricket in the summer. In the spring we had athletics sports day and for a few hours, usually on a cold March afternoon, we raced on a soggy cinder track or, if it was too wet, a hastily laid out grass track on the windswept playing fields. That's where I won the under thirteen 100 yards and the 440 yards. But it was only one day in the whole year, with maybe the odd evening for qualifying heats.

I was still too young for cross country running, a privilege only allowed at that stage of my school career to senior boys. Summer athletics, with matches against other schools and the chance to run distances of up to one mile, was also only for the older boys. But I did do a bit of running, unwillingly and with no pleasure. It seemed at the time almost like a punishment, not for anything I or any of the other boys had done, but to atone for particularly bad weather. It was a sort of human sacrifice, the well-being of the boys sacrificed to appease the weather gods.

When rain or snow or frost made the rugby pitches unplayable, games were cancelled and the boys assembled after lunch in the classroom of their house master for a house run. Dress was not optional. It was standard P.E. kit, i.e. white T shirt, blue shorts, white socks and plimsolls. Anyone wearing anything more would be told sharply to take it off. Having come more or less straight from lunch, where the object of the exercise for most of us, certainly for me, was to eat as much food as possible and, by hook or by crook to scrounge seconds and to sit near anyone who didn't like sausages or who had a reputation for not eating their pudding, most of my blood was circulating too close to my digestive system for ease of movement.

We would sit shivering in the unheated classroom waiting for the house master to send us on our way. I would be feeling lethargic, yawning, and dreaming of a warm bed where I could sleep off the excesses of the dining hall. Then, just as I began to think I couldn't get any colder we were released into the outside. It could have been raining hard, icy, blowing a gale, or even snowing. It was always cold and it was a toss-up which would be worse, to run and get a bit warmer or to walk the whole way and stay frozen. I usually did a bit of both. And I always got a stitch.

What I never managed to do was to run as I had as a child, willingly, with pleasure and with feelings of well-being. It was several years more before I could recapture my enjoyment of running for its own sake. The course for our house runs was only about two miles but it was two miles of extreme discomfort. As an exercise in aversion therapy it nearly worked. It almost put me off running for life, but ultimately it failed. Perhaps, because I didn't try to run properly, I never associated the misery of those runs with the sport that was to occupy so much of my adult life. So I never blamed the running itself for my discomfort. It was not running in the name of sport; it was running as purgatory. And, because I never chose to do house runs - the matter of choice didn't come into it - I could always blame someone or something else.

Despite not enjoying the running that I actually did during this time, I managed to retain my enthusiasm for the idea of running, if not for the practical side. Equally surprisingly, I never lost my ambition one day to be a good runner. But I did very little voluntary running except as part of other sports. I didn't compete more than once or twice a year and then only up to a quarter of a mile, and I certainly didn't train. I didn't even know what training was.

Looking back I think this was a good thing. Early adolescence is no time to be taking anything seriously, least of all something as physical and as competitive as running. Early success often leads to later disappointment while early disappointment can stifle dreams for the future. Either way a potential career as a runner can end before it's begun. I would have been a good candidate for early disappointment if I had entered into competition. I stayed more or less the same size while boys of my own age sprouted out in all directions. I was sure, sometimes, as I looked across the classroom, that I could see them growing as they sat in their desks. Very quickly they could outrun me at every distance just because they were bigger.

Besides which, as the body struggles to develop, as even mine did eventually, it has enough work to do without being encouraged to adapt to any sort of training. I doubt if training can ever harm the developing young person, but it does seem premature to try to hone the body before it's fully grown, rather like painting wood before it has first been shaped and sanded smooth. I almost instinctively knew that my teenage years were not the time to be taking running seriously and I have never regretted that for three or four years I did so little.

I had no idea what was going on in running circles outside my own small world. It was only a long time after the event, for example, that the Rome Olympics in 1960, held when I was just fourteen, exerted any influence on me. Two races from those games particularly inspired me in years to come, though at the time I don't think I was even very much aware that the Olympic Games were taking place. Those two races were the 1,500m, won by Herb Elliot of Australia, and the marathon, which saw the first demonstration of the natural distance running ability of the East Africans, in this case as exemplified by the Ethiopian, Abebe Bikila. I did go, with my father, to watch Gordon Pirie run one day at the White City about this time. I was also aware that the tall figure who was sometimes to be seen jogging around the school playing fields was a certain Mike Wiggs, British international middle distance runner and one time holder of the British 5,000m record. He used our school playing fields to train on because they were a suitably extensive area of flat grassland and he happened to live nearby. Wiggs was guided by Gordon Pirie in the early years of his career and ran in both the Rome Olympics (1500m) and the Tokyo Olympics (5,000m). He set a British 5000m record in 1965, recording 13:33.

Although I had so little contact with the running world and my interest in the sport was very limited through my early teenage years, I had the requisite runner's instincts to be impressed by the proximity of the figure of a famous runner (the said Mike Wiggs), who turned out to have only two legs and to move in much the same manner as myself when running. In fact I couldn't quite understand why he only ever seemed to be jogging. Somehow, when a tall man jogs, it looks even slower than a shorter person's jogging. Obviously, whenever I was walking down the school drive and looked up to see him moving slowly across the grass, I had caught him between faster runs. But it did give me the impression that to be a good runner, first and foremost you have to be built for it. Wiggs was certainly built for it, six foot one inch tall, lean and graceful, in many ways much like his mentor, Gordon Pirie. I am sure that with Pirie to advise him, Wiggs did a large amount of training, but I was never a witness to the fact. The idea of training in any form remained a mystery to me for at least a few more years.

One or two of the better athletes in the school were allowed to use the time available for sport during the summer term to train for their track or field events. This was a privilege given to very few, as it meant them being left unsupervised; there weren't enough school masters to look after athletics on sports afternoons after all the cricket games had been catered for. One boy in particular, the best sprinter in the school (he could almost break fifty seconds for a quarter mile) was often the only one using the track. I would watch him from a distance as I stood idling away a sunny afternoon on the cricket pitch. So, this was training. He spent most of his time sitting on the grass, alternately taking off and putting on his tracksuit. I don't remember him doing very much else. The impression I got was that training was more a mental than a physical thing.

I did establish around about this time, partly through watching Mike Wiggs at close quarters, that, physically, I had the same equipment as some of the world's best runners. So, if I couldn't run it wasn't an anatomical problem. I remember studying a photograph of the Polish runner, Jersy Chromik, in a book on athletics. Chromik was an Olympic steeplechaser and distance runner who flourished in the fifties and early sixties. Three times he held the world record for the 3,000m steeplechase. I didn't choose him in particular to compare myself with. He just happened to be one of the runners featured in the book. But, when I saw the picture, I noticed that, like me, he was slightly built and of average height. When the photo was taken he was at the point of lifting off for his next stride, with one foot on the ground, his right foot, if I remember correctly. I was struck by the fact that his leg looked exactly like mine when I took on the same pose. At that particular point in a stride, when the foot has just landed and the leg is tensed for immediate rebound, the knee is slightly bent and the muscles that support it are contracted. The triangular shaped muscle on the inside of the thigh, just above the knee (the vastus medialis) is particularly prominent. As I looked at my own leg in a mirror, trying to get into exactly the same position without actually running, I couldn't see any difference between his leg and mine, the leg of an international runner and world record holder compared to that of a teenage weakling who lacked enough fitness to run more than half a mile without seeing stars.

Like most teenage boys, I was extremely self conscious about my body, more so because I was so lightly built. I had then, and still have, unusually thin bones. When I buy a watch I usually have to make an extra hole in the strap to make it fit tightly enough around my wrist. For the record, my wrists are just six inches in circumference. I can completely encircle one, with my thumb and littlest finger touching.

I got a huge amount of confidence from knowing that some runners of note were built like me. When I saw Jersy Chromik's leg I thought, 'If that leg can run a world record, then this leg (mine) should be good enough for me'. Of course I neglected to consider that what was inside the leg and attached to the leg also mattered, but, nevertheless, I had placed myself happily on the first rung of the notional ladder to running excellence.

If anything I took this idea too far. Skinniness and a superlight frame became in my mind the only suitable build for a distance runner. Throughout my running career I resented the success of runners who, in my opinion, were over-muscled. Such runners seemed to have the best of both worlds, a body to be proud of and running ability into the bargain. If one of the advantages of being a Mr. Puniverse was to be able to run well, it seemed a fair recompense for what I and others like me lacked in physical attributes. No one should have a muscular physique without paying for it in one way or another. Lack of distance running ability seemed to me to be a fair trade.

Although I never deliberately trained for running until I was seventeen or eighteen, I was an enthusiastic games player and participant in P.E. classes. Anything that was hard and physical appealed to me. I even took up boxing, mainly in order to attend boxing training after school, where we did endless press-ups and sit-ups and arm-jerks and other such exercises. I had four fights in my short career as a pugilist. I won two and lost two, and for many years kept a white T shirt, stained with patches of blood that was not my own. I am not a naturally belligerent person and not in the least bit sadistic, but that T shirt became a source of immense pride and satisfaction for me. It was a symbol of the way in which I could elevate myself from an inferior position by physical effort. The inferior position was mainly in my mind, call it an inferiority complex if you like, but the urge to escape it was always my main motivation. When I discovered that I would never really be a very good boxer I gave up that sport, but the motivation never left me. It was the same motivation that I later channelled entirely into running.

As has already been mentioned, part of this book is a search for reasons and causes. What makes someone devote a large proportion of his or her life to what is at its heart a trivial and meaningless thing like running? I thought I had answered this question in the previous chapter. I took up running seriously because I found that I was quite good at it and it satisfied my need for achievement. As a teenager, I discovered the reason that it satisfied this need. It made me feel less inferior. It even made me demonstrably superior. That is why running became so important to me. I was, in my mind at least, an inferior child, and desperate for ways not to be. Ultimately running became for me the most reliable way to climb out of the inferiority pit, and my teenage years were spent discovering this very fact. I tried rugby but found I just didn't have the build for it. I tried cricket but became bored. I tried football when the school allowed it, but missed out on the formative years and never acquired the necessary degree of skill. I tried a lot of other sports with no real success. I couldn't sing, or act, or play a musical instrument. I worked conscientiously at my academic studies but never saw that part of my life as a route to the satisfaction of my craving for demonstrable success. It was physical success that I wanted.

I was constantly looking for any improvement in what I saw as my lack of development and, if I couldn't find it, then for an area of physical prowess that would make up for it. When the P.E. master summoned one of the better built boys in the class to demonstrate a back press against the wall bars and ran his hands across what he described as the boy's 'lovely flat back' it encouraged me to do my own back presses for weeks afterwards in my bedroom at home. Still my shoulder blades stuck out like chisels and the ends of my vertebrae ran down my neck into a groove like the Grand Canyon.

It wasn't until full adulthood that I came to terms with my given physical build. With a few more added years I did put on a bit of weight and although I still had a stick-like frame everything was more or less the right shape. I could also see that the relationship that I had unilaterally decided was sacrosanct, that between a wiry build and distance running prowess, still held to a large degree. For every good runner who could pass for a rugby player or, in some cases even a boxer or weight lifter, there were half a dozen whom I might have fared well against in a Saturday night brawl. Generally speaking long distance runners are, were, and always will be like Cassius in Shakespeare's 'Julius Caesar', having 'that lean and hungry look.'

Just as Jerzy Chromic's leg gave me confidence so did the sight of top class runners who were even lighter and weaker looking than me. When I did get around to showing an interest in the Rome Olympics, for example, I saw the marathon being won by one of the greatest marathon runners who ever lived, Abebe Bikila, a man who looked in stature a lot like I did at the age of ten. Then there was Sidney Wooderson, one of the greatest middle distance runners this country ever produced, five feet six inches tall and less than nine stones in weight, and the diminutive Bruce Tulloh, European champion at 5,000m in 1962, and so many other famous runners who looked as if a strong wind would blow them off the track.

1963 was a significant year for me. I started running in cross country matches and competed in my first half mile and mile races on the track. I began to attach some meaning to the word training. Running became enjoyable again as a completely voluntary activity. And I became more aware of what was happening in distance running outside the school and on the world stage.

This was still a time when the three main disciplines within distance running were thought of as quite distinct. First and foremost, in what was seen as a hierarchy of importance, came track running, split into middle distance (800m and 1500m, or half mile and mile, and, some would claim, also 5,000m) and long distance (5,000m and 10,000m, or three miles and six miles). The 5,000m, or three miles, and even more so the 3,000m and the steeplechase have always been difficult events to categorise. Are they for the miler, the indisputable middle distance runner, who can hang on for a few more laps, or are they true distance events for which marathon like training is needed? As the sixties unwound this is the sort of question that became, if not answered, then, at the very least, clarified.

After track running came cross country running and after that came road running, which, to many people, meant one thing above all else, and that was marathon running. These latter two categories of running were very much the poor relations of the first. All the big names in distance running, apart specifically from marathon runners, both in this country and worldwide, earned their fame through success on the track. They may have been, and often were, first rate cross country and road runners, but success in these fields, in the eye of the public and the media, could never match their success on the track. To some extent this remains true today, though since about 1990 road running has swept to the fore in a strange revolution that has very little to do with competitive distance running. Marathon running in particular is now probably the most publicised type of running, measured in terms of column inches in newspapers, television coverage and celebrity status.

When I was just starting my competitive running career, middle and long distance running on the track, was seen, not just as a superior class of competition, but as a quite different type of running to either road or cross country, requiring different training, a different type of runner, a different running style, different footwear, and a wholly different approach. Whether a track runner, a 1,500m man, for example, was wise to run cross country through the winter, or whether it would irrevocably slow him down, and whether anyone should mix both racing on the track and on the road were examples of the sorts of question that became material for earnest debate. Some people seriously believed that cross country could damage a track runner's prospects and should be avoided at all costs.

As for road running, for many years that had been the last resort of the older runner, to be taken up when all speed had gone from the legs and all that remained was staying power. It was even thought that long distances on the road could only be tackled by older men with years of inurement to suffering behind them, and their dreams of track successes just memories. It was ironical that just after the second world war there did indeed seem to be some evidence for the idea that young men were unsuited to long distances, and that the advantage was with the older runners. Jack Holden ran his fastest marathon in 1950 at the age of 43. Jim Peters was at his best after he reached 35, and Sydney Wooderson, Britain's premier pre-war half miler, miler and three miler, turned to cross country in 1948 at the age of 34 and won the English Cross Country Union Championship that year. But those and other similar examples had as much to do with the war itself as with any advantage that came with age. A whole generation of runners effectively lost six years of training and competition on account of the war and found themselves having to start their careers again, six years older.

If there is one thing that we can thank the period of my teenage years for, it is the merging of the different categories of distance running into one. By 1970 runners were all basically the same. Running was a single activity, irrespective of the surface on which it was done and to some extent irrespective of the distance covered. As the sixties unrolled enough runners made the grade from top class half milers and milers to five and ten thousand metre men, and even marathon runners, and found acclaim on track, road and country alike, to make the future unity of all forms of middle and long distance running assured.

I recently found a reflection of the view that track running and other types of running were quite separate, in one of my old school magazines. In the December 1961 edition the cross country running report encouraged boys to take up the sport in the new year and concluded: *'It demands no skill whatsoever and requires only determination; and moreover it is excellent training for track events'*. Ten years later this last phrase would have looked a bit silly as, in effect, all it was saying was that running is good training for running.

My running developed, therefore, at a time when attitudes to the sport were quite different from those of today. Everything in my tiny teenage running world came to a pinnacle with the few track events I competed in, track, naturally, being in my mind the most prestigious of the running disciplines. And since the longest of those track events was the mile, I thought of myself as a miler. Even after I had left school I still saw my mile time as the measure of my ability as a runner, regardless of knowing by then that my true talents lay in the longer distances. In thinking of cross country running and road running as very much playing second and third fiddles to track running, despite the fact that I did a lot more of them, I was only reflecting the attitudes I had been brought up with.

Just as I absorbed the predominant views about the relative status of each different type of running, so I was also persuaded towards the most commonly held opinions regarding training. At the start of the sixties I knew nothing about training; I had absolutely no personal experience to learn from. Inevitably, therefore, the first pieces of information I absorbed came from the consensus of the past few years, ideas formed in the nineteen fifties. The debate about amounts and types of training and places to train didn't really heat up until the end of the fifties, so there was always going to be a bit of a time-lag between the development of new ideas and the acceptance of those ideas. To some extent I learned about training for distance running from an out of date textbook.

From the nineteen forties and throughout the nineteen fifties, worldwide, the proper training ground for the track runner was seen, self evidently, as the track. Training on the track was practically all the training that was done by many successful runners. In my mind, as well, it was the only proper way to train for track events. Running on the road and the country was simply not relevant to racing on the track. Besides, running off track was for slower and older runners whose only attribute was endurance. The track became a place where, supposedly, training could be managed using a scientific approach. The basis for the type of training that was almost universally adopted by the best middle distance runners in the immediate post war years, was called interval training. This was the first type of training I read about, and felt obliged to emulate.

Essentially interval training involves running short distances quite fast, over and over again, with a recovery period between each repetition and the next. So a runner might, for example, run twelve repetitions of one lap of the track with a one minute jog between them. The fact that the distances run in this sort of training and the number of times they are run are precise and recordable, as are the times taken for each run and the rest period between each run, immediately gives this sort of training a starting point for scientific analysis, if not a proper basis in science. Whether or not interval training is more scientific than other, less regulated and less recordable types of training is doubtful. The relationship between training and performance will always be an empirical one; what works, works. But interval training, often to the exclusion of almost all other training, brought such success to so many track runners of the forties, fifties and sixties that its influence became incredibly strong and very hard to dislodge, as did its claim to being a scientific form of training.

A number of coaches championed interval training and became famous through the successful athletes they gathered around them. Roger Bannister, Christopher Chataway and Chris Brasher were all coached by the Austrian émigré Franz Stampfl, Gordon Pirie by the German coach, Woldemar Gerschler. The Hungarian coach Mihály Iglói, who was fond of getting his athletes to run very short intervals of 200m or less, had great success both in his native country in the nineteen fifties and then in the USA with runners like Bob Schul (Tokyo Olympic Games 5,000m winner) and Jim Beattie (the first man to break four minutes for the mile on an indoor track).

The case for interval training, done on the track, might have seemed watertight at the time of both the Rome and the Tokyo Olympic Games had it not been for three athletes in particular, and their coaches. The Rome 1,500m was won by Herb Elliot of Australia on a diet of what could be described as free, uninhibited and uncontrolled running amongst the sand dunes of the Pacific coast at Portsea near Melbourne in Australia, under the tutelage of Percy Cerutty, a coach with a horror of the discipline, sterility and boredom of track training. At the same games the 5,000m was won by the New Zealander Murray Halberg, and the 800m by Peter Snell, another member of the New Zealand team who, four years later, in Tokyo, achieved the 800m and 1,500m double.

Both Snell and Halberg were coached by Arthur Lydiard, the man who put the miles into modern training schedules. For any distance, from 800m to marathon, Lydiard believed that a firm base of lots of steady running, including long runs, was absolutely essential, and that faster and shorter work need only occupy a period of a few weeks preceding competition. The very idea of an 800m runner like Peter Snell including ten to twenty mile runs in his training still seems, to this day, somewhat counter-intuitive. Nevertheless it has stood the test of time and is now an accepted part of the preparation of most, if not all middle distance runners.

During the sixties, largely through the thinking, the work and the successes of the likes of Cerutty and Lydiard and their athletes, an alternative to the regimentation of track based interval training became popularised. It seemed to work for runners at all distances and on all surfaces and it did a lot to end the idea of running specialisms. Most importantly, perhaps, it proved that you didn't have to train on the track to be good at track running. This change in dogma freed a lot of runners from dictatorial coaches and from the necessity of access to a track for training and was one of the main reasons for the surge in good runners around that time.

I consider myself lucky that just as I was about to become a proper runner my own views on what running should be: enjoyable, hard but controllable, never forced, self managed rather than inflicted on me by another person, and done in an environment that was itself stimulating, were echoed by others who could plainly demonstrate, either personally or in the athletes they coached, the sort of achievements I could only dream of.

That's why, previously, I mentioned Herb Elliot as a runner whose success at the Rome Olympics had, albeit some years after the event, influenced me a lot. To be precise it was a book by Percy Cerutty, 'Middle Distance Running' that did most of the influencing. I first read it in 1965, just as I was beginning to understand the real meaning of the word training, when I was as enthusiastic about the idea of running as I've ever been. It caught me at a highly impressionable time. I was like a sponge for romantic and heroic notions about running and training and what Cerutty called the stotan approach to living, stotan being a combination of stoic and spartan, a sort of hair shirt mentality, but enjoyable with it. I even took to eating a large bowl of dry muesli as a snack because Cerutty recommended it. *'Here, at Portsea, we believe in letting saliva do its job,'* he wrote, or words to that effect. Try eating dried oat flakes with no liquid and you will begin to understand what stotan means.

What emerged from the sixties was general agreement that neither the very strict, disciplined training of track intervals, nor a more free and easy approach involving lots of steady distance running, was the one and only way for a distance or middle distance runner to train. It wasn't a case of one or the other. Training could be a mix. It could be both free and disciplined. It could be self motivated or enforced. But it had to be above a certain amount if it had any hope of bringing an otherwise average runner to the heights of the sport. Above all the guiding principles of training and the agreed mix that made it up were the same for all, from 800m runners to marathoners. At various times in my running career, in training, I have run regular twenty milers on a Sunday with an international 800m/1500m runner and done 200m track intervals with 10K and marathon runners. No one thought it odd.

My own slow introduction to training came in the midst of the worldwide learning process that was going on regarding training methods for distance running, a process that would eventually lead to the present day consensus. I can probably date my first training run to sometime in 1961. I had reached the age when it became possible for me to run the mile and the half mile on school sports day. I must have been fifteen. My eldest brother told me a few days before I was to run my first ever track half mile that I needed to train. That was all he said and, not knowing quite what he meant, I had to work out for myself what to do. You could say I invented training there and then, in the same way that all previous running pioneers had done.

Simple logic told me that if you try to do in practice what you are trying to do for real that should make you better at it. So, if I wanted to be good at running a half mile race, I should run a half mile as practice. I thought of it as practice rather than training because I had not yet grasped the long term nature of training nor the concept of physical and physiological adaptation that is the intended outcome of training and which itself takes time. So I went for my practice run the evening before the day of my race.

Just down the road from where I lived was a complete circle of road enclosing the local Masonic centre and its gardens and tennis courts. By coincidence the circle was almost exactly half a mile around. I had measured it with my bicycle wheel milometer. I changed into vest, shorts and plimsolls and jogged with my brother down to the circle to run my practice half mile. He would time me. It was dark by this time and very cold, but I was too self conscious in those days to have done it in daylight.

It is strange how, many years after an event, the memory of parts of it, maybe a few seconds only, or just the faintest whiff of it, can remain as clear as when it was formed. It is equally strange how great chunks of it were never committed to memory at all. So I do remember the cold air against my dry throat, the changing light as I passed one street light after another, the mist of my breathing, the constant curve of the road as I negotiated the 360 degrees turn and the feeling of increasing discomfort as the seconds passed. I don't remember how long it took me or what I did afterwards, or anything else really. But that was it, my training for the year.

I don't even remember how I got on in the race. I can find no record of ever having run a half mile race that year, so maybe I never did. One feature of our school sports day was that every event for every age group had to be included in one afternoon. This led to a pretty tight schedule and I could find myself running the 440 yards followed maybe as little as ten minutes later by the half mile. Being as unfit as I was at that age it is possible that, having just done the 440, I was in no state to run again for a good while. Or perhaps the sports day was cancelled that year. Quite often in March there was a heavy frost, or heavy rain, one year a lot of snow, which would mean the events couldn't be run.

It was only when I started running cross country at school, the year before the Tokyo Olympics, that I did any training, in the proper sense of the word, at all. Even then I didn't fully understand the significance of what I was doing. The captain of cross country running, a boy called David Chivers, arranged for us to meet after school, and we would go for a three mile run. I saw it as simply doing what cross country runners did. Rugby players played rugby, swimmers swam, squash players played squash, and cross country runners ran. I should have been less ignorant, but I still didn't think of running as training. I had absolutely no idea as to either the need for training or the dramatic effects on performance that training could have.

With a couple of three mile runs a week plus a race on a Saturday and rugby on games days (nothing, not even cross country running, got in the way of school rugby) I suppose I managed to gain a bit of fitness, but never, in all my time at school, was I properly fit for running. Only someone who has trained hard for a decent length of time can know what it is like to be really fit. I didn't achieve anything like that state until I had left school and was well into my twenties.

How unfit was I in my later teenage years? Compared to most boys of my age I was not unfit at all, and the very fact that I could do reasonably well in cross country races of up to three or four miles and could run a mile on the track in under five minutes suggested I was, if anything, fitter than most of them. But serious runners have to gauge their fitness according to the highest standards, and once I had achieved much higher levels of fitness a few years later, I could see that, despite doing a modicum of training, I was, according to my own adjusted standards, extremely unfit.

The best measure of fitness, of aerobic fitness at any rate, is the ability to recover from severe exercise. If you watch a well trained runner at the end of a race in which he has run to his limit, what is surprising is how quickly he recovers. No sooner has he broken the tape than he is off on a lap of honour. When Abebe Bikila won the Olympic marathon for the second time, in Tokyo, immediately he had finished he entertained the crowd with some warming down exercises, seeming as fresh as at the start of the race. When I was at my fittest I knew that I could always sprint the last quarter mile or so of a distance race to the point of dry retching at the finish, and that I would be back to normal a few seconds later. As a post graduate university student in 1971 I took the train from Brighton to London and ran in the Polytechnic marathon. I finished in well under two and a half hours and returned the same day. That evening I was at a party, raving into the small hours. That's what fitness does. It obviates the power of stressful exercise to have more than a very short lived effect.

By contrast, when I was at school, untrained and unfit, I suffered, the worst horrors of exercise induced stress. I achieved levels of oxygen debt that left me totally bankrupt for hours afterwards. Headaches and vomiting were common outcomes of a hard race. Why I stuck at it I don't know. There is a degree of masochism in all runners.

After one of my school track races, a heat of the mile, held one evening before sports day, I sat on a bench beside the track, unable even to remove my spikes or to put on a track suit. I was bent over, staring at the ground, preparing myself for what seemed the inevitable blast of vomit and the ground below me, closely mown grass, was moving like waves on water. I sat there, fixed in place, for maybe a half hour, head in hands, feeling as if I was floating on water, and suffering from an exact imitation of sea-sickness. The only other time I have ever felt so wretched was after I smoked half a cigar, at the age of thirteen. I thought I was going to die, on that occasion too. Eventually the ground stopped moving and I could walk slowly back to the changing rooms. I had only run four minutes and fifty three seconds!

The strange thing was that, knowing I might suffer in that way, I still looked forward to races over all distances with an excitement that seems totally out of place viewed through my presently tired and seasoned eyes. I became nervous days before a race and absorbed every aspect of the day of a race like blotting paper, so much so that I still remember races and moments connected to races vividly fifty years later.

I remember the waiting around on the bitter, exposed playing fields, wondering if the half hour to my next race was ever going to pass, avoiding my friends for not wanting to talk to them. The pop songs of the time played over and over in my head. To this day I can bring them to mind and immediately be transported back to that place at that time. Three in particular have stuck with me as indelibly as the grooves on a vinyl recording: Bobby Vee's 'The Night Has a Thousand Eyes', Johnny Cymbal's trademark 'Mr Bassman' (You are the king of rock and roll, b-b-ba-b-ba-b-ba-ba) and 'Shop Around' by Smokey Robinson and the Miracles. When I die and my brain is examined those songs will be there, right next to the running centre, which, in turn, is sandwiched between the pleasure centre and the aspiration centre.

I remember coming third in the final of the senior mile and being angry because I had had no choice but to run the 440 yards no more than five minutes previously which, as I saw it, ruined my chances in the longer event. It was also one of the years when the track was unusable, having been turned by a series of frosts and thaws into a jelly. Consequently we ran on wet grass which for me, in my smooth-soled plimsolls, was like a skating rink. It wasn't that I thought I would have won the mile. It was just that I didn't enjoy it because I couldn't do my best. I suffered the same sense of frustration in inter-school athletics matches, when I became old enough to run for the school team. I found myself entered for the 440 yards and the half mile, when what I always wanted to do was to run the mile. It was the price I paid for being relatively fast, even though I was never a sprinter. I felt silly being beaten over a quarter mile by three or four seconds or more, knowing that I would never be able to run much faster. My best time for the distance at school was just under 56 seconds, when good schoolboy sprinters were running close to fifty seconds dead.

The boy who won all the distance events (we thought of the half mile and the mile, as well as cross country, as distance events) in my last two years at school did so for one reason only. He trained. He even ran to school and back. I would see him sometimes crossing the playing fields with a small rucksack on his back on his way home. Had I done the same or even something like it I'm sure I would have been the better runner. As it was, the last time I raced him over half a mile, he only beat me by half a second, 2:8.1 to 2:8.6. Years later I met him and discovered he had never become much of a runner after he left school. But at school he had taught me the power of training.

Because, as a teenager, I didn't really train, hardly at all, and much of my racing was middle distance rather than longer, I rarely had the chance to discover my natural talent for steadier, more measured running. Even when I ran cross country, it was rare for a race to be more than about three miles, and my approach to all races was inevitably the same, start much too fast, continue until oxygen debt set in and then struggle on to the finish as best I could, slowing down all the time. One run, however, did give me a glimpse of my future in running, in the same way that a paper chase when I was still in short trousers had given me a hint of the same thing.

The captain of the cross country team, a ginger haired boy called Christopher Stokes, decided we would all go for a 'long run'. That meant about five miles, the furthest distance I ran in my entire time at school. We set out across the playing fields and through the school gates, about twelve of us, dressed as for a race. Soon thereafter we spread out because we hadn't yet learned the art of running in training as a group, and every run we did together, in due course, became a race. We ran up to Batchworth Heath, where 'Genevieve' broke down in the film of the same name and past the entrance to Moorpark golf course where James Bond played a round with Goldfinger and his caddy Oddjob (Elstree film studios were not far away) and all the time I was running better and better and leaving the others behind. At least two of them would always have beaten me in races.

It was one of those small fractions of history that are not only remembered clearly but which convey influential lessons. I learned that day that I was made for distance running. I wasn't a quarter-miler or a half-miler, not even a miler. I was a long distance runner. I also learned that it was not a good idea to start a race of any distance flat out, but to work gradually into it and, if anything, to speed up rather than slow down. Best of all I was confirmed in my love of running. Running could be stimulating and exhilarating and you could finish it feeling better than when you started. It was also rather nice to finish ahead of your rivals.

I left school at nineteen. I had drifted through a highly influential period in the history of distance running and training theory without realising it, but had picked up a little bit of that theory on the way. If anything I intended to go down the interval training route to fitness, but in that I was probably already out of date. But there was no doubt in my mind that I was going to start training in one way or another - sometime soon, maybe when I got to University. First there were the summer holidays to get through and they were never a very good time for training.

CHAPTER 3
Two decades of progress

'In every field of human endeavour there is a period when more progress is made in less time than in all the years preceding it and in all the years that follow it'.

Anon

If I am right and the peak for distance running in Great Britain was reached sometime in the seventies, the nineteen fifties and even more so the nineteen sixties must have been a period of rapid ascent. In the last chapter I looked at the late fifties and early sixties very much from a personal point of view. I was looking through a teenager's eyes at what was immediately evident to me and was learning about running through my own experiences, rather than by being taught. The sole driving force for my running was my own inclination. Consequently I had little understanding of the sport of running in its more general application and little to say about the broader view. For me it was a period of growing up, of entering and exiting my teens, a period of ignorance slowly assuaged by learning, during which I ran and competed both on the track, over the country and occasionally on the road, at school and then university, more or less in isolation. I had very little idea at this time what was going on in the wider world of distance running. It was only afterwards that I began to put the pieces together, and it wasn't until the very end of those two decades that I became a regular part of the mainline running scene.

In the present chapter I can relive the fifties and sixties with the benefit of hindsight and a clearer understanding of the importance of these two decades to the development of standards in distance running both in Britain and worldwide. One way to point up the progress that was made between the end of the war and the beginning of the nineteen seventies is to refer to my own best performance over the marathon distance. Going solely on times, I would have won every Olympic marathon up to and including 1948, and then again in 1956, assuming, of course, that I had been the only runner of my generation to have had access to the necessary time machine. Had I run my best time during the 1948 London Olympic marathon, again going only according to the clock, I would have won by over ten minutes. The significance of those bald and rather brash statements cannot be over-estimated, bearing in mind that, as I have tried to emphasise time and time again throughout this book, even at my very best, in my own time, I was no more than a good club runner, and there were hundreds of other complete unknowns who were at least as good as me. At the 1960 Rome Olympics, however, I would have been over nine minutes behind the winner, and, at every games since then, with the exception of the high altitude Mexico Olympics of 1968, I would have been no closer.

Jim Peters retired in 1954, having pushed the world's best time for a marathon to what must have then seemed an extraordinary 2:17:39.4. That time remained the world record until 1958, when the Russian Sergey Popov recorded 2:15:17, and it stayed the British record until 1963. By 1970 the world record was down to 2:08:33.6 and the British record stood at 2:10:47.8. In the space of a decade the world record had been improved by nearly six and three quarter minutes and the British record by an almost identical amount. Bill Adcocks had run that British record at the end of 1968 in Fukuoka, Japan and not much more than a year later, on 20th April 1970, Ron Hill ran 2:10:30 in Boston, followed three months later by 2:09:28 in the Edinburgh Commonwealth games of that year. Nor were Hill and Adcocks the only two British runners posting what were world class times for the marathon at the start of the seventies. It had become almost commonplace for the marathon distance to be run inside Jim Peters' British record time of ten years earlier and several men in Britain were approaching the magic five minutes per mile pace for the full distance required to run a marathon in under two hours and twelve minutes.

There is no doubt in my mind that standards in British marathon running progressed more during the ten years or so after the early nineteen sixties than in any other similar period in history. I am aware that Jim Peters, by himself, moved the British record forward nearly twelve minutes in the space of three years in the early fifties, but he was unique amongst British marathon runners of the time. Also it is a lot easier to go from 2:29 to 2:17 than to trim over seven minutes from a 2:17 clocking, as Brian Kilby, Basil Heatley, Alastair Wood, Bill Adcocks and Ron Hill did between them, before the summer of 1970.

It grows progressively harder, naturally enough, to improve on times the faster they become, so it shouldn't surprise us that since Ron Hill's phenomenal Commonwealth games run of 23rd July 1970, a mere minute and a quarter has been knocked off the British record, and it took fifteen years to do it. What that tells us is just what good marathon runners Britain had as long as forty years ago. The world record for a marathon may now be under two hours and four minutes but times such as Adcock's and Hill's are still absolutely top class today.

If the fifties and sixties were a period of rapid improvement in the standard of marathon running in this country does it follow that it was also a time of rapid improvement in distance running in general and in the overall health of the sport? Absolutely. Not only was there a demonstrable improvement in performances at all distances up to the marathon, as well as the marathon itself, both at the very top and in depth, but marathon running by itself was a good indicator of the state of the wider distance running scene. Marathon runners had to come from somewhere, and to record the sort of times that were being run over the marathon distance, runners had to have been doing the sort of training that inevitably made them good three milers, six milers, ten milers and twenty milers. And what were they doing when they weren't running marathons? They were racing over shorter distances, along with a growing number of good to excellent club runners. In those days marathon runners weren't a breed apart. They were just runners, like the rest of us. And we all had a notion to run a marathon, not in the same way that people today aim to 'do a marathon', if only to be able to say that they have done so, but to run it competitively.

I ran my first marathon in 1970, more or less on a whim. I was fit enough at the time to be running ten miles in under 52 minutes, but I was not prepared for nearly three times that distance. But this didn't matter. I was quite happy to enter into unknown territory because I was a runner, amongst other runners, most of whom I knew well, or had come across in races before, or whose names I had seen in Athletics Weekly. Only the distance was unfamiliar to me. Everything else was as it was on any other Saturday afternoon when I had entered a road race. It was just a race, to be run like any other.

I managed to finish in under three hours and would have been considerably faster (to prove the point I ran 2:37:10 in the Polytechnic Marathon less than a month later) except that I spent several minutes sitting by the roadside almost within sight of the finish, unable to get back on my feet because of cramp. Cramp was a new experience for me and I didn't know what to do about it. Now I do. Whatever else you do when cramp strikes you must never sit down. The slightest attempt to raise yourself back onto your feet will set it off again and you become as immobilised as a tortoise on its back.

I must have got up eventually. No one helped me. I hobbled to the finish line with no particular feeling of having accomplished anything special, just relief at getting there and a sense of discovery. Now I knew what running twenty six miles entailed. It was different from any other race, but not so different as to put it in a separate category altogether. I think that's how all my fellow distance runners viewed the marathon then - with healthy disrespect.

The full story of that marathon includes a detail or two that highlights the contrast in attitudes and circumstances between running then and running now. The marathon was the Isle of Wight marathon, more or less a full circumnavigation of the island, starting and finishing on Ryde sea front. It was a marathon with a reputation for being a hard one because of the abundance of climbs up the chalk downland, not the best one, perhaps, for me to choose as my first. But, isn't that the point? I didn't see it as anything special. I certainly didn't have an all out determination just to complete a marathon and to claim huge kudos by doing so. I suppose I took it for granted that I would complete it, in the same way I completed ten mile races and fifteen and twenty mile races. Why wouldn't I? And, having finished it, I expected no special admiration or reward.

I was driven down to Portsmouth, where we were to catch the hovercraft across the Solent, by a fellow club member in a very old and unreliable car that slowed our journey as much as the fact that he had only just learned to drive. We missed the ferry and had to wait for the next. We got changed on the hovercraft and as soon as the doors opened we set off at a run towards the marathon starting line, which we eventually reached and crossed eight minutes after the rest of the runners had left it. I found all this, annoying, yes, but also somewhat amusing. What's eight minutes in three hours? It was odd, the two of us, running completely alone down the wide straight open sea front road, even odder when my club mate decided to try and catch the field much more quickly than I was prepared to, and soon left me behind.

If you look up the results of that race you will find that I was given a finishing time of just outside three hours. To defend myself from accusations of lying when saying that I completed the marathon in under three hours (see above) I merely point to that eight minute delay and subtract it from my given time. It allows me the proud boast that, before turning sixty, I never ran outside three hours for a completed marathon.

The increase in both standards of running and numbers of good distance runners, starting in the fifties and gathering pace through the sixties, was due to one thing only and that was training. If anything distinguished the two decades that marked my progress to adulthood it was the evolution of training. From the end of the second world war, when a few runners in different parts of the world were discovering for themselves the phenomenal effects of lots of hard training, through the first half of the sixties, when the need for such training was still being questioned, to the end of the same decade, when it had been accepted as standard, it was changes to training habits amongst runners at large that caused the upsurge.

By the time I joined the ranks of the good club runners the need for consistent training and lots of it was common knowledge. By about 1970 the pattern of training required to become a world class distance runner was well established and had been adopted by a large number of runners throughout the country. It is basically the same pattern of training both in amount and intensity as applies today and, if the best distance runners are faster now than forty years ago, it is not because of any great change in the training they do. Conversely, if, as seems to be the case, there were more good distance runners in Britain then than now, undoubtedly it **is** due to differences in training. Since the nineteen eighties far fewer runners in Britain seem to be prepared to do the work that so many of us took for granted in our day.

Establishing this optimum type of training was a process spread over thirty or forty years. Before and immediately after the war the running scene was characterised by a few outstanding individuals who held sway either just in their own country or, in some cases, on the world stage, for periods of several years at a time. The explanation almost certainly had to do with training. When the same thing has happened more recently, for example in the case of Paul Tergat who won the world cross country championships every year from 1995 to 1999 and, similarly, Kenenisa Bekele who won from 2002 to 2006, it is safe to say that the dominant figures in question are simply the best runners around, best, that is, in the sense of being the most naturally gifted rather than the product of a particular training regime. It is reasonable to say that because, for many years now, all serious runners have known what training to do and a large number of them have had all the time and resources needed to do it. They have devoted their lives to running and any lack of ability on their part cannot be due to inadequate training. The only things separating the élite athletes at the finish of a race nowadays are differences in natural ability, present state of condition and health, how they went on the day, and, very occasionally, a matter of tactics. Training is no longer a significant variable because there is a consensus about the way in which distance runners should train.

When the world of distance running was dominated by the likes of Paavo Nurmi in the thirties or Emil Zatopek in the fifties, or when British distance running featured Jack Holden and Jim Peters who between them won the AAA marathon every year from 1947 to 1954 and, before that, when Duncan McLeod Wright, Sam Ferris and Donald McNab Robertson shared dominance of the same race between 1930 and 1934, it is far more likely that training made the difference. Of course natural ability will always enter the equation, but before the sixties it was not the case that all runners had reached the same conclusion regarding what training to do, nor even discovered what was best for themselves.

There was still much debate at that time about training methods and tremendous variation in the quantity and quality of the training done by different individuals. In the last chapter I mentioned the contrasting approaches of, on the one hand, the regimented interval type track training that dominated during the fifties and, on the other, the freer, cross country based training that grew up in the sixties. I included a discussion of it there because the respective arguments coincided with my own introduction to training and were the first to influence me. Deciding what sort of training I should do was an integral part of my early career.

Of far greater significance than the type of training, however, was the quantity. Before the nineteen seventies the running world was still very much in the midst of a process of discovery and learning as far as amounts of training were concerned. 'Big' trainers tended to be very much in the minority and were probably seen, despite the obvious success of some of them, as mere crackpots. Worse, they were seen by some as setting a dangerous example. That much hard running was surely not good for anyone. And wasn't it a bit 'over the top' ethically as well as physically? The scene was set for a battle between the contrasting concepts of the more training the better on the one hand and the minimalist approach - as little as was needed to get results on the other.

Take, for example, three outstanding British runners of the nineteen fifties: Roger Bannister, Christopher Chataway and Gordon Pirie. They all held world records at one time or another and they all had plenty of natural ability but, of the three of them, only Pirie ever did the quantity of training that, twenty years later, distance runners had come to accept as normal and necessary. Pirie is quoted (in his biography, 'The Impossible Hero') as saying, at the start of 1954, in an uncannily prophetic statement, *'To achieve a world's best performance in distance running... the athlete must concentrate on training schedules unimagined a decade ago'*. There was considerable discussion in running circles and in the press at the time about the need for the sort of training Pirie was doing. His poor showing in the Rome Olympics of 1960 was even blamed in some quarters on what was seen as overtraining. Some years before that, in May 1953, Norris McWhirter had written, *'Would Pirie do better if he cut down his training to two days a week?'* Runners of my generation can only laugh at the idea.

Bannister and Chataway, on the other hand, did what by today's standards would be considered not nearly enough training. They liked the idea of what was referred to as 'effortless superiority'. Bannister, when asked to write about his training in Athletics Weekly a year or two prior to his famous sub four minute mile, claimed to train a mere three times a week for forty five minutes at a time. Chataway is on record as later admitting, *'...the sort of training we did, one realises, was totally inadequate. I never ran more than twenty five miles in a week.'* He also told Athletics Weekly in 1952 that when he increased his training to forty five to fifty miles a week (still a small amount in today's terms) it *'produced boredom, tiredness and a tendency to get fit too quickly'*. Both he and Bannister believed that a combination of quality rather than quantity in training and fast racing was what worked and that more training simply made you stale.

Here, by contrast, is what Pirie had to say about his training in a BBC radio interview: '*I train seven days a week, sometimes two or three times a day. I start with a one hour warm up, then put my spikes on and do repetition slow and fast runs on the track for an hour and a half and then a half hour warm down*' . That's a total of three hours running, conservatively covering a distance of at least fifteen miles and, if we are to take what Pirie said literally, that he sometimes trained more often than once a day, he was running up to well over a hundred miles a week, maybe even a hundred and fifty. At that time, and by comparison with the amount of training that Chataway and Bannister got away with, what Pirie was doing must have seemed unbelievable.

Maybe it was unbelievable. If the running world in the years after the war was slow to decide what training was most effective it was at least partly because athletes are not very good at disclosing what training they really do. There are two reasons why runners should be deliberately economical with the truth when describing their training. One is the natural urge in a competitive environment to keep their training at least partly secret. If you are better than other runners because you do more training or train harder than them, you certainly don't want them knowing about it. So you understate your training. Then, secondly, and with the completely opposite effect, that of overstatement, there is the need to impress. Everyone who does something hard or otherwise laudable wants others to know just what a tough nut they are, and, if a bit of exaggeration comes into the picture, where's the harm in that?

So maybe Pirie did less training than could be inferred from his radio interview and maybe Roger Bannister and Christopher Chataway did more than they let on. 'Track and Field News', at the time of the Helsinki Olympic Games in 1952 described Chataway as '*the boyish looking student who trains as hard as any but likes to give the impression he doesn't*'. Chataway himself said about Roger Bannister, '*Roger went to great lengths to conceal the amount of training he did. It was a long time before I really understood that he did more than he said he did.*' Perhaps it is equally impressive, if not more so, to achieve world records on very little training as it is to do huge amounts of training, world records or not.

There is an added source of confusion. Not only might runners in the public eye be a little less than totally honest and open about their training, but, whatever picture they present of their training, it is bound to require interpretation. If, for example, I were to be asked to describe my training at any period in my running career I would find it a difficult thing to do, and I would never expect the person hearing or reading my description to get much more than a rough idea of what I did. If I told you that I ran seventy miles a week in training, you would immediately want to know whether that was an average distance or the maximum, and for how many weeks I did it, and did it include every bit of running in the week or just the training running, and how fast was it, and for how long did I run at a time, and so on. I had a friend who was so obsessed with the total mileage he ran in a week that he kept a note of each and every bit of running he did: fifty yards for the bus, up the stairs to the toilet repeated forty or fifty times a week (he always ran, and thought of those short, two steps at a time dashes, I suppose, as his hill reps.), one mile for a game of squash, playing with the dog in the park (a quarter of a mile), etc. That's why he always ran more in a week than I did and why, for all I know, my seventy miles a week could have been eighty or ninety.

Even when I was running at my very best I used to play football once or twice a week. It was madness, for a serious runner, but I loved it too much ever to say no to a game of football. Alfred Shrubb, famous English runner of the early nineteen hundreds, wrote that an athlete '... *should not engage in an actual match* (of football) *however greatly he may be tempted*'. Even had I read that at the time I would have ignored the advice. I played on the right wing and, lacking the ball skills of a Stanley Matthews, a George Best or a Lionel Messi, I relied heavily on the fast run down the line, the pause as the full back came across, the tempting push of the ball to make him think he had a chance, followed by the perfectly timed second push just as he committed himself to the tackle, and the sprint past, jumping over his legs if necessary. It usually worked, but it really tested my fitness and was probably, incidentally, excellent training. Did I count it in my weekly mileage total? I think I used to count a game of football as three extra miles, but it was probably worth a lot more than that. As running was one of the few things I could do well on a football pitch I spent at least half of the ninety minutes doing just that. That's more like seven miles than three. Like Bannister and Chataway I probably underestimated my training load.

Behind any account of someone's training schedule there are unknowns and a lack of clarity. What did Gordon Pirie's one hour warm up consist of? I tend to think of a warm up as continuous easy running. An hour would represent well over five miles, maybe nearer eight miles. But, more likely, Pirie included exercises and stretches as well as running. The same would apply to his half hour warm down, three or four miles running, or what? He doesn't say and we may never know. We are left with only a very patchy idea of how much training he really did.

What can be said for certain, however, is that Pirie did a lot more training than either Bannister or Chataway, quite possibly more than the two of them combined. Even assuming that Pirie was happy to divulge the fact that he trained long and hard and didn't mind if people believed that he did more than he said, while Bannister and Chataway preferred to give the impression of world class performances based on not much more than gutsy racing and an amateurish approach, it is still clear that Pirie did twice as much training as either of the other two. And yet, at the time of the Helsinki Olympics and, four years later at Melbourne, there was little to choose between Pirie and Chataway over 5,000 metres or, for that matter, between Bannister and Pirie over a mile. In a climate where runners with such different approaches and attitudes to training, what could be described as the amateur versus the professional, can each reach the very top of the heap and match each other in races, it is not surprising that there was no general agreement about how much training and what sort of training was right for a distance runner. Only after the nineteen fifties, in a process that was more or less complete by the mid sixties, was the difference of opinion resolved. Basically Pirie was right and Chataway and Bannister and many others with similar beliefs were deluding themselves. The universal and in many ways very simple answer to becoming a good distance runner was a lot of hard training. In 1955 in what amounted to a change of opinion, Chataway himself had said, in the newly revised Achilles Club's standard book on athletics, *'I have no hesitation in saying that the rapid general improvement in the standards of long distance running in Britain since the war is due solely to the acceptance of longer and harder training schedules'.* The very gifted might have got away with less for a while, but in time no one was going to be able to, because, in different parts of the world, runners who were equally gifted were doing more and better training.

The achievements of Bannister and Chataway were, in a way, more remarkable than those of men like Pirie, if their training really was so much less. It points to them being runners with extraordinary natural talent. Through no fault of their own, however, they and other runners who achieved great things with relatively light training (Sam Ferris, for example, won a silver medal in the Olympic games marathon of 1932 and had an outstanding marathon career in the twenties and thirties, all on training that rarely exceeded forty miles a week) did a disservice to the furtherance of the sport of distance running. By perpetuating the belief that the way to excellence was not necessarily through lots of training, they set back the growth in depth of quality runners in the country by about a decade.

Another British runner of the Bannister/Chataway era, probably the world's best cross country runner of that decade, who achieved what he did on a relatively light training regime, was Frank Sando, whose exploits were detailed in Chapter 1. His training is documented by Alastair Aitken on the Highgate Harriers website, www.highgateharriers.org. uk : *'10 miles on Sunday, 5 on Monday, 7 miles fartlek on Tuesday, 3 miles ordinary running on Wednesday, 2 miles fartlek Thursday, rest on*

Friday, race on Saturday. Average miles a week 45.' Even I, at one time, would have called this a light week. Had Sando been merely average in ability he might have wondered whether more training would have brought him to a higher standard. But to win the international cross country championship twice, to win a European bronze medal over 10,000m and to run in the Olympic 10,000m twice, not to mention numerous domestic successes on that amount of training, gave no clue that it might not have been enough, neither to Sando himself nor to followers of the sport. As long as runners like Sando were able to top the heap with the training that they were doing, there was no persuasive argument for anyone needing to do more.

This factor apart, in retrospect it is still difficult to see why it took quite so long for the running world to acknowledge that the sort of training load that became accepted as routine in the seventies, for all but the truly exceptionally gifted, was the obvious, the necessary, the one and only route to excellence. Hadn't Jim Peters clearly demonstrated the fact, and hadn't he learned it from the Finns, Heino and Nurmi and from his arch rival Jack Holden? Peters recounts in an interview with Athletics Weekly: *'I remember I spoke to Paavo Nurmi and asked him how many training sessions he did a week and he said eighteen. I was only doing five! So I knew I had to follow his three sessions per day regime to get anywhere.'* At this point I should add that Nurmi might have been referring to his compatriot Viljo Heino who held the world record for 10,000m twice in the nineteen forties, but, whichever Finn it was who trained eighteen times a week, the point remains the same.

To continue Peters' interview quote: *'So I got up at 5am and went out for a comfortable ten miler at around six minute mile pace. Then I'd get on the train and go to work. At lunchtime I'd pinch some time to go down to the old News of the World track and do my version of intervals. I couldn't see the point of Roger Bannister and people having rests after each effort, because you don't get a rest in a marathon. I did laps in regular times - like 75 seconds - and just kept going. Eventually I was doing about five miles of repetitions on the track. I was so tired, I'd fall asleep on the train after work. When I got home I'd tell the wife, 'Don't have any cooking on, otherwise I'll never go out running,' and I'd go for a fast ten, 55 minutes or under. On Saturday, I'd do cross country hard for two hours, to my physical limit, through hills and mud. On Sundays, I did the marathon but split it into 14 miles in the morning and 12 in the afternoon.'*

Rather confusingly, and proving the point that a runner's account of his training may not be entirely accurate, Peters goes on to say, *'I suppose I used to average around seventy miles a week. The most I ever did was 110, once.'* This, after just describing a week of well over 150 miles! Nevertheless it was clear that, following the example of the great Finnish runners of the thirties and forties, Peters was helping to pioneer, in his own country, the training philosophy of lots of hard running, in his own words, *'as much running as I could'.*

Even before the rise of Peters, Jack Holden was also running over a hundred miles a week. To quote Holden, *'I was the first to run a hundred miles a week in training. Jim Peters wrote to me asking for help and I told him he had to do more and more miles. They all copied me.'* It is surprising, therefore, that, with the evidence of the success of hard training men like these, there was still doubt about the efficacy of the sort of intense training regime that might have looked fairly normal by 1970 but was truly extraordinary in the early fifties.

One reason that runners were slow to see the writing on the wall regarding the almost guaranteed route to improvement through lots of hard training was, and still is, that it takes a massive leap of faith to commit to a long term training regime of mile upon mile of running, day after day, without let up, especially if you have no reason to feel particularly gifted in the first place. If I were to tell you that the way to success in running was to stand on your head for an hour a day, and could only supply you with the flimsy evidence that one or two great runners had done just that and no one could be absolutely certain that they weren't a bit 'you-know-what', would you do it? I don't think so. And if you knew of many good runners who never stood on their heads, you would be entirely justified to ignore my advice.

The situation for an aspiring runner in the fifties, therefore, was that a few outstanding competitors either definitely did large amounts of training, or claimed to do so, or were merely reputed to do so, but that others did much less, and that the superiority of some runners could be accounted for by inborn factors in any case. There was no clear view of the route to success. Some training was obviously necessary but those who did a lot might have done just as well with less. Furthermore the effects of any amount of training take weeks to show; the effects of a lot of training probably take years to materialise to their fullest extent. This meant that there was little reliable reason, and no immediate confirming evidence, on which to base a commitment to training on the scale that is now known to be required. No wonder the creed of hard training was slow to catch on.

Another factor to consider is that Peters and Holden were best known as marathon runners and perhaps marathon runners can be viewed as the tough men of the running fraternity, the slower movers who could only succeed through hard work and who depended entirely for their success on the ability simply to keep going. It would have been hard to convince middle distance men like Roger Bannister and Christopher Chataway that they might also have benefited from seventy miles or more a week training, with long runs thrown in, on a regular basis.

Without wishing to be disrespectful, the signs were there, and can still be seen in the archive film evidence, that Roger Bannister, for one, was inadequately trained. He was famous for his post race collapses. After his 1954 Empire Games mile victory he was, quite literally, carried off the track. It was not merely a sign of someone who had run to his utmost. It was also a sign of someone who, as a result of limited training, was unable to recover quickly from a one hundred percent effort. I wouldn't presume to say as much except that, having at times done a much larger amount of training week by week than Bannister ever did, I know that training to that degree conditions the body to recover almost immediately from all out efforts. If anything, my respect for Bannister is greater because he didn't do all that much training. He was evidently hugely talented and, in my estimation, had he trained as Sebastian Coe and Steve Ovett were doing thirty years later, he might well have been their equal. Surely it must have been noticed that good marathon runners were usually also good at shorter distances. Peters was a first class track runner who represented Britain over 10,000m and a fine cross country runner as well. Jack Holden won the International Cross Country Championship four times before the war. Besides which you have to be more than a hardened plodder to cover the marathon distance in under two hours and twenty minutes. Anyone with the eyes to see must have been able to infer, even in 1950, that large quantities of training brought almost guaranteed success in distance running, and not just at the marathon distance.

Gordon Pirie's British record for 5,000m set in 1956, mentioned in the previous chapter, was not broken until 1965. For almost ten years British performances at 5,000m had more or less stagnated, and only picked up in the second half of the 1960s. By 1980, fifteen years after Mike Wiggs broke Pirie's record, a total of sixteen faster times had been run by British athletes and the British record stood at 13:14.6 to Brendan Foster. Not only does this reinforce the point that the sixties saw the start of a period of rapid advancement in the quality of distance running in Britain, but it fits well with my belief that only when middle distance runners, in numbers, started to train with the same appetite for lots of hard running as marathon runners, did times move ahead apace.

If no other evidence had been available for the benefits of considerable amounts of training, then the case of Emil Zatopek alone would have been enough. Renowned for his brutally tough training (with sessions such as forty times 400m on the track) and hard man approach to his running, he achieved a feat that no other runner has ever equalled (the nearest being Lasse Viren in Montreal in 1976), that of winning Olympic gold medals for all three distance events, 5,000m, 10,000m and marathon at Helsinki in 1952.

What happened during the latter part of the fifties and into the sixties and seventies was that more and more runners took that leap of faith and experimented with the methods that had been pioneered by enlightened, dedicated, or simply eccentric individuals, both runners and coaches, the Heinos, Nurmis, Zatopeks, Holdens, Peters', Piries, Ceruttys and Lydiards of the running world, until the modern pattern of training for distance running had become more or less set in stone. The simple message that read, 'lots of running equals undreamt of improvement', gradually, and with increasing pace, filtered through to aspiring distance runners like a virus.

Before the nineteen fifties it was generally believed that runners were born rather than made and that while training could improve a naturally good runner and bring them to world class, no amount of training was going to turn a tortoise into a hare. During the next two decades, in what amounted to a distance running revolution, runners who were by no means obviously naturally gifted discovered that training could have a much greater effect than had previously been imagined. The longer the distance a runner aspired to race, the greater the improvement due to training became. One still needed a large dose of natural ability to run a fast mile but anyone who could run at all could become a good club runner over much longer distances simply by training hard. This was the seminal message that eventually spread like wildfire through the rank and file of the running community, reaching saturation point sometime in the late sixties or early seventies.

The message gave hope to thousands of 'also-rans' who, like me, loved running and dreamt of greatness but had never thought of themselves as being one of the naturally blessed. I can think of many contemporaries who turned themselves into classy runners by adopting the principle of lots of hard training, when at first sight they had seemed to have little going for them. Had you watched any long distance road race in the sixties or seventies you would have seen dozens of ungainly competitors, some too tall, some too short, some too stocky, some leaning to one side, with stiff limbs, strange arm movements or a crab-like running style, all running times that would have made them world class before and shortly after the second world war. Come to think of it

Zatopek himself was not the most graceful runner, with his lolling head and hunched shoulders.

Without going into detail, which can wait until a later chapter, the pattern of training that emerged and was generally agreed by the start of the seventies for anyone wishing to become as good a distance runner as their potential would allow, consisted of three basic ingredients. They were, and still are: i) lots of running, a minimum total of about seventy miles a week and up to over a hundred miles a week, mostly done at a steady pace, ii) at least one long run a week of about 15 to 20 miles, longer still for marathon runners, iii) some fast running, either repetitions of short to medium distances or continuous runs of up to ten miles run at close to race pace.

This sort of training came together with a philosophy or state of mind that had also been developing over a long period and filtering into the running community, reaching more and more individuals each year, until it became as ingrained as the training itself; running was a part of life. Training may have had its seasonal variation but it was a year-long, day by day activity. It was not something to indulge in when the fancy took. It was as vital as a person's occupation. A runner would no more decide to have a day off training than to miss a day's work. There were no breaks for holidays or for personal reasons. Training and racing merged into one continuous activity. Sometimes it even seemed as if the races and the performances, what at first had been the sole grounds for running at all, became incidental to the training.

The idea that training was an integral part of a runner's life came with the assumption that it brought about continuous, long term improvement. Even when improvement stopped, the same training habit was necessary to maintain the acquired level of performance - hence the 'training trap' that I refer to elsewhere. In short: once a committed runner, always a committed runner. For anyone who embarked on the road of running ambition, following the formula developed in the fifties and sixties, there became no escape.

I managed to reach my own first peak as a runner in 1971. You could say that I had sat out the previous two decades and let the rest of the running world do the experimenting and arguing for me. Then, when I was ready to take my running more seriously, I capitalised on what others had discovered and followed their hard earned example. Actually it wasn't quite like that. Already by the time I was well ensconced at my first university I had done enough running to have developed an instinct for the sort of training that would work for me. Of course I copied other people's ideas, but not blindly. I seemed to know the way I would go, even before deciding precisely which route to take.

At the end of September 1968 I went to a student training camp at Merthyr Mawr in Wales. I was only there for five days but ran eight sessions in that time, a total of nearly sixty miles. I had never before run that much in one week. It may only have been a short period of intensive training but it had a wonderfully stimulating effect on my body. I felt loose and light limbed, more relaxed and definitely fitter, less tired if anything, and invigorated. The day I got back from Wales I ran a relay leg for my club. I remember running particularly well. I knew then that a similar amount of running on a regular basis would be just the thing for me. The only thing that went wrong from then on was that I never had quite the confidence, will power, or time from other things to stick to what I knew would work. I am not, and never was as dedicated as Ron Hill, who has been, throughout my lifetime, the epitome of single minded devotion to running. I lacked the degree of resolve needed to train every single day for years on end, and that makes me ashamed. In my whole running life I could only do in training a reasonable imitation of the truly committed runners, and then only for periods of rarely more than a year at a time.

As well as being the decade that established the required pattern of training that would be followed by pretty well all the best distance runners in the country from then on, the sixties was also the period when the limits were being set. If a hundred miles a week, three sessions a day and hard running into the bargain had seemed incredible in the fifties, the sixties were about to see even more incredible quantities of training tested. It was almost as if the running world, momentarily, in a fit of macho madness, forgot the ultimate purpose of training and embarked on a competition for no more reason than to see who could train the most and the hardest.

Already, in 1965, when I started my first term at University, I became aware of rumours that Mike Turner and Roger Robinson, two of the top runners in the country at that time, both post graduate students at Cambridge University, were running a hundred and fifty miles a week in training. I remember at first thinking that to run that much would be impossible. Then I broke it down to a simple matter of running about twenty miles every day, or two hour-long sessions, and it didn't seem quite so impossible after all. I even wondered whether I could do it, but decided that, although I could probably cope with that sort of physical workload, I could never commit myself to so much time devoted to running. I might last one week, maybe two, but that would be it.

Still, I couldn't help but be impressed. There was no doubt that Turner and Robinson were excellent runners, at the very top of the British distance running tree (Mike Turner twice finished second in the English National Cross Country Championship, in 1964 and 1966) and, if they both felt the need to run so much in training, then who was to say that they had got it wrong? More and more training miles could well be the recipe for greatness, simple as that.

A lot of runners must have thought along the same lines. Extrapolating the idea was the next step that some of them took, leading to the logical but ultimately erroneous belief - the more training the better. A good example of a runner who stretched the limits of conceivable training mileage in the late sixties was the Bournemouth athlete, Roger Matthews, who, seemingly against all the odds, was fourth in the AAA 10,000m championship in 1969, won the selection race for the Edinburgh Commonwealth Games the following year, and became that year's fourth fastest 10,000m runner in the world, when finishing fourth in those games.

I trained with Matthews a few times when I was staying in Bournemouth in the summer of 1969. Once, along with a couple of other Bournemouth runners, we ran ten miles on the road, split into two miles warm up, then six miles hard and the last two miles easy. No one told me we were only doing six miles hard. At eight miles, with two to go, I was ready to give in. I had reached the limit of my ability to keep up with what seemed a furious pace. I decided to drop back. Suddenly the others slowed to a jog and saved me the admission of weakness I was about to make. It was a huge relief. For me that was one very hard run, my only run of the day. For Roger Matthew's it was his third session of the day. Another of his sessions that I joined was on the Bournemouth track; we did 25 x 200m repetitions, jogging diagonally across the inside field back to the starting point between reps. I think we ran each 200m in around 34 seconds. That was Roger's second session of the day.

He was running three times a day in hot summer weather, ten miles to work at 6.30am, a lunchtime session, often on the track, and 12 – 15 miles home in the evening; that's around thirty miles every day, sometimes over two hundred miles a week. The result was that Matthews became permanently, severely dehydrated. For a while he was under observation in hospital but was told to continue his training as usual so that he could be examined in what were, for him, normal circumstances.

What makes the example of Roger Matthews iconic, more so even than his contemporary, and more famous 200 miles per week runner, Dave Bedford, is that he was, or had been, in the words of the well known coach Frank Horwill, 'a mediocre athlete'. He was also a working man who had to fit his three times a day running habit around a five day a week job as a carpenter with Bournemouth council. In this he was like a number of runners of the sixties who between them gradually extended the bounds of what quantity of training was possible for an ordinary amateur runner. It took runners of the seventies and eighties to test these bounds, as it were, to destruction. Where those bounds lay is a question that is taken up in Chapter 7. But, already, at the start of the seventies, it is probable that the bounds had, unwittingly, been reached. Future evidence merely confirmed that, although, the sort of training that Roger Matthews forced on himself can work, it is on the very edge of what is ultimately both physically and mentally destructive. I doubt if a single runner in the world today covers as much as 200 miles per week.

The nineteen fifties and sixties were a truly remarkable period in the history of British distance running. The sport advanced further and faster in that time than during any similar period. It so happened that I grew up, and my running developed contemporaneously with the sport itself, so that we both reached a peak together. In some ways this was my good luck. I often wonder whether I would have been the runner I became had I been born forty years later. I suspect not. I would have run, of that I'm certain, but I would not have caught the infection that caused so many perfectly ordinary working men of my generation to devote large amounts of their lives and energy to the pursuit of what? Fame (but not fortune) for a very few, a sense of achievement, self validation, the odd small prize, medal or trophy, selection for a significant representative team, a report to read in the paper, or a picture to show off, the camaraderie that only those who share the same arduous pursuit can appreciate, friends who understand you because they have the same needs, aspirations and work ethic, an occasional subsidised trip to other parts of the country or abroad and, above all, a totally unrealistic, a mad, absurdly optimistic and hopeful ambition.

All these things are still available to runners today, of course, and some of them are more easily attained. Perhaps that is part of the problem. Nowadays you only have to finish in order to get a medal. You only have to participate to achieve some publicity. You only have to reach much reduced levels of attainment to receive the same accolades that runners of the sixties and seventies sought. Had I started running in the twenty first century I might have become quite good. I might have become good enough to win a lot of the races that are now won in times that show clearly, simply by contrast, how good the glory days of British running really were. But I wouldn't have been as good as I did become. I would always have lacked that compulsion that drove all my contemporaries. The bug that carried this obsession, and that we all caught in the end, originated ultimately from the running stars, the Ron Hills, Dave Bedfords, Ian Thompsons, and all the others, and, since we came into contact with them, both figuratively and literally, on a regular basis, we were bound to catch it sooner or later. Where are the British stars of the twenty first century, the Paula Radcliffes, and Mo Farahs? Coccooned in some foreign land, taking part in quite separate races from the rest of us, completely isolated, bug-wise, from mere mortals like me. It would be hard to catch even the most virulent motivational virus from any of them.

Besides, if I had been born in 1986, rather than 1946, I could never have afforded to become a serious runner. When I started running there was no such thing as a specialist running shoe, what would now be called a 'trainer'. Good, common or garden Woolworth's canvas plimsolls did for every purpose: running, tennis, cricket, school gym lessons, scout camps and summer holidays, and only cost a few shillings. What, I think may have been the very first general purpose running shoes to make it to British sports shops, at least the ones I knew about, appeared in the mid sixties. I bought my first pair in the Turl in Oxford for the memorable sum of nineteen shillings and eleven pence. They were made by the Japanese company 'Onitsuka Tiger' and the pair I bought was the cheapest version, the Tiger 'Cub', very much like a plimsoll with red stripes, though they did have a firmer sole with a slight tread, giving the shoes some grip on wet surfaces. I loved those shoes. Just putting them on made me feel like a real runner. Several pairs and a few price increases later I was running some of my very best times in exactly the same shoes.

I was a student and, therefore poor, but could afford not just a pair of running shoes, but a pair that made me look as much a serious runner as anyone else in a race. Tiger Cubs were everywhere during the sixties, worn by runners of all abilities. Today I would find it hard to find a pair of running shoes with similar status value for less than fifty times the price I paid for my Tiger Cubs. Even taking inflation into account, that's a big difference.

It's still theoretically possible to run in kit costing very little, as most runners did prior to the time I started, but it would take a very determined and self confident person to do so. In an age when image is everything, no one wants to be seen training or racing in anything but the proper gear, and there are armies of sales people, advertisers and others with a vested interest doing everything possible to convince runners that they must have all the specialist kit available. The main purpose of running now seems to be to raise money for the manufacturers. From being a poor man's sport it has evolved into a middle class sport. Inevitably it has lost a lot in the process.

It seems ironic that, as more money circulates around running, as the whole process of being involved in the sport becomes more expensive, as the importance of fashion and image escalates, so average standards have dropped. While runners today care about image as much as about their level of attainment, runners of the sixties cared only about the latter. They couldn't afford (in the financial sense) to care about what they wore or how they looked and, not caring, they could devote more of their intent and effort to the business of running as well as they could.

There was a runner, whom I won't name for fear of embarrassing him, but who may be recognisable to anyone who ran road races in the South of England during the sixties and seventies. In all the times I ran against him, he wore the same pair of shorts. Year after year he wore the same ones. I know, because they weren't running shorts. They were, I think, swimming trunks, the sort that Sean Connery wore in the Bond film 'Dr No', grey-blue, tight and with short legs. The runner in question was better than I was, and I was often in a position to examine his shorts from the rear and wonder how he could run so fast in something so tight. In the 1976 Walton ten, my fastest ever ten mile road race, he finished fourth in 49:19, nearly three quarters of a minute ahead of me. Of two things I am absolutely certain. If any British runner today ran a ten mile race in 49:19, he would be one of the very best distance runners in Britain and, on top of that, he wouldn't be wearing an old pair of substitutes for top of the range, fully fashionable, designed for purpose running shorts.

CHAPTER 4
University

*'If Stanford were a country it would have come
sixth in the Olympics'.*

Fraser Nelson writing about the American universities system.

I left school in 1965 and went to university. It was the making of me as a runner. Universities throughout the British Isles seemed to be the making of hundreds of good runners of my era and had been for many years before that. I have no doubt they continued to be the making of runners long after I left. Either that, or it was a case of accomplished young runners choosing, in their hundreds, to go to university. I think more the former than the latter, though, undoubtedly, there has been an element of success attracting success in the story of the universities' and colleges' running scene. It's the same everywhere. People who are good at something are always attracted to places where there are others who are good at the same thing.

Not only were there a large number of good runners around when I started my university years, who were either university students themselves or had been university students previously, but many of the very best, the winners, record holders and internationals, fell into this category. I haven't all the statistics to prove it but it seemed to me that universities provided a disproportionate number of the top distance runners in the country at one time. Through the sixties, seventies and eighties, on average at least one in five of the top fifty finishers in the senior men's English National Cross Country Championship were students or alumni of universities and colleges.

Perhaps the most remarkable success story, after the Oxbridge trio of Bannister, Chataway and Brasher, came from Cambridge University of the Sixties. To quote from Simon Molden's 'Hares Hounds and

Blues - A History of the University Cross Country Race', *'It is not an exaggeration to say that C.U.H.&H.* (Cambridge University Hares and Hounds) *was one of the strongest, if not the strongest, cross country clubs in the country in the early 1960s.'* Look who ran for Cambridge University at the start of this period: Mike Turner (several times England international cross country team representative), Bruce Tulloh (European 5000m champion in 1962), Tim Johnston (England international over the country, second to Gaston Roelants of Belgium in the 1967 international race at Barry in Wales, and a British Olympic representative in the marathon), Herb Elliot (the same Herb Elliot who won 1500m gold in the Rome Olympics), Tim Briault (another England international), Roger Robinson (who ran for the English team at the IAAA cross country championship in 1966 and later ran for New Zealand), plus several other runners of international standard.

Mike Turner was the driving force behind the success of the Cambridge team of this time. He proved the value of having a group of like-minded runners living in close proximity, training together, feeding off each other's successes and experiences, and working as a team. The same phenomenon is seen today in the training camps set up in countries around the world for the sole purpose of raising the standards of distance running at the very top. It works in Kenya. It has worked in Japan. It worked in Cambridge in the early sixties. In many ways that is why the universities in general have been such a hotbed of promising runners. Even if they are not set up as training camps, that is, in effect, what they often become.

One doesn't have to look any further than that for an explanation of why the universities produced such good runners in the numbers that they did. Any system that takes young people nearing the peak of their physical abilities, puts them into a shared environment, looks after their immediate needs, encourages them to achieve their objectives, manufactures a competitive structure and a team spirit, and gives them plenty of free time, is bound to produce excellence. It only takes one or two single-minded individuals with drive and ambition to start and steer the process, and the enthusiasm and commitment they generate spreads throughout the group. The success that results is like a rolling snowball. Every new bit of snow it picks up becomes part of an ever enlarging mass, developing unstoppable momentum. In time it doesn't matter who started it, or how it started. It becomes a case of perpetual motion. Cambridge University was still attracting good runners years after the heady days of the late fifties and early sixties.

If there is a team leader in the form of a professional coach, so much the better and, if sport is a recognised and formally supported activity within an institution, better still. Groups of runners are quite capable of looking after themselves, but there is no doubt that a bit of outside organisation, even a degree of compulsion, speeds up the process of improvement. Running is no different from any other activity. It can be self-taught and managed through personal commitment alone, but it helps enormously to have a teacher and guide, some extrinsic motivation, and, where the possibility exists, some funding.

This last point can easily be overlooked. In theory running costs nothing. In reality, if running is to be pursued as a competitive sport, it becomes quite expensive. The main cost for any individual or for a club is in entering races and travelling to them, maybe with an overnight stay into the bargain. A university usually budgets for this and each sports club gets an annual amount to cover just such costs. Throughout my university running career I don't remember ever paying a penny towards entry fees, travel or accommodation. This was by stark contrast to the lot of the working athletes of the immediate post war period who had absolutely no financial assistance. In many instances even runners representing Great Britain in international competitions had to pay their own fares to those very events. Imagine that - being picked to represent your country and then being expected to make your own way to the venue and buy your own train ticket!

In 1970, right in the middle of my university days, Ron Hill, himself an ex university student, made the long trip to the USA, where he won the Boston marathon. Was he paid a large appearance sum? Did he get a large money prize? Were even his expenses met? None of the above. There was a fund raising campaign to send Ron to the Boston marathon. A begging bowl was sent around running circles for contributions to the Ron Hill Boston marathon fund! In the Road Runners Club newsletter of August 1970 there is a list of 215 contributors to the fund, mostly individuals, who together raised the grand total of £170. I'm ashamed to say that my name is not on that list. At the time I could barely afford to run my own races. I didn't appreciate it at the time, I pretty much took it for granted, but free competition was a godsend during the seven years I was a university student.

When I started research at my second university in 1969, I bought my first car. It was a cream and pale brown 1962 Wolseley fifteen hundred and I would give a lot to have it still, despite the fact that it leaked like a sieve and seemed to be made as much of rust as solid metal. It was one of the last of what could be called cars with style. It had leather seats and a walnut-faced dashboard. You started it by pushing a button. It always started first time; once on a bitterly cold morning when there was just enough power in the battery to turn the engine over one time only, with a slow groan that sounded as if it came from a dying man; Uu...urgh... brmmm...brmmm, and we were in business. Actually I needn't have worried, because the car had a starting handle and I could afford to run it with an almost totally flat battery.

My car became the cross country team taxi and covered many miles taking myself and three or sometimes four other members of the team to races. I was able to claim a small but adequate mileage allowance from the university and always ended up slightly in profit. You could say that, for a period of a year or two, I was a professional runner. I depended on that petrol money. At the very least my competitive running was being sponsored to the point that my only expenses were for running kit, and for filling myself regularly with copious amounts of food and drink. Students, generally, are not well off. They never were and they probably still aren't. No one today, therefore, can claim poverty as an excuse for the decline in distance running standards since my university days, nor commercial sponsorship and large money prizes for the high standards of the élite. Poverty and high standards went hand in hand in the sixties and seventies. Between 1969 and 1972 I lived on a student grant from the Science Research Council of £750 per year, plus what I could earn by demonstrating and doing a bit of teaching in the summer. I could just about make ends meet. I lived in various shared student flats and houses, ate most of my meals in the university refectory, managed I don't know how to buy and run a car, bought clothes only when absolutely necessary, ran in the same training shoes for sometimes six times the recommended maximum distance (manufacturers and running gurus now suggest you change your trainers every five hundred miles, or what would have been for me at that time, about every two months - I wonder why?) wore running shorts until they were so tatty at the crutch that the two legs were barely still attached together, and never went into debt. I kept a notebook for a while, in which I recorded everything I spent. I would consult my book every so often to calculate whether I could afford to buy a beer or a cup of coffee and whether my outgoings were in danger of overtaking my regular grant cheque. Once I had established that I was always just inside the balance line I threw the book away, but I still had to be careful with money.

Most of us were like that. Perhaps that was the attraction of running as a sport; it didn't cost very much. There was no fancy equipment and no courts or pools or playing fields to hire. If you had a run to do, and the time to do it, you just did it; it was free. Yet, despite their shared impecuniousness, students in all parts of the country reached the very top of the running ladder. A team taken from the British universities and colleges of the early seventies could well have been as good as the English cross country team itself.

One member of that team would have been the best of the lot, namely Dave Bedford, who, in 1971, won both the English National and a few weeks later, the International Cross Country Championship, in San Sebastian, Spain. He was a student at Brighton College, just across the road from Sussex University where I was doing research. For a while we were both in the same club, Falmer Striders, a combined Brighton colleges and Sussex University team. Had I been at Sussex a year earlier I would also have been a Falmer Striders' team mate of another future English National Cross Country Championship winner, Brendan Foster, who studied chemistry at Sussex from 1966 to 1969.

Nor were these the only two English, Scottish, Welsh or Northern Irish international cross country runners who were attending universities or colleges contemporaneously with my own years as a student. Birmingham university was particularly strong during this era, with Malcolm Thomas, Welsh international and winner of the English National Cross Country Championship in 1972, Andy Holden, regular English international cross country team member during the seventies, British Olympic representative in the 3,000m steeplechase and, later, marathon runner of note, Frank Briscoe and Ray Smedley, who were both members of the English team that won silver medals in the World Cross Country Championships in 1974, when it was held in Monza, Italy. There, from a single university, you have the makings of a team that might have been the equal of almost any other club or home international team. Then there were runners of the calibre of Jack Lane, Tony Ashton, Andy McKean, Tony Moore, John Valentine, Greg Hannon, Chris Garforth, Julian Goater, Malcolm Absalem, John Kirkbride and so many more. I mention only those who swiftly come to mind.

Though we students may have lacked ready cash, we had other benefits in abundance. I won't go so far as to say that students don't work hard, but they do have an easy life, more so when living in college, where all meals are provided, rooms are cleaned and warmed, changing rooms with hot showers are readily accessible, responsibilities are limited and time and freedom are always available. Living in digs, outside college, as I did for four years, is not much more stressful. A tenant in rented accommodation doesn't care, beyond his or her immediate comfort, if the roof blows off, if the pipes burst, if the rates bill arrives, or the bin-men are on strike, if the dust builds up to mountainous levels or the garden becomes a rubbish tip. Nothing need disturb the worry-free lifestyle and the training. The student life is certainly conducive to achieving excellence in any sport. It doesn't surprise me that so many students became, in some cases, amongst the best runners in the country, and in many more cases, as I did, good runners of county, rather than international, standard - the classic 'good club runners' of the time.

There is another factor that might explain why so many university students have been good runners, though even to suggest it might put me into politically incorrect hot water. Distance running is a sport where success depends on long term application: on having a goal, on knowing the best way to achieve that goal and on having the determination and confidence to stick at it. It is also, though you might not think so, an intellectual as well as a physical pursuit. It involves a certain amount of planning, reasoning, decision making and problem solving and, dare I say it, intelligence. Aren't these the same necessary requirements for achieving a degree; even more so a higher degree? Anyone, of course, who is able to apply themselves to a long term programme of training using his or her own initiative, university student or not, has to be admired. I hope I'm not being unfairly élitist in this. I am merely suggesting that being at university is an indication that someone has already been through a selection process that concentrates into a particular group such qualities as single-mindedness and work ethic and, therefore, now belongs to a community that is weighted in favour of just those things that it takes to become a successful runner. If anything, top runners who never went further in their education than secondary school, deserve greater admiration simply because, at the most important stage in their development as runners, they didn't have the advantages given to students.

I saw fellow students develop, in an almost automatic response to the warmth of the university sporting climate, from insignificant embryos of runners to competitors of a standard that surprised themselves as much as those who knew them. There was a quiet chap called Dave who came to Sussex the year after I did. I don't think he had done much running before, but he joined the cross country club and ran, not very well, in all our races. For a while he was a bit of a joke, one that, fortunately, he enjoyed as much as the rest of us. After a race we would all have a good laugh about how far down the field he'd finished. But what I loved about him was that he obviously enjoyed his running and embraced it as part of his life with the greatest enthusiasm. I watched him getting better as the winter months went by. He was still no distance runner but, when the cross country season gave way to the athletics season, he revealed a previously hidden turn of speed and became our first string 800m runner, regularly running under two minutes. That's what the university environment could do. All it took was a bit of like-minded company, a shared activity and shared rewards to turn a frog into a bit of a prince.

At the upper end of the achievement scale was another Sussex student who also came to the university a year after me, namely, Adrian Parker. He was a swimmer first, and took up running as a step towards trying the biathlon. He was then head-hunted for the British modern pentathlon team on the basis that he was a good swimmer, and was becoming a good runner. But, although anyone can run and swim using their own initiative, it takes instruction, facilities and expert tuition to shoot, fence and ride a horse.

I only saw him running. He and I ran many races together and for a year or so it never occurred to me to look in front for a sight of his back. But all the time he was getting closer. In 1972 the director of sport at the university, himself an international triple jumper, got together an athletics team to compete in Barcelona against an equivalent Spanish team. Selection criteria were rather loose which meant that the team that travelled to Spain comprised a number of add-ons who had no claim to be members of the university, one of whom, incidentally, was a youthful Steve Ovett from the local Brighton Athletics Club. I think he ran the 400 metres in the Barcelona meeting.

The event turned out to be the last time I beat Adrian Parker in a running race. We both ran the 1,500m. I led most of the way and was disconcertedly aware that I was being closely followed, not only by the Spaniard, who eventually won, but by Parker. It was disconcerting because, according to all my previous experience, he shouldn't have been following me closely. Besides, he was a swimmer. He was built for swimming, six feet tall and muscular with it. He weighed over twelve stones. Harking back to my boyhood convictions, runners were supposed to be slim and weak. Being able to beat big strong men in races was what compensated for their weakness. I think I ran all out in that race primarily to stop myself being beaten by Adrian Parker.

I employed my usual tactic for a 1,500m or mile race, a distance I didn't like because I wasn't really fast enough for it. My lifetime best time for a quarter mile is only a shade under 56 seconds, a time that wouldn't even have allowed me to keep up for the first lap of many a top class 1500m race. My tactic was to run as hard as I could over the third lap, as if it was the last, and try to hang on for the remaining few hundred metres. I didn't do this in order to win, though in a few mile or 1,500m races I managed even that. I did it in order to get the very last drop of effort out of myself and, thereby, to do the best time I could, regardless of the other runners.

Laps went by in 63, 65 and 63 seconds, and still I was leading. I wasn't overtaken until the finishing straight. I wasn't surprised to be beaten, nor disappointed. I finished a mere 0.4 of a second outside four minutes, a personal best time then and to this day; 4:00.4 - such a shame about that fraction of a second. I felt just as Roger Bannister would have felt had he done the same time for a mile at Iffley Road in Oxford on May 6th 1954.

Why was I relieved that it was the Spaniard who beat me and not my friend and team mate, Adrian Parker? Because it is never very nice to be knocked off your perch by someone whom you have seen creeping up on you from an inferior position in the pecking order. Much as you might be friends with someone, you still prefer to preserve the status quo. From then on, however, I gave way to him as the superior runner.

I like to think that, just as he, through natural rivalry, spurred me on to my fastest time for the distance, I might have played some part in what was to come for him in the near future. We didn't train together, but I may have encouraged him to greater efforts just by being there at that time.

Four years later, in Montreal, Adrian Parker won a team gold medal and finished in fifth individual place in the Olympic modern pentathlon event. Judging by the reports of the competition it would be fair to say that he effectively won all three of the gold medals, his own, plus those of the other two team members, because it was his exceptional cross country run and the points it contributed to the team total that gave Great Britain the win. He was first in the cross country run and by such a margin that the team place changed from fourth at the start of his run to first as he finished. To quote from the website www.sports-reference. com: *'With only the cross country event remaining, Great Britain were in fourth place, with all hopes resting on Adrian Parker, rated as one of the best runners in the world among pentathletes. If all went well, the bronze, or perhaps the silver medals, seemed a possibility. With an outstanding run, Parker won the cross country discipline and, against all probabilities, Britain won the gold.'* As they say, 'You couldn't make it up'.

Would Adrian Parker have been noticed if he had not been at University? I can't say. But one thing is certain: had he not been noticed or, by his own initiative, brought himself to the attention of those responsible for the British modern pentathlon team, he would have remained no more than a good swimmer who became a good runner. And, from the point of view of the administrators of the sport of modern pentathlon, where better to look for promising recruits than the universities? Universities and colleges, like schools before them, are the obvious nursery grounds for talent in sports of all sorts.

Nowhere has the concept of organised collegiate sport been instigated to a higher degree than in the USA. The American system, with its treatment of distance running and other sports the same as any other part of the college curriculum, and its awarding of sports scholarships, produced the ultimate training schools for bringing on gifted runners. A number of runners I was acquainted with, and many others I knew simply by repute, took advantage of the offer of scholarships to American Universities, where they were educated and trained in running with the same rigour as applied to their academic work. They had a timetable for training and a schedule to follow, decided by the coach. Training was in groups or what could, more fittingly, be called classes, bearing in mind the context and the way in which they were organised. Missing training was not an option, any more than missing classes in maths or English or any other part of the curriculum would have been. Homework was yet more training, and examinations were races, held on a regular basis.

This somewhat regimented method often turned promising runners into very good runners indeed. Some of the best British distance runners of the second half of the twentieth century were products of the American collegiate system. The same could be said, even more so, of Irish runners. I presume because of the close historical connection and genealogical affinity between Ireland and the USA, some of the first athletes to take advantage of the American collegiate system were Irish. Perhaps the earliest great Irish running success story belonged to Ron Delaney of Villanova University, Pennsylvania. Delaney won the Olympic 1,500m title in Melbourne in 1956 and thus proved the value of the disciplined and carefully stage-managed approach to training and racing that a college environment could readily provide. Nearly thirty years later John Treacy, another Irish product of the American collegiate system (in his case the college was Providence College, Rhode Island) became perhaps the greatest male distance runner Ireland has ever had. His career culminated in the winning of an Olympic silver medal in the marathon at the Los Angeles Olympics of 1984 and before that he had won two consecutive World Cross Country Championships, in Glasgow in 1978 and in Limerick the following year. Both Delaney and Treacy could reasonably be described as products of the American system, but both continued to run successfully after leaving college. I think the same could be said of most runners who spent time in an American College. What this proves is that however intense the training may have been under the collegiate system and however little freedom was allowed, it was not necessarily destructive of motivation. Treacy himself says in an interview for my own club, Annadale Striders Athletic Club in Belfast, when asked what the training at Providence was like, '*The training was excellent. There was great team spirit and it was fun. The training was based on quality and it really was the track sessions that made it.*'

I can imagine those track sessions, though I prefer not to. Nothing can equal a track session carried out with other runners, some of whom might be better or feeling better than yourself, according to a plan that is not your own, for sheer mind and body-numbing hardness. Even now to hear or read something like 'five by one mile on the track' makes me wince. I have always avoided such training like the plague, which may, of course, explain why I was never as good a runner as a lot of others. It is not the nature of the surface or any other peculiarity of the track itself, apart from its confined space, that makes training on a track so hard. It is the facts that it is done under the scrutiny of a coach and other runners, it is imposed and inescapable, it is so excruciatingly repetitive and restrictive - a mile on a track seems so much further than a mile on the road - and it is impossible for anyone with a similar psyche to mine not to turn the training into a competition, with all its associated mentally damaging consequences.

I was interested to discover, from the same interview that John Treacy gave to my club, that one of his training companions at Providence was the English runner Steve Binns. Binns was yet another runner of world class who missed out on public acknowledgement simply because he was a part of the golden age of British distance running and, therefore, just one more bright star hidden in a galaxy. With a best time for the 10,000m of 27:55.6 and having competed for Great Britain at the Seoul Olympics in 1988, his relative anonymity outside the world of athletics enthusiasts confirms two things. One is that distance running has always been and will continue to be a sport of minority interest. The other is that fame and its poorer relation, recognition, are very rarely related to the degree to which they are deserved. There is usually room for only one or two, rarely three (as, for example, in the case of Ovett, Coe and Cram) in the hall of fame at any one time. Steve Binns would have had to share with much better known runners of his day, Brendan Foster and Eamonn Martin, for example, a room to which the media, rather than those who appreciate the sport, has the key.

The success of the American collegiate system in bringing on middle and long distance runners came at a time when the practice of interval training on the track was coming into the ascendency, with groups of runners training together under the watchful eye of the coach and according to his instructions. Again, this was an ideal routine for a college environment. The track was part of the campus. The coach was one of the university staff. Standing by the track with a stopwatch gave him something to do, like a conductor with an orchestra. The groups of runners were already assembled, recruited to the institution by virtue of their promise as runners, some of them subsidised by college scholarships. Their time was the college's time, and enough of it could easily be set aside for the daily workout.

The danger of this form of systematized development of runners is that it tends towards 'one size fits all' training. It's hard to manage a group of runners with a schedule of training and to provide individual training menus at the same time. If the training is geared towards the better runners, as it is likely to be, given that the whole purpose of the system is to create excellence, the weaker ones suffer. For all the athletes who have been made by the American Collegiate system or by any other group training system, especially the most rigorous and dictatorial examples, there are others who have been broken by them.

As I have said elsewhere; if I have one regret about my early running, it is that I never had any guidance or externally applied discipline. I think that, in my teens and early twenties I would have responded well to a benevolent coach who kept me at it and controlled my casual habits where training was concerned. By the time I developed enough experience, confidence and self discipline to stick at it for long periods at a time, without help, I had already missed some of my best years. On the other hand complete independence does bring special satisfaction and ensured, in my case, that no one could have destroyed my love of running through forcing over-hard training on me. I may have been only a sixty watt bulb, when I might have been a hundred, but I was of the long-life variety.

British universities have never taken their recruitment of gifted sportsmen, from all parts of the world, to the levels seen in the American collegiate system, though it was evident in my first year at college that a number of overseas students, mostly postgraduates, chose to come to British universities both to study and for the sport. This was nothing new. Herb Elliot, the Australian Olympic 1,500m champion, was at Cambridge in 1960. Another Olympic 1,500m gold medal winner, the New Zealander, Jack Lovelock, was at Oxford in 1932. What I knew as the PE colleges, Borough Road, Alsager, Loughborough, for example, were well known for always having more than their fair share of good runners. Sporting students were attracted to colleges that had a reputation for sport, a perfect example of positive feedback. At the same time athletic prowess was an advantage when it came to gaining admission, to these colleges in particular, and to universities in general. But it has never been the sole criterion for university admission in Britain.

In the USA, this selection of sporting talent from anywhere and everywhere with the offer of scholarships was, and probably still is, blatant. In effect the American Colleges buy the athletic talent they need for their track teams on the open market, with scant regard for the academic side of a student's life. When Groucho Marx in the film 'Horse Feathers' goes looking for two famous football players for his college team and finds Harpo and Chico instead, it may be farcical, but it has a grounding in truth. American college sports teams, including track, are managed in much the same way as an English premier league football team, where players are actively sought out and paid for and are as likely to come from Africa, South America or Asia as anywhere in Europe and, least likely of all, to come from England, Scotland, Wales or Northern Ireland. Chelsea, I believe, once put out a team in which every single player was a foreigner; or was it Arsenal, or Manchester United? It makes little difference.

What goes on and has gone on in universities and colleges in the USA may seem irrelevant to the running scene in Great Britain except that it has had at least two profound influences. The first is to demonstrate that an expertly managed system for producing good runners, even if it is a bit mechanical, can really work. The same principles are seen in 'schools of excellence' in all sorts of sports, and in the training camps and improvement programmes that have been set up in different parts of the world to advance running standards. It is no coincidence that different nations come into the ascendancy in distance running, for a period of a few years at a time, not with just one runner, but with several together, Finland in the nineteen thirties with the 'flying Finns' and again in the seventies, and Italy in the eighties, for example. Hungary, Poland, East Germany, Spain, Portugal, Japan, China, USA have all flourished at different times and, of course, Kenya and Ethiopia in the nineties and beyond. For the same reasons British running clubs go through periods when they are immensely strong, times when the club training set up, inspired by the presence of one or two top class runners, is working exceptionally effectively. When Brendan Foster was Britain's top 5,000 and 10,000m runner, he trained with a Gateshead A.C. crowd who were almost a who's who of British distance running. Which came first, the runners or the club set-up?

The second influence of the American collegiate system is that of globalising running. When Ron Delaney went to America in 1950 to run for Villanova University it must have seemed an incredibly adventurous thing to do. Just after the war and for years afterwards athletes were very much home birds. Home was where they lived, and home was where they trained and ran. Any jaunt abroad was solely for the best runners on international team duty. It may have seemed a slightly unpatriotic thing to do, to deliberately go to another country to train. In some people's opinion it may have almost amounted to a form of cheating. Years later it hardly seems to matter where runners do their running, where they live and where they train. The best British distance runners are now routinely based abroad. The country you run for, if you are of international standard, has become a purely political formality. One of our best distance runners of recent years, John Brown, who was fourth in the Olympic marathons of both 2000 and 2004, running for Great Britain, and who held the British 10,000m record before Mo Farah broke it in June, 2011, emigrated to Canada in the second half of the nineteen nineties and, when it seemed that he had been forgotten by his country of birth, became a Canadian citizen. That is how fickle the concept of nationality and running for your country has become. John Brown did nothing wrong. It was just the way he was perceived by the public, the media and the administrators of the sport, one moment lauded for his great performances as a British runner, the first to seriously challenge the Africans, the next, ignored simply because he had gone to live elsewhere and, finally, forgotten, because he was no longer British.

The exodus of promising young runners to the American universities, the peak of which, in my perception, coincided with the peak of British distance running, may not have been the first, nor the only influence diluting the importance of nationality and domesticity in running, but it played its part. It helped to dissociate the home based running scene from what was happening globally and thereby diminished the importance of many of the significant running events held on British soil, which were, more and more, being seen as very minor, parochial competitions, unless, of course, they happened to be one of the new breed of multi-participant, money-spinning, big city road races. Globalisation, in my view, has been one of the primary causes of a decline in standards of British distance running. Once a sufficient number of Britain's best runners had moved more or less permanently abroad, the aforementioned John Brown for example, and other top marathon runners, such as Geoff Smith, Steve Jones and Paula Radcliffe, to the USA, it had begun to seem practically necessary to emigrate in order to be any good. No longer was it considered possible for any home based runner to reach the top. So not so many tried.

My time at university was not remotely geared to running in the way it might have been if I had had an athletic scholarship to an American college. All the guidance I obtained in my running came indirectly, by a slow process of osmosis. It came from fellow students, from taking part in races, from watching other people running, from reading and talking about running and through all the other processes by which we learn, without actually being taught.

When I first arrived at university I was lucky enough to find myself in the same college as three or four fellow students who were much more serious and practised in their running, and much better, than me. Through them I learned the basics of training, the advantages of training in company, the ethos of a shared sense of purpose and the proper way to be serious about running. All through my school years and, if I'm being honest, throughout my first two years at university as well, my approach to running was dilettantish. I ran when I felt like it, or when there was a race to run. I had no particular aims, no long term plan of training, no weekly schedule to keep to and no targets in mind. Left to my own devices, at weekends and during the time between terms, I did very little training. I did belong to a club and competed occasionally for it, but I did so on the basis of residual fitness from term time running, natural ability and youthful resilience. There was no question of meeting regularly with other club members for training. It was a fifteen mile round trip from my home to the club headquarters and I had no transport and no spare money to pay for train or bus fares.

My development as a runner from my first to my last year as a university student was primarily an evolution of attitude. During those years at university (seven in all) I changed from someone who liked running but still didn't appreciate the need to work at it in order to get anywhere, into what could be described as a serious runner. What kept me going during the early transitional period was the fact that, despite being untrained and undisciplined, I remained quite a good runner and, most of all, I constantly day-dreamed about running success. That was the key to my education in serious running, my desire to be a good runner never wavered. My fellow students were my tutors and my coaches. I learned from each of them. I may never have had a coach, in the proper sense of the word, but, in a way, I had many coaches. It's just that none of them realised the influential role he played.

When runners get together for training, or just socially, everyone gains something from the others. It may be ideas, instruction, good example or bad example. Just as I learned that, if I wanted to improve, I had to be more serious about my training, others probably saw me as a lesson in how not to approach their running. For all I know some much better runner than I was might have benefited from my weaknesses of character at that time as much as I benefited from his strengths.

Meeting up for joint training can be just the push one needs to get out at all. It's hard to break an appointment. It helps a lot, especially on a long run, to have company. Time passes much quicker when you're sharing an activity. After training we would often stay together for a drink or for a cup of tea in someone's college room. Training became as much a social as a purely physical occasion. All these things happened because a university is a place where everyone lives in close proximity and can usually be free at the same time. There are very few strings attached to a student. I could arrange to go for a run with one or two of my college mates, more or less on a whim. I'd bump into them in the morning; 'Fancy a run this afternoon?' 'OK. See you at three o'clock.' Because there were no lectures or classes at weekends everyone could be available for a long run. Sundays, especially, could be a rather boring and lonely day. Going for a run in a group made it more enjoyable.

I was especially lucky, not just because there were good runners in my own college, but because in the university as a whole there were some extremely good runners. During my four years at my first university, I came across and, on occasions ran with, several internationals and discovered, just as I had noticed as a teenager that Jersy Chromik's leg was the same as my own, that they were just like the rest of us, only better runners. It is said that you are grown up when you realise that your parents are ordinary people. Similarly, when you realise that the best runners around are ordinary people, you have become a grown up runner. I became a grown up runner in my first year at university though it took me another two years before I acted like one.

I can now see the steps in my running education, all climbed at university, stretching out quite clearly behind me. I matriculated in October 1965 along with another student, called John, who was to become a top class cross country runner, never quite international standard, but almost so. He was to win the Oxford/Cambridge cross country race in1968. Because he was in the same college, he became the first person to influence my running. I very quickly realised that he took his running very seriously and when I learned that he had run a mile, while still at school, in 4:25, or thereabouts, I was impressed. I think my best time for a mile at school was 4:53. He was, perhaps, the very first influence causing me to connect running performance with dedication to training.

In one day he altered for ever my concept of a long run. Before I met him the furthest I had ever run continuously was five miles. A standard run for me at that time was about three miles and I wouldn't always run even that far. John led me and a couple of others on an out and back course totalling nine miles. I noted in my diary that I had run **nine miles!** Interestingly I found it quite easy, even though it was nearly twice as far as I'd ever run before. Looking back now, I smile. Not so many years later ten miles had become my most usual training distance. There came a time when 'long' didn't even start until fifteen miles. But it was only with the help of a fellow student that I gained the confidence to run that sort of distance routinely.

One afternoon, in my second year, I ran out of the city, up the river Thames towpath, planning to cross the river at Wolvercote and come back along the other bank. I was doing a few faster efforts during the run and one of these brought me to the road bridge that I was going to cross. As I stopped to open the gate onto the road another runner appeared from the opposite direction. He must have seen my final sprint to the gate. It was his idea that we run back together. When I suggested I might be going a bit slowly for him (because I knew exactly who he was) he didn't seem to mind, so we ran back to the edge of the city where I went one way and he went the other. He wanted to do, as he said, 'a bit more'. The runner was Fergus Murray, who had come from Edinburgh University to Oxford to do a year's postgraduate Certificate of Education course. Fergus Murray was one of Scotland's most outstanding distance runners. At the time that I bumped into him on the Thames towpath he had already represented Great Britain in the 10,000m at the Tokyo Olympic Games of 1964, and was an established cross country runner of some class. Four years later he represented Scotland in the marathon at the Edinburgh Commonwealth Games, finishing 7th in 2:15:32.

'So what?' you might say, 'we've all bumped into famous people by chance at one time or another.' In which case, you would miss the point. The point is that I learnt something from the experience and I absorbed something that contributed to changing me from a casual to a serious runner, not there and then - it was no conversion on the road to Damascus - but in due course. As we ran together down the river I could sense that while for me this run was a one-off, a day's indulgence, something that I felt like doing but hadn't planned on doing until moments before I set off, for Murray it was just another brick in the training wall. For him it was a tiny piece of a long process of conditioning, leading him back to a place that he had already visited, but that I couldn't even see from where I stood.

When we separated and he said he would 'do a bit more', I knew, without asking, that he had planned for that day a run of a certain distance. I ended up running about seven miles. He might have covered ten, twelve, fifteen or more, I don't know. But I'm sure it was a distance that he had decided on beforehand as part of a training plan. I'm sure also that he would have been out again the next day, maybe later that same day, and again would have known what he was going to do. I might have run the next day, I might not have. I really didn't know. Whatever I did I wouldn't have decided until the next day.

How did I gather all this from such a brief acquaintance? I knew all about myself, of course, and what was in my head, but how do you see inside someone else's head after running alongside them for a couple of miles with only a few words exchanged? For a start, his running was business-like. I could tell that it was done as a routine. The difference between his running and mine was the same as that between work and play. The very fact that he was happy to run with me, whom he didn't know, at my pace, suggested that the run was not important to him except as a small part of something much bigger. Every run I did at that time was an event in itself. I never looked further ahead than the next day or the next race. I was still treating running as a hobby rather than a job.

And then, of course, running with one of running's greats was another chance to prove to myself that I was superficially not a lot different from him. For two miles at least we ran at the same pace, almost stride for stride and I found it easy. He didn't seem too worried about that.

In the AAA track championships three miles event of 1965, just over a year before we ran together, Fergus Murray had finished sixth behind the winner, Ron Clarke of Australia, in a time of 13:21.2. Clarke had recorded 12:52.4, the first time anyone had broken thirteen minutes for the distance. By a strange coincidence a year later Clarke also won the race, this time slightly slower in 12:58.2 and was followed home by another Oxford University runner, the South African postgraduate Henk Altmann, who recorded 13:15.8. In 1967 Altmann ranked eighth in the British Commonwealth over three miles and seventh over six miles with times that would look very respectable even today. He would have been a much better known runner had South Africa not been effectively deprived of international competition due to the political stand against apartheid. Lo and behold, when I first arrived at the university, there was Henk Altmann running in university events, sometimes in the same races I ran. If I went to the track to change for a run, he would sometimes be there, or, if it wasn't him, it would be some other good runner doing interval training, pounding the same cinder pathway that Roger Bannister followed over ten years earlier, quite literally following in his footsteps.

Being thrust into an environment shared by top class distance runners, running the same races, changing in the same changing rooms, showering in the same showers, where training was an accepted part of some students' lives, and where there was an implicit and open invitation to the likes of me to emulate them, became, perhaps, the biggest influence on my running life. By the time I left my first university and started a research degree at Sussex I had matured into what could be described as a serious runner. I had been extremely tardy in reaching such a place. I was twenty three years old and had only just begun to see running as an uninterruptable part of my day to day life. I had got together with another running student in my fourth and final year before changing universities and begun to run more or less every day, up to fifty or more miles a week, but still with long breaks for no good reason. Between February 23rd 1969 and March 28th, for example, I note from my diary that I ran only twice. Why? I have no idea. It was a weakness that, as I started at Sussex University, I was determined to cure.

As a postgraduate research student my life was totally different. Gone were the three terms, Michaelmas, Hilary and Trinity (Christmas, Easter and Summer) and the long holidays in between. While I adhered to the university terms I was actually in college less time (three eight week terms) than away from it. Once I started at Sussex, however, I was in the same position as any working man, five days a week, forty eight weeks a year, which made adhering to a training routine much easier. If you want an everyday training pattern, first establish a workaday life style. You could say that, alongside the advantages of a student life I now had the advantages of a settled pattern of living. For nearly a year I trained without a significant break, up to seventy miles per week, sometimes more. Admittedly I slacked off for a couple of weeks in August, 1970 (summer holiday) and, again, over Christmas, but at the start of 1971 it was back to the grindstone and towards some of the best performances of my life. I can explain those performances, for example my thirteenth place in the Finchley 20, winning the Middlesex championship in the process, very simply. I had a settled and largely stress free life, I was more or less at my physical peak, I was highly motivated, I had learned what I needed to know about running and, most of all, I had put in about eighteen months of consistent training. That's what university did for me.

CHAPTER 5
One day in October

*'...beautiful, natural and spontaneous, not like now, when
everything is inflated, blown out of proportion.'*

Ottavio Missoni, fashion impresario and runner, recalling the
1948 London Olympics.

In the introduction and elsewhere in the book I make the bold claim
that the sport of distance running in Britain reached a peak around
1970, maintained that peak for between ten and twenty years, and has
been declining ever since. The coincidental but exact parallel with
my own life as a runner was the stimulus that encouraged me to start
writing in the first place.

There were two things that I wanted to communicate before anything
else. One was the evidence that brought me to this conclusion. I needed
to convince the sceptical that the running scene really did flourish, for
not much longer than a quarter of a century, starting in the late sixties,
in a way that is now just a memory and that the whole idea is not just
based on the nostalgic ramblings of an old man wearing rose coloured
glasses. The other thing that I was very keen to describe was the nature
of the peak. What was it like to be a part of the glory days for British
distance running? Why were those two and a half decades so special?
Why do so many other runners of my generation talk about those times
with such reverence, tinged with implied criticism of the running scene
of today?

I used the case of the Finchley 20 in the introduction as my strongest
evidence for a decline in standards in distance running in this country.
Elsewhere (in Chapter 9) I compare the present day Great South Run,
the self-proclaimed 'world's premier ten mile road race', with one of
the best ten mile road races of the seventies (but still quite ordinary by
the standards of its day) and conclude that there has certainly been no

improvement in nearly forty years, and pretty well all the large number of changes that are evident are not good ones. I mention briefly the fact that the men's British marathon best is now coming up to thirty years old. In the first chapter I talk about England's and Great Britain's record in the World Cross Country Championships, a story of a great fall from the heights if ever there was one, from the very top to nowhere to be seen. Here and there you will find other pieces of evidence. There is, I think, room for yet one more piece here.

Taking the British all-time rankings list for 10,000m, i.e. the fastest runners over the distance in order of time, quickest first (Mo Farah: 26:46.57), and selecting the top 150, then dividing it into decades, what do we find? Before answering that question, however, let's think what we might expect to find. If standards had remained the same during the last fifty years we would expect each decade to have thrown up roughly the same number of the top 150 times, exceptional individuals having come to the fore at a constant rate. That would be an unlikely scenario simply because standards usually keep increasing, in which case we would probably expect more top ranked 10,000m runners to appear in each successive decade, least in the sixties and most in the last decade. The actual results, on the other hand, point quite clearly to a peak in the seventies and eighties. Of the 150 top individuals, 5 set their best time in the 1960s, 46 in the 70s, 44 in the 80s, 31 in the 90s and only 16 between 2000 and 2010. Looking at those statistics in a slightly different way it can be seen that in the twenty years before 1990 almost twice as many of the all-time top 150 British 10,000m runners ran their best times as did so in the two decades since.

Going through exactly the same process with marathon times we find almost the same picture, but with a huge peak (73 out of 150) in the nineteen eighties. Comparing the twenty years preceding 1990 with the same period following that year, the numbers of runners qualifying for the present all-time list of top 150 British marathon runners are respectively 95 and 43. It's hard to wriggle out of statistics like those.

Now to the second of the two things I especially wanted to communicate. What was it like, being part of the glory days for British distance running? For me, one day tells it all. It was Saturday 27th October, 1973. The place was Harlow in Essex and a seminal event in the sport of British road running, specifically marathon running, was about to take place. I was there, and, in a sense, I was part of that event, though about as much a part of it as a film extra in a crowd scene or the goal posts in a football match. That was the day a more or less complete unknown, running his first competitive marathon, won the AAA Championship race and, with it, selection for the team for the Commonwealth games that were scheduled for Christchurch, New Zealand, the following January. His name was Ian Thompson and in the words of Athletics Weekly, reporting on the race a few days later, *'Who is the fair-haired, moustachioed athlete who has just won the AAA title in such authoritative style? He is Ian Thompson. Again one might ask, who is the fair-haired...?'*

I had gone to Harlow for a training run. I had entered the marathon but had no intention of running the whole way. I planned to run twenty miles, then make my way to the finish to watch the outcome of the race as it unfolded. I have no idea what sort of misguided optimism gave me this idea. How would I be able to get to the finish before the leaders did so? I must have imagined that there would be some sort of short cut or that I might get a lift. When I reached twenty miles I expected the leaders to be about ten minutes ahead of me and for them to have not much more than another twenty minutes to run. So I had to get from the twenty mile point to the finish in less than twenty minutes. Needless to say there was no short cut and no lift and I missed the finish and all the excitement and talk that immediately followed it. I would have got there quicker if I'd just kept running. As it was that's more or less what I had to do. The shortest distance from the twenty mile point to the finish turned out to be precisely six miles, three hundred and eighty five yards.

I had to wait, like most of the other runners, for the press reports of the events that I had missed. And what a story! A journalist's dream, the unknown underdog, the ordinary runner, the also-ran who decided to run just to make up the club team, the pedestrian, mildly talented club runner who miraculously discovers a previously undemonstrated, exceptional gift, turning from Clark Kent to Superman beyond a certain distance and beating the best in the land in the process.

In this case the best in the land happened to be Ron Hill, winner of the previous Commonwealth event held in Edinburgh in 1970. Hill was a legend in his own still active life time. In the Edinburgh Commonwealth Games race he had run the phenomenal time of 2:09:28, and had won the Boston marathon three months before that in 2:10:30. Although not quite the runner he was in 1970, Hill was still the odds-on favourite for the Harlow event. Less than two months previously he had won the Enschede (Netherlands) international marathon in 2:18:06, a slow time by his standards, but clearly run with an eye on the imminent Commonwealth trial race. No one runs an all-out marathon two months before a more important race over the same distance, and one has to assume that Enschede, from Hill's point of view, was a practice race, completed well within his limits. Hill ran well at Harlow, finishing in 2:13:22, an excellent performance on a hilly course, but ultimately finished merely the runner up. Thompson's beating of Hill by over forty seconds added one more layer of incredulity to an already mind-bending happening. The winning time was, at that time, the fastest debut marathon on record.

To say that the result of that race was inspirational to all aspiring marathon runners would be a colossal understatement. It was a validation of the whole ethos of competitive distance running, of the hard work, the dedication, the excitement and the pure enjoyment of the physical act of running, whether it was one's own or someone else's. For a while on that day and during the furore that followed it, runners like me **were** Ian Thompson. By that I mean no disrespect to those other more famous names who ran that day, not even Ron Hill. We had been him and them before, and might well be again, in our fantasies, but, for now, we were Ian Thompson. We knew what it felt like. We had felt the same on many a training run, smooth, easy, flowing along, as if running was no effort at all, and able to go on forever. We may never have experienced the same degree of success in a race nor found such sudden fame but still we knew what it would be like. It happened to Ian Thompson and, in a way, it happened to us as well.

The sad thing is that it couldn't happen now, nor ever again. An advert inviting entries for the 1973 Harlow marathon appeared in Athletics Weekly, October 13th, just two weeks before the race. The closing date for entries was October 15th and the entry fee for individuals was 25p. How ridiculous that appears today, with entries for big marathons closing or the entry limit being reached sometimes months before the event and entry fees of £30 or so being commonplace.

Here's how it was in the seventies. You fancied a race in a week or two's time so you looked in Athletics Weekly, the runner's bible and, as far as I knew then or know now, the only source of such information in those days. You might have wanted a six miler or ten miler or even a marathon. You sent off a letter and, if you were honest you enclosed your entry fee and a stamped addressed envelope and that was it. Or, if you were a regular club runner, you simply told the secretary that you fancied a run in a particular race and left the entry to him. Club secretaries usually made a standard entry for all major events in any case, the usual suspects being entered whether they liked it or not. Club funds covered the cost and block entries were charged at a discount. As an impecunious student for seven years through the late sixties and early seventies and running more or less independently of a club (though I was a member) I used to take a less gentlemanly approach by sending an entry with no entry fee, promising to pay on the day. I rarely failed to appear for the race and always paid when I did, but I simply couldn't afford to lose an entry fee if, for example, I got injured or had a cold, or for any other reason couldn't run. I was never rejected because I had not pre-paid and I don't remember ever having been unable to enter a race because I was a day or two late with my entry.

In 2012 I entered a marathon for the very last time. It was the Belfast marathon, to be run on May 7th, and the closing day for entries had been April 6th. Even as I entered, using the Belfast city marathon online service, I wasn't sure whether I would run or not. I was about as fit as I could have been but I knew I was not really able to run a marathon. To do one, yes, but not to run one. I was in that limbo state between dreams and reality. I wanted to run, but considering my age (65) and the difficulties I had coping with training, I had to admit that I probably couldn't. I had stiffened up badly in a half marathon at the end of March, running the last three miles as if both legs were in plaster. Every joint and every sinew ached. I imagined running twice the distance and had to admit that, as far as hoping to run the marathon was concerned, I was in a state of denial. But I entered anyway. It cost me £35.50.

Then, on Friday 13th March (yes, it really was) I fell in my own front room and hit my back so hard on the corner of a table that, for a while, I couldn't move. I think I cracked a rib. The next day it took me twenty minutes just to get out of bed. Every time I got myself into a position from which I thought I might be able to raise myself and applied the necessary effort I was struck with a crippling pain that forced me back to the starting point. Getting onto my feet became as much a mental as a physical puzzle, like working out a complicated route on a map, trying first this technique and then that method, with the necessity of not crossing any pain barriers. For a week I was virtually immobilised. Only the thought of my £35.50 kept my marathon intention alive, barely so. When the day came I didn't even try to run. There was no point starting. Is road running now a sport for the well off? Who can afford to commit themselves to regular entry fees of this magnitude, weeks or months in advance, knowing that a no-show doesn't mean a refund?

In entering races without pre-paying, as I always had done in my heyday, I felt justified, both in protecting myself from the loss of a non-refundable entry fee and also in considering that the relationship between runners and race organisers was one of mutual respect and mutual dependence. Neither could do without the other, and there had to be a bit of give and take on both sides. Things are different now.

The story has it that Ian Thompson entered the Harlow marathon at the last minute as a team filling make-weight, which, if true, means that his entry was posted a matter of weeks before the event, possibly even as little as twelve days before and that it cost him or his club, Luton United A.C., very little or perhaps nothing at all. If the club had entered a team and Thompson was simply filling a space there would probably have been no additional fee. That is why the same circumstances could not happen today. The AAA marathon championships have, since 1983, been incorporated into the London marathon and, while club and serious marathon runners do not have quite the same problems getting a place at the start as the fun runners or the aspiring marathon runners with no demonstrable form, it is still not easy, nor cheap, certainly not the casual last minute process it was for even important races in 1973.

Suppose an Ian Thompson run-alike appeared today and thought he might have a crack at the AAA marathon championship, held in conjunction with the London event, which he had heard was being used as a selection race for the Commonwealth Games or, indeed, the Olympics. First he would need to decide months in advance. Then the hard bit; he would have to persuade the organisers that he should get an automatic entry on the basis of being quite a good club runner, but with no previous form over the marathon distance, nor even the half marathon. That might not be as problematic as I imagine, but it would need a lot more enterprise than simply registering on the website, sending a letter or making a phone call. The entry fee would have to be paid, non returnable, of course. It would be an amount that would make a lot of people think twice.

Then, with success and a place in the field, what sort of race awaits our modern day Ian Thompson? No real race at all. He would not start along with the so called 'élite athletes' who, to all intents and purposes and often quite literally have their own separate race, but in amongst the masses, like the population of a small country, who run, walk, limp, hobble or conga their way to the finish but who largely don't race at all, not in any competitive meaning of the word.

The London marathon and all the other big city marathons are extreme cases of the way in which the sheer size and popularity of events and the change in attention from running and racing to simply participating, has smothered all trace of the sport and the atmosphere and the seriousness that was exemplified by the Harlow marathon of 1973. But almost all road races held in Britain since the nineties and into the twenty first century show the same effect in less exaggerated ways.

In 2008, for example, I had thoughts of entering the British Masters Championship marathon. I learned that it was to be held in conjunction with the New Forest marathon. That was my first taste of how things had changed. I was quite surprised to find that the British Masters Athletics Association did not stage its own marathon championship but farmed it out to an already scheduled marathon with all its fun and charity entries included. I almost gave up there and then. I was, after all, a serious (though by that time very slow) marathon runner, looking for a proper race where all participants were there for the same reasons, all starting on equal terms and roughly from the same start line.

I delayed deciding whether to enter until near the closing date for entries, which was several weeks before the day of the race. Even though I tried to enter before this date I found that the field was already full and entries were no longer being accepted. Again I was surprised. When the New Forest marathon was adopted as the official British Masters Championship no guarantee had been arranged for entry for registered masters runners either before or after the advertised closing date. The championship had become totally annexed by another entirely separate event. In a sense it had ceased to exist. It was as if the British Masters Athletics Association had invited me to a private dinner and then sent me out to a popular restaurant on the off chance I might find a table free.

If the serious competitive side of marathon and distance running in general has now become submerged under a whole new public interpretation of the sport, there was no hint of this change in 1973. At any road running event, from the biggest marathon in Britain that year, the Harlow marathon, to the smallest club run, you would only find serious runners.

I make no excuse for using the term 'serious runners' to describe those who ran for the reasons I ran, to achieve their best and to work hard in training and in races for no other reason than to be competitive. I use the term only to distinguish runners like that from those who run for fun, for the satisfaction of taking part and finishing, regardless of how well they run, or for any other reason that is non-competitive. Many such runners are probably very serious, but not about competitive running.

The outward contrast between any big city marathon of today and the Harlow marathon of 1973 is so great that it hides the fact that the superficially less grand, less publicised and altogether less appreciated event was by far the more important, measured in terms of British distance running. It was also, for any fan of distance running, an infinitely more exciting race. A marathon like the London marathon is now an almost unbelievably vast display of pomp, publicity and popularity but, in road racing terms, it has a hollow centre. Remove the invited (and well paid) élite runners and all the non-serious runners, and those who simply want to be able to say that they ran it, and what is left is a reasonably but not very high standard marathon race, fairly ordinary in fact by nineteen seventies' standards. The serious British runners in today's London marathon, competing in the AAA's championship, must often be wondering exactly what race they are in, and who they are running against, and whether anyone else even knows what's going on, or gives a damn.

The Harlow marathon, as were all other equally important British marathon races of the time, was the total opposite of the modern big city events. All the gold and glitter lay on the inside. The strangest thing about such races was how superficially low-key and insignificant they were, and how little attention they were paid by the media and the general public. The Harlow marathon that year was the sporting equivalent of an FA cup semi-final. It was the selection race for the

Commonwealth Games, the next most prestigious event in British athletics after the Olympics. You would think that fact might have added a bit of extra glamour to the event, that there might have been a few banners and advertising hoardings about, a television crew with their encampment of service vehicles parked close to the finish, crowds of people thronging the course, rows of portable toilets, kiosks and tents for officials to officiate from and commercial interests to advertise in and from which to dispense drinks and food and balloons and T shirts, with loud speakers, and music, in fact all the razzamatazz of any modern day running event. I don't remember any of it. Harlow may have been, like the similarly understated selection race for the Montreal Olympics, the 1976 Rotherham marathon that was held two and a half years later, an extremely significant race, but it was not a conspicuous race, nor a big race. Three hundred and fifty one runners entered the Harlow marathon in 1973. Compare that number with the thirty thousand or so participants who start the London marathon each year. You can't. There is no comparison. If, however, we remove the invited élite from the London marathon of 2010, for example, and focus only on the British runners, those who would have been eligible had the marathon been a selection race for the British team for a major games, we find a very different comparison, one that is easily made. The 'winning' time in London, 2010, was 2:13:40 (Andrew Lemoncello). In Harlow it was 2:12:40. Eight British runners broke 2:20:00 in London, twelve in Harlow. Forty runners finished in under 2:30:00 in London, fifty one in Harlow.

If you had been able to pick out the tiny kernel of the 2010 London marathon, therefore, in the form of the British Marathon Championship, from the massive flesh of the big occasion and its countless impenetrable distractions, you would have found a race similar but of a slightly lower standard to the Harlow event of thirty six years earlier, bearing in mind that Harlow was a hilly and, therefore, slower course (I know it was, because I ran twenty miles of it). London, on the other hand, is well known as a fast marathon. As if to rub in the comparison based on performance, Ian Thompson went on to win the Christchurch

Commonwealth games marathon in 2:09:12, still one of the fastest times ever run by a Briton.

Anyone who ran in that Harlow marathon, or who went to the race to support or to watch, will know that it was just like any other road race of the time. There was nothing to tell the casual observer that it was in any way special. There was a certain sameness about road races, and cross country races, that belied the fact that some were more important than others. There was never any gloss, however many star runners were present. For competitors the experience was the same whether it was a small local race or a big event like the National Road Relay, the English National Cross Country Championship, the Inter-Counties twenty mile race or a vital selection race like the Harlow marathon.

In a contradictory way, the low-key nature of running events during the peak time for British distance running was one of the reasons for high standards. Phenomenal runners like Ian Thompson emerged, like diamonds from the mud, because that was the only way any brilliance could make itself noticed. There was no alternative source of lustre, from publicity or media hype, celebrities or shiny pound notes, and no other way to attain acclaim than through running well and racing hard. To be anybody at all in that environment you simply couldn't afford to aim for anything less than the very best.

I hated race days, up to the moment the running started. I hated the prelude: the travelling, the changing, the counting the minutes until the start, the warm up, the nervousness, the milling around at the start, the smell of the toilets and the liniment, the shifty looks that were exchanged, the final stripping off for the start, wondering what to do with the outer layers, and then the start itself, always too fast, always hazardous, always like a crowd of unruly children let out of school. None of this was in any way different at Harlow.

We changed *en masse* in a local school. It was almost always a local school. Leisure centres were not as common then as now. You found a space on the bench and, if you were early, as I often was, you just sat there, or dumped your bag and looked for the toilet. If you were lucky, and early enough, you could get in without queuing and before the pervading reek of loose bowels filled the whole area. You sometimes even found some toilet paper still in the dispenser. Wise runners brought their own.

You might ask why runners can't go to the toilet before they travel to a race. The answer is that they can and they do, but a combination of nervous and hormonal messages telling the body to get ready for action insist that they go again. The closer the start the more insistent the urge becomes. Even if you don't need to go you'd better do so, just in case. The alternative, especially in a marathon is a 'pit stop', or worse. There is no, way to be delicate about the fact that two hours hard running can reduce the bowels to an open tube of oozing liquid, assuming there was anything still in there to start with. Many a runner in an important race, when confronted with a choice between stopping briefly for relief or keeping running has decided just to let it go. Women runners, who usually wear tight fitting shorts, have been known to lift the elasticated lower edge with their fingers to let the evil liquid out. It's not a pretty thought, but it's one of the unpleasant realities of what can be a tough sport.

At the weekend there is no heating in schools. Where we changed was cold. The concrete floor was hard and so were the wooden benches. As other runners arrived we started to get changed. People wandered around in various stages of dress and undress, shirts over running shorts or running vest over trousers, socks on or socks off. Strong smelling liniment was rubbed onto legs, vaseline applied to nipples and groins and in between toes. Some people tape their toes with plaster. Runners went through their various static stretches and individual rituals. Mine was to keep untying and retying my shoe laces until I had arrived at the perfect state of tightness. A shoe will rarely come off or even move around on your foot while you run, but it can easily be laced up too tight. I once ran the whole of a twenty mile race with one shoe lace undone. It didn't seem to make any difference. When I run with a shoe that's too tight, however, it results in pain caused by the different parts of the foot not being able to move freely.

I remember Ron Hill himself (no VIP treatment for him) wandering around the Harlow changing room chatting effusively to everyone around him, wearing nothing more that his running shorts. His chest was round, like a barrel. That still strikes me as odd, not Ron Hill's chest, but the fact that he was mucking in with the rest of us, feeling the same hardness and coolness, smelling the same smells, having to find a hook for his clothes and a space on the bench for his bag. In a way his very presence, having to run the race just to be selected for the Commonwealth Games, said a lot about the way the sport was viewed and managed. There was no presumption of superiority. If Ron Hill, arguably at one time the greatest marathon runner in the world, and still one of the best at the time of the Harlow race, wanted to run in the Commonwealth games, he would have to earn his place just like anyone else. The slate was wiped clean, all his previous performances, including his outstanding win in the previous Commonwealth Games had been rubbed out. No one got special treatment. There were no exceptions. The selectors were only able to defend such a strict policy, which did cause quite a bit of debate at the time, because of the richness of distance runners in Britain in the early seventies.

In 2012, on the other hand, at the time of the selection race for the London Olympics, which was that year's London marathon, only one place in the marathon team remained unfilled, subject to the Olympic standard of 2:12 being reached. Even the runners vying for that place had already been determined. Only six British runners lined up with the élite field. Had the selectors already decided who might get that last place, or were there only six runners in the whole country who considered they might have a realistic chance? And what about another Ian Thompson? Where was he?

How ironic, therefore, in the Harlow race, that the very thing should happen that would justify Ron Hill's presence, and the need for him to be selected on the day's result: the sudden appearance of a new talent to beat Hill and to win a coveted place in the GB team. I wonder whether Ian Thompson also, as I did, saw Ron Hill in the changing rooms and got some inspiration from the knowledge that no one there would be considered any better than the rest until the race was over. Whenever I have lined up at the start of races alongside some of the best runners in the country, or even in the world, it has given me a lot of confidence. I know they will beat me, but, for a moment or two, just as we wait for the gun, we are equals.

It is the same in training. Without wishing to impress with a list of famous names (famous that is to anyone of my generation who had some interest in British distance running) I have at one time or another run alongside a number of very good runners in training, some of the very best, and got far more from it than the physical effects. Perhaps the most surprising thing, and the thing I was most gratified by, was the realisation that they were as pleased to have me to train with as I was to train with them. However good a runner may be, he or she still has the same needs as any other runner, still welcomes company, still finds training hard and is still just one of the crowd. It was also, of course, quite encouraging to be able to keep up with such good runners in training. I am almost afraid to say that sometimes it seemed a bit too easy.

I originally called this chapter, as a descriptive working title, 'How it was.' It reminded me that I was trying to convey something of the atmosphere, the sense of community, the extremes of shared motivation and the flourishing nature of the running scene in the nineteen seventies. My account of one day and one race can only go so far towards that aim for the simple reason that by far the more important part of the running scene happens in the days and weeks between races. Training with other runners is a part of it. The fact that some of the very best runners in the country trained regularly with less talented companions both reflects the egalitarian camaraderie that existed and was also undoubtedly a contributory factor towards the great depth in running standards at that time. Many good club runners, myself included, owed at least part of their success to once or twice weekly, communal training sessions, in the company of runners of all standards. Every Sunday, in Belfast in the early eighties, I used to join a group for a long run. As we picked up more and more runners along the way, the throng swelled, until we resembled a small army storming down the pavements. One regular member of that group was Greg Hannon, British AAA marathon champion in 1979 (see Chapter 10). No such groups of runners are seen nowadays on the roads of Belfast, and Greg Hannon, if he were still running as well today, would probably be living abroad.

As I pointed out in the last chapter, the tendency in the last decade of the twentieth century and beyond has been for the best runners in the country to become isolated from the rest, even, in the case of the very best, those of world class, isolated from the country itself. They live abroad, they train with their own group, they rarely compete in domestic events. Like the rest of the world's élite, they are professionals. For the average, locally domiciled runner, the club runner, the junior, and the up and coming runner, this is a deprivation of inspiration. It can only lead to an impoverishment of the sport.

A fair amount of the training we did during the glory days of British distance running, more for some than for others, was done in company, with clubs and club runs and training partners and training groups and, however hard it may have been at times, it was a greatly enjoyable social activity. The running scene had its own grapevines, both spoken and written. The running magazine, 'Athletics Weekly' became, for me and thousands like me, as essential a means of communication as the telephone, the radio and the television. It brought all the isolated pockets of runners throughout the country together into a single running community. This gathering of like-minded athletes, who all lived for running and put their hearts and souls and a large part of their lives into it, formed a society that grew to a peak in the seventies and eighties, thriving in a way it has never thrived since. It was both the reason for the high standards and a consequence of the same thing. There was an overt devotion to a shared objective, hard work, competition, aspiration and imitation, communication and, above all, a sense of community; all extremely infectious things.

I forget the start of the Harlow marathon except that it was at a sensible time of day, 1.30pm. Most road races started around that time. Participants had the whole morning to get to the venue, time to digest their breakfast and be fully awake when called upon to run. Even the slowest runner wasn't going to take much longer than four hours for the marathon distance, leaving the course virtually clear by early evening.

I can see why big marathon events now start ridiculously early, but it is not for the benefit of the runners. The idea for early morning starts may have originated for that reason, however. Sometime around about the mid eighties, or it might have been earlier, television commentators began to condemn the organisers of big events for scheduling the marathon to start in the middle of the day, and their views must have eventually had some effect. Their particular concern seemed to be for the runners themselves and the effect of heat on their performances and their well being. Running for any length of time in the heat of the day was considered a risky thing to do. Perhaps the runners themselves were consulted. Some runners may well prefer to run a marathon in the early morning, especially in hot countries, but at least as many, me included, would consider an early start a bigger problem than hot weather. A number of Olympic Games have been held in very hot places. Rome in 1960, for example, was notably hot, and the marathon was held after the heat of the day had dispersed. The race finished in darkness. Other Olympic Games marathons, on the other hand, have been held during the day in hot conditions and have passed off without many problems. As recently as the summer of 2013 the World Championship women's and men's marathons were held during the hottest part of the day, amidst much critical comment from the British TV coverage. Admittedly, times were slow, but no one died. Joan Benoit made no complaint about her win in the 1984 Los Angeles Olympic marathon, run in temperatures approaching 30 degrees Celsius. Ironically that race was started in the early morning.

During my marathon running days it was accepted that running, even marathon running, was not like cricket or tennis. Rain didn't stop play, and neither did hot weather. Only once do I remember a race being cancelled due to weather conditions. It was the Mitcham 15 road race, and ice on the roads was the reason. If a marathon had to be run on a very hot day then so be it. It was the same temperature for everyone, and bringing the start time forward three or four hours was going to cause far more problems than it solved.

No one, to my knowledge, complained about the starting time at Harlow. I can hardly imagine the complaints that would have been made had that marathon, with all its domestic importance, been scheduled for a 9 am start. I think a boycott would have been on the cards. One of the big problems for organisers of national competitions, even in a relatively small country like Great Britain, is to find a venue that is fair to everyone, whichever end of the country someone has to travel from. That is one reason why the National Road Relay Championship is held each year at Sutton Coldfield in Birmingham, a good, central location.

Of course, ultimately, complete fairness is not possible. I came to Harlow from Somerset, a journey of about a hundred and fifty miles. Others came from the North of England, from Wales, Scotland and from even further afield. I'm sure a number of entrants would have travelled the previous day and spent the Friday night in Harlow itself. They had to do so at their own expense, possibly losing a day's pay into the bargain. If the race had started at the sort of time big road races start nowadays, we all would have had to do the same thing. I think that would have rendered a race such as the Harlow marathon, with its importance for selection and its status as the AAA Championship, open to accusations of favouritism towards the south of the country and towards the better off amongst runners. A lunchtime start at least helped to introduce an element of fairness by giving a large proportion of the field a decent amount of travelling time.

I'm sure that the majority of serious runners would prefer to run any race at least three or four hours after their normal getting up time, whatever the weather. Starting a marathon at nine in the morning, as I did the last three times I competed in one, is not only close to a physiological impossibility for some, but is also a logistical nightmare.

Do you arrive the previous night and stay somewhere, or do you get up in the middle of the night to make the journey to the start? Do you have any breakfast? The main reason that big marathons now start so early is that the majority of participants take so long to finish. It's got very little to do with the possible dangerous effects of hot weather and it shows no regard for runners' travel arrangements or body clocks. The lot of the serious competitive runner has been sacrificed to the democratic principle.

Are modern day big city road races, therefore, not fair, as far as different entrants are concerned? I'm afraid not. And when entry to a particular race is the first step to something that, in competitive running terms is vitally important, such as an individual or team championship or selection for a more important event, they are grossly unfair. They are a two day commitment for most participants and they represent a quite considerable expense, as well as a big inconvenience. They discriminate heavily against those who are not well off, those who don't find it easy to free themselves for two whole days at a time, even over a weekend, and those who are interested in a domestic running competition and nothing else.

Because I wasn't intending to run the whole course at Harlow, as I previously explained, when the field assembled at the start I kept well back from the line. Had it been a six or a ten mile race in which I expected to do well I would have been toeing that line along with everyone else who didn't want to run one inch further than necessary. Now, of course, in big races every runner wears an electronic chip that activates the timing process as the starting line is crossed. So there is no real need to worry that you'll lose a few seconds by not starting slap bang on that line.

It's still important, however, if you're serious about a race, not to get caught behind slower runners at the start. This was not a common problem at any time during the period when I was running well. It seems to be a latter day annoyance faced by runners at the start of races. When every single runner in a race was there to run as fast as possible, according to their own acknowledged place in the pecking order, there was a surprising degree of discipline before the gun was fired.

I must have run more than two or three hundred road and cross country races between 1970 and 1990. A lot of them had large fields. All of them would have had a field of at least thirty runners. Yet I don't remember a single serious incident of pushing or impeding or jumping the gun or of much slower runners placing themselves in front of faster ones. The penalty area on a football pitch when a corner is about to be taken is a war zone by comparison with the starting area for a distance race, despite there being far more runners in a far smaller area than football players in a penalty box. I think that says something about the running community during those years. There was a strong sense of fairness. No one wanted to take advantage of others because to do so would be to devalue their own performance. If, latterly, in one of my rare outings in a race I have found myself having almost to force myself through a picket line of joggers and even young children to make any progress at all in the first mile, it is partly because of my own over-developed and by now anachronistic sense of fairness, partly because of the increased size of fields, but mainly due to ignorance on the part of other participants. The joggers and fun runners are simply unaware that others may be taking the race seriously.

Only once was I party to a disaster at the start of a race. It was a six mile road race in the South of England. I was expecting to run quite well and eventually I did finish in the first half dozen. So I was up there at the start. Just before the start time, the field of about fifty runners was ushered to form a line across the whole width of the road. It was a two lane rural road with little traffic. What traffic there was had been temporarily held up both behind us and in front of us by race officials. I don't recall any police presence.

The gun, or hooter, or whatever device was used to start the race sounded, and the whole field took off in a mad dash down the full width of the road. At almost precisely the same time, about fifty yards in front of us, a string of horses, carrying mostly young girls, emerged from a gateway and turned in the same direction we were running. Luckily there was a wide grass verge on that side of the road. Nevertheless the horses panicked and broke into a frenzied gallop, the second stampede of the day; first us, and then the horses. I saw at least one child thrown off and others being carried away at great speed on completely uncontrollable animals. I'm ashamed to say that my only thought was whether the race would be interfered with. There was nothing we could do, and nothing we wanted to do, other than to continue our own equally uncontrolled rush, which is what we did.

I don't know whether anyone was seriously hurt in the incident. It turned out that the riding school involved had been notified of the race and, in a way, therefore, was itself responsible. I learnt two things. One is that a serious runner during a race has concern for one thing only and is oblivious to anything or anyone else to the point of total selfishness. I have even seen a runner jump onto the bonnet of a car and off the other side when someone drove out of a side road in front of him. Good for him! The other thing I learned is that a frightened horse can run considerably faster than I can, even when I'm almost flat out.

After the orderly start and nearly two and a quarter hours of running, what awaited Ian Thompson when he had completed his amazing marathon debut? There was no digital timing device held aloft by a giant triumphal arch, just a plain white tape across the road. There was no glamorous girl to hang a medal round his neck or drape a silver blanket over his shoulders. No one was giving out bottles of water or energy drinks. There were one or two photographers and journalists, probably only local ones, a small group of race officials recording numbers and times and a small crowd of applauding onlookers, separated from the course and from the runners as they approached the line only by their own self discipline; no metal barriers, not even a rope or a line of plastic tape.

A running race is, after all, a very simple affair. It starts, the runners sort themselves out according to how well they run, and then, for each individual in turn, according to their ability, it ends. The bare minimum of officials is needed to send the runners on their way, to direct them the right way, to see that the race is run fairly and that no one cheats or breaks the rules, and to record the finish. It is the same whether it is the Olympic marathon or a small club race.

During my best running years, starting in the late sixties and continuing for over twenty years, I ran a race of some sort most weekends, and the odd race during the week as well. In 1970, for example I ran a total of 47 races of varying distances from 2,000m to a marathon and in 1976, at a time when I was working on Saturdays and had to look for races taking place on a Sunday, I ran 41. In this I was typical of most club runners. If anything I was a fairly frugal competitor compared to others. Racing, for many, was as regular a part of running as training was, two equal and inseparable parts of the running way of life. We could afford to race so often and so carelessly because it cost so little to do so, and no one made it into anything bigger or more important than it was.

Inevitably some races were taken more seriously than others, though not necessarily by the same people. Some races might have been seen merely as an integral part of training, a test of fitness, a debt of duty to the club, a practice race for something more important or an excuse for a social outing. But always, sooner or later, came the races that really meant something to the individual. The strange thing was that there was very little to distinguish the important races from the unimportant ones, and little rhyme nor reason behind one runner deciding that one particular race was more important than another, while another decided the opposite.

The 1973 Harlow marathon was, in many ways, a typical road race. For me it wasn't even a race. It was my long run for the week, combined with what I thought would be the chance to get involved in the big occasion, both as participant and spectator. It turned out, with all its ramifications and despite its simplicity, to be the most iconic race I was ever privileged to be a part of. To this day it encapsulates for me everything that was good about the sport of distance running at the start of its twenty year peak. In terms of the history of British long distance running it holds a key place in the archives.

CHAPTER 6
The good club runner

'Where are all the good club runners?'
Television commentator during a recent big city road race.

I was never a star and this book, thank goodness, is not the autobiography of a star. The best that could have been said of me was that I was one of those by now almost mythical beings, so loved by TV commentators, a 'good club runner'. The good club runner was very much a feature of the boom years of British distance running. There were so many of us. That was what most characterised the running scene in the sixties, seventies and eighties, the number of good club runners. There must have been ten times as many as today.

This is the big contrast between running then and now, the huge difference in strength in depth. I have already spelled this out in the introduction, and elsewhere. Whenever I ran in a road race I knew I wouldn't win, unless it was a small, local race. I expected to get in the first dozen in a lot of races but I knew I would have some stiff competition, wherever I finished. A few seconds let up was likely to make the difference between maybe fifth and eighth. A bad run would bring me down half a dozen places, but an especially good run was only ever likely to bring me up a single place.

Because most serious club runners competed regularly in their local area, doing the same races from year to year and travelling far only for major events like the National Cross Country Championships and the National Road Relay, the AAA marathon and the Inter-Counties races, it was usual to meet the same competition in race after race. Perhaps this got a bit boring. It became a little too easy to predict where you were going to finish and one glance at the list of entrants was enough for you to work out how many runners would beat you. But there was always the element of surprise and there was always room for individual improvement. For example, between the years 1973 and 1977, I moved from 23rd to 19th to 8th and finally 6th in the Mitcham 15 road race (which at some point became the Mitcham 25K road race and later had to be put to rest, along with so many other road races, as the roads became more and more congested). The Mitcham 15 was a race, like many others, with a long tradition, and a record of top class entrants. It was held in January in the south London area, around the suburban roads of Surrey, attracting a large entry from all the London clubs. It was a race I ran most years, as did a number of good runners that I knew well, and my progression gave me some measure of the fact that I was getting better.

That was the challenge, to get better and to keep getting better. Doing the same races year after year and running against the same competition made it easy to gauge progress. Every runner was doing the same thing. Everyone in every race was looking at the opposition and challenging them anew. 'You beat me last year, now see if you can do it again.' It was due to this covert in-fighting, and to the sheer numbers of good club runners and to the somewhat parochial nature of all but the most important running events that the running scene was thriving and those active in it were so well motivated. If you ran badly in a race and were beaten by someone whom you normally beat, then you went away and trained harder so as not to let it happen again. If you surpassed your own expectations you thought, 'If I can improve like that, then why not even more?' So you went away and trained harder.

Some runners, often the better ones, preferred to keep their powder dry and their prowess a secret until they were ready to display it on their own terms. They would train away for months at a time, not exactly in secret, but without advertising their intentions. Then they would appear for a race in their own good time and, if all had gone well, they would make a few heads turn with a display of unanticipated success. This was most satisfying for them but a little disconcerting for those of their opponents who had calculated, to within a place or two, where they were about to finish in the race.

I am thinking, for example, of a good friend of mine, called Bill, whom I met in 1969 and ran and trained with many times between then and the early nineteen seventies. I know he trained a lot. Reputedly, when I met him, he was doing up to 150 miles per week. He ran to work and back and I would see him at lunchtimes running around Stanmer Park, the park that adjoins the campus of Sussex University, where we were both working at the time. I couldn't mistake him. Whatever the weather he wore an old orange anorak, the sort that had a waterproof lining that eventually perished and cracked until the material became good only for keeping the wind out.

I learned from Bill the wisdom of dressing for training with comfort in mind and acquired a similar anorak myself. It was a blessing when the rain drove against my chest or a biting winter wind cut through me, though quite why Bill wore it on hot sunny days, I don't know. This was before the advent of breathable fabrics or, if they did exist at that time, they were far too expensive for the average runner, living on a working wage or, in my case, a student grant. The sort of anorak we wore was either completely waterproof and air tight when it was new or, as with Bill's, reduced with age to no more waterproof than a thin cotton jumper. When I ran for any length of time in the one I bought, even in cold weather, I used to sweat profusely and a pool of sweat would collect in the elbows. When I stopped I would straighten my arms, each in turn, loosen the elastic at the wrist with my finger and let the sweat run out onto the ground before I took the anorak off. Sometimes there was almost enough liquid in each elbow to fill one of the third of a pint milk bottles that were a daily feature of my school days. Because I was unable to wash the anorak very often, it began to smell, a breathtaking reek of ammonia and rancid sweat, so strong that I kept it in the garage and only put it on immediately before I ran. When I came back from running, I drained it of sweat and hung it up to fester until I next needed it.

Bill used running, as I often did, as a means of getting around, and was once stopped by the police as he ran home in the early hours of the morning after seeing his girlfriend. I suppose there is something suspicious about a young man running through the streets at one o'clock in the morning for no apparent reason. But for Bill it was all good training and it had a purpose, to get into the best possible condition for the races that he wanted to run.

In 1970 he trained throughout the autumn and the beginning of winter before venturing out in December for his first race for months. It was a big South of England road race, the Farnham to Guildford 'Hog's Back', one that was always well supported by some of the best road runners in the country. It was a good example of the sort of race that is run by many of the same people each year, in which everyone knows everyone else, at least by sight, and every competitor before the start has a fairly accurate idea of his finishing time and place. Bill was about to inject a sense of unfamiliarity into the mix.

A group of four led the field after the first mile, having gone off fast and drawn out a gap on the rest. Three were well known home-counties runners, perhaps not quite of the very highest national standard, but certainly good enough to have surpassed the average good club runner category; solid, 48 minute ten mile performers. The fourth was Bill. The reporter for the magazine Athletics Weekly understood the situation well. Referring to the three better known runners in the leading group he wrote, '... *have raced against each other several times this winter. Yet they kept on asking one another who the white vested runner wearing 33 was. For* (Bill) *was a complete stranger to them and they couldn't understand what he was doing challenging for the lead.*'

I can imagine it. It's disconcerting to be running alongside someone who is a complete unknown to you, especially when you feel, however unjustifiably, that he has no right to be there. It makes you wonder whether you're not running as well as you think you are. Just the unknown dimension is enough to put you off your stride. Bill finished third in the end but it took a record time for the course to beat him.

There was really no reason why Bill should have been '*a complete stranger*', either to his opponents in the Hog's Back race or in the eyes of the Athletics Weekly reporter. In February that same year Bill had finished second to Dave Bedford in the Southern Cross Country Championship, beating both the runners who finished ahead of him ten months later. He was by no means unknown to anyone who followed athletics closely and who possessed a memory span of longer than a few months. By the end of his career Bill had reached the heights of British distance running, with a British vest for the 3,000m steeplechase and several top places in prestigious road and cross country races. How could a runner of his class have effectively been forgotten simply because he hadn't raced for a long time?

The reason was that, despite his being such a good runner, it was impossible for Bill to stand out quite as brightly as he certainly would today. He was one of hundreds of good club runners who briefly touched the very edge of the topmost class at that time. British distance running was populated by such large numbers of people like Bill that no one could remember them all. When I look back at the results of races that took place in the late nineteen sixties and during the seventies, results that I have pasted into two large scrap-books covering all my running years, I see countless names that I have forgotten, all good club runners, many of them considerably better than I was. I recognise the names. I recall them when I see them, but if I were asked to list them all now, with nothing to refer to, I would come up with no more than about one in ten or twenty. That, to me, is a measure of the breadth and depth and strength of good club running between 1965 and 1985.

When I was running at my best, popular road and cross country races were continuously eventful. There was rarely a gap of more than half a minute between places. Runners would be finishing within a few seconds of each other and spectators were treated to numerous finishing straight battles and sprint finishes. Because the outcome of a single duel fought over the last few hundred yards of a race could decide the team places, even, in some cases, which of two clubs became the winning team, these minor place battles were as fierce as any. There was as much excitement, therefore, in races, lower down the field as at the front and all because of the strength of club competition and, in turn, the large number of good club runners.

For the sake of the uninitiated a word of explanation is needed regarding the scoring system for club competition. In any road or cross country race a set number of runners make up a team. Each runner scores his or her finishing place in the race, one for first, two for second, three for third and so on. Usually the first six from one club to finish complete the scoring team and their individual scores are added together to give the team total. The team with the lowest points score wins. It's as simple as that.

There is no special weight given to finishing first, or second, or anywhere else, meaning that in the race, where club team places are concerned, there is no more significance attached to the individual finishing line battle for first place than to any other similar fight for places lower down the field. It is commonplace in races for the team positions to be decided by the outcome of a sprint to the line for maybe twentieth or thirtieth place, or, in big races like the National Cross Country Championships, something like the hundredth or two hundredth place. This system of scoring and its arithmetical logic inevitably means that all declared club runners in a race have reason to run as well as they possibly can, knowing that wherever they finish they have an equally important contribution to make to the team score. This even applies to those who don't actually make the scoring six.

Here another word of explanation may be necessary. Although most usually the first six runners to finish for a club form the scoring team, the club can enter up to nine runners into a race as its declared team. The club can also enter any number of runners more than the nine that make up the declared team but these additional runners either run as individuals or as part of a second or 'B' team. At the end of the race, three of the nine 'A' team runners, because they have been beaten by six of their own team, become 'non-scoring'. Their places in the race are not added to the final team score. But they are not taken out of the calculation for other club teams' additive scores. So they can still beat members of another club's team and in so doing add one more point to that team's total score. This may sound complicated but it's not really, and the outcome is beautifully pure and fair and highly conducive to the production and motivation of good club runners.

Suppose, and many times I was in this sort of position, you are half way through a race and you know, or are told from the side lines, that you are the seventh runner in your team. You look ahead and can just see your club's sixth runner, presently the last scorer for your team, about ten places in front of you. You are fairly sure you're not going to catch him and, therefore, you'll finish the race as a non scorer. Do you give up? Like hell you do! Not only is there personal pride at stake but you still have a part to play in the team competition. Just because it looks as if you're not going to score yourself doesn't mean that you're not ahead of or can get yourself ahead of someone who is going to score for an opposing team. Every place you can gain on a scoring member of another club is another point added to their total. In short you're still just as contributory a member of your own team as anyone else.

It's the job of club supporters, coaches and managers to make rough and ready ongoing calculations of team scores during the race and relay the information to their team from the sidelines. If that information is accurate and well transmitted it can give a team a big advantage, but it's not an easy thing to do. It requires a nimble brain and nimble legs to do the calculations and get around the course and communicate with the runners. When done well it's a great stimulant to a competitor. It's easy for a runner in a big race to become like an extra in a large crowd scene in an epic film, anonymous and lost, both physically and competitively. In those circumstances it helps greatly to be told, if you can hear what the team manager is shouting at you, that you are a hundred and fiftieth, and fifth scorer and that the team is ten points up on its arch rival. It immediately puts your running into a context that gives it purpose.

I have experienced running in a vacuum and the way it can de-motivate. What a difference information from the sideline would have made that day. It was the one and only time I ran in the English National

Cross Country Championship, in 1968. The championship that year was held at Sutton Coldfield, Birmingham and the race was won by Ron Hill. This was not the infamous Sutton Coldfield National, the day that a blizzard turned so many competitors into frozen jellies. That was four years later in 1972 and won by the Welshman, Malcolm Thomas, of Thames Valley Harriers (see Chapter 13). The one I ran in was on quite a pleasant day. The ground was mainly dry and owing to the nature of the gravelly heath-land paths I decided to wear my flat-soled running shoes. I never liked spikes and I think, at the time, I couldn't afford a pair in any case.

An hour before I was to run myself, I watched Ian Stewart, one of the few British runners ever to win the International Cross Country Championship, which he did in Rabat, Morocco, in 1975, on his way to winning the junior race. I was standing by the water splash as the runners came through. I gained some inspiration as I saw them do so, and I suppose I was quite keen to run myself at that point. I would try to do my best, but I was not really excited about the prospect. I didn't see a lot of point in taking part in a race in which I would do well to finish in the first three hundred (I actually finished 374th). It was not a time when I was running particularly well and I was certainly not there to satisfy any great urge or ambition of my own. I was making up the club team and I was prepared to run hard for the club, but that was my only motivation.

It was not uncommon for more than one thousand runners to take part in the senior men's race at the English National Cross Country Championship. The estimate for the entry for that year's race, according to the previous week's Athletics Weekly, was 1,346, bearing in mind that not one fun runner set out to run nine miles round Sutton Park that afternoon. Every competitor was what could be described as a serious runner, even the relatively slow ones.

Immediately, in such a mass of runners, it's easy to get lost and beset with a sense of insignificance. As we lined up at the start, in ranks, each club a file of runners standing in likely finishing order, two questions sprang to mind for someone like myself, a middle to lower order finisher; what am I doing and why am I doing it? I'm afraid I was never a very staunch or enthusiastic club runner, especially when I had no personal ambition in relation to a particular race.

We started, and the field spread out into a long procession, two or three abreast, knees almost touching the backs of legs in front. It was hard to run at my own pace, impossible to pass anyone except by breaking into a sprint when the opportunity presented itself, and difficult to keep from stumbling without keeping my eyes glued to the ground right in front of me. Very quickly I became absorbed into what seemed a continuous conveyer belt of runners, endless in front of me and endless behind me.

My shoelace came undone and for a while I ran with the laces flapping. But they were long laces and there were many feet hitting the ground around them so I stepped sideways, knelt down and tied them again. I suppose it took less than ten seconds. I have no idea how many runners passed me in that time, I estimate perhaps twenty or thirty, but, when I started running again, I noticed absolutely no difference; the same endless stream of runners ahead and the same behind. At that point I gave up. I didn't give up running or even trying, but I did give up competing. I simply didn't see the point. It didn't matter one jot whether I finished 374th, 274th or 474th. I vowed to myself that I would never again run the English National until I had a reasonable chance of finishing in the first one hundred.

Ironically, in 1976, and again, in 1977, two of my very best years, I calculated, on the basis of good finishing places in the Midland Cross Country Championship (14th in 1976 and 11th in 1977) and tenth fastest long leg in the Midland Road Relay in 1976, that I could well have finished in the first one hundred in the National. Still I didn't bother to run it. There's something very unattractive, almost dispiriting, about a race with so many people in it. For the élite it's different, of course. Being near the front of a procession, when you can count how many are ahead, is not the same as being in the middle.

Only in those boom years could a runner of my standard have felt like that about any British distance running race. I look at the results of races of distances above five miles run since about 1990 in Britain, and, without wishing to be big headed, running at my best, I could have won most of them. That is not so much a tribute to me. It is a tribute to all the good club runners of my generation, amongst whom I was just middling. I can only have ever felt, as I did at Sutton Park, that there was no point in running the English National Cross Country Championship because a hundred or more good runners would certainly have beaten me. Then, of course, there were the hundred or so that would have been not very far behind me, all good club runners too, and the hundred or two hundred behind them. I don't know where it stops but as I pointed out in the introduction, the number of British distance runners who were prepared in the period of thirty years or so, starting in the sixties, to train regularly and intensively, and to compete at the highest level, and who reached a standard that would place them well up the finishing order in any race run today, is nothing short of a phenomenon.

Of course you can't have good club runners without good running clubs. In my competitive days I ran for three clubs: Hillingdon Athletic Club, based in Ruislip, Middlesex, (Hillingdon A.C. was formed by the amalgamation of Finchley Harriers and Ruislip Northwood A.C. in 1966), Westbury Harriers in Bristol, and Annadale Striders A.C. in Belfast. They were all strong running clubs. The fact that I was usually no more than about the last scorer in a six man team for any of them says a lot about the strength in depth of distance running during my better years.

Hillingdon A.C. was one of many strong clubs in the greater London region and Westbury Harriers held a similar place in the South West and Midlands. Neither was ever consistently the best club in the area. Annadale Striders, in the much less populated area of Northern Ireland, on the other hand, was one of very few clubs in the region, and for many years was the outstanding club in the province, though it still could never be said to have had a monopoly. When I first arrived in Belfast it was Duncairn Harriers who dominated running events and only later did Annadale overtake Duncairn. It was in the nature of running clubs and athletics clubs to wax and wane in their relative successfulness over the years.

In London, where I started running, competition for top spot was fierce and the strengths of the various clubs rose and fell almost yearly: Hillingdon, Ealing and Southall, Hercules Wimbledon, Blackheath Harriers, Thames Hare and Hounds, Shaftsbury Harriers, Thames Valley Harriers, Southgate Harriers, Highgate, Ranelagh, Epsom and Ewell, London Irish, Belgrave Harriers, Borough of Enfield, South London Harriers, Herne Hill Harriers, Mitcham, Essex Beagles, and others to whom I apologise for forgetting them. Almost every outlying town of any size also had its own club: High Wycombe, Brighton, Crawley, Windsor Slough and Eton, Watford, Basingstoke, Aldershot (joined with Farnham), Portsmouth, Reading. The names trip off the lip of my memory with such ease and with them, by automatic word association, the names of famous runners or runners who were, like me, in the context of team competitions just good club runners: Shaftsbury: Dave Bedford and Julian Goater, Blackheath: Bob Richardson, Hercules Wimbledon: Bob and Dave Holt, Belgrave: Gerry North, Ealing: Mike Barratt, and so on. Every club, at one time or another, had its star or stars. Sometimes a club had more than its share, for example Portsmouth A.C. in the sixties, with Bruce Tulloh, Tim Johnston and Martin Hyman, all international distance runners of the highest class.

I could say the same for the Midlands and West of England in which area of the country I ran between 1972 and 1978. Only the names would change. And, had I lived in the North of England or in Scotland or Wales, things would not have been any different. Throughout Great Britain during my competitive running years there were numerous thriving running and athletics clubs with something like a dozen or more good club runners in each. As I ask elsewhere, which came first, the clubs or the runners? I don't know and it doesn't matter. Many of the clubs have a long history, as the names 'Harriers' and 'Beagles' suggest. Many were solely running, rather than all-events athletics clubs. Thames Hare and Hounds, for example, is still just a club for runners. Most clubs, even the older ones, are still in existence, but inevitably they have evolved, along with the sport itself. For four decades these clubs and the rivalry they built up were the fire that heated the sport of distance running and gave rise to the profusion of good club runners of between thirty and fifty years ago.

So what is a good club runner? There is no definition and even to try to define the phrase by times and performances would miss the point. Of course, a good club runner has to be good, but that is a relative term. I can say without hesitation that the good club runners of yesterday were better on average than those (the few that are left) of today, but I cannot set a standard above which someone is good and below which someone is no longer good. If I were forced into a definition it would hinge on whether a runner was serious or not. A serious runner is one who strives to become as good as possible and to do as well as possible in competition. Being a good club runner is more a matter of attitude than of performance.

It is also, to some extent, a question of lifestyle. Running, to the serious runner, is more than something to enjoy on an occasional basis, like a game of golf or a day's fishing. It is a habit and a commitment, the exact opposite of a fad or a leisure activity. Above all it is a permanent way of life.

You will have gleaned a little about me as a runner from what I have said already. Because I am putting myself forward, somewhat presumptuously, as a representative of the good club runners of the sixties, seventies and eighties, and rating myself as something like average in that respect, you need to know more precisely what sort of runner I was. I will tell you only on the basis of communal bragging. If you know about me then you'll know about all those good club runners who were about my standard, a little less, perhaps, about those who were clearly better than me, and something also about those whom I could probably beat but who were, nevertheless, deserving of the same praise. They may not have been international runners, Olympic or Commonwealth Games representatives, or famous names, but they deserve some acclaim. If they had little acclaim in their day they should certainly have it now, when any one of them would stand out like a beacon in the diluted standards of today's running scene.

Here then is a profile of what you might describe as a typical good club runner of the peak time for British distance running. At my very best, probably when I was in my mid twenties and again at thirty and thirty one, (my career was one of periods of feast and then of famine over a large number of years) I estimate that I was one of the best one hundred or so runners over distances greater than three miles in England, possibly in Great Britain.

My best performances came in road races. I liked the predictable surface, the instant response as each foot hit the ground and the instinctive reaction of the muscles, tendons and ligaments to the impact, turning the direction of movement through one hundred and eighty degrees in a space of time so short it was hardly noticeable. One moment the foot is poised an inch above the ground, the next it is rising at speed into the air and nothing seems to have happened in between. There is no pushing and no pulling, just a light bounce, and forward motion is seemingly uninterrupted. It's like running on wheels.

Cross country, on the other hand, was never my style, though I ran quite well in a number of races, usually when the ground was firm and dry. I welcomed a heavy frost on the day of a race that would turn the mud into concrete and allow me to wear my beloved road racing shoes. I loathed mud and uneven ground, what is often described as 'real cross country', as if that is some form of commendation, and I felt that a point came when cross country running was no longer running, more like wading and wallowing and sliding and getting stuck. Running was never designed to be a pulling exercise, hardly even a pushing exercise; it is or should be all about bouncing and flowing with absolutely minimal muscular effort. I was a road runner first and foremost who ran cross country because everyone else did.

In that respect I was like a number of good club runners. We each had our preference. Some runners took their aversion to cross country to the point that they were rarely to be seen competing anywhere but on the road. Outside their speciality they were practically unknown, even in running circles. And since road running, with the exception of the marathon distance, was the poor relation of track and cross country, with little or no international competition and few high exposure events, those who chose it in preference to other types of distance running (not forgetting that other extreme form of running, fell running) remained out of the limelight. Who, for example, other than fellow road runners, people who lived in the same area and distance running anoraks, knew anything of Bournemouth's Barry Watson until he won the AAA marathon in 1976, and earned a place in Great Britain's team for the Montreal Olympic Games. For many years before that, he had been one of the country's archetypal and best road runners, well known to all other road runners in the south of England and always on the periphery that separated the good club runner from the full international.

At the other extreme I can think of several cross country runners who were hardly ever seen in road races. They were often the annoying runners who beat me hands down over slimy grass and ploughed fields but whom I knew I would leave far behind on solid ground; a case of horses for courses. And then there were the extremists, the hill runners and ultra-distance men. But scratch off the veneer of difference and we were all the same at heart, good club runners with the same commitment and the same motivation.

Certain of my performances stand out because they represent what I now believe was my ultimate potential as a runner. At some stage in a running career, usually as it comes to an end, everyone who ever took the sport seriously asks that most difficult of all questions, 'Could I have been any better?' It's a terrible question to even contemplate because the very fact that it has been asked means not only that there is doubt about the answer but that it is too late to do anything about it anyway. I have now come to terms with the question and with what I believe is the answer. The more time that passes the more confident I become in the answer and the more at peace with the past that makes me.

Over distances up to a half marathon I don't think I could have been much better, whatever I had done by way of training. I could have been more consistent but in one or two races I think I reached my limit. These are the races that stand out in my memory and define my place in the hierarchy of good club runners.

In the summer of 1969, while still at my first university, I went to Reading for a 3,000m track race. I had been training consistently for twelve weeks, running something like fifty miles a week including a lot of fast running and a number of track races over a mile and two and three miles. I had won a mile race in what was then a personal best time of 4:21.5 three weeks previously. Even so I was amazed to run 8:31.6 for that 3,000m. It was not my distance. I was flat out the whole way. It was a triumph of will power over oxygen debt and, having never again got close to that time, I think it was about as fast as I could ever have run, or ever could run for the distance. The eventual winner was Gerry Stevens of Reading Athletic Club, a British 3,000m steeplechaser. The amazing thing was that he, along with half the rest of the field, only overtook me on the last lap. Perhaps they were taking it easy.

Trying to explain it years later I can now understand that I had youth on my side (I was twenty three), I had been doing a lot of racing in the weeks preceding the race and the distance was sufficiently short so that weeks of really big mileages probably wouldn't have made me any faster. In a way I had proved that there was some truth in the Roger Bannister and Christopher Chataway approach to training. It had brought me to what I still consider was my absolute peak at that sort of distance.

The same applies to my near four minute 1,500m that I recounted in Chapter 4, definitely very close to my absolute limit. I might have spent years trying to break four minutes for the distance and might have done so had it been my most precious objective, but it wasn't. And I knew that whatever I had done in the way of training and racing I would never have broken four minutes by more than one or two seconds. Four minutes for 1,500m, by the way, is worth about 4:16 for a mile.

I never ran a serious 800m. I was simply never fast enough. I left school with a best time of 2:08.6 and didn't even start another 800m race until, one day in my late thirties, I lined up alongside a group of proper middle distance runners, all height, athleticism and muscle, for a go at the distance. I have no idea why I did, unless it was for points in an athletics match. It was farcical what some of us runners would do to add a point or two to the team total in athletics matches. Very few teams can find a competitor or, if required, two competitors, for every single event. In one of my college matches a fellow runner volunteered for the pole vault. On finding that pole vaulting was trickier than he had imagined, he asked could he do it without the pole? He then proceeded to win the 3,000m walk, another event he had never tried until that day.

My expedition over 800m was nearer to what I was good at, but still very much not my thing. I remember sprinting for a lap and going through 400m in 58 seconds, about two seconds outside my fastest time for the half distance, at which point I started to laugh. It was all so ludicrous. I had run to half way practically flat out, and wasn't even well placed. But I was fit, as only a well trained distance runner can be, and in a way that certainly didn't apply when I was at school. I got round the second lap without collapsing completely and finished in 2:1.8. That time, incidentally, went a long way to convincing me that middle distance runners would do well to train in a not dissimilar way to distance runners. I know that I could never have run that fast over 800m without the background of lots of miles and lots of hard intervals that was designed to bring me close to my potential at distances up to the full marathon. Almost by chance the same training enabled me to run 800m in a time that, given my relative lack of basic speed, was pretty impressive. Compare it, for example, with Sebastian Coe's former world record, set by a man who could run 400m ten seconds faster than I could. There is an uncanny equivalence.

In October 1976, after a whole year of uninterrupted training, averaging about sixty miles a week, I ran the Walton ten mile road race in 49:52, finishing nearly a minute and a half behind the winner, Tony Simmons of Luton United Athletic Club. That was the only time I ever achieved a sub fifty minute ten miler over an accurately measured course. It was like running a ten thousand metre race and just keeping going. At the end I knew that I could not have run faster, not in that race nor any other and that I had earned a label that said, 'forty nine minute, fifty two second ten miler, at his very best'. Over thirty five years later I consider that label to be about right. I deserved it, I'm proud of it, and I don't think I could have improved it. Had I been able to, I think that subsequently I would have done. All through my thirties, during which period I trained harder and more consistently than ever before, I could usually run between 50 and 51 minutes for ten miles, but never bettered that Walton ten time.

In 1983, at the age of thirty six, I was second in the county Antrim half marathon, in 1:05:57, having passed through ten miles in 50:06. It was the same year that I achieved my best position in the Northern Ireland Cross Country Championship, ran in the World Cross Country for the first time, and set my fastest time for the marathon. It was one of the best running years of my life.

Only over much longer distances, twenty miles and marathon do I think I failed to do myself justice, but then not to a degree that gives me sleepless nights. Every distance runner knows that the further the distance, the greater the contribution made by training. My best marathon time was set after what was, for me, about as much training as I could take, thirty eight weeks of up to over eighty miles per week with ten long runs of between twenty and twenty five miles and plenty of fast stuff (see Chapter 8). I don't think I could have done much better at the time. But it happened in 1983, when I was already thirty six years old, and I know that the same amount of training ten years earlier might have given me a slightly faster time. If I were to guess at what sort of marathon time I might have run, with youth on my side and with the benefit of the maximum amount of training I was capable of, I would say that I might just have dipped under 2:20. But 2:10 or 2:15? No way.

So there you have it. That's the sort of good club runner I was. Along with every other good club runner, after a few years reaching a plateau of performance, I settled into my place in the hierarchy and strived to stay there just as I had strived to reach that place to start with. Of course we all hoped for improvement but the phenomenon of the plateau, recording the same sort of times over the same distances year by year, when experienced for long enough, convinces even the most optimistic runner that real improvement is no longer a reality.

A cross section of the mass of good club runners of the peak years would have shown a core of people like me who had reached their potential, who posted the same times each year, who accepted that they would never be very much better but, nevertheless, were happy and determined to work just as hard to stay where they were for as long as they could. On the periphery were those who were new to the game and about to move through, some to dizzy heights, others to their place in the middle of the core. Very few left altogether until the natural process of deterioration with age pushed them down to the bottom of the slope and into retirement. Longevity of career was always a feature of the good club runner.

For the majority of good club runners, running became the defining feature of their lives. They were runners first and other things second. I have often puzzled over the urge to discover what people 'do' as if this is all one needs to know about them. As contestants introduce themselves on TV quiz shows (of which I am a great fan) they do so according to a standard format: 'I am so-and-so and I am a teacher, a police officer, a secretary, a journalist, or whatever'. They may be asked what they do in their spare time, this being, by implication, a less important part of their lives. Only at this point is it permissible to reply 'running'. When I was a lecturer and introduced myself to groups of teachers on one of the college's in service courses, I used to come out with a list of things that I did, including running (it was a long list because I always had far too many interests) and ended by saying, 'and, in my spare time, I teach science.' It was meant as a joke but I was also making a keenly felt point. Teaching was not what I was, it was simply what I did, and then only some of the time. I had to earn a living, after all. Running on the other hand was me. I did it because I couldn't not do it.

Occasionally an exceptional individual burst through from the mass and emerged at the very top, having graduated from good club runner to the élite. The first time I won the Yeovil 10, in June 1976, I was followed home by a certain Steve Jones from Swindon Athletic Club. I had met him before in races. That same year he was one place behind me in the South West Counties AAA Cross Country Championship and appeared in the results as Stan Jones, much to the amusement of his club mates. 'Get up there, Stan!' they shouted at the medal giving. At that time he would have fitted well into the good club runner category and it seemed likely that he might stay there for the rest of his career. After all it's very unusual for anyone to make the sort of leap that he was about to.

Eight years after I beat him at Yeovil, the same Steve Jones was 186 places and three minutes and twenty eight seconds ahead of me when he finished third in the World Cross Country Championship in New York. Carlos Lopes of Portugal won the race and second was England's Tim Hutchings. Steve Jones was representing Wales and I was running for Northern Ireland, the country that adopted me in 1978 when I moved there to a new job. Two years later he set a world's best time for the marathon in Chicago, 2:08:16, followed by an even faster time in the same city the following year, 2:07:13, still the British record.

Though less well known outside running circles than, for example, Ron Hill, Charlie Spedding (London marathon winner in 1984 and Olympic bronze medallist the same year) or John Brown (twice fourth place finisher in the Olympic marathon), Steve Jones could justifiably claim to be Britain's best ever marathon runner. That makes me suitably mortified that I had originally thought of him, in a condescending way, as no more than a promising young runner just reaching good club runner status.

The strange thing is that Steve Jones, the up and coming club runner of the mid seventies and Steve Jones, the world class distance runner of the nineteen eighties was not only the same person in the literal sense, but was also the same in my mind and, I would guess, also in the minds of all runners who had witnessed his rise to fame, the same in every way. The small matter of some improvement in performance was neither here nor there.

The running community as I knew it was a continuum, from slowcoach to élite. In a sense every one of us, from the top to the bottom, was a good club runner. As one runner improved he didn't change. He still worked hard, as we all did, he still hoped to get even better, as we all did, he still got nervous at times and felt vulnerable, he had good days and bad days, experienced triumphs and disasters. Who can forget, for example, the sad sight of Steve Jones finishing the 1986 European Games marathon in 20th place, crawling onto the track towards the finish in the sort of distressed state that runners of his class were not supposed to get into. Perhaps that particular demonstration of fallibility endeared him to more runners watching than anything else he did. In the space of one bad race he attained good club runner status again, having lost it briefly amongst the clouds that are exclusively the home of the élite.

Because big road races today often have a separate contest for the élite, a fundamental distinction has been created between good club runners and élite runners, a bit like the much older distinction between amateur and professional. Once that line was drawn, sometime in the last decade of the twentieth century, it destroyed the sense of shared aims and a shared sport within the whole body of competitive runners and removed some of the soul from the sport of distance running. It is at least part of the reason that there are fewer good club runners around today than years ago.

I often wonder whether there is a personality type associated with distance running and whether the decline of good club runners in general in the last few decades has something to do with the inability of a shared personality to adapt to the changing running scene. In pondering this question I am very aware of the likelihood of falling into the trap of attaching my own psychological strengths and weaknesses to all fellow runners, on the basis that because we share the same passion we must also share the same personality. I know that is not true. The range of personalities amongst all the runners I have ever known seems as wide as in any random group of the same size. Nevertheless I still feel we must have a number of psychological traits in common.

For example, what about 'the loneliness of the long distance runner'? This phrase implies, quite mistakenly, that runners, because they go for long runs, often by themselves, are lonely. Non runners imagine that it cannot be possible to run alone for up to two or three hours without becoming bored and in need of company. To them, needing company is the same as being lonely. I have never been lonely while running. Probably ninety percent of all the running I've ever done has been on my own.

If anything, running is an escape from loneliness. When I first went to Sussex University in the autumn of 1969 the only accommodation I could find, in my urgency to find anything at all, was a tiny bedsit in a long row of terraced houses in the inner suburbs of Brighton. I hadn't had time to make friends and, outside the working day, it was a very lonely few months for me. One evening, purely on a whim, I put on my running kit and ran into the darkness, westwards along the wide coast road towards Shoreham-on-sea, Worthing and Littlehampton, until I thought it best that I turn round and run back. I did about sixteen miles and it was the least lonely and most enjoyable hour and three quarters of the whole day.

I think all runners who are willing to make the necessary commitment to training that being a good club runner entails benefit from being able to survive and even enjoy their own company for long periods of time. It is possible, of course, to train in company, but not always. My guess is that most serious runners, past and present, have always done a large part of their training by themselves. Perhaps I carry my introversion to extremes, and I cannot assume that everyone who regularly runs for long periods of time on their own does so with the same sense of relief, freedom and comfort as I do. But I guess, again, that a large proportion of those same runners always enjoyed running on their own and, maybe, all distance runners do share a high degree of stoicism and self reliance.

Once again we come back to motivation. To do anything for hours at a time, devotedly and with effort and concentration, requires a driving force. Above everything else the good club runner has to be highly motivated. Whether motivation necessarily precedes enjoyment of running, or whether the two form yet another chicken and egg partnership is a moot point, but the two things indicate another shared aspect of personality amongst serious runners. All good club runners are good at sticking to a long term training task to the point that it becomes practically impossible to abandon it. If I had to answer the question posed at the head of this chapter, 'Where are all the good club runners?' I would say, quite simply, 'Their motivation has gone'.

CHAPTER 7
Six rules of training

'Eddie, you have to train to train.'
Good friend and fellow runner.

As I outlined in Chapter 3, the business of training for distance running has taken about a century to evolve from a haze of general ignorance, lit by isolated beacons of individual effort and idiosyncrasy, to the point where it is hard to see how it can progress any further. Training theory and training practice have become so refined and so universally agreed that the history of the development of training is like that of converting muddy fields of beet into bags of pure white sugar, freely available in any amount from any supermarket. We now take training for granted. All runners are fully aware that they need to train and they have a fair idea of how much they need to train if they are to become any good. No runner today has any excuse for not knowing roughly what form that training should take. Yet still the most frequently asked questions in running circles are about training; what training do you do, does he or she do, should I be doing? And the most written about topic in modern running magazines is training and training schedules. It's as if the clearer our knowledge of training becomes, the more we wish to mystify it. If we pretend that we still don't know the answers, then perhaps we can avoid the unsavoury truths about training. Having effectively found the holy grail of training for distance running, we feel compelled to look for another one, an even holier one, one that is easier to stomach. The indigestible fact is that to be any good as a distance runner it is necessary to train long and hard. It is taxing, time consuming work. It tests one's resolve and physical reserves to the limit. There are no short cuts. To some extent the more you put in the more you get out. Yet, still, runners look for secrets and elixirs and ways to make training easier; and there are plenty of people willing to sell them such things.

Recently I joined a group of runners for training on a Wednesday evening. I had come back to serious running more as an experiment than for any other reason. I was curious to know what I could do at my age. Also I wanted to be able to give up running, if it came to that, on a high rather than a low point. So by degrees over three or four years I revived my tired old body to the point that I could consider running with much younger people. Originally I joined other runners because I wanted company on a long run. I was going to do a bit before meeting them, run with them for six or seven miles, then do a bit more by myself. I soon abandoned that idea when it became clear that I had to run as hard as I could just to keep up with them. So Wednesdays became my burn-up session, what would now be called a tempo run, but which I still refer to as a hard run. My long run would have to wait for another day.

On only my second evening with the group I was asked straight out what my best time for a marathon was. I explained that it was a long time ago but couldn't avoid giving a straight answer (my best marathon time was 2:24:24 in 1983). Immediately I was asked what I had had to do to achieve that. It was an interesting and, in some ways, curious response from young runners fairly new to the sport. It was said in exactly the same way that someone might ask how much I had paid for something that was obviously very expensive. There was the unquestioned understanding that to run a good time for a marathon it was necessary to do a considerable amount of training, more perhaps than my running companions would consider doing themselves and, at the same time, there was the attitude that training was a sort of price to pay for achievement, the greater the achievement, the higher the price.

I later realised, from other things that were said, that these runners had a very measured approach to both training and competing, one that was more relaxed, more mature even, and quite different compared with my own. If a certain amount of training was the price you paid for reaching your potential I was never willing to haggle or to come away with less than I wanted because I couldn't afford it. I just paid the price asked. Here, however, were runners who were happy to set their own price limit and to be satisfied with what that amount could afford. It was almost as if, in asking what training I had had to do, they were asking if I didn't think I had paid too much. As a product of the running peak of the seventies and eighties, when no one that I ran with questioned the amount of training that simply had to be done, I took some time to adjust to this new outlook on running.

When, later, I thought about it, I began to wonder whether, all my life, I had been wrong about my running and had spoiled it with ambition. Ambition, except for the very few, is almost bound to be thwarted at the end, and the price paid is invariably too much. If I had set myself more easily attainable targets and done only the training that was necessary to achieve them, might I have enjoyed my running more? I don't think so.

What was different about my contented young running companions and me was that, as far as their running was concerned, they were firmly in the driving seat. They could go exactly as fast or as slow, and only just as far, as they wished. I, on the other hand, had always been driven. I trained because I had to. I had places to get to and a time to be there. I enjoyed my training, as they obviously did, but it was, first and foremost, a means to an end, and I spent all my running life adjusting my training, upwards, downwards and sideways, in a continuous attempt to achieve the very best that I could. Even after the age of sixty I couldn't contemplate any other approach to my running.

Implicit in my attitude to competitive running and in my running companions' reason for training and in the question I was asked, is what could be called the first rule of training:

Rule No. 1: IF YOU TRAIN YOU GET BETTER.

That is the most encouraging thing about running. Improvement is absolutely guaranteed if you train. I can say that with complete confidence of not giving anyone false hopes. There is no question about it. However little training you do, if you do any at all, you will run better and more easily as a result. Initially, if you've never trained before, it doesn't really matter exactly what that training is. It's probably best if it's some form of running but even that isn't essential. A lot of runners cycle as part of their training. Walking is worthwhile, especially for those who are starting from a very low level of fitness. Plain, steady running is as good as anything. No one needs worry about the finer details of training until some basic fitness has been established.

I could go on and say that the more training you do the more rapid will be the rate of improvement and the better you will get. Most of the time I would undoubtedly be right, but I would be sailing dangerously close to a serious misrepresentation. It is a fallacy to state, without qualification and with no limits, that the more training you do, the better you get because (and here lies the fatal flaw) it is only true up to a point.

When Bruce Tulloh ran across America in 1969, from Los Angeles to New York, a total distance of 2,876 miles, the jury was still out on the sort of mileages distance runners should be doing in training, 25 miles a week, 50 miles a week, 100 miles, 150 miles, 200 miles? And, if 200 miles a week, why not more? Tulloh effectively answered that question. In crossing America on foot he averaged over three hundred miles each week for over nine weeks. There was no evidence he was a better runner when he had finished than before he started. Quite the reverse; that amount of running over that length of time had done far more damage than good. Tulloh had been injured and exhausted and reduced to a state which made running at any speed problematic. No one would have expected anything else.

Tulloh's purpose in running three hundred miles a week was to cross America in a shorter time than anyone else had done before. In this he succeeded. The training effects of the running were clearly not a consideration. But a number of other distance runners also tested the point of diminishing returns, deliberately running huge mileages in the hope of becoming better runners. I have already told the story of Roger Matthews in Chapter 3. Dave Bedford was another, more famous, example. Bedford, one time holder of the world record for 10,000m, winner of the English National and the International Cross Country Championship in 1971, running phenomenon of his time, had already extended the bounds of reason by contemplating running 200 miles a week in training and sometimes actually doing so. It seemed absurd and yet he provided evidence that it could work. While he may have demonstrated that covering two hundred miles per week was not impossible and even for a while that it might have been effective, he failed to convince the running world that it was necessary. Ultimately he showed it to be counterproductive.

Derek Clayton, the British born Australian who set a world best for the marathon of 2:09:36.4 in 1967 and bettered that with 2:08:33.6 in 1969, also sometimes ran over two hundred miles a week, and averaged between one hundred and forty and one hundred and seventy. He, like Bedford, was plagued with injury problems that eventually demanded surgical treatment. In the nineteen eighties Alberto Salazar, one of USA's greatest distance runners followed the same pathway to self destruction. In the words of 'Men's Running' (Dec/Jan 2012), *'He became a slave to mileage, churning out ever greater distances in the belief that only through filling his legs with the hugest loads possible would the greatest improvements arrive ...wrecking himself with training weeks in excess of two hundred miles'.* Had these great athletes been content to run no more than a hundred miles a week, or perhaps a little bit more, my belief is that they would have been just as good. But then we would still not know where the limits to training mileage lie. It took runners like them to test the effects of ever increasing mileages in training for others to benefit. We owe them a lot.

Common sense alone would have put the phrase 'up to a point' into the second rule of training. Those who tested the doctrine of ever more miles in training to its logical conclusion simply hammered the phrase home so firmly that no one would ever again think of trying to remove it. The second rule of training, therefore, becomes:

Rule No. 2: THE MORE TRAINING YOU DO, THE BETTER YOU GET - *UP TO A POINT.*

Nevertheless, even without its qualification, there remains a lot of truth in this second rule. The problem is in defining the point up to which it applies and above which it does not. If there were a single such point that applied across the board it would be quite easy to define, but there isn't. It is a different point for each individual and can only be found individually. For Bedford, Clayton and Salazar I would guess that it lay around a hundred and fifty miles. For me it was about eighty miles. For someone who is not a naturally gifted runner it might be only twenty or thirty miles.

It is also a different point for the same individual at different stages in his or her running life. A beginner cannot do as much training as the same person can cope with two or three years later. The point when more training no longer leads to more improvement, therefore, not only needs to be identified in the first place but needs continuous adjustment as a runner gets better over time. I'm afraid that if you want to find that point for yourself you will have to do so by trial and error and keep doing so year by year. Err on the low side and you might wonder for the rest of your life whether you might have been a better runner. But, err on the upper side and you could destroy your running and any enthusiasm you ever had for it.

This brings us to the third rule of training:

Rule No. 3: ALL RUNNERS HAVE THEIR OWN TRAINING LIMIT.

This is where the subject of training changes from being exceedingly simple to being extremely complicated. It is made complicated by the fact that every runner is unique. Runners vary hugely, physically, physiologically, psychologically and in their lifestyles. Consequently only the most general of principles, such as those encapsulated in rules 1 and 2 above, can be applied to all runners, and why it is up to each individual runner to discover the training that best suits them. All that a hundred years of experiment in training methods, the results of other people's successes and mistakes, has done for present day runners is to give them the knowledge, on which to base their own learning process. It cannot be prescriptive.

If we think of training and performance in mathematical terms, there are three variables to consider. First there is a runner's genetic make-up, what can be called natural ability, impossible to measure, but usually fairly obvious to gauge. Let's call it NA. Then there is training, T. Finally there is performance, or how good a person is at running, as measured by times and positions in races. This can be P.

The simplest relationship between the three variables, one with which no one would argue, is the equation:

$$NA + T = P$$

In other words, how good a runner you become depends on your natural ability and the training that you do. In this case NA and T are what are known in mathematics as independent variables, while P is the dependent variable.

As far as most people are concerned this is about the limit of their thinking on running ability. It's the basic assumption behind all arguments about the effectiveness of training, the superiority of one runner over another, even the ethics of the principle of judgement based on performance. Still today, to some thinkers, the very idea of training, especially when it is done in a committed and highly strenuous way, is close to cheating. Let natural ability alone dictate the outcome of competition.

The equation also contains the seed of a very common fallacy, one which can be seen wherever discussions take place as to why some runners are better than others. The fallacy involves the temporary forgetting of the first factor in the equation, namely natural ability, the unchangeable genetic gifts that make someone a good runner, and the consequent elevation of training to the sole determinant of performance. Hence the misguided believe in the equation:

$$T = P$$

For example, in trying to explain why runner 'A' is better than runner 'B', the reason will be found in the fact that runner 'A' does more or better or simply different training. What follows is the second and worse part of the fallacious argument. For runner 'B' to become as good as runner 'A', all that is necessary is for 'B' to do the same training as 'A'. QED!

If the relationship between training and performance were this straightforward it would follow that the best runners would simply be those who did the most training or, if not the most training, then the best training. Even though this is blatantly not the case it is still presented as a serious contention whenever the issue of training for distance running crops up. If you think this is an exaggeration, you only have to read any of the numerous articles in running magazines that attempt to explain why the Kenyans and Ethiopians dominate the world in distance running. The main reason found is always that they do a lot of hard training. This leads to headlines such as 'Train like the Kenyans', with the implication that if we Europeans were to train as hard as the East Africans we would be just as good.

This sort of argument, wherever and to whomever it is applied, fails to recognise that performance, the P in our equations, can itself be an independent variable and, at the same time training, T, can be a dependent variable. This gives us an alternative formula:

$$NA + P = T$$

In simple terms, how much training you do or can do is determined by how good a runner you are. The relationship between training and performance is reversible. Each can be causal. Each can be the product of the other. They are inseparably bound, like the proverbial chicken and egg.

Every serious runner does, not so much the training that is suggested by theory, certainly not, slavishly, the training that some much better runner does, but the best training that he or she **can** do. It's really very obvious. When I read that Haile Gebrselassie (one time holder of the world's best marathon time) included runs of three hours or more at sub five minutes per mile pace in his training, I knew where I had gone wrong. My best marathon was over twenty minutes slower than his. Clearly this was because my longest runs in training were only about twenty three miles and done at a mere six minute mile pace.

I simply cannot emphasise this point enough. To train long and hard you have to be a good enough runner to be able to do so. The training that some world class runners do is way beyond most runners' ability, however hard and for however long they might try to emulate it. All anyone can do is to train consistently and progressively until a point is reached beyond which it is either impossible or counterproductive to do any more. Wherever that point turns out to be, it will eventually be reached by anyone who is determined enough to find it. That's when you know just how good a runner you are, or ever could be.

This elementary fact was brought home to me very clearly when, at the age of fifty nine I resumed what I considered to be serious training with a view to becoming 'good for age'. My attitude was the same as it ever was. I was going to train regularly, long and hard, in the certainty that I would gradually improve. I was aware that I couldn't hope to do the amount of training I had done as a younger man nor would I do it at anything like the same pace, but I saw no reason not to aim for a somewhat similar training régime.

Four years later I had nearly achieved my aim but I had discovered the manifest truth that, although I was the same person, I was no longer the same runner as in the past. And I could no longer do the same training. I was runner 'B' when I had been runner 'A'. I managed to average about fifty miles a week in my build up to a marathon in 2011, but that was only two thirds of the weekly mileage that I did in the seventies and eighties. Because I was now running bulk training miles in between seven and a half minutes and eight and a half minutes, I was actually running for a longer time each week than previously but that, in turn, meant that long runs (15+ miles) had become like an all day event. They were considerably harder than they had been and took a lot more out of me. At times I wondered whether I was in danger of doing myself serious harm by trying to emulate myself at half my age.

It would have been pointless to tell runner 'B' (my 64 year old self) to train like runner 'A' (my thirty year old self). The fact was that runner 'B' was no longer runner 'A' and simply couldn't train like him. In the same way, there is no point telling someone to train like the Kenyans if that is itself impossible. It is more the case that if you want to train like the Kenyans, first you have to be a Kenyan.

I have to qualify the point a little. As you train so you get better. As you get better you are able to train more and harder. As a good friend and top class runner once said to me (quoted at the start of this chapter) *'Eddie, you have to train to train'*. So whereas a beginning runner cannot jump straight in at the deep end, embarking on a ferocious training regime in imitation of élite runners, it may be possible to reach the same or similar end point after a period of years of progressive training.

I estimate that it took me three years to progress from an average twenty year old runner to what I took to be my potential as a distance runner and to a level of training that I hardly improved on during the next twenty years. I still think three years is about the length of time a runner just beginning to train can expect to wait before the dreaded performance plateau comes into view.

My comeback as a near sixty year old took about the same time. Perhaps it was a bit longer. If so, I put that down to age. At forty three I more or less gave up competing. I tried a couple of comebacks as I joined each new veteran age group. But effectively I didn't run at all consistently for fifteen years. That put me back to the beginners' ranks and I needed those three years to build up to the point that I could train every week at what I considered a reasonable level, stay free of serious injuries, not get too tired or physically or mentally depressed and, above all, enjoy my running with that almost forgotten sense of ease and fluidity.

Every runner who sticks at it long enough will go through the same process that I went through, first as I entered my early twenties and then, again, as I turned sixty. Consistent training will bring about steady improvement which, in turn will allow more training and a higher level of training, leading to even greater improvement. It's a wonderfully motivating process of positive feedback that, unfortunately, has to come to an end sooner or later. How do you know it's come to an end? When, whatever you do, your performances do not improve and, if you try to do more or harder training, you find that you can't. You break down, you get injured, overtired, unwell, slower rather than faster and, worst of all, just plain fed up.

Training is easy when it seems worth it, when it's within your compass, can be done without ill effects and when you can see measurable improvement or simply have confidence that it's working. It becomes a little bit more difficult to stick to when it becomes obvious that your performances are plateauing out. At that point it is necessary to adjust to the idea that it's just as worthwhile to maintain an acquired standard of performance as to have reached it in the first place.

Between 1971, when I experienced my first real running peak, and 1988 when increasing years began to slow me down, I got neither significantly better nor worse as a runner. At the same time I lost none of the motivation that got me there. In some ways you can be even more determined to hang on to what you've got than you were to get hold of it in the first place. To reach a peak as a runner can be the beginning rather than some sort of end point. For a start you have a reputation to keep up. Your training so far is like hard-earned money, saved in the bank. Now is the time to spend it and to reap the rewards of all that work, always bearing in mind that if you want to go on spending, you have to replenish it at the same time. In other words you still have to train.

This is what I call the 'training trap'. Running, including training, is a source of great pleasure. If it weren't, no one would do it. Running well is even more pleasurable. The fitter one becomes, through training, the more enjoyable running is. Conversely if you stop training and let yourself become unfit, running becomes hard work again. A run that you would have breezed through when fit can now leave you tired, stiff legged and a little queezy. Where's the pleasure in that? So you become trapped in an endless routine of training, just to be able to enjoy running to the full. Training is not just a device to get you to your potential, it is just as much a necessary means of keeping you there.

A perfect example of what I mean by a performance plateau comes from my own record in running the Hyde Park relay in the seven years 1965 to 1972. The Hyde Park relay is for university and college teams, over six laps around the Serpentine Lake in London's Hyde Park, each lap of about three miles. It's held annually in February. My times for the three miles in successive years were as follows: 16:16, 15:26, 14:47, 14:29, 14:24, 14:14 and 14:24. That is a plateau! And, had I continued to run the same relay leg every year from then on for the next ten years I doubt if I would have beaten my best time nor been much slower than my last appearance in 1972, which happened to be a repeat of my time in 1970.

Training had got me to the top of my personal plateau and only much the same training could keep me there. The point I am trying to emphasise is that the plateau is not just a performance plateau. It also represents a training plateau. At the start of my first year at university in 1965 I ran relatively little and not very consistently, perhaps, on average, fifteen or twenty miles per week. By 1968 I was a lot more consistent in my running and had reached over thirty and up to sixty miles a week, most weeks. When I changed universities in 1969 I really got down to serious training and averaged over fifty miles a week for periods of months at a time, with regular weekly mileages of seventy or more miles. Had I tried to do that sort of intensity of training in my first year at university, or even before that, I suspect I might not have been running at all four years later.

If you study the performances of famous runners you will find the same plateau effect. I am looking, for example, at the appendix of Brendan Foster's autobiography, 'Brendan Foster', in which he lists all his major race results from 1962 onwards. I note that in 1969 he ran the Hyde Park relay but got round considerably faster than I ever did. His time was 13:33. More relevantly I also note that between 1973, when he ran his first track 5,000m, and 1978 when the appendix closes, he ran 17 significant 5,000m races, fastest 13:14.6 in 1974, and slowest 13:54.8 in 1973. Eleven of those races were run in between 13:20 and 13:40.

Foster's plateau, for a plateau is undoubtedly what the results point to, was achieved with considerably more training than I ever did. Exactly what that training consisted of can also be found in his autobiography. In preparation for the Montreal Olympic Games where he finished third in the 10,000m in 27:55 and fifth in the 5,000m (13:26.2 with an Olympic record 13:20.4 in a heat) he was running well over one hundred miles each week, up to as much as 130 miles some weeks. He remarks at one point, *'Feeling as if I'm doing as much running as I possibly can, getting sick of all the running without variety...'*

Surely Foster had reached his limit, not just in terms of times over measured distances, but in his tolerance of training. Can anyone who reads what his training involved at that time seriously believe that yet more training could have improved his performances? A performance plateau, to my mind, is the very best evidence that a runner has achieved what his god-given gifts have allowed him to, no more and no less.

You may be wondering by now why the currency for training for distance running is miles per week. It is just for convenience sake. It is assumed that the bulk of a runner's training is straightforward running, usually done at a steady, comfortable pace, in my case, when I was younger, about six minutes per mile. A typical week's training for any runner would comprise at least half to three quarters of the time spent doing nothing more elaborate than plain, simple running. It is also assumed that at least some of the week's mileage will be done as interval type running, short distances run quite fast, with a breather between each repetition. Even so, this type of training can still be recorded quite easily as the total mileage covered. Non-running activities such as drills or weights, or time on a cycle machine can be converted to mileage equivalents, based on time and effort involved. So, miles per week becomes a reasonably good, if not entirely accurate, yardstick for the amount of training being done. It may only be a rough and ready measure but it's the best we've got.

Merely counting miles, however, says nothing about the intensity of training. At the very beginning of the twentieth century, when the whole concept of training was in its infancy, a much advocated part of a distance runner's training was not running but walking. Alfred Shrubb, Britain's outstanding runner of the nineteen hundreds, wrote regarding 'training for a long-journey race' (i.e. a marathon), *The principal item is walking'*. He went on to suggest a sixteen-mile walk on three or four days a week, plus two or three walks of half that distance on other days, and one run of sixteen miles. This regime would be increased after six weeks and, for about the next month, each week's training would consist of one or two runs of twenty or even twenty five miles, and long walks of up to twenty five miles on the other days.

That pattern of training has the runner covering a weekly mileage of between 80 and 150 miles, but most of it is walking rather than running. Elite distance runners of today are doing similar mileages, but it is all running. I don't think any runner nowadays would count walking miles towards the total weekly training mileage. It must be obvious to anyone that Shrubb's recommended training for a marathon and the sort of training done by more recent runners, starting in the nineteen forties and fifties and routinely since then, despite the equivalence in distance, are by no stretch of the imagination the same.

In the early years of my own experimenting in training there was a fashion for what became known as LSD. Depending on where you got your information from, LSD stood either for long, slow distance or for long, steady distance. The distinction was never clear as both slow and steady are pretty much indefinable descriptive words. Come to think about it, so is long. The principle behind LSD, however, was clear enough; training for distance running should consist of just running at a nice easy pace for lots of miles. It was during the height of the LSD craze that the figure of 100 miles a week achieved an almost mystical significance, a bit like the figure of four minutes for a mile.

Up and down the country, during the sixties, seventies and eighties, runners of all abilities were religiously churning out the magic hundred miles a week, without ever running either hard or fast. It kept them injury free, never grossly over-tired or run-down and, in theory at any rate, full of pent up energy for races, energy that hadn't been expended unnecessarily in training. It might have been exceedingly boring but it did seem to work.

In November 1970, Cliff Temple, the well known athletics journalist, in an article in Athletics Weekly titled 'An end to the daily grind', asked the question, '...*how many* (runners) *are actually thinking of anything deeper than the comforting figure of one hundred miles a week?*' It seems bizarre for anyone to think of running one hundred miles a week as comforting but I knew and every other runner like me knew what that comfort consisted of. To run a hundred miles a week was never a guarantee of success but it was a proven route to success for some and it was a certain way of getting rid of feelings of guilt and 'what-ifs?' There is no comfort for a keen runner in doing less training than is believed to be necessary. I never ran a hundred miles in a week, let alone week after week for months on end. The most I ever ran in one week was 94 miles. That is why I still wonder what might have been the result for me of a one hundred miles a week schedule. Yes, it would be comforting to know that I had once tried it.

The main point of Cliff Temple's article was not to question the wisdom, the necessity even, of running one hundred miles a week. At the time this was more or less taken for granted. What he set out to do was to counter the objection that not many runners could fit in what amounted to almost fifteen miles of running every single day by suggesting that the target one hundred miles could be covered by running just four days a week, the bulk of it in just three long runs of nearly thirty miles each. To this day I don't know whether he was absolutely serious or whether he was being satirical, pointing to the absurdity of making training mileage the objective itself rather than merely an effective route to improvement. Either way, knowingly or unwittingly, he managed to make the point. There was no magic in the figure one hundred and no purpose in merely achieving that figure for its own sake.

I knew a runner for whom a hundred miles a week became an obsession. He had to cover exactly one hundred miles each and every week, not ninety nine or one hundred and one, but precisely one, zero, zero. His week ended on a Sunday so, however many miles he had run by Sunday morning, he would make up to one hundred on that day. If he had been particularly keen during the week he might even get a day off but, more often, he found himself having to make up a deficit of well over twenty miles in one day. But he always seemed to manage it. I don't think he was ever an especially good runner.

Another runner of the same mind, but this time one who **was** especially good was Barry Watson, British marathon representative at the 1976 Montreal Olympic Games. If you watch footage of the start of that particular Olympic marathon, which is available on YouTube, you will see Watson leading the field out of the stadium. When he was interviewed by Athletics Weekly about his training he said, '*I run exactly one hundred miles a week*'. That might appear, like Ron Hill's insistence on running every single day of his life, a mindless compulsion, but for someone who has worked out that something like one hundred miles a week is the amount of training that is right for him, it is actually easier to aim for the exact round figure, one hundred, no more, no less, than to be content with a more approximate figure. In the same way, it is easier to go for a run if you have arranged to meet someone at a specified time than if you can choose to go out at any time of the day.

If lots of steady running worked for some runners, then so had a diet of short sharp training sessions worked for a large number of others, with very few miles covered in total. This less-but-harder formula was exemplified, for example, by runners who subscribed to the philosophy of interval training, with fast running over short distances. Clearly, mileage alone cannot begin to describe training fully. One mile walked is not the same as a mile run slowly which, in turn, is not the same as a mile run hard.

Which brings us, by a rather long winded approach, to a fourth rule of training:

Rule No. 4: A LITTLE BIT OF HARD RUNNING IS LIKE A LOT OF EASY RUNNING.

This is a very rough and ready rule, open to much interpretation and qualification but it makes sense in two ways. Firstly, based on my own experience and the evidence of the careers of many very successful distance runners, the same training effects can come from the two very different ways of training, lots of easy running or a lesser volume of hard. But, and here comes the second piece of sense incorporated in the rule, you cannot do as much hard running as you can easy running. It's simply not physically possible.

That could explain why, even in recent times, top class runners seem to do very different amounts of training, despite performing at very much the same level. Those who do very large total mileages most likely do the bulk of it relatively slowly whereas runners who do what might be considered, by today's high standards, a conservative weekly mileage (that is, less than a hundred a week) are probably incorporating more hard running.

Of course, it's not quite that simple. Slower running has different training benefits compared with faster running, and vice versa. There are risks attached to large amounts of running, whatever the pace and other quite separate risks attached to running hard. Different people have their own preferences as to the type and amount of running they do. We all have our strengths and weaknesses as runners and our own preferred events. Even though basic training for distance running is the same whether the distance raced is one mile or twenty six miles, no one would expect a miler, for example, to do exactly the same training as a marathon runner.

There are two more rules of training before we leave this chapter. They are so closely linked as to be, as it were, joined at the hip. They apply to two features of training that have already been mentioned, namely, consistency and progression. The simpler and predominant rule of the two can be expressed thus:

Rule No. 5: TRAINING IS A LONG TERM AFFAIR.

In other words it is the exact opposite of my first concept of training, demonstrated by my practice half mile run the evening before my first race over the same distance. Training is not the same as practice. A better alternative word for training is conditioning, because it implies the same slow process of physical change. The effects of training may sometimes seem almost supernatural and unrelated to bodily changes (after all, a runner emerges from a winter of hard training looking little different from before, with no obvious outward sign of his newly acquired powers) but, in reality, the effects of training are as physical as the healing of a wound, or a loss in weight as a result of dieting, or the massive increase in muscle bulk of body builders due to pumping iron, or simply the adolescent growth spurt. It's just that most of the changes brought about by training for distance running are internal and invisible.

They can also be long lasting. I sometimes wonder even whether some of the physical effects that many years of training have wrought on my body are more or less permanent. At my very fittest my pulse rate at rest was about 45 and occasionally it dropped below that. Once, while I travelled on a bus from Exeter to Torbay, I measured it at exactly 40. Lowering of the pulse rate is a well known and lasting effect of hard training and is a sign of a larger and stronger than average heart. Forty or more years later my pulse is still usually below sixty and I am quite sure that when I die the post mortem will find a larger than normal heart inside me. It may take a long time to strengthen the heart to that degree, but it takes even longer to undo the good work. Obsessive fears about losing hard won fitness because of a few days missed training are invariably unjustified.

The simplest principle of training is that if you stress the body it adapts in such a way that the next time you do the same thing it's better able to cope. If you lift heavy weights, for example, the muscles respond by getting stronger. The next time you lift the same weights the work is easier and you find you can lift even heavier weights. Of course the process of adaptation takes time. My adolescent half mile training run would never have done me any real good, not by the next day. But it might have helped me run better a month later.

Pretty well all the adaptations that bring about an improvement in a distance runner's performances are related to the body's capacity for producing energy in the running muscles. As practically all the energy used in distance running comes from the oxidation of sugar in the muscles, the key adaptations are those affecting the supply of oxygen to the muscle cells. Without going too deeply into the physiology of running we can sum up the main changes that occur as a result of training and see that they all help to facilitate the movement of oxygen from the air to the muscle cells, via the lungs and the blood system. It will also be obvious that these changes are physical ones akin to growth, slow to develop and slow to reverse.

So, for example, the heart gets stronger, pumping more blood with each stroke, the blood's oxygen carrying capacity increases, more blood capillaries develop, especially within the running muscles, the exchange of oxygen between the blood and the muscle cells becomes more efficient, the muscle cells grow more of their energy producing organelles, called mitochondria, the systems for getting rid of waste products of exercise get more effective. The net effect of these and other adaptations is that the body becomes able to utilise oxygen at a higher rate. Being able to use more oxygen in a given time means being able to produce energy at a higher rate, which, in turn, means being able to run a long distance faster. No runner need understand what is going on in his or her body. It is enough to know that all these beneficial changes are the inevitable effects of training.

There is a measure of the rate at which a person can use oxygen. It's called VO2Max. (the maximum amount of oxygen that someone can make use of in the production of energy in a fixed time, expressed as litres of oxygen per kilogram of body weight per minute). It's an interesting measure because it can be seen to increase dramatically as a result of a training regime, and its value relates almost directly to running performance. Good distance runners have high values of VO2Max and slower runners much lower values. You could say that a person's VO2Max is a predictor of their running performance and you would be right, to a degree. But it is not an infallible guide to performance, just a good one. In 1987, when I was tested as part of a project involving some Northern Irish distance runners, my VO2Max was measured at 74, quite a high value for any runner. But the best marathon runner in the province at that time, who could beat me by five or more minutes, had a lower one. Surprisingly enough both Frank Shorter and Derek Clayton also had recorded values lower than mine. As I indicated, it's not an infallible measure of performance by any means. It goes to show that the best attempts of science to make the study of running and training for running precise and predictable are never wholly successful.

An immense amount of physiological research has been carried out on the effects of training and on the relative merits of different training regimes for distance running. There is still a general belief that if training is scientifically based it must be better than training done without supporting experimental evidence. So we have endless published scientific papers on the training effects of short fast runs compared with longer slower ones, of short rest periods between repetitions or longer ones, running uphill as opposed to downhill or on the flat, running once a day or twice a day, of having rest days or not, stretching or not stretching, stretching before training or after training, static or active stretches, long runs of less than twenty miles or more than twenty five miles, and so on, and so on. The result? Total obfuscation. Month after month the popular running magazines contain articles that contradict previous ones. The tide sways continuously between one type of training and another, and always with the relevant and apparently incontrovertible scientific backing.

As a scientist myself, used to the nature of scientific research, I would say that training for distance running is, like any such extremely complicated area, highly resistant to the precise delving of scientific method. Worthwhile conclusions emerge with great difficulty and are rarely particularly precise. The experimental processes for much of the research that has been done are poor by scientific standards.

Experimental groups are usually too small. Controls are inadequate. Experiments are not carried out for long enough. There is a lot of bad science involved in such investigations, and a lot of unjustified conclusions drawn. In short, the bulk of such research is pretty much worthless. Some of it is undeniably of value in advancing our academic knowledge of human exercise physiology, but very little is of much good as a direct and useful guide to what training a runner should be doing.

I am, on the other hand, a firm believer in empiricism, especially when it is applied by the individual to the individual. That is why I have always worked out my own training for myself and by myself, based on the simple empirical principle that I do what works for me. Just as the whole of the twentieth century was one worldwide experiment in training for distance running, my whole running life has been my own personal experiment into my own training. Of course I have considered the scientific evidence but, if someone quotes a piece of research that tells me I should do this or that in training, I don't believe it unless, firstly, it makes sense and, secondly, I have tried it, or enough other runners have tried it, and found that it is effective. I am much more inclined to listen to advice from someone who speaks from experience of running at a high level themselves, whether it is backed by scientific research or not.

My own, some would say heretical, view is that to improve as a runner and to reach your potential, or as near to it as makes very little difference, it doesn't matter exactly what training you do, provided three things apply. Firstly, almost all of it should be running rather than weight training, or calisthenics, or cycling, or swimming, or any of the other forms of exercise that athletes sometimes indulge in. Secondly, there must be enough of it, at least three or four hours of running per week, up to nine or ten hours, or even more and, lastly, a good proportion of it should be in the range of vigorous to extremely hard. If those three things apply the precise details of individual sessions are not going to make any difference.

I recently, for example, read an article in a running magazine detailing ten sessions designed to improve someone's 10K time. Every session was basically the same, a number of repetition runs, from 400m to a mile. But each individual session was made to seem strikingly unique on account of the details: 4 - 5 x 1 mile in session three, as opposed to 8 - 10 x 1K in session six, threshold effort (whatever that is) for some efforts and 10K pace for others, sometimes 75 - 90 seconds recovery, at other times two minutes recovery, and so on. Up and down the country there may now be runners of all abilities following those schedules to the letter and finding that they work wonders. Of course they work; it's all good training. But, really, do the exact particulars matter in the least? My simple view is that the body records and responds to two things only during and after a training session. They are the intensity of the exercise and the duration of the session. Vary all the variables by all means, if only to allay boredom, but don't concern yourself over whether to do three four minute repetitions or four three minute ones. As for how hard to train, rely simply on what it feels like and what you want it to feel like.

One of the best pieces of advice that I have ever been given, with which I totally concur, came from an international marathon runner with whom I trained briefly in the summer of 1969. He and I and another couple of runners had just completed a ten mile road run, not fast but at a good steady pace. It was a hot summer that year and I remember the sweat dripping off me as we jogged to a halt after an hour's running. 'That's all you need to do,' he said to me. 'Just do that every day.' A year later that was more or less what I was doing. I would leave my work in the Sussex University biology labs in the late afternoon, walk up to the University changing rooms, run from there up the slope of the South Downs to Blackcap, along the ridge of the Downs, descending into the valley of the River Ouse, turn on the outskirts of Lewes, then back along the main Brighton road to the university campus at Falmer. That was ten miles. I did that more or less every day for several months and achieved a performance peak that I may have equalled since, but have never very obviously surpassed. The success of that training regime, dull and unadventurous as it may seem, lay not so much in the exact detail, as in the quantity, which was nothing to brag about, but was nonetheless quite considerable and, most of all, the consistency. For nearly two years I hardly took a break from running of longer than a few days, and then only for very good reasons, and averaged about fifty miles a week throughout that period. If fifty miles a week sounds rather little, in the light of what I have said about the obsession for one hundred mile weeks that was current at that time, bear in mind that to **average** that much running requires a considerable amount of making up for weeks when a cold, or a slight injury, or some other pressing cause led me to a very much below average mileage.

I have already said that, in my estimation, starting from scratch, an untrained adult (who, incidentally, is likely to have a VO2Max of around 45 for a man and 35 for a woman) can expect to reach something approaching his or her potential after about three years of regular training, rarely less. As rule No. 5 stated: Training is a long term affair. As if in an echo of this principle, Ron Hill when asked why British runners weren't as good as they were 40 years ago, replied that today's athletes need patience. He added, *'People look for shortcuts today. It may be a lack of talent, but it's certainly a lack of perseverance. It took me five years to improve from 2:14:12 to 2:13:42, then years more to get to 2:11 in Fukuoka, then to 2:10 in Boston in 1970, and finally to 2:09 in Edinburgh.'* He didn't add how long it took him to reach 2:14:12 in the first place, but the message is as clear as crystal. Habitual hard training over a period of many years is the way for a distance runner to achieve his or her full potential. It is a message that could not have come from a more authoritative source. Ron Hill is famous for never having missed a day's training in his whole, very extended career.

Roy Fowler, another great British runner of the sixties, said much the same thing. *'Don't forget, most athletes will do this* (train twice a day) *for six or seven years before they win so much as an area title.'* Hill and Fowler and I are in agreement. It is years of uninterrupted training that produces the best results. No runner or coach, however, could have come to this conclusion before the end of the nineteen sixties.

The evidence just wasn't there. But, by the seventies, the concept was, I think, more or less taken for granted by all serious runners.

Rule No. 5 has to be expanded to include a very important principle that is implicit in it. In fact, the idea is so important that it deserves a rule of its own, the last of the six rules that form the title of this chapter, the rule that clings to rule 5 like butter to toast:

Rule No. 6: TRAINING SHOULD BE BOTH CONSISTENT AND PROGRESSIVE.

I call this a single principle because the two things, consistency and progression, are themselves so closely linked as to be almost inseparable. They are like pounds and pennies. Look after the consistency and the progression will look after itself. Consistency means keeping the training going, week by week, month by month and year by year. Better to do a little every week consistently over a long period than to have training binges followed by lean periods during which the benefits of previous training are undone. Progression lies in gradually increasing the amount and/or intensity of training, again over a long period.

You may think that progression comes wholly from conscious choice, from sticking to a plan which dictates that as time goes by you increase your training bit by bit. This can be the case, but, more often, progression is an inevitable consequence of consistency. It is impossible to train consistently without also training progressively, though with consistency alone, you may not achieve quite the degree of improvement that is possible with a bit of planned progression thrown in.

Suppose, for example, completely unfit and new to training, a person decides to go for a run three or four days a week. Three miles might seem a reasonable distance. At first it will seem hard enough, but if that runner keeps it up, those slow three mile runs will gradually become so easy that they no longer seem like training at all. Even if there is no deliberate decision to run further or more often in training the pace of those runs is bound to increase. As the pace increases the runs take less time and the temptation is to run a bit further each time. Soon running becomes such a pleasure that the frequency of runs increases.

And so training automatically becomes progressive. Consistency brings about improvement and improvement leads to progression. When some additional, planned progression, increasing even further the length and frequency of runs or, deliberately, the speed of running, for example, is incorporated into training, improvement happens even more quickly. But consistency comes first. Progression, planned or automatic, follows in its wake. The rate of progression cannot be forced but is determined solely by the rate of improvement. As someone trains consistently over a long period of time that person slowly becomes a better runner and, referring back to the point made earlier in this chapter, being a better runner they can now do more and better training.

Where does it end? Sometimes I have felt that there is no limit to improvement as, week by week, training seems to become easier and easier and my body becomes ever more finely tuned, my pulse lower and lower, my breathing less and less perceptible, my legs feeling lighter and lighter, my recovery faster and faster. But it has to end somewhere and, whatever bodily feelings may be telling you, it does. The proof of the training is in the performances, and they will tell you eventually that a limit has been reached. Try upping the training by all means but that too has a limit, a fact that has already been acknowledged in rule three of training.

Every aspiring runner can only be guided by the long history of distance running and what training other runners have done. There is no foolproof one-size-fits-all recipe for success. And there is no compulsion. All runners have the right to decide for themselves what best suits their needs and ambitions, their likes and dislikes, their lifestyle, and what works for them. The process of arriving at the perfect training regime takes a long time. You may never get there and when you do you may find that it still needs to be changed. All I can do here is to recall what I have found out about training over the years, and what did and didn't work for me. The next chapter, therefore, is a personal account of training; what I did, why I think I did it, whether it was worth it; that sort of thing.

CHAPTER 8
Training myself

'I did it my way.'

Frank Sinatra song. Lyrics by Paul Anka;
music by Claude Francois and Jacques Revaux.

I'll try to answer the question that I was asked by my latter day training companions, as recounted at the beginning of the last chapter. What had I had to do (their words) to run a marathon in 2:24:24? Taking into account my previous comments about the difficulty for any runner to describe with honesty and accuracy the nature of their training or, in the words of the court, 'to tell the truth, the whole truth and nothing but the truth' and the problems of interpretation for anyone trying to understand what that training actually entailed, I'll be as open and truthful as possible. I hope I can give, not just the facts and figures of my training, but everything else that could be remotely relevant. Above all I'll try to make sense of it. The whole idea of training, carried to the extent that committed runners can carry it, may seem to many people a form of madness, but maybe a full account accompanied by an attempt at finding reason behind the madness will open the door to some understanding, even on the part of a running lay-person.

I didn't come to that marathon as a newcomer to the distance. It was about the tenth marathon I'd finished. I had done three marathons already within the previous year, all in around 2:34. It followed at least eight years of fairly consistent training and periods during my running career when I had reached a standard that I was never later going to excel. I was already a hardened runner, thirty six years old with thousands of training miles under my belt and some performances in races that I am proud of to this day.

You could say, therefore, that what I had had to do to run my best ever marathon was spread over many years and that no part of it could be separated from the rest and held up as the significant determinant of my performance. Nevertheless, there was something special about my preparation during the nine months prior to the 1983 May bank holiday Monday, when the marathon was run.

In the first place, all that time, I had the race in mind. It was my prime goal and had been so for a whole year. Rarely did I plan my training around a particular race but I had realised, after many years of failing to plan for important events, that to do so, especially in the case of a marathon, was practically essential. It was necessary, not only for the achievement of a goal but also in order to get total satisfaction from that achievement.

My goal was to run a marathon in the sort of time I believed I should be capable of. I worked out, basing my estimate on my times over shorter distances and the times for a marathon that other runners whom I considered to be about my standard had done, that I should be able to run the distance in about the time I eventually achieved. Anything under 2:25 would have pleased me. Tellingly, as it turned out, I knew that a time near 2:20 was beyond me, and I would be foolish to contemplate it. So my final time represented complete satisfaction in fulfilling my goal and perfect validation of the training I set myself during the build up period.

Another factor that made my build up special was that I knew exactly what I was doing. Over the years, I had perfected my training. I had achieved a fine balance between doing too little and doing too much. The amount I did was effective and was never more than I was able to keep up, week after week, month after month. Over and over again I come back to the same question regarding my training, the question that itches like a bad rash and is never answered and never goes away; could I have done more and could I, therefore, have been better? Just thinking about that question constantly, preferably during rather than after the training, can help keep the training process effective and within bounds.

When I look at my training diary now I am happy in the belief that I could not have done more, at least not with any beneficial effect. I was never a hundred miles a week man and I reasoned that, for me, this would not have been the way to greater things. The standard mileage in training for the great distance runners of today seems to be around one hundred and twenty miles a week, but they are the best. Some of the very best reputedly did less. Steve Jones, for example, still British marathon record holder, was reported as running a mere eighty miles a week. In other words his training was not a lot different from my own and, having seen an account of what he did in the weeks leading up to the 1984 Chicago marathon, which he won in 2:08:05, I would consider that to be a fair comment. Why he ran the marathon more than sixteen minutes faster than I did, I cannot say.

For me to have run more than I did in training would have necessitated running twice a day most days of the week. To do their hundred or more miles a week the best runners usually include a daily steady or easy run of about five or six miles, often done in the early morning. That daily run immediately accounts for between thirty and forty miles for each week, before the main training starts. So, excluding these runs, they are only covering much the same as I was each week, about seventy or eighty miles.

I decided, and I still believe it was a good decision, that short extra runs that merely add to the week's total, without having any specific training effect are a waste of time. They are often referred to as 'junk miles'. I consider them a hangover from the obsessive days of a hundred miles a week being the one and only key to greatness. The important thing was to get in your hundred miles. Never mind the quality, feel the width.

Moreover, the price paid for twice daily training is huge. It involves a lot more than twice the effort. Sometimes it's hard to find the opportunity to run just once in a day, remembering that the professional runner is a very recent invention and, even now, very few runners have the luxury of being able to revolve their lives around their running rather than vice versa. However long or short a single training session may be, there is an added time before it and after it for changing, showering, warming up and cooling down. Those of a hygienic disposition will want to wash their kit after each run, so that twice daily training doubles the amount of washing to be done. A simple calculation will tell you that to train twice in one day can add about an hour or more each day to the time taken up by running, even before adding any actual running time. That seemed to me an absurd waste and I very rarely tried to fit in more than one training session in a day.

You could say that in deciding to limit my training to one session a day I was showing a lack of commitment. That would be a fair comment. But it was an eyes-open admission on my part that my commitment to running ended at that point. To run once a day, almost every day of the year, for several years put together, was my limit, both physically and psychologically. I had a life to lead and a job to do on top of my running, and I never really believed that yet more training would have made me a better runner.

The only exception to my general rule of sticking to once a day training came when I was getting back to running after a lay off. One of my weaknesses as a committed distance runner was that sometimes I wasn't committed. I would get so sick to death of running or so stressed by other things in my life that I would go AWOL and simply stop training, sometimes for long periods. In May 1984, for example, after the most disappointing marathon I ever ran, I kept the running going for a couple of weeks, like a fast moving vehicle, unable to slow down without first dissipating its momentum, and then stopped almost altogether for nearly four months.

I had trained long and hard for that marathon (it was the Belfast marathon of 1984) and was in the best shape I'd ever been in. That led to feeling just too good during the race and over-reaching myself. I blew up badly at about twenty two miles and barely got to the finish line. It seemed such a waste, all that training for nothing. For me it was like a form of post traumatic shock. Running seemed pointless. It had taken me six months to get to a high point, the like of which I had never quite reached before, and two and a half hours to plummet to the depths of disappointment. Physically I had lost nothing but mentally I was totally drained. For weeks afterwards I had as much interest in running as a sloth. You can read about that particular marathon in Chapter 10.

Whenever I came back to training after a lay off, because I was temporarily not fit enough to carry on where I'd left off, I found it necessary to do shorter than usual runs and sometimes to run at lunchtime as well as in the evening. In this instance, following my marathon disaster, it was still just summer, and on hot days I would return from my first run of the day, shower and, all too quickly, head for the staff common room (I was a college lecturer at the time) for a bit of lunch. Because I hadn't had time to cool down properly I would immediately start to sweat profusely. I would feel the sweat dribbling down my forehead and cheeks, my back and neck. Sweat has an irritating habit of tickling. I would become embarrassed in the company of colleagues and would sweat even more in response. I had to casually mop my brow with my handkerchief or a paper napkin when I thought no one would notice. I could feel my armpits and the back of my shirt becoming saturated. As soon as I had finished my lunch I would rush away into the relief of the outside air.

When I returned to the office that I shared with a colleague, who was later to become my head of department, I draped my wet running kit over the radiator. I always used to do that until the day I found a note from her saying that the smell of my running things made her sick. That was reason enough not to fit in a lunchtime run.

Inevitably, sticking to running once a day meant that my weekly mileage was limited but I held to the philosophy that as I was training for distance running and in particular the marathon distance my training sessions should reflect what I was trying to do in races. Unless I was particularly tired or short of time or easing up for a race, my minimum training distance was ten miles and I would often cover up to fifteen miles at a time without thinking that I had done a particularly long run. A hundred miles a week works out at just under fifteen miles a day, not an unreasonable amount of training to do in one session. I never achieved the magic one hundred miles, partly because I sometimes had a day off during the week, but I did once run ninety four training miles in a week in only seven sessions.

Two other considerations influenced my decision not to train more than once a day, a decision I stuck to throughout my running career. One was that I never deliberately ran slowly in training, that is, any slower than I felt like running. Of course, if I was very tired or physically or mentally low, I might run slowly, but otherwise I would always adopt a good pace and often run fast and hard in training just for the joy of it. Consequently all my training running was good training running; no junk miles. When I trained with other runners, some much better performers than I ever was, I was often surprised at just how slowly they ran. This was most noticeable on long runs. I realised that, even if I was running a twenty miles or longer training run, I would instinctively adopt the pace that came naturally to me, the same steady pace I used for six mile runs, for ten mile runs and for all other distances, except when I was deliberately running hard and fast. In my best years this was six minutes per mile pace. For a long run, twenty plus, this was considerably faster than most writers on the subject would have recommended for a runner of my ability. I think I was someone who by nature trained quite hard. Therefore I could get away with fewer miles in total.

The other factor was mentioned by Cliff Temple in his piece on running a hundred miles a week in only four sessions (see previous chapter). He made the point that one long run has a greater training effect than two sessions totalling the same distance. With this I totally concur. I base my belief in this idea, not so much on logic as he did, but on personal experience. I never ran better than when I was running distances of more than ten miles at a time, irrespective of total weekly mileage. One ten mile run is worth, not two five mile runs but, in my experience, more like two six or seven mile runs and one twenty mile run is worth more than any number of six or seven mile runs, unless they happen to be run so close together that they might as well be continuous. I never ran truly well at any distance until I was doing a regular weekly long run, long being anything over about eighteen miles. Years ago I gave up calling a fifteen miler a long run.

That, therefore is the background to the specific training I did prior to running what is still my best time for a marathon. I had come to what I considered the right form of training for me. I believed in training once a day, primarily for practical reasons but also, so I thought, for good reasons of effectiveness. I believed that training should be just that. Running by itself was not good enough, which is why I never took to running to and from work.

I tried running to work and back for a while but I sensed it was not working. I was running, but I wasn't training. I was using my body but not my mind and I have always felt that when the mind is dissociated from the task in hand (i.e. in this case, training) the result is a degree of inefficiency. My purpose in running to work, especially that outward journey, and running home from work, was to get to my destination. The purpose was not training and, therefore, the running was not a hundred percent effective. At least, that is what I felt.

When I am asked that common but rather, to my mind, silly and needless question, 'What do you think about when you're running?' I should really reply, 'Running'. What else should I be thinking about? If I'm not thinking about running then perhaps I should be. And, if I am, then I can be content that I am getting the most out of my training. Running is a thinking activity. If you train without thinking about training you're not putting everything into it and you will not get everything out of it.

Another reason I never took to running to and from work was that I am not an early morning person (early morning being any time before 11am). The last thing I want to do at eight o'clock in the morning is to run. When I did do it for a while the distance to work was about four miles and the road climbed up and over a ridge of the South

Downs before descending to the university changing rooms, where I used to leave my work clothes overnight. I would have a light breakfast immediately before starting the run in. However slowly I ran and whatever I had had for breakfast, by half way up the hill I started to see great big patches of light in front of my eyes, as if I had just been dazzled by a bright light. They were usually orange-red in colour, like the setting sun seen through a winter mist, but they could change shade as I ran from dark purply-orange, to almost white. They would shrink and grow and change shape. If I shut and screwed up my eyes they would become more clearly defined against a black background but oscillate slowly inwards and outwards. They didn't worry me, but they certainly didn't make running to work a pleasure. When I got over the brow of the hill, after a minute or two of downhill running, they always faded away.

If my body was so stressed in the morning that I couldn't even do a short, easy run without my blood not knowing which bits of the body it was best to go to, I can't have been doing very effective training. So I gave up running to work and back as a bad job. The evening or late afternoon is my preferred training time. Probably at least half the training I have ever done has been after work, with a meal, a relaxing evening and a night's sleep the only things to follow that day. When I ran I could concentrate on running and I could take as long as I liked over it. Training is like eating; it should never be rushed.

I believed absolutely in the value of distance in training, not total mileage necessarily, but long individual sessions. I knew that, when it came to a marathon, the distance itself, the twenty six plus miles, was my greatest weakness. Only twice in my life have I finished a marathon with 'something in the tank'. More usually I was a 'get to twenty and survive' sort of marathon runner, not a recipe for a good time, nor a satisfying run, nor self justification.

I knew the importance, the absolute necessity of consistency in training and of a long term approach. I had contemplated the goal of a May marathon as early as August the previous year and planned a training build up starting initially from about the same time and, in deadly earnest, at the beginning of January. Nor did this build up start from the bottom rung. Even as I embarked on it in the autumn of 1982, I was in form for a 10K time of around 31 minutes.

In the nine months before Monday May 2nd I averaged 66 miles per week, and in the four months leading to that day the average was 72 miles per week, with the biggest week at 88 miles. For the final six weeks I averaged 79 miles per week. I know that put beside the hundred plus training miles per week of the best marathon runners those mileages look a bit conservative, but it was all I could do, and I still believe it was all I needed.

I even wonder whether the better a runner you are, the more training you need to do. I have already spelt out the rather obvious truth that only a very good runner is capable of doing the amounts of training that good runners do and, on this basis, I believe that the training I did at my best represented the greatest amount that someone of my absolute standard could and should have managed, but is there yet more to the difference in amounts of training that runners of different abilities do? Had a really top class runner done exactly what I did and no more, would he have been as good as he was, or only as good as me, or somewhere in between? Had I tried to emulate the training of the best, I don't believe I would have been one of the best myself, but what about the other way round?

When I ran, say, ten miles in training it was harder for me than the same run would have been for a much better runner. Consequently it would have had a much greater training effect. So my seventy to eighty miles a week was equivalent in its effects to a top class runner's one hundred plus miles per week. Perhaps we should feel sorry for the very best runners. The poor élite runners of this world not only do more training, but **require** more training than the less gifted! Like a knife made of hardened steel they need a lot more sharpening than us soft steel runners. But their edge is eventually that much keener than ours. It brings us back to the same old question: which came first, the runner, or the training?

Whichever way I look at it now, I come to the same conclusion. I did the training that was right for me, it was the most I could do, and it brought me to the point that I was destined to reach. The only pity is that it took until I was in my mid thirties to find out and the only remaining question that I still dwell on is whether, had I trained during my twenties as I did in my late thirties, might I have been a better runner? Much to my regret I think the answer to that might well be yes. But, hey, we all could have done things differently with hindsight.

My weeks of training in the build up to my best marathon all shared a similar pattern, which was:

Monday: a 'tempo' run of around 10 miles usually done in about 55 minutes.

Tuesday: a session of repetition runs of between a quarter of a mile and a mile and a quarter, e.g. timed hard runs of 1 min, 2 min, 3 min, 4 min, 5 min, 4 min, 3 min, 2 min, 1 min, with a jog in between. Total distance, including running there and back, 13 miles.

Wednesday: 15 or 16 miles steady.

Thursday: often a rest day, or an easy run, 8 - 10 miles.

Friday: steady run, 8 - 10 miles.

Saturday: race or short intervals, e.g. 12 - 20 x 400m flat out hill runs. 10 miles total.

Sunday: 20 - 24 miles.

If I look in detail at one particular week I think I could describe it as 'typical'. Take the week beginning Monday 7th March 1983, for example. It was the week after the Northern Ireland Cross Country Championship where I finished sixth, my best ever placing, earning me my first World Cross Country vest. The World Cross Country race was held on 20th March that year at Gateshead.

The day after the Northern Ireland championship race, the Sunday preceding the week I'm about to describe, I did a twenty one mile run in 132 minutes. I must, therefore, have started the week fairly tired, though I can't have been so tired that I bothered to mention it in my diary. I was fairly used to the level of training I was doing, with a race or two thrown in, so maybe I was no more tired than usual. Tiredness becomes an integral part of a training regime, an accepted part of life, and not something to remark on every time it becomes noticeable. Brendan Foster is quoted as saying, '*A runner goes to bed tired and wakes up tired.*'

On Monday 7th March, the first day of my representative week, I ran for ten or eleven miles steady and remarked that I was a bit stiff. Stiffness, especially as the years accumulate, is another thing a runner takes for granted and learns to ignore. There seems to be no obvious relationship between the type and amount of running that has previously been done and the stiffness that results. I have sometimes felt stiffer after a day off than after a very hard race. In fact, to get rid of stiffness the best remedy is sometimes a fast run. It doesn't make a lot of sense, but nor do a lot of the peculiarities of running. I've learned never to make predictions about how I'm going to feel or perform nor to look for patterns in my running or links between different aspects of it.

I did that run, partly at least, over the country, which means it must have been during the day. More usually, through the winter at any rate, I would have run on the Belfast roads, after dark. In all my years running I have probably done more than half the miles along urban roads, by the light of street lamps. That has always been my preference. To this day the eerie pale orange glow of sodium lights shining through a cold fog evokes just one thought, the memory of my nightly runs. Once darkness falls distances seem to shrink and time stands still. Darkness was, to me, what seemed a protective cocoon. I ran with it wrapped around me, in my own introverted little world. I loved that feeling of isolation combined with exhilarating physical activity. Once I got into my evening run there was nothing I would rather have been doing. I can honestly say that I looked forward to it; my day would not have been complete without it.

When, in 1972, I was appointed to my first teaching post and moved to live in Street in Somerset, I didn't think for one second about my training. Only after I had settled in did I realise how lucky I had been to find a small country town where I could run for ten miles after dark, along lit streets, without covering the same ground more than once. The reason for this was that no more than a couple of miles from Street lies the similarly sized country town of Glastonbury and, connecting the two, is a well lit main road with wide pavements. So every evening I could run round my own town, down the main road to Glastonbury, round it, and back to Street. That was ten miles, and all by the comforting glow of street lamps. That was the bulk of my training for six years. I often wonder whether I would have done the same sort of training had Street been completely isolated or, worse, if I had lived in a tiny country village with virtually no street lighting. As I have said, I have always got more enjoyment from running on roads at night, by means of artificial lights, than from any other form of running. Running down country lanes in complete darkness doesn't bear thinking about.

The week I am recounting started uncharacteristically, with a run over the country. I forget why. My usual Monday run when I was living in Belfast was a route that I must have covered hundreds of times; just over ten miles, along urban dual carriageway and city roads, bordered by wide pavements and shopping precincts, and suburban residential streets. I called it my Newtownards Road block because that's where it took me: along the Knock dual carriageway till it hit the Newtownards Road (4 miles), down towards the city, across the suburbs that ringed Belfast at a radius of about two miles from the centre and then, at 8 miles, up towards where I started, my home on the side of the hills that border Belfast on its southern edge. Newtownards is a small town at the top end of Strangford Lough, about ten miles out of Belfast.

Mondays was more often the day when, if I was going to do one that week, I did a tempo run, or, in my vocabulary, a hard run. On those occasions I timed myself. Quite often I ran under fifty five minutes for that block and reckoned it had taken at least a minute longer than if it had been exactly ten miles. In completing the course I had to cross eleven roads, which inevitably slowed me down somewhat. Having measured it in different ways, on the Ordnance Survey map and by driving around it in the car, I reckoned it was closer to ten and a quarter miles than ten. The fastest I ever ran it in training was 53 minutes exactly.

On Tuesday 8th March I ran the Newtownards Road course and included between three and four miles of 'fartlek'. Fartlek is a Swedish word meaning 'speed play' and, for want of a more precise translation, I have always understood it to mean running as you feel. It is the opposite of steady running. You might run fast for a minute or two, then you run quite slowly to recover, then you are off again, not quite so fast, but this time for longer, maybe half a mile or more. You know you're going to put some effort into the running but it is done *ad lib*. There is no plan. You literally run as you feel. Because fast running is interspersed with slower running, fartlek is much the same as interval training. Physically and in terms of training benefit there is probably nothing to choose between fartlek and interval running, but psychologically they are worlds apart.

It is clear who is in charge of interval training. It is whoever decided on the exact content of the session, it is the clock and the distance to be run and the number of repetitions and the sheer rigidity of it. In some ways this is its strength. There's no cheating it and no escape from its sadistic clutches. Even if you, yourself, have decided what it will involve, you are still its slave, surrendering your free will to it and compelled to carry it out to the letter. No wonder it works.

But it also saps you of your own will power and the joy you have in running. It is not a form of training that is easy to stick to for long without losing enthusiasm and inspiration, however successful it may seem to be. Fartlek, on the other hand, puts the runner firmly in the driver's seat. However hard the running is, it is always the product of the runner's own choice. And there is always an escape route. If I set off, for example, on part of a fartlek run, intending to run really hard for the next four minutes, I know that I don't have to. Invariably, however, I do. But, even as I run, as it gets more and more difficult to keep it going, as I force myself onwards and long desperately for the four minutes to be up, I am still a free agent. Any effort I make is still due to my own free will. That is a great weight off the mind.

One of the counter-productive effects of training is tiredness. Mental tiredness, or staleness, is far more damaging to a training regime than physical tiredness, and it is important to do everything possible and to play whatever mind games are necessary, in order to stem the onset of mental fatigue. That is why I always steered clear of the regimentation of the track and the discipline of a coach and preferred training by myself according to the fartlek philosophy. It was the key to sticking to my training, week after week and month after month, while remaining keen and fresh.

When I moved to Belfast my new club coach asked me to show him what sort of training I had been doing. All I had recorded was a pattern of daily runs of about ten miles each. He wasn't impressed, saying that I should have been doing more faster running. It did seem rather monotonous on paper, a schedule of nothing but steady running. But I knew that a lot of it was fartlek and within the 'steady' runs there would have been a mixture of harder and easier running. It was simply that I hadn't recorded it. My running was, and to some extent still is, all done in the spirit of fartlek. It was self inflicted, free from pressure, mind soothing, motivational, all those things, but hard nonetheless.

Another thing I neglected to tell my new club coach was that I usually ran at least one race in a week. Races were my fast sessions. If a 'tempo' run, as a faster than usual run is now called, is good for you (such runs are generally considered an essential part of any runner's training) then a race must surely be equally good for you, if not better. That was certainly my thinking. I am amused when I read training advice in one or other of the running magazines, specifying this or that distance run at a particular race pace, for example, three by a mile run at 10K pace, five miles run at half marathon pace, ten miles at marathon pace, and so on. If it's so important to run at race pace (which I'm sure it is) why not just run races, as I and so many others like me did on a regular basis? And, if three miles at 10K pace is good training, surely 10K at 10K pace is even better?

An odd thing about training at race pace, whatever the distance of that race might be, is that it's considerably more difficult than racing at race pace. Had I set out to run in training a typical 'race pace' session of four by 1 mile, each in five minutes, at a time in my career when I was regularly racing 10K in around 31 minutes (which is a little under five minutes per mile pace) I'm not sure I could have done it. Even if I had managed it, I know it would have been an extremely hard session and mentally particularly tough. I never really understood why that should be, but it is a fact. Roger Bannister records in his autobiography, 'First four minutes', that in December 1953 he embarked on a series of training sessions, each of which consisted of ten quarter miles run one after another on the track, with a two minute interval between them. Each repetition was done initially in 66 seconds, but through January and February they got faster until, by April, he was managing them in 61 seconds each but, in his own words, '... *however hard we tried it did not seem possible to reach our target of 60 seconds.*' Isn't that almost inexplicable? A matter of weeks before attempting (and succeeding) to run four quarter miles without a break, each in 60 seconds or less, Bannister couldn't run ten quarter miles in 61 seconds with two minutes rest between them! But it's a phenomenon that all serious runners will have experienced. Once you put on your racing shoes and the gun goes, the quarter miles and miles tick by at a pace you could barely keep up for a single one of them in training.

Knowing that this is the case gives me a slightly suspicious view of some of the recommended training sessions that feature so commonly in modern running literature. Often, I think, they are designed by theorists rather than practising runners. What looks good on paper is quite different when you're dressed in wet weather gear, it's freezing cold, and the wind is blowing, and you don't have the advantage of the powerful stimulant of the racing environment. I strongly believe that at least some training has to be done significantly faster than race pace and, if that means reducing the distance run in a session of intervals or repetitions to 400m or even 200m then that is better than trying to run miles or half miles and managing a pace that is not a lot faster and may even be slower than race pace. You can always do more of the shorter intervals, with a much briefer rest between one and the next. There must be a lot of runners out there who have never run faster in training than in races. They are missing out on a very important part of a training plan.

Going back to my Tuesday run in the week in question, it was a fartlek run of just over an hour over a continuous road course. During the ten and a bit miles run I managed to do ten hard efforts. I didn't record how far those efforts were but they would have been, on average, about eight hundred yards. That was typical.

On Wednesday 9th March I ran steadily for 14 or 15 miles, a single run. I never possessed one of those gadgets that are commonplace these days and tell you how far you've run and at what pace and exactly where you are if you get lost. I don't think such things were available in 1983, so I often didn't know precisely how far I had run. I recorded a figure that was an intelligent guess based on how long I was running and my knowledge of distances in my own neck of the woods. I think I tended to err on the low side when recording distances run. So it is more than likely that I ran fifteen miles that day.

On Thursday 10th March I had a day off. I was never afraid of taking a day off during the week, as long as it was my decision, made for a good reason. Usually it was a Thursday, but I never planned ahead that I wouldn't train that day. I left the decision until the day itself. That way I could still run if I felt like it and it gave me a sense of being in control of my training. The reason that Thursday tended to be my day off stemmed from the need to ease up for important races. The obvious day to rest prior to a Saturday race might seem to be Friday but ever since I noticed that I ran better in races if I had trained the previous day I decided to have a rest two days before a race, that is if I had one at all.

To some extent all runners in training become beholden to the training rather than being in charge themselves. Training becomes a habit that it is impossible to escape. The training plan becomes set in stone: so many miles a week, one or two sessions every day, a long run on Sundays, a track session on Tuesdays; stray from it at your peril. To take a day off is a terrible show of weakness and leads to unremitting feelings of guilt. Once you display such weakness it seems that you've undone all the weeks of training that you've already amassed. When, months later, you run poorly in a race it's because of that single lapse. I know those feelings. I have been obsessive too.

That is why I allowed myself a day off occasionally. Many weeks I didn't take it. But the choice was always there if I needed it. It proved to me that I was master of my training rather than the other way round. It was the fartlek philosophy of free will again. Self inflicted discipline is painless, because you know you can always switch it off.

Giving myself the choice of a day off was one of the numerous mind games that I mentioned that runners play with and against themselves to keep the training going, and to keep motivated. I saw it as a sort of reward for having trained hard the previous few days and a minor guilt trip from which I would redeem myself by training harder after it. It was the same as someone on a strict diet indulging in a cream bun once in a while. There were also real practical reasons for a day off. The daily grind of training is physically tiring, and, worse, it is very costly in mental energy. Sometimes a runner needs a rest. The art of taking days off is to recognise the difference between really needing them and just giving in to a lack of will power.

On Friday 11th March I did a steady run that took 75 minutes so I called it between eleven and twelve miles. The route took in some hilly country so I know, without specifically remembering the fact, that it would have been quite a hard run. Belfast is at the mouth of the River Lagan, with hills on both the Southern and Northern sides. As I lived on the side of one of those ridges it was difficult to run in any direction from my house without incorporating some stiff climbing somewhere along the route. That being the case, it is odd that, throughout my running career, I have always been a hopeless uphill runner.

On Saturday 12th March I had no race so I did what I thought of as one of the most important sessions of my week. It was the nearest I got, on a regular basis, to interval training, though I ran it according to the best principles of fartlek, over parkland and forest trails, according to my watch, yes, but with no measured distances involved. Essentially what my Saturday training comprised was a run of about ten miles during which I ran hard, in fact more or less flat out, for periods of from seventy to eighty seconds, anything up to twenty times. I managed always, partly by design and partly through chance, to do most of the hard running uphill. I suppose, therefore, it could be called my weekly hill session. Hill running has always been a much recommended form of training for runners at all distances. On this particular Saturday I note that I only did ten such hill runs, but covered the same distance as usual.

This particular session, that I call 'one of the most important', might seem a little out of place in what I am citing as a training schedule for the marathon. Its likeness to running a dozen or so flat out, one lap intervals round a running track might suggest it was more suited to a middle distance runner. There's no doubt that I ran every one of those just over a minute long intervals almost as fast as I could, to the point of having to stop with my hands on my knees, my legs like jelly, my head bowed and my chest heaving. But I was absolutely convinced that, in their way, they were as useful in preparing me for a marathon as were my long runs. I had come to that conclusion after years of experimenting with my own training, applying what I saw as physiological commonsense to the business of conditioning the body, relying heavily on my own experiences. It was the same thinking that brought me to the general principle of the last chapter's Rule No. 4 of training, 'A little bit of hard running is like a lot of easy running'. At the end of any hard, hour-long training session I don't think the body knows precisely what it has done, only that it has worked very hard and been under stress for that length of time. But, and this is the most important point, only by running absolutely flat out in training, or as close to it as possible, can you ever get the body to experience that degree of stress. And the only way to do that and survive is by running relatively short intervals. By stringing them together into a continuous ten mile run, with the minimum necessary recovery between them, I tricked my body into thinking that it had not only run as fast as it could, but had done so for an hour.

Finally, Sunday, the day of my regular long run; today, the 13th March, I covered more than twenty two miles and was running continuously for about two hours and twenty minutes. I always considered the long run to be the most important ingredient of my training. I would have held the same view even had I been a middle distance runner with no intention of ever running a marathon. Of course, for a marathon, you have to prepare with runs that approach the marathon distance, but a long run in training is far more than just specific marathon preparation. It has effects that show in subsequent running at all distances. It builds a kind of endurance that doesn't come from any other type of training. As hard as it can be to complete a long run, especially on your own, and when the weather is not conducive to enjoyable running, I knew that I had to do a good number of them in the weeks leading up to a marathon, if I was to get the most out of myself. This was to be the eighth long run (twenty miles or more) I had done so far in my marathon build up and there were another four to come.

A lot of serious marathon runners, perhaps even most, feel the need to do at least a few over-distance runs in the weeks leading up to a race, runs of up to thirty miles, or well over three hours duration. The most I ever managed in training was twenty five miles. Why didn't I ever run further? The answer to that question is simply that I couldn't. I did what I could and, however much I might have agreed with the theory of running even longer runs than I did, maybe just one over-distance training run, there was no point in running part of the way and walking the rest. Perhaps if I had run much slower than my normal long distance pace I could have managed thirty miles, but that was not my inclination. The irony is that when I resumed marathon running as a sixty year old I found myself on occasions running for well over three hours in training, a greater length of time continuously running than I had ever previously managed, but only covering nineteen or twenty miles in the process.

That concludes a typical week. I did six sessions and ran a total of 79 miles. At least two sessions included some fast, hard running. Had I added a daily easy run of four or five miles to my schedule I would have been up there with the élite, but only, I think, in my training.

What is difficult in training is keeping it going. It is easy if you're physically up to it to do a lot of running, including a fair amount of it at a fast pace, for a few days on end, for a week, maybe even two or three weeks, but, after that it becomes harder. What at first, viewed with enthusiasm and resolve, seems exciting and rewarding, quickly becomes a chore. And yet doing a good amount of training week after week over a very long period is what brings results. As explained in the last chapter, the purpose of training is to cause physical and physiological adaptation and that takes a long time. To some extent the process never reaches a conclusion. So it's essential to keep the training going. Months are better than weeks and years are better still.

When I first ran well at distances of more than six miles, so well, in fact, that I surprised myself, I immediately looked for the reason in the training I had been doing. It was in 1971 and I had just won the Middlesex twenty mile road title, in what is still my best ever time for a race of that distance. You could describe that race as my big breakthrough as a long distance runner. What had been the key to it?

At first sight it seemed that I had been doing no more training than during the previous two or three years but, taking a closer look, I noticed that I had trained without a break for fifteen weeks prior to the race. I hadn't done a huge amount, averaging only 53 miles a week, but I hadn't wavered. Never before had I trained quite so consistently. Even before that period of fifteen weeks I had been training fairly regularly the whole year, but still with my very bad habit of taking whole weeks off, sometimes two or three weeks, during the summer holiday and at Christmas for example.

Later in my career I would have thought there was nothing special about a fifteen week stretch when I never eased up my training but at that time when I was still in my twenties, it was unusual. It was probably the longest I had ever gone without a significant break and it was undoubtedly the reason I ran exceptionally well. I had discovered the holy grail of training for distance running; consistent and protracted training.

The sad irony for me is that only now that I am too old to hope to run at anything like the standard I once reached, for the first time in my life I have everything I need to be able to train as much and for as long and as consistently as I like. I am retired and settled down as firmly as a limpet on a rock. I am mostly stress free. I have freedom and choice. I have no money worries. I live in close proximity to some of the best training grounds, both day and night, that I have ever come across. I have a comfortable home with a power shower that I often use just for the sensual pleasure of it and an excellent, reliable washing machine and drier. My wife gives me companionship and support. I have no significant emotional entanglements. I have time; time to run and time to recover and time to do the few things that I still have to do, and still time in between. Those are the things you need to train consistently, without sacrifice.

When, in 1972, aged 26, probably at my absolute physical peak for running, I ceased to be a student and got my first job as a teacher in a secondary school, I ran very little. For a year I averaged less than twenty miles per week and for three whole months I didn't train at all. The reason was quite simply that I had too many other things on my mind and occupying my time. Despite the popular belief to the contrary, teaching is a very hard and time consuming job, especially for a beginner. No allowances are made for the fact that you're new to the job. You are handed a full timetable the day you start and you just have to get on with it. I worked every hour of the day, from nine in the morning to nine, or even later, at night. I hardly had the opportunity to fit in the basics of life, let alone any running. I even had to work on Saturdays. The school in which I taught had Saturday morning classes, and games in the afternoon. Quite often Saturday would be the longest working day of my week. I would teach in the first part of the morning and then, later in the morning or immediately after lunch I would be driving the school cross country team to a competition that might have been fifty or more miles away and, that same evening, I would be driving the team home and doing the rounds of the boarding houses delivering the boys to their beds. It was sometimes after ten o'clock before I reached my own home. Did I then get changed and go for a run? No. The next day, Sunday, I would be working a full day preparing for the following week.

It was only after that first year that I resumed training conscientiously, fitting my running into the time between the school day ending and the evening meal. My wife used to beg me to go out running so that she could eat before seven o'clock. A simple recipe of a daily evening run of about ten miles and a longer one on Sunday initiated what became the best few years of my running career.

My transition from state supported student to independent working man came as a shock and made me realise how difficult it is for the average runner to stick to a serious training regime while, at the same time, working full time, supporting a home and family, managing other commitments and interests, keeping fed and clean and entertained, and generally having a life. I gained a new and much greater respect for the pioneers of distance running, the runners of the thirties, forties and fifties. Here were men who ran in training more than I ever did, who worked a long day, who earned nothing from their running, who had very few days off in the year (at least I had the school holidays) and who lived before the days of instant hot water, central heating, cheap, runner-friendly clothing and automatic washing machines and clothes driers. For that first year as a teacher, when suddenly plunged into similar, though maybe not quite such demanding circumstances, I found I couldn't do anything approaching what they had done.

How things have changed! Mo Farah, before his double Olympic triumph at London in 2012, is quoted in a Radio Times of August 2012 as saying, '*I wake up, run, have breakfast, sleep, gym in the afternoon, another run in the evening. That's it, nothing else.*' Compare that with a quote from one of Britain's outstanding distance runners of the sixties, Roy Fowler, taken from 'Masters Athletics' magazine, Summer 2012, '*The British athlete gets up in the morning at 6.30, does his 8 to 10 miles, comes back, washes, shaves and goes to work. He has about half an hour for dinner, and then at night he is on the highway again.*' Much was written both before and after the London Olympics about the sacrifices Mo Farah had made to be where he was. Well maybe he had made what other people saw as sacrifices, but they seem to me to have been small sacrifices compared to those made by earlier runners, none of whom could look forward to any monetary reward and most of whom got meagre reward of any description. Did I, an average distance runner with no real hope of ever becoming a star, make sacrifices? I made changes to my life, I made commitments, but I never thought of them as sacrifices. I don't suppose Mo Farah thinks of what he had to do as making sacrifices either. I know who had it easier.

Only a sense of time running out gave me the incentive to restart my running life after my teaching job brought it to a temporary standstill. Approaching my thirties I felt it was a case of now or never. Somehow I had to fit my training around all my other commitments, however difficult that was going to be. Nothing short of the most drastic of circumstances would interrupt the training. It would simply become another necessary part of my life. Not being able to find time for it would not be an acceptable excuse. I would be doing no more than hundreds of other runners were doing and had done in the past, even though it would be a new experience for me.

There is no secret to doing something that is difficult, and for which there are any number of reasons for not doing it. It is just a case of will power. First you decide you want to do it, really want to do it, really, really want to do it. Then you plan what needs to be done, and you work out whether it's going to be possible to do it. Finally you resolve to do it, and you get on with it. That's more or less what I did in September 1973. It was the first mature decision I had made in my running career.

CHAPTER 9
The sport changes

'Fings Ain't Wot They Used T'Be.'

Frank Norman musical.

When my father retired he moved to Dorchester in Dorset and, although I never lived there myself, Dorchester became the family home, the place for regular visits and Christmas gatherings. Over the Christmas and New Year period in 1986 I was staying in Dorchester and trying to keep my running going during quite a successful winter season. I was displaced from my usual routine, away from my normal training routes, and had already lost a day's training through travelling, with another lost day to come for the journey home.

It's hard for a runner to keep to a schedule and to maintain the edge on his fitness while away from home. There may be nowhere to change and shower, or to wash and dry kit. Sometimes it's impolite to those with whom you are staying to make time to run. It may be difficult to find the opportunity to do any running at all or a place to do it. Ron Hill, who prides himself on his unbroken record of running every single day for the whole of his long career, resorted to jogging around airport lounges and hotel corridors when he was travelling, in order to maintain the sequence.

I understand that. Although all reason and logic tell you that a day off running is not going to affect your fitness, and any lost miles can always be put back later or banked beforehand with an extra run in the days leading up to a trip, an enforced rest always plays havoc with the mind. Runners become so obsessive about their running that, when they go twenty four hours without any training at all, through no choice of their own, they start thinking that they are back to square one. All those months of training suddenly seem to have gone to waste because something has stopped you running on one day. It doesn't matter whether it's an injury (though injury never stopped Ron Hill), an illness, an emergency or just the fact that you're driving all day, from Stranraer in Scotland to Dorset in the south of England, for Christmas.

A moment's thought makes this irrational concern appear as ridiculous as it is. It would probably take several weeks of inactivity to damage a trained runner's fitness significantly and anyone who, like me, sometimes takes a day off by choice can't complain about a day off forced on them. Even so it's a mind thing, a matter of confidence, self esteem and reassurance. Running regularly and keeping to a training routine becomes a runner's comfort blanket. Remove it and the runner is suddenly bereft of the familiar and warming habit that supports his confidence.

It's also a conscience thing. Training requires discipline and persistence. If you don't keep it going as planned you have failed in your resolve and shown weakness of character. The result is a disproportionate degree of guilt. Ron Hill is an intelligent man. I am quite sure his determination to run every single day had absolutely nothing to do with a belief that his physical condition would suffer if he gave way to even the most difficult obstacle to his daily run. Sticking to your training at all costs may not be physically essential but psychologically its importance cannot be over-estimated.

One thing that I found very effective in keeping myself both physically and motivationally in shape when I took a travel break was a race. There's nothing like the prospect of a race to focus the mind on running. A race makes at least one day a running day. It defines a time and a place when running is certain to get done, and it makes it easier to train on the days preceding it as well. It's hard, once you're committed to a race, to find an excuse not to do it and it's hard not to take it seriously enough to be concerned about what shape you're in at the start.

Wherever you go in the UK there's usually a race organised somewhere within easy reach almost any weekend of the year. Dorset is no exception. Several times, when staying in Dorchester at Christmas, I ran the Poole 'Round the Lake' 10K race which was held each year on Boxing Day. Poole is just a short drive from Dorchester and this event became my regular means of keeping myself in a running frame of mind over the Christmas break. I ran it in 1986. Boxing Day that year was on a Friday.

I had also discovered in the same year another race, an eight mile road race, that was to be held on the following Sunday, the 28th of December. On the basis that, if one race is good for keeping the running mind and body in tune, then two must be better, I entered this one as well. It was organised by Bridport Lions Club and run on a point to point course from West Bay, a small coastal town very close to Bridport itself, to Beaminster, another small town, about six or seven miles directly inland, and a few hundred feet above sea level.

I remember very little of the race itself. There was an impetuous young chap who flew off at the start and after a mile or so was well in the lead. I wondered why he was so far ahead and whether I shouldn't try to catch him before it was too late. I felt tired but, even so, I should surely have been nearer the front. I had finished third in Poole two days previously and earlier that same month had run under 31 minutes for 10K, so I was confident of finishing well up. Following this short period of self doubt, having come through the initial period of discomfort that accompanies any race, and now well into my running, I became almost disinterestedly fatalistic. Eight miles is a long way, plenty of time to catch up, if ever I was going to.

From then on it was an enjoyable, hard run in the country. I caught the early leader quite soon after his first mad rush and half an hour later entered Beaminster square in the lead and a minute ahead. It's always nice to win, even if you haven't taken the race very seriously and even if the field is not the strongest you've ever encountered. But I had taken what I saw as the ethos of the race seriously. To me it was a proper race and I had run it as hard as I could. I had been competitive. I had relished the sense of invincibility that came as I realised I had a mile or so to run and was well enough ahead not to be caught. I had thrilled at the feeling of running strongly and fluently. And I had considered and respected the other competitors as runners, like myself, participating for exactly the same reasons and for no other.

Five days later I was disabused by the Western Gazette. I was a relic who should have known better than to take what was a 'fun' run as a serious race. I should have realised that the real purpose of the run was to raise funds for local charities and that those, like myself, who were not sponsored were failing to enter into the proper spirit of the event.

To quote from the report of the run, headlined 'Running for fun is getting much too serious', *'Serious competitive runners outnumbered fund-raising entrants by more than three to one in Bridport Lions Club's Christmas fun run on Sunday. The trend, which is not welcomed by officials, has put a question mark over the future of the popular annual event. From the outset, the run was meant to be a light-hearted way of raising money. Now it is fast becoming a serious athletic event.'*

I have no complaint about the fact that my view of a road run was different to that of the organisers. I just wish I'd known from the outset and hadn't had to find out from a newspaper report almost a week later. It was a shock. I had been living in a road running shell that was now rudely breached. Until that moment I hadn't the faintest inkling that there was any other way of looking at a road race than how I looked at it. I had been introduced, somewhat belatedly, as if to a blast of cold water, to a new era of running events.

Although unhappy with the outcome of the Bridport Lions Club's event I never felt that I, nor any other serious runner, was made to feel unwelcome that day, merely out of place. The official quoted in the Gazette went on to say, *'We do not mind it becoming competitive but we like the majority of runners to be sponsored.'* For the organisers to say they didn't mind the event becoming competitive was disingenuous. Hadn't they made it pretty clear that they did mind? They might as well have laid on a vegetarian feast and said that they didn't mind a few carnivores joining in. The truth about serious runners in a fun run, as

I discovered, is that the organisers don't know what to do with them.

The putting on of a hybrid event like the Bridport Lions Club's one, and the ambiguity of attitude to serious runners was an early expression of the belief that organisers of road races could have their cake and eat it, that serious running and fun running could cohabit and that, in a strange synthesis of two quite opposite approaches to the same activity, each could support the other.

We see the same belief taken to its logical conclusion in the big city marathons, the half marathons and other road running events of today. At one extreme are the mass participants, hoping just to finish and raise some money for the charity of their choice or grab some publicity. At the other are the professional, élite runners having a race of their own with a separate start and separate media coverage. So much attention is paid to these two extremes that the middle, what little still exists of runners running for running's sake alone and still striving to compete, is virtually ignored.

At the Bridport Lions Club's run I represented that middle part. The two extremes had not yet materialised in such a minor event and in what were the early days of the evolution of the road running scene. The fun runners raising money were not yet all that different from me and, at the other extreme, the invited élite runners didn't exist. In a sense I was both the middle and, at the same time, the élite extreme, in embryonic form. I was running hard to escape the challenge for attention from the fun runners behind me but not fast enough, nor in a classy-enough race, to earn attention on my own terms. Obviously no one had come to Bridport or Beaminster on the Sunday after Christmas to see an averagely good runner win a low key road race. Why should anyone? I certainly wouldn't have expected it. More to the point, that was not why I entered the race.

The phenomenon of an exhibition race, held in conjunction with an established road race and involving some of the best runners in the world is a relatively recent one. It has only been made possible by the large amounts of money generated by the big road races enabling the payment of appearance fees and cash prizes. At the same time it is something that has been made necessary in order to stop the race, as opposed to the whole event, being completely overshadowed by the mass participants. Imagine how little interest there would be in, say, the London marathon race, if it consisted only of a domestic field and was likely to be won in around 2:20. As a spectacle vying for publicity and media attention, it wouldn't stand a chance.

If the race, again as opposed to the event as a whole, is not to be about as insignificant as Icarus in Breugel's 'Landscape with the fall of Icarus', it has to be a display of road racing exciting enough by itself to compete for the public's attention against the draw of the mass participation festival. It has to promise fast times and a show of running at its absolutely very best. It may involve a mere handful of runners, against many thousands making up the mass field. Those thousands of fun, charity and novelty runners are variously and colourfully attired, with a host of fascinating and often heart rending stories to tell. The élite race has only one thing to offer the spectator - running. No wonder it has to be top class to be noticed at all.

To me it is ironical that, however massive the fun running side of big road races becomes, it cannot exist without the presence of a race held concurrently. It is an admission by those who would take over the sport of running and turn it into a vast media carnival that without the competitive component in its purist form, i.e. a straightforward running competition, there can be no event at all. A mass participation procession of thousands of fun runners through the streets of a town or city, it would seem, cannot be justified, even by the organisers, without the supportive accompaniment of a proper race.

As the carnival side of road races has grown, so have the élite races had to keep pace. It is as if the sheer mass of the fun event can only be balanced by ever more amazing feats of superlative running. For a thousand fun runners entered, an event needs a winning time of something of the order of under 2:20 for a marathon or 1:05 for a half marathon for parity, while twenty, thirty, even forty thousand fun runners, as participate in some of the really big events, demand something much better, several runners under 2:07 or 1:01, with the realistic expectation of a world record. Woe betide an organiser who gets the balance wrong. It is essential that the fun runners, even those who barely run at all, maintain the illusion that they are competing in a race, and it is essential that the media can continue to pretend that their own attention is primarily directed at the sport of running.

In short, the role of the staged élite race in big road running events is to add gravitas to the occasion and to give it serious running appeal. The role of the masses is to make the event what it is designed to be, a big dazzling show for the public, and, of course, to enable the organisers to pay the large sums of money required to attract the best runners in the world.

Charlie Spedding, bronze medal winner in the 1984 Los Angeles Olympic marathon and winner of the London marathon in the same year, wrote in his book, 'From last to first', *'Road racing used to be a serious sport for competitive runners, but it has been hijacked by charities and overweight joggers.'* He came in for some criticism for saying that. Yet, what an apt word to use - hijacked. It describes perfectly the taking over of a long established, albeit minor sport, with a resident and enthusiastic following, by outsider interests for purposes totally unrelated to any that may have been associated with the sport in its original form and it leaves absolutely no doubt as to which type of running came first, which was the incumbent and which the gatecrasher.

If you think that the change in the nature of city road races is not really significant (it is still about running, after all) then consider the advent of wheelchair racing. Fun runners may still be going through the motions of running, even when dressed in costumes that make it all but impossible to progress at much more than a shuffle, but movement in a wheelchair bears no relationship to running whatsoever. Even so, all big city road races now include a wheelchair race. If that is not a clear case of hijacking I don't know what is. It may be a commendable and welcome extension to an event but, from the point of view of the serious runner, like any irrelevant addition, it amounts to a distraction, a dilution and a devaluation.

Charlie Spedding, of course, was one of the élite. At the time he won the London marathon he was unwittingly and, had he realised, I am sure, also unwillingly, a part of the staging of big road racing events primarily as public and media spectacles. He was part of the top end of the field that was so essential to balance the huge counterweight of the mass participants.

Luckily for him he was good enough to take some of the limelight for himself, deservedly so. His role, along with that of the other élite runners (Ingrid Christiansen from Norway won the women's event that year), aside from running his own race and gaining selection for the Olympics, was to authenticate the event as a bona fide and extremely classy marathon race which just happened to have attached to it, in parasitic fashion, a cast of thousands.

The real victim of this duality of élite running side by side with fun running is the mid-field, what used to be the backbone of any running event and the totality of most, the good club runners, those who wish to race in the proper spirit of competitive running. As fields in the big televised events are stretched at each end, from thousands to tens of thousands at the slow end and from good runners to ever more élite runners at the fast end, it is the middle that takes the strain. With so much to fascinate, to amaze and to delight at the two extremes, near superhuman racing at the apex, smiling waving crowds and fancy dress, charities and human interest at the base, there is no longer any place, nor any need for an ordinary race in the middle. And so, often enough, there isn't.

Any aspiring runner who wishes to indulge in the purity of the sport, to train hard, to enjoy running for its own sake, to compete in races with an eye to nothing other than doing well and improving, and who decides to enter one of the big events, the London marathon, or the Great North Run, for example, will find numerous barriers getting in the way to what should be a very simple goal. This point was made in Chapter

5, in relation to the AAA Marathon Championships. By incorporating the AAA marathon into an event (the London marathon) which is so much more, and, therefore, paradoxically, so much less than a serious and, in the context of the sport, definingly important race, the relevant authority has shown an appalling abdication of responsibility for the wellbeing of the sport. Ultimately the phenomenon of the big city road races will be the death of road running as a serious sport in this country. I doubt if there is any longer a single marathon staged in the UK that a hopeful marathon runner might enter that does not incorporate at least some of the trappings of a typical mass participation event.

When a small field of runners lined up for the first running of, for example, the Finchley 20 in 1933, or, similarly, for any road race of the early twentieth century, it didn't share the event with something else. Any interest there may have been in the race was not sidetracked by other things going on at the same time and in the same place. No one had even thought of running as a means of raising money for charity. No one ever dreamt of running just for fun, or of running in anything other than vest and shorts. If anyone at any stage in the race started to jog or walk, it was because he absolutely had to. It was like that in all the races I ran in the sixties and seventies and for a number of years after. I only noticed the start of the hijacking process in 1986, though it was initiated in this country some years before that. It was not a good feeling, having to adjust to running no longer being the most interesting thing about a running event.

Although I never thought that I had been unwelcome in the Bridport race I was unsettled by what I read in the Western Gazette. I knew I had no apology to make to the organisers any more than they or the journalist who quoted them owed me and all the other runners who took the race seriously an apology. On the contrary, I am grateful to have been educated in the changing face of road running and to have been a part of a process that had probably started years earlier but was about to change the sport almost beyond recognition. It was a learning process for both of us. I and others like me had to learn to share races with fun runners and charity raisers even though we might have felt that our sport, one with an established structure and a great and hard earned tradition, had been hijacked for other purposes, while organisers of events had to learn how to persuade potential entrants that an apparently unrewarding and somewhat masochistic activity can still be worthwhile, even fun, once the seriously competitive part of it ceases to be a motivating factor.

When my eyes were opened by the Western Gazette reporting the Bridport Lions Club's run I felt a bit like a man who finds his wife in bed with someone else. First there is the shock of revelation, then a sense of betrayal and finally an ominous vision of the future. I should have seen it coming but I hadn't. The concept of a fun run was too obvious to escape the notice of publicity seekers and money raisers. Running events had an established place in the sporting calendar. If not, they were easy to organise from scratch, as many were. In fact, to be fair to the organisers of fun runs, including those responsible for the Bridport run, most such events, if not all of them, were new events. They were planned and introduced as fun runs rather than serious races and maybe we, the serious runners, were the interlopers after all.

That would be a fair assessment of the early days of fun events were it not for two things. Firstly every fun run that has ever been staged retains the pretence, the format, the basic idea of a running competition, something stolen from a centuries old sport where the sole point of interest lies in the order in which competitors complete the course. And, secondly, as the fun run notion gained ground, it became virtually impossible for any race, even long standing events that were a staple part of the sporting calendar, not to develop a fun component or, at the very least, to accept that a hefty proportion of entrants would be there for reasons that owed very little to the sport of competitive running.

I sometimes wonder whether the same sort of takeover could have happened to any other sport. Would horse racing tolerate the Epsom Derby, or the Grand National fields being followed home by a mass of cart horses and children's ponies, gaily decked with coloured coats, balloons and ribbons? Would Henley Regatta appreciate a large flotilla of dinghies, canoes, rowing boats and makeshift rafts slowly making their way up the course behind the international rowers, and would the motor racing circuits of the world tolerate participation in a Grand Prix by almost any form of motorised road vehicle? Running has been extremely easy to hijack. It is so simple, ultimately so appealing though, at the same time, not obviously very exciting, and it has so few rules. That has been its weakness.

Even the rules that do apply to the simple business of road running are conveniently ignored in order to smooth the forward motion of the show business omnibus. Wasn't Dorando Pietri disqualified as he approached the finish line of the 1908 Olympic marathon because he was assisted over the line and, thereby, broke the rules? But if I wanted to enter the London marathon with a friend dressed as a pantomime horse, that would be fine. I could push him from the back until half way and then we could change over for the second half. If you think I'm joking you may be interested to know that in the London marathon of 2012 two brothers from Surrey completed the course in a new world record time for a pantomime horse. The horse was called Bonzo. Bonzo trotted 4:49. But did his back legs assist his front legs? That is the question.

I was probably about ten years late in recognising that a change in the sport of running was imminent and about five years late in seeing that the change was happening in this country. For the origin of the change we need to look across the Atlantic and if the seed of change was planted at a particular time it was probably about 1972. In that year Frank Shorter of the USA won the Olympic marathon in Munich. The possibility that an American might win any marathon at that time was similar in credibility to the idea of a Briton winning a ski jumping event. Despite the success of Billy Mills and Bob Schul in the 1964 Tokyo Olympics at 10,000m and 5,000m respectively, the USA simply did not produce distance runners, any more than Great Britain produced ski jumpers.

Then, out of the blue came, not just Frank Shorter, but Bill Rodgers as well, an equally outstanding marathon runner, winner of the 1975 Boston marathon and the 1976 New York event, with times close to 2:10 on both occasions. Shorter went on to win the silver medal at the Montreal Olympics four years after his Munich triumph. Rodgers won the New York marathon again in 1977, 78 and 79 and the Boston race in 78, 79 and 80. There were others too; Kenny Moore was fourth in the Munich Olympics, Dick Beardsley came first equal in the inaugural London marathon and, then, on into the eighties and beyond, came a number of great U.S. distance runners including the remarkable Alberto Salazar, who set a world best for the marathon of 2:08:12.7 when winning in New York in 1981.

But it was the American runners of the seventies who signalled a change in public attitude to the sport of running. Suddenly running in the USA was respectable. More than that, it was something to be proud of as a nation, and something to aspire to. By itself this renewed appreciation of running within the USA might merely have given the sport a more enthusiastic public following and greater media coverage. But something of far greater import was taking place. It was the start of the jogging boom. People didn't just want to follow distance running, to read about it and to watch it, they wanted to run themselves. So began the transition from running being a tough and highly competitive activity, popular within a very small body of highly driven, slightly eccentric individuals, indulging in what most people saw as self imposed cruelty, to running as fun!

The jogging craze, call it fun running or recreational running if you like, started in the USA and spread to Britain and the rest of Europe within a few years, so that by 1980 it was well established and seemed here to stay. I've mentioned one factor that may have been partly responsible for it, the success of American runners in the Munich Olympic marathon. But no such craze, one that sweeps across a whole country and then across half the world and involves thousands of people, is ever set moving by a single happening. Several things have to come together to provide the impetus for such a movement, and, of course, the time has to be right.

Frank Shorter and others may have shown that running could be exciting, nationalistically gratifying, highly admirable and something really worth trying to emulate, but it took something else to get across the message that running could be the two things that would prove to be crucial in firing the jogging boom and, later, in changing the sport of running for ever. Those two things were, firstly, that running was good for you and, secondly, that it could be enjoyable. That's what jogging was all about: easy running that made you feel good, made you fitter and healthier and longer lived and was fun to do.

One other factor added fuel to the jogging boom, so much so that the craze spread at a speed and to an extent that no one could have anticipated. The added impetus came from the accoutrements of running. In 1960 Abebe Bikila showed that an Olympic marathon could be won using nothing more than a pair of shorts to protect his modesty and a vest to show his nationality and on which to pin his number. What craze in the modern age can survive with no more attached paraphernalia than that? Where is the commercial interest to exploit? Where can any money be made?

As if in answer to the business world's communal prayer, Bill Bowerman, coach to the Oregon University track team, using Kenny Moore's foot as a model, designed the running shoe that became the prototype for one of the first trainers made by the sports company 'Nike'. Nike shoes went on to become fashion statements. For every pair that was ever worn in anger, many others were worn for appearances only. The very word 'trainer' is now a generic term for a design of shoe, irrespective of whether it is ever used for training. By the end of the seventies, running gear had become 'cool' and sexy, and running proved an excellent excuse for wearing fashionable running gear. Wearing the gear was just one more way in which running could be fun.

It didn't stop with shoes. This is what the modern day fun runner is using, in one capacity or another, and paying heftily for, in pursuit of his or her hobby:

1) not just one pair of shoes, but shoes for every occasion: for training (stability, motion-control or shock-absorbing) and for racing, for cross country, for trail running, and for road running, for ice and snow and, most recently, so called bare foot shoes (how oxymoronic is that?);

2) running socks and long, compression socks;

3) what I used to call tracksuit bottoms, then became tracksters or jogging bottoms, and are now more like a circus performer's tights and are called leggings;

4) running shorts, if that's what they are still called; they seem now to be more like a diver's or surfer's wet suit, cut off just above the knees;

5) running pants (actually I made this up but I'm sure someone has tried to convince gullible runners that ordinary pants, or no pants at all are inadequate for the properly equipped - no pun intended - fun runner);

6) running bras for the ladies;

7) sweat-wicking running tops of all descriptions: long sleeved, short sleeved or sleeveless, lightweight or thermal, black, white or multicoloured, plain or hi-viz;

8) running jackets (what I still call anoraks) - ditto;

9) running gloves and, I notice lately, what appear to be long socks for the arms, without the feet, of course;

10) running hats; white peaked for the summer and Ali G-style for those cooler days (a variation is a headband that keeps the forehead and ears warm but allows the top of the head to 'breathe');

11) running sun glasses (which, I have read, are not only essential, but quite different from ordinary sun glasses, just as running socks are not the same as ordinary socks);

12) nasal strips to keep the nostrils flared (as if we don't have a mouth to breathe through);

13) copious amounts of water in plastic bottles, some of which

are doughnut-shaped for ease of carrying while running and others that are so state of the art that they calculate when you need to drink and tell you to do so (by the way, bottles and other containers for water are now referred to as hydration systems);

14) energy drinks, gels and energy bars, isotonic drinks and recovery drinks (what's wrong with a pint of beer?);

15) a belt with pockets to carry said drinks, bars, etc.

16) a running rucksack, if there's not enough space in the belt; even, and I have seen this item seriously reviewed in a popular running magazine, a rucksack with a water reservoir;

17) a running watch or, better still, a satellite navigation 'watch' that calculates distances run and times run and the pace at which you run, monitors your heart rate and, I suppose, tells you where you are when you get lost;

18) earphones to plug into your iPod;

19) all the latest running magazines obtainable, which rely for their very existence on the fact that runners today feel they really need everything that has already been mentioned.

If you sense a degree of scepticism and ridicule in this list it is entirely intentional. It is not that none of these things are necessary. Some of them are absolutely so. It's more the idea that something quite ordinary, like a drink or a snack, a pair of socks, a pair of gloves or a woolly hat, has to be specially designed for runners. I never wear, nor ever wore, sun glasses, but if I did feel the need to do so while running I would just pick a pair off the shelf. But then I would be told by that month's running magazine that I had been very foolish.

As to the cost of all this running gear; it is immense. There is a premium attached to anything using the label 'running'. A pair of running socks costs three times as much as an ordinary pair of socks. A pair of top of the range trainers costs an average person's daily wage, or two days' wage for a pensioner like me. Jim Peters wore plimsolls from

Woolworth's and so did I in my early years. It's odd that I and many others like me managed to run to a respectably high standard with little more kit than Abebe Bikila wore in Rome. In 1960 there was no money to be made out of running. Today the business of making money is what drives and controls the sport.

By 1977 in the USA jogging had taken off to such an extent that Jim Fixx's book 'The complete book of running' became a best seller. Who could have envisaged a book on running becoming a best seller before jogging (BJ) caught on in such a big way? Was there even enough material to fill a book on running BJ?

The jogging boom might have existed side by side with serious competitive running without the two becoming involved in the same events, just as recreational swimming coexists with swimming in lanes in Olympic pools, kicking a ball about the park with league football, rambling with race walking, touring cycling with the velodrome, and going for a drive in the country with motor racing. There was no need for existing races to absorb the growing army of joggers nor for fun running events to try to be anything other than what they were intended to be - running just for fun. The present generation of big road running events, each one an uncomfortable amalgamation of the two incompatible sides of running, like a two-headed monster, the separate heads fighting one another for attention, might never have come into being. I would have preferred it that way. But the change has come and there is unlikely to be any going back.

One only has to look in a small amount of detail at any big road race, more particularly one of the famous televised races, to see in exactly what ways road running as a sport, and as individual events, has changed over the last thirty or so years, bearing in mind that the first London marathon was staged in 1981, based on the model of the New York marathon, an event that had already been held each October for a number of years. The 1981 London marathon was probably the first mass participation event of its kind to be held in Britain. It set the pattern for all future ones.

Some of the changes to road running races were very obvious and happened suddenly. Over seven thousand people participated in that first London marathon. Before then it would have been unimaginable to have a field of more than a few hundred in a single road race. Thirty years later the London marathon attracts over thirty thousand participants.

But let's look at another recent event, the Great South Run of 7th November 2010. I choose this race mainly because I have only quite recently watched it on television. Also it is a ten mile race, a distance that is rarely run nowadays but was staple fare to all road runners throughout most of the twentieth century. How does the race that is described by its own publicity machine as 'the world's premier ten mile road race' compare with an important ten mile event of thirty five years ago? I am thinking specifically of the 'Crest Homes' Walton 10, run on October 17th 1976. This was the race in which I broke fifty minutes for an accurately measured ten miles for the first and only time in my life and which, for that reason, holds special significance for me. It also happened to be a very good race with an especially high class domestic field. I can confidently hold it up as a fitting symbol of what could well have been the very peak time for British distance running.

The differences between the two events are so many and so great that it would take a book by itself to catalogue and analyse them. Some of these differences are of no consequence, some of them, in that they have brought the activity of running to a wider audience, may have been beneficial to the sport, but most of the changes, by themselves or through their long term effects, have been detrimental to the sport in its pure form.

There are, oddly, one or two crucial similarities. Both races were held in the very south of England and would, therefore, have tended to attract participants mainly from that region. This was more true for Walton, where only a quarter of the first fifty finishers came from clubs based anywhere outside the English home counties. The Walton 10 was very much a regional ten mile race and can be seen as having been representative of no more than perhaps a quarter of the running talent in the whole country at that time.

If we remove from the results of the Great South Run all the foreign and invited runners, including the élite British runners who were based outside Great Britain and ran because they were invited and paid to do so, we are left with a race of roughly equal quality to the Walton 10. Walton was won in 48:29 by Tony Simmons. The GSR would have been won, after removing the invited athletes, in 48:22. The last person to break fifty minutes in the GSR finished 18th in the full field, or 10th after the same adjustment for foreign and invited runners. In Walton eleven finished under fifty minutes (I was tenth). Two races, therefore, in British terms, of very similar standard.

So no improvement in domestic fields in thirty five years? Has the sport really not progressed at all in that time? Well actually no. A comparison of the Walton 10 of 1976 and the Great South Run of 2010, from a domestic point of view may, if anything, seem slightly to favour the running of today, until you delve further back into the finishing order. The land inhabited by men running between fifty and sixty minutes is much more thinly populated in modern ten mile road races compared to events like the 1976 Walton 10. The one hundredth finisher at Walton ran 55:55. In the GSR the same placed runner was almost exactly six minutes slower and, therefore, well outside one hour. Did two hundred run under one hour at Walton? I don't know, but it wouldn't surprise me. It is worth noting also that the Walton event made no claim to be any more than a run-of-the-mill, if somewhat above average, ten mile road race and had none of the pretentions of the GSR to be the world's or even the country's premier anything.

A more detailed picture of the decline in distance running standards is given in the introduction, using the Finchley 20 as an example. The strength in depth, the territory of the 'good club runner' is what has shrunk so much. That has been the greatest change.

Many of the big and obvious differences in the organisation and staging of important road races as exemplified by a comparison of the two cited ten milers are largely superficial: the vast increase in numbers, the introduction of élite runners, the run for fun element and the fancy dress and novelty angle, the media interest, the number of spectators, the cost to enter, the restricted total number of entries and the much earlier closing date for entries, the goody bag and the medal for everyone, the earlier starting time and the money prizes and appearance fees of today's races.

But being superficial doesn't mean they are inconsequential. The big question that needs to be asked by the sport of distance running if it has any concern for its own future is, 'Where are the good but less than élite runners in a race like the GSR and what's in it for them anyway?' At Walton in 1976 they had the stage to themselves. No one questioned why they were there. Motivation was not an issue in any doubt.

Just as the London marathon is now the venue for the AAA marathon, the GSR, I learned, almost as an afterthought on the part of the television commentator, was the deciding race for the English Ten Mile Road Race Championships, except it wasn't. Because the field was so large it was sent off in waves; first the élite women, about twenty of them, then not until several minutes later the élite men, about forty, who 'led out the masses', including the serious but non-élite runners of both sexes. Positions in the English Ten Mile Championships, presumably, had to be worked out from finishing times in order to take into account the results of two separate starting lines, the élite and the non-élite.

For the better than average but non-élite female competitors the situation must have been even more insulting and demotivating than for the men. In the 2010 GSR there were no more than twenty élite women runners. That is a very small field for a ten mile road race and yet, even so, no other runner was allowed to take part in their race. The essence of a race, especially for a championship, is for the whole field to start together and for the runners to compete for the entire time they are running, side by side or in procession makes no difference, but always with the knowledge that they are all in the same boat. The race is, or should be, the same for everyone.

By assembling an élite field, one that is exclusive, and largely composed of imported runners, the organisers of a road race are effectively saying to the domestic competition, 'You are neither good enough nor interesting enough to take part in the real race.' They might as well go on to say, 'and, if you insist on running solely for the reasons people used to run road races, we don't really need you in this event at all.' This presumption of inferiority, which is now a feature of all the big road races, is what is doing most damage to the sport of distance running today. Why bother running a race if you've already been dismissed as being not worth any consideration? Since writing this I have watched the 2013 London marathon. The women's élite race involved just twenty one runners and was started one hour before the rest of the women set off. There were, therefore, just as in the GSR two quite separate races for women, one for a relatively tiny group that was considered worth any notice and another for those delusional women who thought they were competing in a serious marathon race.

Perhaps that is the worst thing that has occurred within the sport since the beginning of the eighties, a complete loss of respect and consideration for serious competitors. Today you get more respect if you walk a marathon dressed in some absurd costume and raise hundreds of pounds for charity than if you train hard and run hard and have some ambition and believe in the sport above the show and find satisfaction in the very pure and simple business of a running competition.

In some spheres the lack of recognition granted to serious runners of below élite standard amounts almost to a complete denial of their very existence. I sometimes wonder myself if such people still do exist. In January 2013, I picked up a glossy supplement in the supermarket, one of those publications that is too big to be a magazine but not substantial enough to be called a book. It was entitled 'Women's Guide to Running'. Curious to know what strange difference there might be between women's running and my own sort of running, I flipped through the pages and came to a section 'Why Run?' There were ten reasons given, all, without exception, to do with running being good for you: for the heart, for the brain, the hormones, the bones, the mood, and so on. Clearly in the running world that spawned this booklet the concept of running for competition and in order to be good at it seems to have been completely unheard of. It was an admission that the new running, the type that had taken over from the old, was different in kind. It was not a sport; it was a lifestyle, and within it there was no place for serious, competitive runners.

On the Thursday prior to the 2013 London marathon the Daily Telegraph devoted two pages of its sport section to a preview of the race. The main reason was that on the previous Monday two bombs had been detonated at the finish of the Boston marathon, killing three people and severely injuring many more. Would the London marathon, only three days ahead, also be a target for terrorism? Would the participants be safe? Hidden in the body of the report was a very short paragraph that disclosed as clearly as anything could, though written with absolutely no intention of doing so, the very point I am trying to make. There it was in black and white, *'In addition to the élite athletes, in excess of 37,000 recreational runners are due to take part in the 26.2 mile race from Blackheath to The Mall'*. By 2013 it was official; in public and press perception you were either élite (which means in the context of the London marathon able to run a marathon well under 2:20 and probably considerably faster than that) or recreational. There was nothing in between.

It is the backbone of the sport of running that has had to bend and adjust in order to fit in to the major events. At one time road races allowed themselves to accommodate a few fun runners and some novelty acts, and why not? There appeared to be no harm in letting these less than serious runners tag along behind the main field. But, within a few years, the also-rans became the majority in any road race field. To balance the two separate points of interest, serious and fun, athletes of higher standard than home based runners were invited to compete in races. At every stage it was the serious sporting runners who suffered. At Walton in 1976, I seem to remember, everything was as easy as it could have been: the entry, the parking, the changing, the start, the course, the finish, the results, everything. The organisation was done to accommodate the runners. It was not the other way round. Now it has become so difficult for intending participants to meet all the requirements of the organisation of a major road race that, for many, it can hardly be worth the effort.

In 1982, on the 3rd May, Belfast put on its own city marathon. It has been held every year since. I ran in that first event and I ran in several more. I even ran in 2011, aged 64, though I didn't finish because I developed an excruciating pain in the arch of my left foot and had to drop out at the half way point. The history of my own city marathon epitomises the evolution of all big road races since they started to change dramatically over thirty years ago.

The Belfast marathon was always intended to be first and foremost a city event rather than just a running race. That was in direct imitation of the London marathon and, before that, the New York marathon. It was a particularly poignant initiative in Belfast, a divided city, just emerging from the worst of its troubles. I could ask why Belfast had to choose a marathon rather than some other type of event as the centrepiece for its annual festival of reconciliation. Ultimately it did nothing to raise the standard of distance running in Northern Ireland. But it was only doing what several cities and towns had done before.

No one had the illusion that it was being done for the sport, though the general feeling was probably that the sport might benefit through greater exposure. If running as a sport was ultimately to be the victim of its own exploitation as a means of celebrating a city, the organisers of these events were not to know at the outset. Although, in my opinion, there is a direct causal relationship between the new breed of big city road races and the decline in strength of British distance running, it was never foreseen and was certainly never intended.

The first Belfast marathon was run, I remember, on a very windy day. It was not pleasant, and the conditions made the distance seem even greater than what, for me, was always a few miles too far. The field was mostly from Northern Ireland and the South of Ireland and, although I'm sure there would have been some fun runners there, I didn't notice a massive presence. The race was won by a local man, Greg Hannon, who in the summer of 1979 had become AAA marathon champion and before that finished fifth in the Commonwealth games marathon of August 1978. He ran 2:20 in Belfast. I finished 11th in 2:32:45.

At the end of that day I felt that I had just participated in an ordinary road race, much as I might have done on any other day in my home town. Only the distance was not normal. The people I ran with were the usual crowd, the organisers and marshals were people I knew. I wasn't aware at any point that I was taking part in an entirely different type of event. Maybe there were more spectators, more vociferous support from complete strangers, more atmosphere and more column inches in the local newspapers, even some TV coverage, but that was all. There were no obvious indications of the changes that would come in the following years.

The second Belfast marathon was similar, still a largely regional affair with the emphasis on the race for the top places. But, within two years, the feeling was that a day of this significance to a city the size of Belfast could not be supported by a race of such relatively minor standing. The organisers were beginning to realise that if you take an event that would never normally attract much attention as the basis for a festival for a city's entire population to remember, once the novelty value has worn off, you are left with a bit of a damp squib. Much as I love running and as enthusiastic as I am about it, I would be the first to admit that it is not intrinsically a very exciting activity to watch.

Reports of the 1987 Belfast marathon were particularly damning. Under the heading, 'Best forgotten?' a reporter wrote, *'The Belfast marathon is doomed, finished and best forgotten. That was the clear message to emerge from yesterday's 26.2 miles trek over the stamina sapping distance. There was a lack of atmosphere and appeal and the race was one bore from start to finish. There was no home town hero and yesterday's eventual winner was unheard of. In the wake of a bitterly disappointing event one question remains unanswered, why do the organisers go on?'*

Actually there is another question that this sort of reaction provokes and leaves unanswered, one which comes to my mind every time I watch a big road race on television or read reports or previews in the papers. It is this. Who is an event of this sort for? Is it for the sport and for the runners, or is it for the general public, the organisers and the media? As the mass participation road race machine has gathered momentum over the last decade or two that question has become a 'no-brainer'. The obstacle course confronting a runner of average ability, but with the sport in his or her soul, is enough to make the keenest person think twice: the need to enter an event sometimes almost a year in advance, the greatly inflated entry fee, the lottery for places, the registration, usually a day or two before the race, the ridiculously early time to be out of bed on the day itself, the journey to the start, the crowds, the standing around in any weather, the need to pee or poo and nowhere to do it or a queue almost as long as the race itself. And, added to that, there is the lack of consideration and lack of any recognition paid to that runner as a sportsman; as a fundraiser perhaps, as someone with a sob story perhaps, as someone who is getting married during the race or carrying a tray with a wine bottle and glass on it perhaps; not as a celebrity, which he or she is not, nor an élite runner (ditto) and, the saddest part, definitely not as an individual with only an interest in competitive running to offer as their story to the media.

Returning to the Belfast marathon; ironically the next year's event, after the *'best forgotten'* one, namely the seventh Belfast marathon, was contested by one of the most home based fields there has ever been and turned out to be an extremely exciting race, reminiscent of marathon races of earlier years. It was won by a mere four seconds in 2:19:00, not a very high class time by today's standards, but good enough for a second division marathon. I retained my veteran's title, finishing tenth in 2:29. Most impressively 124 runners finished inside three hours. I remember it as a great day, one which took me back ten years or more and dispelled any ideas I may have had at that time that the sport was changing at all.

Still this wasn't good enough for the organisers, who went on in the following years to turn the Belfast event into a smaller version of London, with the emphasis on mass participation, charity fund raising and non running-related public interest. Professional runners, mostly Kenyans, were introduced to guarantee at least one respectable time for the course, and a walk and a relay race were initiated, the relay race to run from the same starting line and at the same time as the full marathon.

I take particular exception to inviting outsiders to a local race, be they Kenyan, British or from any other part of the world, for the sole purpose of raising the standard of the event. Nothing could so clearly show the lack of appreciation shown to those runners who have a right to call an event their own. Even if 'foreign' runners are not approached directly, as soon as a suitably sized prize pot (£1,000 to the winner of the 2010 Belfast marathon) is introduced to any race there is no doubt that it is there to attract peripatetic, professional runners. I have nothing against runners travelling to races outside their usual range on their own initiative, just for the kudos of doing well, or for a change of scene. I've often done it myself. But the blatant importation of one or two 'stars' for image improving purposes, or the unsubtle dangling of a cash bait in the wider running ocean, cannot be good for the sport at a local level.

Nor did I like the introduction of a relay race to the Belfast marathon day. To those starting the full distance, the presence of relay runners was just one more sign that they were no longer the main, or even particularly important players, in the day's events. At any stage in any race it is nice to know whom you are competing against. In a marathon, where gaps between runners can extend to distances measured in hundreds of yards and fractions of a mile, it is helpful to know who is ahead and who is behind. But when you are surrounded at all stages by relay runners, however well they are distinguished from the marathon entrants, it becomes very difficult to place yourself in relation to the competitors who matter to you.

When I last finished the Belfast marathon in 2010 I was being passed by relay runners even in the finishing straight. I was barely running at this point and hadn't been moving much faster than walking pace for a couple of miles. But I couldn't jettison my competitive instincts. Everyone and everything that came past me gave me another sharp wound to my pride. As soon as they were in front of me I knew they were relay runners, but the hurt had been done, and couldn't be undone. I wondered why they were there. Surely any team of five people can run the marathon distance quicker than one decrepit old man? I achieved my second slowest ever time for a completed marathon (3:41) and still beat some relay teams. Shame on them.

When the organisers incorporated the relay did they think of the effect on the marathon runners and did they consider whether the presence of non participating runners during the course of a marathon championship (the Belfast marathon is the race for the NI Marathon Championships, just as the London marathon is the race for the AAA Championships) might compromise the legitimacy of that race?

Events like the Belfast Marathon, the London Marathon, the Great South Run and the Great North Run are now so far removed from their source of inspiration, the plain and simple road race, they have become unrecognisable. The new generation of big city road races are much like modern supermarket food: manufactured to appeal to the general public, advertised to the hilt and appealing to the lowest tastes, over-packaged, full of additives, attractive to look at but lacking in nourishment, harmful if indulged in to excess, and, worst of all, bearing no resemblance to real food at all.

But what of road races and other running events that have been around for a lot longer? I ran the Finchley twenty again in 2011, the seventy eighth running of the event. I have to say that the only really obvious difference I noted, compared to the same race in the nineteen seventies, was in the quality shown in the result, poorer, as expected. So there are still races that are relatively unadulterated by all the trimmings associated with the big events. There is a niche where the sport is changing much less than elsewhere.

This is even more the case with cross country. No one has yet been able to convince the fun runners to join in cross country events in the same way they have taken to the road. Cross country is cold and dirty. It's hard to televise and hard to present to spectators and it's ... well, it's just plain hard. That's why I never much liked it. But cross country and, to a lesser extent, what still remains of traditional road running may ultimately be the saving of the sport of running as it was when it was invented. When the public are tired of watching an endless succession of almost superhuman African runners winning staged road races, pursued, a great distance behind, by a mass of jogging, walking and waddling humanity, cheering and waving and grinning at the television cameras, perhaps that particular offshoot of running will die away, and some interest will pass back to the minority sport of running for running's sake.

CHAPTER 10
The Marathon

'Ze pace; is it too fast?'

Emil Zatopek to Jim Peters during the
Helsinki Olympic marathon.

The most famous, the most historical, the most fascinating, the most appealing, the most dramatic, the most addictive of running races and, at the same time, the most frustrating, the most cruel, the most unforgiving, the most hateful and the plain daftest of races - the marathon. It's the only race distance with its own generic name, or any name at all for that matter that isn't simply the place where the race is held or the club that organises it or a person it commemorates or its sponsor and a distance in miles or kilometres. The half marathon doesn't count because without the marathon there could be no half marathon. As for that other oxymoron of the running scene, after bare-foot running shoes, namely the mini-marathon, it's just an insulting title, like calling a very small person a mini-giant, or a very dim person a mini-genius. It's an insult to the marathon and disingenuous to everyone with an interest in running.

The marathon is far too long a distance to race in the same way that distances up to half its length can be raced. In Olympic competition the next furthest distance run, the ten thousand metres, is less than a quarter the length of the marathon. And what of the marathon distance itself? It's absurd; twenty six miles, three hundred and eighty five yards, supposedly fixed at that idiosyncratic figure because, at the London Olympics in 1908, the marathon finishing line was moved so that the race could finish beside the royal box at the White City. The only significance that story now retains is as a reminder of the dominant role Great Britain played in the history of athletics. The whole world still sets the marathon distance at such an inconvenient measurement, and all because of a small organisational adjustment made in London over a century ago.

I call the distance absurd and daft, however, for another reason. The person who originated the marathon, the Frenchman Michel Breal in 1894, either just hit on somewhere around twenty six miles as being a good distance for a long distance race by chance, or was a sadist who knew exactly how far an average runner, even a well trained one, can run without using up all their stored resources.

This is what makes the marathon such a cruel and unforgiving distance. For a large proportion of runners, from mediocre hopefuls to some of the very best, the marathon is simply too far. Whatever these runners may do in training they will never be able to race a marathon as others can. They can run one all right but in competition, particularly competition at the highest level, they cannot really race the whole distance. I know only too well because I am and always was a typical example of the type of runner whose maximum race distance lies at about twenty miles, perhaps even a little bit less.

As far as the marathon is concerned, therefore, runners come in two types, those who can cope with the distance and those who can't. The path to marathon success is strewn with the shattered remains of top class ten thousand metre runners who tried the longer distance and failed. During the seventies and eighties, whenever a major games appeared on the horizon and competition for places in the British team for the distance events on the track was intense, a number of hopeful ten thousand metre runners entered the marathon selection race (usually that year's AAA Championship) as a sort of insurance policy. If they didn't get one of the three ten thousand metre team places, maybe they could still go to the games as a marathon runner. The surprising thing is how rarely this ploy worked. Almost invariably, at least before the mid nineteen eighties, the British marathon team was composed of specialist marathon runners rather than ten thousand metre runners trying to move up.

The list of British runners known for running marathons superlatively well, and for little else, is a long one. The classic example, the marathon runner *par excellence*, was Ian Thompson, whose story was told in Chapter 5. From virtual obscurity as a track and cross country runner and with a lifetime best time for ten thousand metres of 29:33, he leapt to fame in 1973 with wins in the AAA marathon and the Christchurch Commonwealth Games marathon the same year. In the latter race he set a new British best time for the marathon of 2:09:12. That is the sort of time that a runner of his no more than average shorter distance credentials is simply not supposed to be able to do. At the time of his marathon debut his best five thousand metre time was 14:05, ranking him a mere ninetieth on the British all time list, his best ten thousand, 30:10, (which he did later improve), and his best ten miles on the road, 49:49. These are all good times, but they do not point to a runner capable of covering the marathon in under 2:10, or anywhere near it. Ron Hill's best under-distance times were considerably faster, including a world record ten mile track time of 46:44. But Ron Hill never ran quite as fast as Thompson over the full marathon distance. How do you make sense of that?

Clearly Thompson, more than perhaps any other British marathon runner before or since, had the right running style and the right physiology for the distance: the ability to keep going at close to the pace he would run over distances a fraction as far, without tiring, slowing down, or running out of energy. As if to prove the point, in 1980, he moved up to ultra-distance races and won the London to Brighton race that year, a distance of over fifty miles. He was quite simply a natural long distance runner.

Although Ian Thompson's ability to run for a very long distance without suffering to the same degree as other runners may have been acquired through training, this cannot be the whole answer. Other runners, who did just as much training, never managed to achieve quite the same staying power. If you think the secret lay in Thompson's especially long training runs, further than marathon distance and run almost as fast as race pace, I would refer you to the point I make in the chapter on training (Chapter 7). Ian Thompson was able to do a weekly twenty eight mile run at close to five minute mile pace, partly because of the training he had done previously - that goes without saying - but, first and foremost, because he was Ian Thompson. And, if I might make again the same point I made in Chapter 7 in relation to Haile Gebrselassie's long, fast training runs; in my training for the marathon, every Sunday, I ran only 20 to 25 miles at about six minutes per mile pace. Twenty five miles was the most I ever managed. The distance never got any easier and I was never able to increase it. Had I been able to, I wouldn't have needed to, if you see what I mean. My interpretation of those observations is very straightforward. I am neither Ian Thompson nor Haile Gebrselassie.

The list of the top British ten thousand metre runners of their time who made it to the highest grade as marathon runners, by contrast, is quite short. It should include Ron Hill himself, who finished sixth in the ten thousand metres in the Mexico Olympic games and only then went on to gain a much more prominent reputation as a marathon runner, with a best time of 2:09:28. Then there is Steve Jones, present British Marathon record holder (2:07:13), who deserves greater recognition for his exploits on the track (best 10K of 27:32); Charlie Spedding who won the AAA 10K in 1983 in 28:08, won the 1984 London marathon and was third in the Los Angeles Olympic marathon the same year; John Brown, fourth place finisher in successive Olympic games marathons, Sydney in 2000 and Athens in 2004, and the predecessor to Mo Farah as British 10K record holder (27:18); Eamonn Martin, winner of the 1993 London marathon, with a best 10K of 27:23; Richard Nerurkar, fourth in the Seoul Olympic Games marathon (best 10K, 27:40); and Geoff Smith, best known for his exploits in marathons in the USA (best 10K, 27:43.6). I might also include Paul Evans whose fastest marathon, in Chicago in 1996, was 2:08:52 and best 10K, 27:47.8, and Alister Hutton who won the London marathon in 1990 (2:10:10) and has a best 10K time of 27:59.1. But I would then, I think, be guilty of reverse argument by turning marathon runners into 10K men, just as I may already have done in the case of Charlie Spedding. I don't think anyone would argue that Spedding, Britain's second fastest ever marathoner, was primarily a 10K type of runner turned marathoner rather than an exceptionally gifted marathon runner in the first instance, cast in the same mould as Ian Thompson. Had he never turned to the longer distance his career would undoubtedly have ended in the vast hall of great but forgotten British distance runners. Instead he found the perfect niche for his ability and achieved lasting fame.

If that seems enough names to disprove my point, think of all the great 10K runners who either tried the marathon and failed by their own high standards, or who never tried it at all: Gordon Pirie, Dave Bedford, Dick Taylor, Brendan Foster, Ian Stewart, Mike McCleod, Mike Tagg, Nick Rose, Steve Binns (a 27:55 10K runner with a one off 2:13:32 marathon to his name - but, then, one good marathon hardly makes a marathon runner), Julian Goater, Lachie Stewart, Roger Matthews, all in their day amongst the best 10K runners in the land but not, it turned out, marathon men of note. I could even add to that list Dave Moorcroft, who once held the world record for 5,000m, except that he never to my knowledge ran 10,000m on the track. But although primarily a middle distance runner, 1500m being his main event, he had the stamina to run well over the country and in 1976 finished second in the English National Cross Country Championship. I think, therefore, he counts as an outstanding British long distance runner who never progressed to the marathon, as does Tim Hutchings, another top class British Middle distance runner who ran with great success on the country, finishing second in the World Cross Country Championships of 1984, in New York, and 1989, in Stavanger, Norway.

If the response to the very idea of a middle distance runner like Moorcroft and Hutchings or, indeed, Brendan Foster, who started his career as an 800 and 1,500m runner, all three of whom seemed happiest at distances below rather than above ten miles, becoming marathon runners, is one of derision, I would reply, 'Rod Dixon'. Dixon, a New

Zealand runner of the seventies and eighties, came to fame as a 1,500m runner, then moved to 5,000 (just as did both Foster and Moorcroft), won (strictly speaking he was only a guest in the race) the English National Cross Country Championship in 1973, beating none other than Dave Bedford into second place and in 1983 won the New York marathon in 2:08:59. His was possibly the greatest range of distances run in world class times of any athlete before or since, proof that it is possible to combine ability at distances below a mile with whatever it is that enables someone to maintain world class pace for the full marathon. He must be the only athlete ever to have competed for his country in the Olympics at 1,500m (a bronze medal in 1972) 5,000m (4th place in 1976) and marathon (10th place in 1984).

Then there are those, again a number of British distance runners, who moved from great successes at 10K and cross country to the marathon, and almost made it, but not quite as emphatically as they might have hoped: Dave Black, Bernie Ford and Tony Simmons are three who spring to mind. How galling it must have been for a man like Tony Simmons, fourth in the Olympic 10,000m in 1976, second in the world cross country championships in 1969, and second in the European 10,000m in 1974, with a best time for the 10K of 27:43.6, to get so close to the peak of world class at the marathon distance but ultimately not to reach it. And how much more galling to be beaten by runners in a marathon who would never have got close to him at shorter distances.

He won the 1978 AAA marathon in Sandbach, Cheshire, in 2:12:33, a feat that surely confirmed him as a great marathon runner. But did it? Based on his best10K time, using the calculation I'm about to describe, Simmons might have conservatively expected to run 2:10:00. Although his Sandbach time made him Britain's sixth ranked marathon runner at that time, he could not have been said to have fulfilled his apparent potential. He said himself after his AAA Championship win, *I'm not a marathon runner yet*. I regret to say that, brilliant runner that he was, and, ironically, brilliant marathon runner that he was, he was probably right. He was always a better shorter distance man than twenty six miler. When he was ranked sixth on the British all time list for the marathon, he was sandwiched between Don Faircloth, ranked fifth and Jeff Norman, seventh. In the context of races other than the marathon, had either of those two great British marathon runners ever been heard of?

Top distance runners who never became top marathon runners have ample excuse. Someone who is top class at shorter distances can be forgiven for not wanting to run marathons at all, or for running one, just to see, and then saying 'never again'. Why work so hard, and run more than four times as far, for less reward than you have already got by running 10Ks? To run marathons seriously you have to know instinctively that you are at least as good at them as at shorter distances. You have to have a feel for them, an urge to indulge in the romance of the marathon and to rise to its very special challenge. Most of all you have to feel it is worth the extra effort to train for the marathon, either because you won't be content until you try, or because you believe you will be relatively more successful at the longer distance. I suspect that all the top class shorter distance runners who were found wanting over the marathon knew, even if they couldn't admit it to themselves, either before they tried it or very soon after they had done so, that they were not really marathon runners.

We now (2013) have the interesting prospect of Mo Farah, double London Olympic gold medallist at 5,000m and 10,000m, moving up to the marathon. He is reported to be thinking of competing in this event in the Rio de Janeiro Olympic Games in 2016. Will he be the best marathon runner Britain has ever produced or will he join the list of great shorter distance runners who never quite made it at the longer distance? I stick my neck out later in this chapter and predict that no one, at least not in the foreseeable future, will run under two hours for the marathon distance. I would be chickening out if I weren't to make some prediction regarding Mo Farah. In my view he will undoubtedly run a good marathon, if he decides to try, but he will not beat the best. I shall be delighted if I am proved wrong, and I will take little pleasure from being right, but I say it with some conviction. Mo Farah has two weaknesses, in my opinion. One is that he is too fast, and flat out speed and the special endurance needed for marathon running rarely go together. The second is that he runs with a long stride. He lopes along rather than tripping along with the quick staccato rhythm of most of the best marathon runners. When he wants to speed up he simply opens his legs still further. It is an extremely effective way of moving over middle and slightly longer distances but it's hard to maintain for the really long distances. I look forward to being shot down, and, if I wished to give myself the riposte that I perhaps deserve, I would say the same name that I used before in a similar context - Rod Dixon.

When I glibly said that there are two types of runner, those who can run a marathon and those who can't, I was exaggerating. There is, as with all such things, a continuum, with Ian Thompson at one end and, without wishing to name anyone else for fear of causing offence, someone like myself at the other. One way to predict what time you can expect to run for a marathon, if you've never done one, is to take your best 10K time and multiply it by a factor of 4.7. This will give you a rough estimate of your prospective time, a time that you can reasonably expect to be able to do, rather than one that might turn out to be a trifle optimistic. Or, if you have run both 10K and a marathon, and reverse the process to get the value of your own personal conversion factor, it will tell you what sort of marathon runner you are; are you a runner who just goes on and on, like Ian Thompson, or are you, like me, one who hits the wall with a bang at about twenty miles? For Ian Thompson the value is less than 4.4. Mine is 4.7. The lower someone's conversion factor, the better a marathon runner he or she is.

I may be wrong but I am inclined to think that a runner's personal 10K to marathon conversion factor is fairly immutable. You can improve your times at all distances through training, but you can't turn yourself into a natural marathon runner if you're not one. If we take the present men's world record for ten thousand metres and multiply it by 4.4 (Ian Thompson's conversion factor) we get a marathon time of about one hour and fifty six minutes. I don't believe anyone will run a marathon in that time, at least not in the foreseeable future, because I don't believe anyone can combine that sort of 10K speed with the natural marathon runner's ability to keep going at close to his maximum shorter distance pace. Making predictions based on times for other distances is a very inexact business in any case, and it has to take into account the obvious fact that speed and endurance are not happy bed mates. If they were then we would look no further than the best 100m sprinters for our best marathon runners.

Up to now I've written almost as if all distance runners are male. That has been largely for convenience of writing. Also, being a man myself, I can only speak from experience of men's running. A third reason is that, when I started running it was, to all intents and purposes, a male dominated sport, and, fourthly, most of what applies to men applies equally to women. But here we have come to an exception, and I have to make a distinction. Based on the 10K/marathon conversion factor women are much better marathon runners than men.

When Paula Radcliffe won the London marathon in 2003, in 2:15:25, for a while I didn't believe it. How could any woman run that sort of time for a marathon when the women's world record for ten thousand metres was slower than twenty nine and a half minutes? With a best 10K time of 30:38, Paula has a conversion factor of 4.46, way below some of the fastest ever male marathon runners. If she had herself been the 10K women's world record holder (29:32 at that time) the value would be 4.62, compared with the equivalent for men (world best marathon time divided by world record for 10K) of 4.7. Looking at performances of other female marathon runners in general, their marathon times seem to be disproportionately impressive compared with their shorter distance performances. From a personal viewpoint, if I were running at my very best today I could compete with the fastest women in the world at any distance, from 1,500m up to twenty miles, on the track, road or country, with a fair chance of beating them, but in a marathon, I would expect to lose.

Here, for example, is a comparison between my best times for various distances and those of the American runner and holder of five US records, Deena Kastor. Kastor won two silver medals in the World Cross Country championships, in 2002 and 2003, and the bronze medal in the Athens Olympic Games marathon in 2004. I just happened to come across a list of her personal bests and was struck by the similarity with my own, that is until I came to the marathon. I have recorded the differences in our best times as F where I am faster and S where I am slower:

1,500m: 7.4s F. 3,000m: 11.6s F. 5,000m: 14.6s F. 10,000m: 8.3s F. 10miles: 1min 39s F. Half marathon: 1min 37s F. Marathon: 4min 48s S. I think that is as good evidence as I can find to prove my point.

Whatever physiological advantages Ian Thompson was blessed with, and however he achieved his unmatched running efficiency and his immunity to the exhausting effects of the marathon distance, he shares his gifts with women runners in general. Since the early 1970s, when women were first able to run marathons in official competition, I can't remember a single dramatic example of a female runner hitting the wall in the way so many men have done in famous races. When I watched the inaugural women's Olympic marathon in 1984, run in the heat of Los Angeles, already twenty five degrees by the time of the eight o'clock in the morning start, I never doubted that the winner, Joan Benoit of the USA, who took the race by the scruff of the neck from the gun, would keep going, without faltering, right to the finish. Women marathon runners, I had learned, the good ones, were automatons. They set off at a pace and kept to it until the end. While men were still prone to blow up in marathons (though this is far less common in the case of élite male runners in more recent times), women rarely seemed to do so.

Two marathon races, one that I took part in myself but failed to finish, and one that I watched on television, were classic examples of head to head contests between a true marathon runner and a shorter distance specialist who had decided to move up. In each case the marathon runner won.

The first, the one that I watched but didn't run, was the European Games Marathon of 1969, held over the classic Marathon to Athens course. The contest was between Great Britain's Ron Hill, whose marathon career may not have reached its peak by then, but was well enough established to mark Hill out as an experienced, top class marathon runner, and the Belgian, Gaston Roelants. Roelants came to fame as a 3,000m steeplechaser, holding the world record and winning the gold medal for that event in the 1964 Olympic Games in Tokyo. He was also probably the best cross country runner of his time, with four wins in the international championships of 1962, 67, 69, and 72. I saw him win in 1967, when the race was held in Barry in Wales, a race, incidentally, that Ron Hill also ran. Here was a man with obvious track speed and with strength and endurance enough to beat the world's best over six or seven miles cross country. He took to the marathon in the late sixties, finishing eleventh in the Mexico Olympics of 1968, in a mediocre 2:29:05. This was not a particularly auspicious start to a marathon running career for such a classy distance runner, certainly not a sign of a great future at the event, but for that maybe the altitude problem in Mexico was to blame.

In preparation for the Athens European Games he had reputedly been doing a lot of training and, given his background and recent form, there was no reason to suppose he couldn't become the next great marathon runner. Bill Adocks had run the same course in April that year in 2:11:7. It was now September, and perhaps Roelants was thinking in terms of a similar time. As if anticipating such a feat, he opened up a good lead at 30 km and held it until near the finish. Ron Hill later admitted that he was running for the silver medal after Roelants disappeared in front of him. When I watch a race on television, particularly a marathon, I identify so strongly with the participants that it is as if for the moment I am inside their minds and inside their bodies, experiencing every feeling of elation or fear, superiority or exhaustion. As the TV camera followed Ron Hill gradually catching the slowing Roelants in the last mile of that race, I was alternately, as I watched Hill, filled with the thrill of knowing that now, after miles of not even considering the possibility, I could win and, switching to Roelants, the awful realisation that after thinking I was going to win, that I wouldn't.

I know where my sympathies lay. As the camera followed Hill's forward leaning figure, striding strongly on, it picked up the forlorn Belgian in the distance, desperately trying to maintain his lead but, by that stage, completely unable to prevent the inevitable. I knew what it must have been like for Roelants. However much I looked forward to a British victory and a personal triumph for Ron Hill, a man I much admired, it was Roelants I was urging on. It seemed so miserably unfair to be beaten like that.

The race was a classic case of a man who could not quite last the distance being run down by someone who could. It confirmed that the marathon is a different class of race from anything shorter and to be good at it you have to be a special sort of person. It's not enough to be fast over shorter distances, even if those distances are well into the realms of what can be classed as long (Roelants held world records for 20 km and one hour). It's not enough to do masses of training. You have either to be born with, or somehow acquire, a particular gift, one that Hill had and Roelants did not.

Roelants never quite made it as a marathon runner. The silver medal he won in Athens was his best place in a championship marathon, though he ran a better time in the Rome European Games in 1974. He finished third in that race in 2:16:30, which may well have been his career best time for the distance. Then there was his Mexico Olympic Games eleventh place finish, fifth place in the 1971 Helsinki European Games in 2:17:49 and a d.n.f. in the Munich Olympics of 1972. Anyone else might have been justifiably proud of a record like that, but for a runner of his stature, one of the very greatest distance runners of the sixties, it can only have been a big disappointment.

The other race, the one that I started myself but didn't finish, was the 1979 AAA Marathon Championship, held that year around country roads on the outskirts of Coventry. This turned out to be a contest between a man whose fame as a runner hinged almost entirely on his prowess at the marathon, and a top class British cross country and 10K runner, making his marathon debut.

The proven marathon man was Northern Ireland's Greg Hannon, who had been the first UK runner home in the previous year's Commonwealth Games in Edmonton, Canada, where he finished fifth in 2:17:25. Although an excellent cross country and track runner with a fine record of performances over road races at shorter distances, it was as a marathon runner that he ultimately became best known, most famously as a result of the race he was about to win. Had it not been for his performances over the marathon distance and for his becoming AAA marathon champion in 1979, with a time that then ranked him ninth on the UK all time list, he would have gone down in the history of British athletics as yet another good, but not great, distance runner.

By comparison, the man with whom he was about to have a neck to neck battle for over twenty miles in the Coventry sun was a giant of track and cross country. He was Englishman Bernie Ford, who had been either first (twice) or second (four times) in the previous six English Cross Country Championships, and had represented Great Britain in the ten thousand metres in the 1976 Olympic Games, finishing eighth in the final. In that memorable race, when Lasse Viren won his third Olympic gold medal for Finland, Ford had recorded 28:17.8 after running a remarkably consistent 28:17.4 in the heats. Those times, not to mention his life time best of 27:43, put him firmly amongst the world's leading 10K track runners, less than three years prior to his marathon debut in Coventry. Greg Hannon, on the other hand, could never claim, at any time in his career, to have been such an élite ten thousand metre runner.

The situation was, therefore, that in covering just over twenty six miles on an undulating, three lap course, on a hot day, in the midlands of England, Hannon, the eventual winner, was always running much closer to his race pace at shorter distances than was Ford. According to all logic Ford should have won. But logic cannot be applied to the marathon. The winner is the runner who can do what Hannon did that day, to run as close as possible to his theoretical maximum pace for the distance, based on times over shorter distances, and remain strong right to the end.

The race was hard. I know that from my own experience. There were some tough hills and the day was hot. A number of runners dropped out, myself included. By fifteen miles Ford and Hannon were on their own, running side by side. By twenty miles they were three minutes ahead of the rest. Soon after twenty miles Hannon surged on an uphill stretch and was away. He beat Ford by just over a minute, 2:13:06 to 2:14:15. The third placed runner was over five minutes behind.   Ford didn't blow up. He didn't hit the wall. He simply found, over the last six miles, that twenty previous miles of, in his own words, 'reasonably comfortable' running could bring you to a state where it becomes impossible to do any more than just keep going. Hannon, on the other hand, could 'surge' and cover the 6 miles 385yards (a little over 10km) in 31:36, despite having run the same twenty miles much nearer to his maximum shorter distance pace. That's what distinguishes a true marathon runner from any other, the ability to absorb the distance, to dispense power and energy frugally so that there's always plenty left, to run mile upon mile without ill effects and to do this when running at a pace that, for you, is faster than logic says it should be.

Reporting on the race, the Athletics Weekly correspondent wrote of Bernie Ford, '*it was a momentous start to what could become a sensational career as a marathon runner*'. Sadly this prophecy never really came true. Ford did run 2:10:51 in Fukuoka, Japan, later that same year, but it was the pinnacle of his marathon career, rather than a sign of more to come. Besides, with his 10K credentials, it was no more than he might have expected. He was one of the three British marathon representatives at the 1980 Moscow Olympics, along with Ian Thompson and Dave Black, where all three failed to finish. Perhaps I am being unfair to Bernie Ford; nevertheless I still think of him as an outstanding distance runner who tried the marathon, rather than an outstanding marathon runner. Neither he nor Black, another world class ten thousand metre runner who took to the marathon, ever achieved the sort of consistent success at the marathon that their 10K class promised. My interpretation of the relative failure of outstanding ten thousand metre and cross country runners to transfer effortlessly to the same superiority over twenty six miles lies in the absence of what could be called the Ian Thompson factor.

At the risk of stating the obvious, it is the distance of the marathon that makes it unique. It is a race that cannot be approached in the same way that other races can be approached. In any marathon there is a relatively high drop-out rate. When the weather is hot or the course is particularly tough there can be a very high drop-out rate. Runners don't drop out for fun. They drop out either because they literally cannot continue or, more often, because they are in distress, and they have slowed down so much that there is no point in carrying on. If they were to continue they would only suffer more - and for what? There might be some reason to finish a first marathon at all costs, just to do so, or to finish for a team place, but for a serious runner, once the damage has been done, the race is already over. There is no shame attached to dropping out of a marathon. It is like leaving a girl alone when she goes off and marries someone else.

I have dropped out of several marathons and I have reached a point in a number of others when, in different circumstances, I might have dropped out. Sometimes keeping going becomes the easiest way to reach the finish. There's not a lot of point dropping out when you're five miles from the end of the race, in the middle of nowhere, with no hope of a lift; it's far simpler just to struggle on. Other times, maybe, I should have dropped out, but kept going to preserve my place.

I was fourth in the Welsh marathon in July 1976, having been leading up to about nineteen miles. If there had been more people ahead of me with a couple of miles left I might have stopped. I think I would have been wise to stop, even before that. But I struggled on at a snail's pace, first to preserve second, then third and ultimately fourth place.

My time was 2:34:02 but would have been around 2:25 if I hadn't hit the wall. In my diary I wrote afterwards that I had felt good until eighteen miles. Things went to pieces from there on. It so happened that there was someone doing a medical research project at the event, taking blood samples and weighing runners before and after the race. Between the start of the race and the finish I lost eight pounds, and I was later informed that my blood had accumulated almost unheard of amounts of waste products, mainly urea, I think. On the way home I slept on the back seat of the car (I was so colourless my wife thought I was dead) and on arrival I went straight to bed. When I tried to drink a glass of water, just pure water, it shot back out of my stomach as if from a power shower. I couldn't take in any liquids at all until the next morning, and I was probably more severely dehydrated than I care to know.

At the start of any marathon, therefore, every competitor is asking the same question, 'Will I finish?' One sure way to guarantee finishing a marathon is to run very slowly, and, if that is your only aim, just to get round, then a marathon is really pretty easy. If you can run at all and you don't care how long it takes, covering twenty six miles on foot is not a problem.

To digress for a moment; I happened across something in the British running magazine 'Running Fitness' recently that summed up the complete change in attitudes to marathons, between the time that only serious competitive runners entered them, and the present 'anyone-have-a-go' marathon scene, as perfectly as anything could. It was the first sentence of John Brewer's 'Home Brew' column. John Brewer is a professor of sport and, at one time, was director of the Lilleshall Sports Injury and Human Performance Centre. By chance I ran alongside John for nearly three laps of the 2011 Finchley 20, the very last twenty mile road race I ever ran. He was most agreeable company.

To quote from John's column, *'I was contacted recently by the BBC who asked me whether it was possible to run a marathon without doing any training.'* I assume that John hadn't made this up. The question falls into the same category as one that was asked by a boy at my primary school of a professional horn player who had visited the school to give a recital. For years afterwards the headmaster warned children of asking anything similarly silly; 'Can you play the horn while chewing gum?'

John, being a decent chap, gave the BBC a fair and honest answer, making the very two points that brought me to this. Firstly, and again I quote, *'Consider the facts: a brisk walk at 4mph will cover the distance in six and a half hours.'* I take this to imply that, of course, you can complete the distance without training if that is all you want to do. Secondly, John replied, *'...there is a distinct difference between running a marathon competitively and completing the distance.'* I bet that surprised the BBC.

Before this digression I said that all runners at the start of a marathon are wondering about whether they will finish. It goes without saying that I was thinking only of serious runners, those who line up on the starting line hoping and aiming to run as good a time as possible, trusting that the training they've done and their own quota of natural ability will allow them to maintain the pace they choose, all the way to the end. And, by 'wondering whether they will finish', I don't mean simply reach the finish line, I mean **run** to the finish line. A degree of slowing down still constitutes finishing, but complete collapse and being reduced to a jog, a shuffle, or a walk doesn't count.

This is where the race becomes a guessing game, and the reason I have come to hate the marathon as much as I love it. Success at the distance, assuming the preparation has been done, is all about pace judgement. Every mile has to be run at the pace that is right for you. Get it too fast by a matter of seconds and you will slow down drastically over the last few miles. Get it too slow by the same amount and you will forever afterwards wonder whether you could have run faster. I leave it to you to decide which is preferable.

For my part, I give you what could be called 'a tale of two marathons'. In one I got it very wrong, and suffered the biggest disappointment of my running life. In the other I achieved a major triumph, but also got it wrong; or did I? I shall never know. That is why the marathon is such an enigma.

In the1983 Belfast marathon I had run my lifetime best time, 2:24:24. I didn't do a lot of running the following summer but at the end of August I resumed full training and was already thinking in terms of a faster time in the next Belfast marathon in May 1984. By the middle of January I was starting my real build up towards that date. I followed more or less the same pattern of training as I had done the previous year, as outlined in Chapter 8. If anything the Tuesday sessions were more intense with, for example, six or seven hard efforts of between three and four minutes. The Saturday fartlek runs were also harder. Typically, on Saturday, I would cover sixteen, mainly uphill, flat out efforts of at least a quarter of a mile each. I was also doing more long runs, and adding a couple of miles to the longest. A typical week would see me running sixteen miles on a Wednesday and twenty three on a Sunday. This was the year when, starting on Monday12th March, I managed my biggest ever week's mileage, 94 miles in seven sessions. This was achieved primarily by running 23 miles on Wednesday and 25 on Sunday. In short, between January and May I did more and better training than at any time in my life. I averaged 76 miles per week and did 25 runs of fifteen or more miles with twelve of them over twenty.

It worked! I retained my place in the Northern Ireland team for the World's Cross Country Championships in March by finishing eighth in the selection race. The local press headlined the report of the race and the selection process, 'Old hands make New York trip.' (I was 37 at the time). The trip itself was an experience. I would not have missed it, but it came as an unwelcome interruption to my training for the marathon. Then, in April I ran 14:37 for a 5,000m road race, and 8:45 for a track 3,000m. Fast times (for me) over short distances have always been a good indication of my state of fitness. By the time of the Belfast marathon I was in the form of my life and I knew it. I could feel it in every part of my body.

That's where it all started to go wrong. Had I lined up on May 7th for a 10K race or a ten miler or a half marathon, I feel sure I would have set a personal best. When you run any of these distances it doesn't matter too much if you go too fast at the start. You soon realise the mistake, take a bit of a breather and continue just that tiny bit slower. As the miles go by you run continuously at the fastest pace you can hold without falling into oxygen debt. You teeter on the edge of too fast, but never contemplate deliberately slowing down because you might not be able to hold that pace for the whole distance. If you do slip over the edge briefly, maybe on an uphill stretch or in overtaking someone, you simply recover and, seconds later, get back to the business of running as fast as you can.

A marathon cannot be like that. Anyone who adopted the same approach, the all out from the start approach, the run as fast as the body will allow approach, would be lucky to reach half way without ending in a heap. Even before the gun fires a marathon runner has to reach a decision; how fast to run? I had always believed in running as I felt and letting my runner's instinct dictate the pace. That was the problem. I felt good, far too good. It was my undoing.

Looking back I think I could have run around 2:23 that day, possibly a little faster. That would have meant a pace of just under five and a half minutes per mile. I should have made that calculation before the race and stuck to it. I knew I could maintain five and a half minute mile pace for the full distance, because that's what I'd done the previous year. Even just one second per mile less would have reduced my best time by almost half a minute.

But I felt so good! I ran as far as half way with the leading group, mostly, in my childlike enthusiasm, at the head of the leading group, not at just under five and a half minute per mile pace but at nearer to five and a quarter minute per mile pace. It was so easy, and so exhilarating. As the miles went by I didn't see any reason to do anything other than more of the same. At half way I broke away and was followed only by the eventual winner. We led the rest of the field by about a hundred yards. At fifteen to sixteen miles he overtook me and drew away. I wasn't slowing; he had speeded up. At the finish, for him, the clock showed 2:18. From then on, once he was gone, for the next five miles the course was mainly uphill. I began to find the pace a little less easy, but only because of the gradient. I still felt fine. I passed the twenty mile point in what was the fastest I had ever run for that distance, 1:46:05. That's still sub 5:20 mile pace, potentially around 2:20 for the full marathon.

I hadn't begun to slow noticeably and, although I knew that I would begin to slow in due course, I was still quite confident of a personal best time. A mile later that confidence had gone. I began to struggle. The eventual second placed runner came by, and I could do nothing about it. I forget, or prefer to forget, the next five miles. I know that the distance from twenty miles to the finish took me nearly fifty minutes. For much of that time I was almost within sight of the end, immobilised by cramp, just as I had been when I ran my very first marathon on the Isle of Wight. My finishing place and time? Twenty third in 2:34:21.

I ran every day for the next eight days, including a 'quite brisk' ten miles on Wednesday, just two days after the race, and a track 3,000m in 8:40 on Saturday. Physically I was practically unaffected by the marathon, but mentally I was shattered. Emotionally it was like the end of a passionate love affair. I had invested everything. I had hoped for so much. For nearly two hours I had felt on top of the world and then, in the space of two miles, I had lost it all. The thing I loved so much had gone and was never coming back. I carried on running for another three weeks, more out of habit than for any other reason, like a headless chicken, flapping its wings. Then I more or less gave up running for four months. What was the point?

I learned from that bitter experience that marathons cannot be run with the heart and the body alone. The head is also involved. Less than ten seconds per mile too quick - that's no more than three percent- is all it takes to turn potential success into disaster. Never mind how easy it feels, if it's too fast on paper, it's too fast. You won't notice the effect of too fast a pace creeping up on you until it's too late. Proper pace estimation is a fine calculation, but one that marathon runners ignore at their peril.

This is, as I said, a tale of two marathons. The second was also the Belfast race, the 1987 version. In June 1986 I became a veteran. In those days a veteran runner was anyone over the age of forty. Now you only have to be 35, and are called a master runner rather than a veteran. I prefer the former state of affairs. In June that year there was to be an international veterans team challenge marathon, held in conjunction with the Potteries marathon in Stoke on Trent. I decided that I would set my sights on that race as my target for the year and that I would use the Belfast marathon as a practice run to test my form and, I hoped, to give me confidence for what I saw as the main event. It was four years since I had run my best time for the distance and three years since my last marathon outing, the same very disappointing race that I've just described. I was nearer 41 than 40. Nevertheless I had noticed no decline in my running. Life and training continued as if time had stood still. On 11th April I had been first vet home in the Pearl Assurance half marathon in Belfast in 68:35. I was running well.

For the Belfast race I teamed up with a friend of mine who was, or had been, about the same standard as me and we agreed, at my suggestion, to run 5:40 miles. That was a pace I knew I would be able to keep up without difficulty and with the prospect of being able to finish the race without slowing down, for a time around 2:30. If I accomplished that, I would be well set for a marathon a month later in a time a few minutes quicker. That was the plan.

Strangely, it's not in the least bit difficult, provided there isn't a strong wind and the course is not very hilly, to run to a set pace, within a certain comfortable range, almost to the second. We ticked off 5:40 miles like two well oiled and calibrated machines until ten miles (56:10). At that point I felt my friend having some trouble keeping up, so I continued without him, 5:40 miles to 15 miles (1:24:20), 5:40 miles to 20 miles (1:53:20). I was all on my own (the field was particularly thin that year) and it was as if I was on a long, lone training run. It felt just the same as that, no pressure, no stress, just comfortable, smooth, rhythmic, enjoyable running; tick-tock, tick-tock, this is easy, this is nice!

At twenty miles I had a discussion with myself. I had achieved what I had set out to do. I had proved that I was well capable of running around two and a half hours, even though I still had six miles to go. I knew I had that much running still in me. I could sense it as surely as a car's petrol gauge can show how much fuel is left in the tank. I was as full of running as at the start of the race. Why keep the brakes on?

I pretended I was just starting a 10,000m race, and let go. If I recall one thing on my death bed it will be the last six miles of that marathon. I ran as fast as I could, not as fast as I dared, but as fast as I could. A cyclist came alongside and kept me company for a mile or two. Otherwise I was alone. There was no one behind me that I knew about and, even if there had been, he wouldn't have been able to keep up. I couldn't see anyone ahead, though I half expected to do so at any moment. With the finish line in sight I was sprinting. I could have gone on. I had run the stretch from twenty miles to the finish, the same stretch that had taken me nearly 50 minutes three years previously, in 32:38. My finish time was 2:25:58, which was and for all I know still is a Northern Ireland veterans' record.

Had I blown a golden opportunity? Had I run too conservatively early on and right through to three quarter distance, and thereby sacrificed my chance of an even better time? I have no idea. All I do know is that, taking what was for me a calculated safe pace of five and a half minutes per mile as a starting point, ten seconds per mile less led to failure on a grand scale while ten seconds per mile more led to success, yes, but also to questions that could never be answered and to an almost equal sense of frustration.

In any belief system, code of ethics, or principle of fairness, it cannot be right that it is possible to reach a point a long way before the finish of a marathon when you can't run any longer but neither is it right that you can finish a marathon with running still left in reserve. Ideally you should expend your last iota of energy and hit the wall just as you cross the finish line. The finish line and the wall should be in exactly the same place. To run the perfect marathon you have either to be very lucky or have so much experience and knowledge of your own capabilities that you know exactly what pace to run at. Only if you are exceptionally lucky and are not like other runners can you take a marathon, quite literally, in your stride, treating it like any other race, knowing that in turn it will treat you no worse than any other race. No wonder you can get to hate the marathon. The worst thing is that it takes about two hours of running to discover whether your pre-race guess-work regarding pace was right or wrong. That's a long time before finding out that you've made a mistake, especially when it's too late to do anything about it. Daft, cruel and unforgiving, that's the marathon.

How did I get on in the Potteries marathon? On Monday 1st June, two weeks before the race, I set out for my last preparatory long run. No more than half a mile down the road I felt a pain in my foot. The foot is like a bone necklace that has become impossibly and intricately tangled. There are so many joints and threads and sinews in it, and the stress on it during running is so forceful that it is a wonder that it doesn't get hurt more often. Because my long run was so important, or so I thought, I ignored the pain and did as I had planned, twenty miles at a steady pace. It was madness. My foot didn't stop hurting until the beginning of December.

But I kept up the training, despite the pain, and finished the Potteries marathon in 2:30:00. It was only the second time I had ever run a marathon and still had plenty left at the end, only this time it was the injury rather than a deliberate decision on my part that stopped me running too fast early on. It merely confirmed that a comfortable pace is the secret to fending off the wall. But, still, to finish a marathon with something in reserve seemed almost as big a disappointment as not finishing at all. Of the twenty or so marathons I've ever completed I don't think I was happy with a single one.

When I look back now, nearly thirty years later, to the best marathon I never ran, the one that swallowed up all my greatest hopes, the first of this tale of two marathons, strange as it may seem, I have no regrets. I think I know what I might have done that day. I certainly found out what I obviously couldn't do that day. I couldn't run 2:20. I think I could have run about 2:23, maybe even 2:22. Sometimes to know what you can't do is as gratifying as knowing what you can and to find out what that is you have to take risks. I'm glad now that I once did.

Things have changed in the last twenty or thirty years. At the front of marathon races fewer runners seem to blow up dramatically, even when running times that are considerably faster than the best times from my day. Most élite marathon runners have run world class times for ten thousand metres. Many championship and big city marathons are won with a real race over the last six miles or so, rather than by the best survivor. I see a lot of runners striding to the finish in the same way I had done in Belfast in 1987, but much faster. I see very few runners at the head of the field finishing in a truly distressed state. I can suggest what has changed: professionalism, better training, better coaching, more research, better support, new nations supplying more runners; there are a number of possibilities. I don't intend to pursue them here.

In Britain little has changed. Steve Jones still holds the British marathon record, after nearly thirty years. He proved in the 1986 European Championship marathon that even the very best can hit the wall if they misjudge the pace. The tendency now is for the majority of runners in the big, mass entry marathons, to aim for nothing more than to finish the distance. Over-ambition is, therefore, less commonly seen. Runners are more scared of a bad experience and of not finishing than they are of not doing themselves justice. I said before that distance runners of my generation had a healthy disrespect for the marathon. I still think that's true, but they also understood it. It's not just a feat to be accomplished, like climbing Mount Everest. There are no prizes just for doing it. It's a race. What makes it unlike distance races of shorter duration is that to do it well requires a special aptitude that runners possess to different degrees. The history of marathon running in this country and worldwide has been, like the history of training, one of discovery. Who has that special aptitude and who doesn't? Not me, I'm afraid.

CHAPTER 11
The World Cross Country Championships

*'I am pleased to send warmest greetings to participants in the
XII International Amateur Athletic Federation's World Cross
Country Championships. You have my very best wishes for an
enjoyable contest.'*

President Ronald Reagan; introduction to the programme
for the 1984 New York staging of the event.

There are certain events on the world distance running calendar that accurately reflect the history of the sport, record its progress, and show the shifts in predominance from individual to individual and from nation to nation. There are the famous international marathons that were held each year long before the new generation of commercialised big city marathons: the Boston, the Fukuoka, the Kosice, the Enschede, the Karl Max Stadt, the Polytechnic, the Manchester Maxol marathon, to name a few of them. Then there are the Olympic Games and, more recently, the Athletics World Championships and, of lesser importance because of their restricted participation, the Commonwealth Games (originally the British Empire Games), the Pan American Games and the European Games and, in my view, the most revealing of the lot, the World Cross Country Championships. I consider it the most revealing for at least three reasons. It is an annual event rather than a four yearly or biennial one (though it may soon be biennial), it focuses on distance running and nothing else and it is very much a team event, giving every country the chance to show its strength in depth in different age groups, as well as the very best of its complement of male and female runners.

The title World Cross Country Championships came into being in 1973 when the IAAF (International Association of Athletics Federations) took on the administration of what had, since 1903, been the International Cross Country Championships. Effectively, the event remained the same, though it drew its competitors from a much wider range of countries. Today the word 'World' in the title is unarguable but in its early days the International Championships involved very few teams. For many years it could hardly even have justified the title of European, let alone World Cross Country Championships. It should, more accurately, have been called the 'British home countries and one or two European ones Cross Country Championships'. For the first twenty one years only six nations took part. In 1958 the first non European country, Tunisia, entered a team, followed in 1959 by Morocco. South Africa competed in 1962, New Zealand and Algeria in 1965, USA in 1966 and Canada in 1969. By 1981 there were twenty seven countries with full teams competing in the senior men's race. Today the championships has become one of the greatest athletic events of global proportions in modern sport, all the more so for being packed into one day of hectic participation or, since the introduction of the short course events, into just two days of competition. In 2000, when the championships were staged in Vilamoura in Portugal, what was a then record number of 76 nations participated.

And yet in essence the World Cross Country Championships, for all its expansion, betterment and added grandeur, hasn't changed since its origin. This is why I like it, why it shows up modern, synthetic running events for the pretence that they are. Only serious runners take part. Each nation contributes, as far as possible, its best teams. Every race starts from a single starting point and at the blast of a single horn or the shot of a single gun. Every competitor, from the best to the slowest is there simply to run as well as he or she possibly can. With teams from the best running nations in the world and others from the very least significant competing in parallel, inevitably there is a huge difference between first and last, but there is no artificial line separating the élite from the masses. However stretched out the field in any race becomes, however fierce and brilliant the battle for first place and however slowly the back markers plod, it is always a homogeneous affair. Even the TV commentators, in the absence of much else to talk about, have to resort to drawing their inspiration from the races themselves, none of which, they discover, perhaps to their surprise, are different in kind from any pure distance running competition. The world event is a sort of throwback to running as it used to be.

My own association with the World Cross Country Championships and its predecessor, the International Cross Country, covers the whole range of possibilities: devotee, historian, spectator on the course and via the media, participant (I ran in three WCCC's) and finally, course steward, when the event came to Belfast in 1999. That is why this chapter has a place in what is supposed to be a personal history of the sport of distance running in Britain. The championships have been a part of my own running history, from inspiration, to high point, to fond memory. They remain for me a gratifying reassurance that the sport of distance running is still out there, as pure as it was in 1980, 1970, 1960, and before.

When the International Cross Country Championships came to Barry in Wales in 1967, I had my first experience of the event in the flesh. I and my girl friend, now my wife, and a couple of friends drove to the venue, parked somewhere and walked on to the course. It was that simple. OK, it was 1967 and for all its importance within the sport it was still quite a minor event in overall sporting terms. It was no first division football match or international rugby game. There was no entry fee for spectators nor any restriction on access to the course. Security was a concept that had not yet been invented. I remember wandering about amongst the runners as they warmed up for the main event. My wife asked Ron Hill for his autograph. 'It'll be a pleasure,' he said.

When the race was in progress we stood on one side of a tape or a rope, I forget which, while the runners passed by the other. It was just as it had been when, aged five, I had seen Jim Peters run in the Finchley twenty. A group of runners would race by, the ground vibrating to their footfalls. Their breath would break the air beside my face, drops of sweat sparkled momentarily, an occasional grunt or gasp rang out, a fleck of phlegm flew past, a spray of liquid mud, a fragment of turf, all so close, for a moment we were part of it. For me it was nothing new, and yet it was. This was no ordinary event. This was the greatest cross country race in the world that year and running in it were many of the greatest cross country runners of the time. Barry was one of the four International Cross Country Championships that was won by the Belgian, Gaston Roelants. Oddly all four of his wins were on British soil: Sheffield in 1962, here in Barry in 1967, in Clydebank, Scotland, 1969, and in Cambridge, in 1972. Second at Barry was the English runner, Tim Johnston. Ron Hill finished 11th.

I have watched a lot of cross country races. I have run in many more. They are all inspiring, but this one was more so. I was just approaching the point in my running life when I was on the verge of becoming serious about the sport. I was at an extremely impressionable stage. Watching the cream of the world's runners at close quarters was a very potent stimulus.

Strangely, watching some of the world's more ordinary runners was also stimulating, perhaps, in some ways, even more so. As Roelants passed by me at Barry, for the first and subsequent times, his running fast and graceful, then as his followers came by in turn, successively less and less fast and graceful, I built up an overall view of the range of running ability on display, a continuum of running performance, from best to, if not worst, then to very much less than best. This is something only a spectator can have - a total view. When you are competing in a race, especially a big one like the World Cross Country Championship or the English National Cross Country Championship, you are aware only of what's going on immediately around you. The leaders could be two or three minutes ahead, and might as well be in a different race altogether. Behind you is somewhere you never look in any case. Even as you finish you have no idea what has happened in the race as a whole, only that you just managed to outsprint the man who might have been Swiss or maybe Danish (I have a red and white vest that I swapped for my own Northern Ireland team vest after one of the World Cross Country races that I ran and I'm still not sure which country it's from) and that you were probably somewhere between two hundredth and three hundredth. It's almost as if you haven't experienced a race at all.

The spectator, meanwhile, has seen the whole thing, displayed as a series of significant moments, like a comic strip. It's a much better way to see a race and gives a far better understanding of what is going on. I deplore the modern tendency to film distance races for TV viewing by following the leaders with a camera car. It may get good close up shots of the more famous runners and the right atmosphere of cutthroat competition and all out effort, but it leaves the viewer with absolutely no idea of what's happening in the rest of the race.

As I watched the Barry field pass me on what may have been the last lap, long after Gaston Roelants and Tim Johnston and the other top placers had gone by, my inspiration changed from straightforward admiration of excellence to what could be called the inspiration of negativity. In simple terms some of the runners (yes, even in the International Cross Country Championship) were, or looked, so bad that there had to be hope for me. Surely I could become at least that good one day? I remember in particular a tall man with an odd, leaning forward and slightly sideways running style coming by. To reach where I was standing he had to mount a slight rise. For him it seemed to be the last straw. As he drew alongside me he almost stopped. Only his forward lean kept him moving and on to the downhill part. His whole body was as white as his vest and shorts, and he gasped in air with a ghostly moan. I wondered if he ever made it to the finish line. Yet for all his apparent poverty as a runner at that moment, he became as much my inspiration from then on as did Roelants himself. Years later in Northern Ireland I met and ran with and became friendly with a tall man about ten or fifteen years older than me. At one time he had been one of the best runners in Northern Ireland and a very good marathon runner. There was something a little familiar about his running style. Could he have been? No, that would be too much of a coincidence.

The World Cross Country Championships, to this day, are almost unique amongst great sporting events in accommodating both the very best and the more mediocre together, simultaneously in the selfsame competition. I know this from personal experience. The three times I ran in the Worlds: in Gateshead in 1983, New York in 1984, and Neuchatel, Switzerland in 1986, I was respectively 202nd, 186th and 247th. I ran well in those races. I am proud of all three performances, despite being behind the eventual winner to the tune of a good four minutes on each occasion. I couldn't have expected to be any closer.

In Gateshead I ran with a slight injury, a sharp pain in the foot but, by ignoring it, I managed to finish ahead of some of my own Northern Ireland team mates. On paper I should not have done, but I did. In New York, paper proved accurately prophetic, and I was beaten by every single British runner bar one. I won't name that man. He deserves better treatment. Two years later, at more or less the same time as I did, he entered the veteran's ranks, and was instantly by far the best veteran distance runner in Britain, beating me soundly in several races. I think he must have had an uncharacteristically bad run in the New York World Cross Country. In other words, by rights, I should have been the last placed British runner in that race. Yet, still, I ran well. I did more than that. I ran very well, probably as well as in any other race in my life. I accepted that I was the slowest of the Northern Irish contingent, which meant that I was automatically the slowest of all the British team representatives, and it didn't bother me. All I could do was to run as well as I possibly could, which I did. As someone's school report once said, 'I regret to say that your son has achieved his potential'.

Only by moving to Northern Ireland in 1978 did I get the chance of competing in the World CCC. That's not why I moved there but it was certainly one of the perks. I might have made the English team at one time had it been expanded to about a hundred members, but at the normal number of nine, with one travelling reserve, there was never the remotest chance of my ever getting into it. In England I was a small fish. In Northern Ireland I was in a small pond. That's the only reason I became a Northern Ireland international but never an English or British international. The difference in population size between the two countries was immediately a terrific spur to my running. I started to be well placed in races. I even won the odd race. I read my name more often in the local press. There were one or two newspaper features about me. When I made the team for the WCCC for the last time in 1976 the Belfast Sunday News carried a piece entitled 'Eddie caught out', about the fact that I had had to cancel a fishing trip because I was unexpectedly selected for the Northern Ireland team for the Neuchatel WCCC. The feature, a real space filler if ever there was one, almost amounted to my life story.

My change of domicile, my move to Northern Ireland and what emanated from it, taught me a lot about motivation. Trying to make the international team, by itself, became a reason to train especially hard and diligently. In England it would have been a laughably unrealistic goal for me to aim to make the international team. And no one, except perhaps a fool, strives for an unrealistic goal. Even in Northern Ireland, for the first five years before I had really settled down, I didn't see myself getting into the international team and didn't, therefore, make it one of my prime objectives. Only when I realised that it was a realistic aim did I train towards it. Then, each time I made the team and ran in the World Championships, I focused on a private race between me and the other Northern Irish runners. That way I could put my performance in a context I understood, and not be demoralised by being beaten by a large margin by some of the world's best runners, or submerged in a seemingly infinitely sized field of runners to the point of meaninglessness as I had been in my only outing in the English National Cross Country Championships.

This approach worked well in my last appearance in the World Championships, in 1986, in Switzerland. Again, on paper, I was the slowest of the team, but I ended up fifth finisher and would have been fourth Northern Irish runner had one of my team mates not found a little extra speed in the last fifty yards. I was especially pleased with that run. I was thirty nine years old and it proved to me that not only was I running as well as ever but that I had retained my tendency to run well on the big occasions. It has always been a puzzle to me why anyone should do anything other than rise to the occasion. I tend to think that, unless there is some good physical reason, it should be impossible for anyone to have a so called bad run. I proved this to myself several times, with unbroken strings of good performances in cross country and road races. I still believe that with the right mind set there is no excuse for not reaching one's potential in races and that the more important the race, the better one performs. Nevertheless a lot of runners do 'freak out' on the big occasion. The fact that they do and I don't has always been a factor in my favour.

Watching the Barry race had been a great inspiration to me and so was the next International event at which I was a spectator. In 1976 the championships again came to Wales, to the hilly turf of Chepstow race course. I went to that event dressed in running gear, to watch the races and follow them from point to point, completing my day's training in the process. My inspiration on this occasion, something that stayed with me for years after and can, to this day, spring to my mind and immediately refresh memories of that wonderful running decade, came from seeing a small and quite beautiful man from Portugal dominate the senior men's field. His name was Carlos Lopes, and he was just at the start of his long and prodigious career at the top of world distance running. Because his win was so unexpected (even I, who thought I followed athletics closely, had never heard of him) it was that much more impressive. It was not unlike Ian Thompson's victory in the 1973 Harlow marathon for its inspirational value.

Lopes went on to win two more World Cross Country Championships, at New York in 1984, and in Lisbon in 1985. But he will be best remembered for his Olympic marathon gold medal from the Los Angeles games of 1984, and for his silver medal in the Montreal Olympic 10,000m in 1976. For a brief period in 1985 he held the world's best time for a marathon, having run 2:07:12 in Rotterdam.

If I were asked to name the best distance runner of the 1980s I would um and ah for a while and probably answer, 'Carlos Lopes'. I would admit to a certain bias but I would be perfectly willing to justify my choice. The bias would come partly from my experience of first seeing the man dominate the Chepstow WCCC race. If I say it was love at first sight I trust my meaning will not be misinterpreted. He ran as I had always wanted to run, as I sometimes imagined I was running, effortlessly and perfectly. For a small man he had a seemingly immense stride. That was because he bounced off the ground rather than pushing off it, raising both arms on short downhill stretches like wings, as if he was about to fly, then ascending the hills as if, perhaps, he really could.

Then, to add to my bias, there were a number of small coincidences that sometimes made me think that Lopes had been especially provided as my own personal inspiration. He and I were born within eight months of each other. We made big breakthroughs in the same year, 1976, and both continued to run at our best well into our thirties. Lopes was 37 at the time of his Olympic marathon win. I was the same age, less a month, when I ran my best time for the distance. When I first competed in the World Cross Country Championships at Gateshead, Lopes was second. The following year he won the race and autographed a programme for me. I am not normally an autograph hunter, but seeing him in the hospitality suite after the race and imaging this fanciful link between us, I couldn't resist asking.

Lopes always ran as I believed a runner should do, making a big effort long before the final few hundred yards. He was a front runner, as I always tried to be, even when he didn't win. In the marathon at the Los Angeles Olympics he broke away with a mile or two to run and came in well clear of John Treacy of Ireland and Britain's Charlie Spedding. At Montreal, in the 10,000m final, he led for the last two or three miles of the race and managed to beat Brendan Foster for the silver medal, but failed to stay ahead of Lasse Viren. But what an admirable effort, worth ten times more than following like a shadow on the off chance of winning with a sprint finish.

Lopes was the last European to win the WCCC, apart from the Moroccan born and nationalised by marriage Belgian runner,

Mohammed Mourit. Lopes represented the end of an era and the beginning of a new age of world distance running, an age which very quickly became totally dominated by African runners and remains so to this day, with no likelihood of any change in the foreseeable future.

Around the same time that Lopes was winning his last WCCC title, England's standing in international cross country declined very rapidly. In 1976, at Chepstow, when Lopes won so dramatically, England's Tony Simmons was second and England won the team event. They did so again in 1979 and 1980. In 1982 in Rome and 1987, in Warsaw, England could still manage to win silver medals in the men's team event, but between those two years the best England could do was 6th. The following year, 1988, the four home countries were no longer able to enter separately but competed as a combined United Kingdom team. With what should have been added strength, the new team managed second place in 1989 (Stavanger, Norway) and third in 1992 (Boston). Since then the men's team has never been in any of the medal positions and has often failed to get in the first ten teams.

I don't think I could have been very much inspired by any of the latter day WCCCs, certainly by none that took place after 1990. Part of my inspiration from watching the race at Chepstow was dependent on my ability to relate to runners I knew of and who came from places I knew. Even though Lopes would be my abiding memory from that day and my main inspiration, the fact that he beat Tony Simmons into second place had a lot to do with it. Tony Simmons was the man, you may recall, who won the best ten mile race I ever ran. I didn't know him personally but it was not difficult to imagine that under different circumstances he might, perhaps, have been at the same school as me or lived in the same town or run for the same club. I had been to school not far from Luton.

As long as England did well in the WCCC there seemed to be some link to my own ambitions. As long as English runners (and I still was one at that time) could mix it with the best in the world, they retained the ability, not just to inspire, but to add realism to inspiration. True inspiration has to retain a dose of truth and a modicum of hope. England's last team win was in 1980. After that it became very difficult for any British runners to gain inspiration that was wholly or partly based on national identity.

England's history in the WCCC is second to none. Between 1903 and 1973, in which year the International Cross Country Championships became the World CCC, England won the men's team title 43 times out of 60, and provided the individual champion on 35 occasions. Most of those victories could be explained on the basis that there were so few countries competing but by the time England won the International CCC for the last time before the fixture transformed itself into the World CCC, this explanation was wearing a bit thin. Up to the beginning of the 1980s England was, quite simply, the best cross country running nation in the world. Another small European country, Belgium, might have had a claim to that title but, on balance, England wins.

Quite why Belgium was, for many years, along with Great Britain, such a premier cross country running nation is a mystery to me. France was almost Belgium's equal but lacked consistency and didn't have stars of the calibre of Gaston Roelants, Karel Lismont, Eric de Beck and Leon Schots. But where were Germany, Italy, and the Scandinavian countries, to mention but a few? It is odd how one country can build up a reputation for doing something particularly well and keep that tradition going over decades for no apparent reason other than habit.

The inauguration of the WCCC, the same event as previously but with a new name and new management, initiated a somewhat delayed revolution in cross country running. Whether the name change simply mirrored something that was about to happen or whether a more overtly global approach to what had been a very European sport brought about the change is hard to say. For a few years, really until 1981, things carried on in a superficially similar way. The cognoscenti of the sport might have noticed some odd events, like sun spots auguring a storm: New Zealand winning the men's team race in 1975 in Rabat, Morocco and an American (Craig Virgin) winning the race in 1980 in Paris and again the next year in Madrid, for example. But these small details were insignificant compared to what was about to happen.

In 1981, two years before I first took part in the WCCC, with a record number up to that time of 39 countries competing, the men's team championship was won by Ethiopia. Ethiopia went on to win the next four men's team championships. Only England in her heyday could previously claim five victories on the trot. It was the start of the complete ownership of cross country running on the world scene by the East African nations. Ethiopia arrived at the party first and was then joined by Kenya. The two of them simply took over the house, filled the rooms and shared all the glory, hardly letting anyone else through the door.

I don't intend here to attempt to go into the reasons for the African takeover of all distance running events, track, road and cross country. To me the prime reason, and I say reason in the singular on purpose, is glaringly obvious, but I shall leave its discussion until the relevant chapter (Chapter 15). For the time being let the facts speak for themselves.

Between 1981 and 2011 (there was no event in 2012) every single men's WCCC team competition has been won by either Ethiopia or Kenya. During those years, in 23 out of the 31 of them, the individual winner of the men's long course race has come from one or other of the same two countries. Only two of the other eight winners were not of African descent. They were Craig Virgin of the USA in 1981 and the afore-mentioned Carlos Lopes in 1984 and 1985. Khalid Skah who won in 1990 and 1991 is Moroccan, Mohammed Mourhit (2000 and 2001), though running for Belgium, is Moroccan born and Zersenay Tadese, winner in 2007, is Eritrean. I would guess that such domination of any sport to which every nation in the world has equal access by just two countries (and where they failed then the holes in their domination being patched by others from the same continent) is unique. Kenya is the more dominant of the two, having beaten Ethiopia to the team title 24 times to 7. Domination to that extent by a single country in a sport that requires no apparatus, no facilities, no elaborate kit, no specialist nor difficult to acquire skills, no obscure tradition, no access to the sea or freshwater, to snow or mountains, no large source of finance, in fact nothing other than men and women with legs and feet, is not just unique. It is other-worldly. No wonder it has spawned a whole industry of hypothesis and investigation. What makes the Kenyans and Ethiopians such good runners? I know, but I don't think anyone else really wants to. The story and the theories it generates, not to mention the messages it sends, each with its attached moral, are far too good to be brought to an end with an answer.

The East African dominance is equally true in road running and in distance races on the track, but it is most obvious in cross country. It is the WCCC, more than any other event that has brought it to such a point of undeniability. It is not uncommon to see a leading group in one of the WCCC races of perhaps two or three dozen runners that includes the whole Kenyan team and, quite likely the whole Ethiopian team as well. It is the sheer numbers in a cross country race, and the tight packing of smaller but still large numbers at the head of the field, that makes the phenomenon so clear. The greatest number of runners from one country that can be seen in, for example, the leading group in an Olympic 10,000m, or even a major games marathon, is three. Perhaps the nearest thing to the display seen in the WCCC of numbers of Kenyan or Ethiopian runners in the leading group, with the odd Ugandan, Eritrean, Tanzanian or Djibutian thrown in, comes in the big city road races. And then, usually, three of them are pace makers!

The East African takeover of the WCCC in particular has had some profound and unforeseen effects. For me it has been nothing but magnificent. My love of running extends no further than to run as well as I can myself, irrespective of the opposition, and to admire the best runners I can possibly get to see. If all those runners come from one or two countries I'm not in the least bit put off. My only complaint, which I'm sure I share with most aficionados of the sport, is that it does get a bit boring. Even I have to admit that a running race is not just a display of excellence. It draws at least some of its interest value, and most of its ability to excite, from the element of uncertainty. Let the best man and the best team win, by all means, but let there be some variety of identity of the winners.

Soon after the finish of the Tokyo Olympics what is reckoned to be one of the best films made of any sporting event went on general release. It was Kon Ichikawa's 1965 film 'Tokio Olympiad'. I rushed to see it, of course. I think it was showing at the Harrow Dominion but I can't be certain. There were about half a dozen cinemas within easy reach of where I lived at that time, in the suburbs of northwest London: the Granada, also in Harrow, the Langham in Pinner, the Gaumont, later to become the Odeon, in Rayners Lane, the Embassy in North Harrow, the Ideal in Eastcote, to name only the ones I remember. They were all wonderful examples of flamboyant thirties architecture, many of them thankfully still preserved, though not for the same purpose they were built. I visited them all on many occasions.

I mention the film here because it constituted my visual introduction to the man I consider to be the first of the great African distance runners to star on the world stage, namely marathon second time Olympic winner, Abebe Bikila. I suppose, strictly, the first African runner of note who achieved global recognition and medals at international level was Alain Mimoun, winner for France of the 1956 Olympic marathon in Melbourne, Australia. Mimoun was Algerian by birth and, therefore, as African, in the continental sense of the word, as any Kenyan or Ethiopian. But, in the context of the present superiority of East African running nations, Abebe Bikila remains the undoubted precursor.

I suppose you could say, therefore, that, as I watched Bikila in Ichikawa's film in 1965, I was getting a glimpse into the future of distance running. And, more than forty years later, as I get my annual dose of the WCCC, or watch one of the big city marathons, I am seeing more or less the same thing, men and women who are made to run doing what they do best, with grace and ease, and in the process showing anyone who might be watching that runners of their type, from their part of the world, have no equal and probably never will have.

Ichikawa made good use of slow motion, whether it was in filming the raindrops bouncing off the track on the morning preceding Lynn Davies' long jump win, or Bob Hayes getting to his blocks in the 100m final, or the sweat dripping off Abebe Bikila's nose and chin during the marathon. Bikila was filmed in profile, running from left to right. His head filled the screen. He cast worried glances at the camera for its invasion of his privacy. He held his head drooping slightly as if it was an effort to keep it upright. So when he looked sideways he also looked upwards, the look of someone who doesn't want to be scrutinised. The filming was almost too intimate, too close and too revealing. His mouth hung slightly open, the lower lip projecting and vibrating slowly with his rhythmic breathing. That's when the sweat drops fell, to a rhythm of their own. It is said that Ichikawa kept the focus of his film more on the atmosphere of the games, and the human side of the athletes. If this was indeed his purpose, then he very much succeeded. To one extremely impressionable nineteen year old it was a life-lasting stimulant, this glimpse into the very being of a great runner.

When the film rebounded into normal speed with a crash of noise, the true pace of Bikila's running appeared. It was a surprise and a revelation. The ponderous yet balletic slow motion suddenly burst into the pitter-patter rhythm of effortless five minute miling. Bikila was in a class above his opposition in that race, finishing more than four minutes ahead of the field and setting a new Olympic record and world's best time. And, just to prove that there's no truth in the saying that no one remembers who's second, it was Basil Heatley of Great Britain. Third was Kokichi Tsuburaya, running on home ground, who four years later committed suicide. The idea that the reason for his suicide was the shame of being overtaken by Heatley in the Olympic stadium, in his own country in front of thousands of his own countrymen with little more than a hundred yards left to run, turned out to be sufficiently attractive to make it so in popular mythology, though life, or in this case death, is rarely that simple.

I don't know whether Abebe Bikila ever ran in any international cross country races. I don't think so and it doesn't matter in any case.

His only relevance in this chapter is that whenever I watch superlative running from the East African nations I remember that piece of film and get the same kick as I did then. Perhaps the nearest I got to being so thrilled by one person's running was when Sammy Wanjiru became the first Kenyan runner to win the Olympic marathon in Beijing in 2008. It was the uninhibited nature of his running as much as the end result that was so impressive, what seemed much too fast a pace on a hot day, with the half way point reached in 1:02:34. But then, perhaps more impressive still, was Wanjuri's strength in the last two miles. He showed no signs of slowing down, when to do so would have lost him the race. I shall never tire of being thrilled by what seem almost super-human demonstrations of running talent, and I suspect that in future they will all come from runners of African origin. I have no complaints about that.

If the rise of the East Africans had nothing but stimulating effects on me, the same cannot be said of its effects on others. I have no doubt that the onset of a virtual monopoly of major distance running events by an endless supply of lean, elegant, magnificent runners from Kenya, Ethiopia and a few other African nations knocked the stuffing out of British running, and did the same for the sport in most European countries. When it happened, running had already become a global business. It was no longer good enough, either for individuals or for national federations for runners from a particular country to be good by local standards. It was only worthwhile to be the best in the world. And the Africans had made that no longer possible. For non-African runners and running organisations it had the same effect as Amundsen's flag at the South Pole had had on Captain Scott and his team. What was the point anymore?

Mark Butler, BBC Sport athletics statistician, reporting on the 2010 WCCC in Bydgoszcz, Poland, put it well. *'In recent years the number of European entrants has declined and only 18 out of 50 eligible European countries competed this year despite the championships being staged in the heart of the continent.'* And later, *'It seems that this dominance* (of the African nations) *is alienating the rest of the world when it comes to entering a championship,'*. He added, in agreement with my view, *'but nothing should detract from the quality of the winning performance, even if the victorious nations are somewhat predictable.'* and continued with the mirror image of my own thinking, *'I would argue that a man like Kenya's Joseph Ebuya* (the senior men's long race winner that year) *has risen from poverty to become world champion at the age of 22. This is World Championship competition at its purest, and the sight of masses of Kenyan and Ethiopian vests at the fore of a world-class distance race remains one of the greatest in world sport.'* Amen to that.

The modern era of distance running has created, in non-African countries, an ever decreasing élite of professional runners who can call themselves world class, who can earn a living from running, who can live where they like, who can train whenever and however they like, who are invited to races rather than having to find races that suit them, and can be rewarded with money prizes, sponsorship, advertising revenue and fame. In Britain at any one time there might be a mere one or two, at very most three, such runners of each sex. Why are there so few? Partly because the mass of African runners, who are mostly better than the best non-Africans, has filled the space available, but also because up and coming British runners who could in different circumstances graduate to that élite and who, fifty years ago, when the élite in Britain comprised ten times as many runners, probably would have done, do not see it as a realistic possibility. I don't blame the Africans for any decline in running in our part of the world, not directly. But I do blame the way in which the African dominance, combined with the dubious 'winning is everything, second is nowhere' attitude and the defeatist view, 'if you can't beat them, don't even join them', have taught our runners simply not to bother.

In 1999 the WCCC came to Belfast. It was not the first time that the international event had come to what is now my home city, but it was the first time it had been held there under the present title of World CCC. The International event took place in Belfast in 1910, 1920, 1938 and 1956. In both 1910 and 1920 it was held in the very park, Belvoir Park, no more than half a mile from my front door, where I walk my dogs every morning and where I've run many training miles over the years and competed in one or two races as well.

The course in 1999 was laid out in another Belfast Park, Barnett Demesne, two miles from my house, a very large area of woodland, meadows and traditional suburban parkland: asphalt paths, mown grass, ornamental and native trees, playing fields and masses of bulbs flowering in the spring. The whole area lies on the slope of the north side of the River Lagan valley, so there are some very steep hills. Perhaps so as not to antagonise the runners too much, the course avoided the worst and longest of the hills but still incorporated some short but steep uphill sections and some steeply cambered stretches. Inevitably it was a lap course. With it being essential to design a course for such a prestigious event that can be easily televised, it becomes impossible to have one that is too far-reaching or that cannot be covered by a camera mounted on a moon buggy. That is the real reason that major cross country races, including the one in Barnett Park, are always run over several laps of a course that is rarely much more than a mile and a half in length, and why the runners in Belfast were able to avoid some of the more hilly parts of the park. The senior men's event comprised a starting distance of 460m followed by five laps of 2,308m, giving a total of 12,000m. The women and junior men ran the same starting distance and four slightly shorter laps for 8,012m and the junior women ran one lap less than the senior women and junior men for 4,236m. The two days of competition also included men's and women's short course events, 4,236m in each case. For the most part the running was over the parkland and playing fields rather than the more country areas that were available.

As a rule cross country races these days are so routinely run over playing fields and parks, that I now associate such places with running. As soon as I get anywhere near a large mown area, especially when it has several inches growth of grass on it, I imagine myself running around or across it. Wet grass, soft earth, worm casts, dandelions and plantains, white painted boundary lines and touch lines, and goal posts mean one thing to me - running. Indeed I may actually be running on such a place at the time my mind makes the association, or have run on it at some time in the past. The Belfast WCCC course covered ground that I had trained and raced over many times, and on which I continued to run many more times after the event was over. At a guess I would say that at least three quarters of all cross country races are now run over such ground.

The days of 'real cross country', one lap, or point to point courses, with hedges and ditches to negotiate, rough ground and ploughed fields and hills so steep that they have to be scrambled up, are over. I say good riddance, but many runners wouldn't agree. But, even I, who love the flat firm surface of a tarmac road, have little respect for so called cross country courses that are like slightly untidy running tracks. When I ran in the New York WCCC, at The Meadowlands, the course was a bit like a dust bowl, dry, flat and featureless. To make it a bit more interesting there were some straw-bale and log barriers to hurdle and a man-made hill; you could feel the dirt covered boards vibrating under your feet as you ran up it. It reminded me of those laughable 'outdoor' scenes in old movies that were so obviously shot in the studio.

At least Belfast provided a cross country course that was almost natural. Despite its part managed nature it contained real grass, real mud, real trees and real slopes. The asphalt paths, perhaps the most obvious evidence of human interference, were well covered with thick layers of bark chippings that were still there two days later, having survived the efforts of thousands of pairs of flying feet to destroy them. Paul Tergat of Kenya, the winner of the senior men's race, on the eve of the race, described the Belfast course as *'the toughest I have ever seen'*. It may seem that to run over well kept grassland cannot be tough but, if you had seen the course at the conclusion of all the races you would not have described any part of it as well kept grassland. Even by the end of the first day of racing (the men's long course race was the very last race on the second day) there was barely a blade of grass visible through a continuous mass of wet and sticky mud. Then there were the hills, short certainly, but steep and as muddy as every other part. Parts of the course ran across the slope. Running on a sideways camber can be even more difficult than straight uphill and, incidentally, is an excellent way to get injured. I don't think Tergat was exaggerating. I wouldn't have liked to have run on that course in those conditions.

In a strange way it made me feel quite proud. For the best cross country runner in the world at the time (he had already won the event four times in a row; this was his fifth successive victory) to describe the course in that way was quite a compliment. I thought of it as my course though, of course, it was nothing of the sort. I neither owned it nor had anything to do with choosing or designing the course, but it was my neck of the woods and I knew it as well as anyone there and better than most. I felt as if the England cricket team had turned up to play a test match on my back lawn. Despite the fact that I hate mud and hard cross country courses when running myself, I can appreciate the challenge they present, and was gratified to hear that challenge acknowledged by the world's best.

I had volunteered along with about three hundred and fifty others like me to help with the management of the two days of racing in Belfast. In return we were each equipped with a pair of trainers, navy blue track bottoms, a bright orange hooded top and a T shirt in the same colour, courtesy of Adidas, the sponsors. We had a couple of training days to meet and be instructed in what we were to do as part of the organisation of the races. My specific role, along with two other stewards, was to control the funnel that led the runners as they crossed the finish line in an orderly line to the check-in point. If you have never seen the finish of a big cross country race you won't know what I'm talking about. Let me explain.

As the runners approach the finish line of a race the course widens out so that there is no need for bustling and barging, and one runner is unlikely to impede another. At the finish line itself there is usually about five metres width of space. Even if four or five runners cross the line almost simultaneously it is not difficult for someone to record the numbers on their vests and their finishing order, but mistakes can be made, and a check is needed. So the finishers are ushered into a funnel of tape, so as to keep them in a neat line or queue, in the order they finished. Once trapped in this way, like sheep or cattle going for tagging or worming, in single file in a narrow taped off passageway, their places and numbers can be recorded at relative leisure. Often each runner is handed a numbered disc as a record of the finishing position.

Problems arise when runners are finishing one on top of another at the rate of perhaps one every few seconds. The funnel becomes overloaded and the area just beyond the finishing line begins to resemble a motorway pile up. This is where the clever bit comes in. My job was to swing a piece of rope from one side of the finish line to the other, thus changing a right hand funnel into a left hand funnel. I would let perhaps ten runners into the right hand funnel and then, seeing a gap in the line of runners approaching the finish I would move the tape across to the other side and admit the next dozen or so into the left hand funnel. By distributing the finishers alternately, some to the left and some to the right, we avoided pile-ups and confusion in recording finishing places. Of course now it's all done electronically, but having a back up, human-dependent system is still a necessary belt and braces policy. What a catastrophe it would be, for example, if the chip timing system failed one year in the London marathon.

The 1999 Belfast WCCC confirmed the domination of the Kenyan men about as emphatically as it was possible to do. A Portuguese runner, Paulo Guerra, was third, but he was surrounded by Kenyans. Following Tergat in first place came Tergat's team mates in second, fourth, fifth and sixth. With four to score, Kenya, of course, won the team race with a mere 12 points. It almost defies belief.

Overall the two days of racing proved, once again, that the African nations had no equal anywhere else in the world and that wherever Kenya was deficient Ethiopia could usually step in. There were six races in all: men's long and short, women's long and short, and junior men and women. In the team competition Kenya won three gold medals and two silver, Ethiopia the reverse, two gold and three silver, plus a bronze. In the individual battle for medals, without bothering to distinguish between gold, silver and bronze, Kenya won eight out of a possible eighteen medals and Ethiopia five. I suppose someone might point out that both nations could have done better, but, surely, any nearer than this to a complete monopoly of medals is almost unimaginable. And it has been the pattern for all WCCC events since the end of the twentieth century, and seems to be set to continue that way into the foreseeable future.

Strangely, I wasn't inspired by the Belfast edition of the WCCC. For a start I was well beyond the age for inspiration. I was 53 and, if I remember correctly, going through a fallow period where running was concerned. But I was excited. I had volunteered to help with not a second's thought or hesitation. I would sooner have refused a free ticket to the Olympics. And I was affected by being so closely involved in the event. It was the first time I had watched the Africans in the flesh. When I had been in the same race as them, at the WCCC events of 1983, 84 and 86, I would have needed binoculars to see them. But here I could watch them as I had watched Gaston Roelants in 1967, and Carlos Lopes in 1976, close up and personal. It had the same effect on me as having run with top class runners at university. It made the world of the élite that much more ordinary, though still wonderful, if that is not too much of a contradiction to understand.

As I stood beside the hill that formed the toughest part of the course in Barnett Demesne and Paul Tergat passed me for the second or third time, in the lead and obviously having run faster up to that point than anyone else in the field, he was finding it hard. The mud and the incline were having the same effect on him as on everyone else. In short, he looked human. His win was no less impressive, perhaps more so, but, for a moment at least, the sight of him struggling (there's no other word for it) brought his world of running a little bit closer to mine.

CHAPTER 12
Races

'In real life, of course, it is the hare who wins'

Anita Brookner.

It might seem that the be-all and end-all of competitive running is to be found in races. Without races there is surely no point in being a competitive runner at all. And aren't the two things, races and competitions, the same anyway? Isn't success in races what justifies all the time and effort and emotional energy put into training? Isn't it what makes the whole business worthwhile? It must seem so, at least to any observer of the sport.

Viewed from the inside, however, it's not quite that simple. For a start most races, for most runners, are not really races at all. They are time trials. When I look back at all the races I ever took part in, hundreds, maybe even over a thousand races, at all distances from seventy five yards up to a marathon, I can think of very few in which I can honestly say I was racing, rather than just running as hard and as fast as I could. 'What's the difference?' you might well ask. The difference is absolutely fundamental. Success in a race is measured simply by your finishing position, irrespective of how well you ran. It is about whom you beat and who beats you. Ultimately it is about who wins. For spectators and commentators, and followers of the running scene, more often than not, it is solely about who wins. Hence the exaggerated and, in my view, misplaced importance attached to winning races: 'winning is everything', 'winning is all that matters', 'no one remembers who finished second', 'they can't take a gold medal away from you' and so on; all hollow reflections of the winning cult.

As recently as September 2013 Mo Farah was reported in the Daily Telegraph sport section as saying, in reply to those nay-sayers who still reserved their judgement on his greatness and cited the fact that he is a long way short of being the fastest man in the world over either 5,000m or 10,000m in support of their view, *'Times are nothing. They are there to be broken whereas gold medals can never be taken away from me.'* It is an old and to my mind rather illogical cliché and, more to the point, it can only be applied to those who win. For the rest of us, for the masses of runners who never win gold medals, it is meaningless. Times are all we have to reflect our achievements. So times are what we strive for in races and, almost as an incidental by-product of a good time, comes a good position, maybe even on those special, very rare occasions, a winning position.

I have won some races in my time. I may or may not have run particularly well in those races. I am not denying that winning is special and does score a lot more points in the morale and gratification tallies than finishing anywhere else, but by itself it's really a rather valueless concept. What if, for any of the races I won, someone had turned up who was considerably better than me? Would I have still won? Obviously not. Would I have run as well? Yes, and quite possibly even better. I remember my wins in races with great pride and clarity, but I don't necessarily value them as highly as other performances, events (call them races if you like) in which I finished well behind the winner but ran particularly well by my standards.

Winning a race, whether it's between just two people or has a cast of thousands, is an achievement permitted to one person only. If it really were all that mattered, the one and only reward that made a runner's life worthwhile, it would be the death of the sport. Why would the rest of the field even bother? At the peak of long distance running success in Great Britain there must have been hundreds of serious competitive runners who trained with the same commitment as the very best, who entered races week after week, who ran as hard as anyone and who never won a thing. Try telling any of them that winning is everything. It would be the same as telling them straight out that they were all completely stupid. At least I had the good fortune to win a few races in my career, but only perhaps a dozen or so over thirty years. That makes winning worth diddly-squat.

At the start of a typical track, road or cross country race there may be five or six runners who think they might win. The rest, numbered sometimes in hundreds, including me on many occasions, know that they are not going to win, they don't stand an earthly. But they are still just as keen to run to their limit. They will be running for the best time and, consequentially, the best position, they can attain. Other runners in the race may become temporary pacemakers or windshields, to be used selfishly or they may provide a needed challenge, a spur to run harder, or in a long race they may become friendly companions, to share the strain and help with the concentration. But this form of racing between runners down the field is different in kind from the race for first place. I don't even refer to it as racing. There are no tactics. No one can afford to run any slower than the optimum. To do so would be to lose place after place and add seconds to the finishing time.

Whenever I watch the leading group in a distance race I think to myself that, in that pack, there is at least one person who, at the end of the race, will not have run as hard as he or she could have done. It is more than likely that there is more than one person in the group not running as hard as possible. The one person who I usually know isn't doing so is the one who will ultimately win, though I can't necessarily identify him yet. He may have an excuse. But the others who are underperforming are gambling. They are gambling their chance of a result to be proud of, the best result they could possibly achieve, against the chance of winning. You won't find any of that kind of thinking going on lower down the field. It could be argued that those not involved in the race (for first place) are running in a more honest and admirable manner. Once the mind is free of any thoughts of winning, competing becomes a much simpler matter and motivation can do its job uninhibited.

For me the classic instance of a race in which the eventual winner was the right winner, while almost the whole of the rest of the field gambled away their chance, not of winning, but of performing to the very best of their ability in the hope that they might win by, as it were, sleight of hand, was the 1976 Olympic 5,000m final. It was a race that stirred the souls of all iconoclasts of tactical dogmatism. Watching such a tactical race irritated people like me, who would rather see someone run as fast as possible than watch runners stake everything on the off chance of winning with a sprint finish. The ending of the race, when the dust had settled, proved completely satisfying because the best man won. Everyone who gambled lost. It was a race that could only have happened because there were a number of so nearly equally matched runners, all of whom thought that winning was the only thing worth doing, and who were deluded into believing that they would be the one to do it.

With one lap to go in that race the leader was the eventual winner Lasse Viren of Finland. Grouped behind him, like a pack of dogs snapping at his heels, in what would be described by pundits and commentators as the 'right' positions, maybe even the 'best' position, were all the fancied runners, with their famous finishing speeds awaiting imminent release: Dick Quax and Rod Dixon of New Zealand, Klaus-Peter Hildenbrand of West Germany, Willy Polleunis of Belgium, Brendan Foster and Ian Stewart of Great Britain. Even at that point it must have occurred to each of them that they were not all going to win. For them the race had become almost a lottery, not simply who could run the last lap fastest but also who could find the clearest and shortest route to the finish. I doubt if any of the chasing group gave much thought to Viren himself, the man in the lead. Wasn't being in the lead the very worst place to be at that stage in a race? And had anyone ever seen Viren sprint?

For Viren, however, the task was simplicity itself. He didn't have to run faster than anyone. He merely had to stay ahead, which he could do by running the last lap, not faster, but just slightly slower than everyone else. He had the advantage of having to run precisely 400 metres, not a centimetre more, with no one in front of him to get in his way. The fact that he won the race by doing precisely that, should have raised a huge question mark over the whole concept of the right tactics for a middle distance race.

By a strange coincidence, no sooner had I written the above than I sat down to watch the final of the men's 5,000m at the London 2012 Olympics. It was as if the spirit of Viren had taken over the body of the new Olympic champion, Great Britain's own Mo Farah. Coming off the first bend into the back straight of the penultimate lap, Farah was running on the shoulder of the leader and the race began to take on a sense of real urgency. Up to that point it had been a dawdle, that turned into a canter at 2,000m, then a gallop at 3,000m and, now, it was beginning to mount to what was obviously about to become a flat out sprint. With what could have been an ominous piece of bad advice, with memories of the Montreal 5,000m final springing to mind, the commentator cried out, 'now hold that position, Mo'. Mo Farah had two things in his favour at that point, which happily proved good for him and good for British athletics. He's an intelligent man and, secondly, he was brimming with confidence. So, very sensibly, in my opinion, he disregarded the pundit's advice, and with over six hundred yards to go he took the lead and he kept it to the finish. The last lap was run in 52.9 seconds. Consider, for a moment, what Mo would have had to do had he not taken the lead before the last lap. He would have had to run further than 400m over that lap, probably in an even shorter time than he did, not beyond him, but a tall order for even the best runner in the world. Like Viren before him, on the day that mattered, Mo Farah was the best runner in the field, and knew how not to make his winning any more difficult than it had to be. Had he lost, of course, his tactics would have been heavily criticised. 'He took the lead too early,' everyone would have said. They would have been wrong, not because the end result would have proved them so, but because, by taking the lead when he did, Mo Farah, win or lose, took the shortest route to the tape, just when fractions of a second and fractions of a yard were about to make all the difference.

And here's another thing for the dogmatists of tactics to think about; when Mo Farah took the lead he handed his 'good position', that is on the shoulder of the leader, to someone else, someone who now became the one in a good, or the best position. But we know who won, don't we? It's a good thing that there have been distance runners like Farah and Viren to demote the whole idea of stereotypical tactics in races to its proper and very insignificant place.

Without the obsession with who wins, races are just a measure of ability. In a sense they are a necessary evil. True, without them, the sport would be pointless, but, even in their absence, runners could still get personal satisfaction from improvement, from getting fitter and fitter, faster and faster. Time trials could replace races. It would still be possible to compare one runner with another, again by means of recorded times over measured distances, even if the two runners never met in the same race. This is what happens in a relay race which is, in effect, a series of individual time trials and can be just as suspenseful and exciting as a straightforward race. If you believe, as I do (mentioned in Chapter 1) that competition has more to do with the individual than with the matching of runner against runner, then races could, at least in theory, be dispensed with altogether. The only losers in that case would be the non participating public. The role of races in running, especially what are regarded as the most important races, is primarily for spectators, not for runners.

Perhaps the erosion of the significance of races has already happened for the majority of runners today. Entrants to the big city road races, those who are seriously competitive at any rate, are almost all aiming for nothing other than a personal best time. Finishing positions in races with fields of such magnitude become meaningless. Is one thousandth this year better than one thousand one hundredth last year? Who knows? And if you're in the middle of it all, and running somewhere amongst the top thousand, and someone passes you, do you see it as having lost a place, so respond to the challenge with increased effort? I doubt it. You are not in a race; you are in a time trial, a very personal one at that.

When I competed regularly in road races there was a direct and very overt relationship between places and times, one that wasn't hidden by sheer numbers of competitors. The places we finished, even for the tail-enders, were worth fighting for. Tenth is a lot better than eleventh. Even forty ninth is significantly better than fiftieth. Only in the very biggest races was it possible to become submerged into a state where places and times and the very concept of racing became indistinct. It was usually quite easy to see the whole field as part of the same race, for competitors and spectators alike. Even if, as so often happened, a distinct leading group emerged, and the race for first, second and third separated itself from the race for other places, it was always part of the same event and everyone could identify with it. Not so nowadays, impossible in events with two or more separate starts.

I never really enjoyed races. I suspect that a lot of runners have felt the same. They were too much like exams. You had to do them and, of course, it was good to do well in them, but if there had been some other way to be measured, it would have been preferable. When I was young I made up for my fear of races with ambition and nervous excitement, but, by the time I was over forty and had lost all my compensatory enthusiasm, I used to line up at the start of a race, saying to myself, 'I don't want to do this.' The shorter the race the less I enjoyed it. That explains why, in later years, I rarely entered races shorter than a half marathon. When asked why, I explained that long distance events, and in particular the marathon itself, were the only ones in which I could run within myself, without going too slowly. It was the intense, mind-sapping, throat-drying pace of shorter races that I hated, however often I mimicked the same thing in training. Sometimes I explained that I preferred to run marathons because they were easier, but people thought I was joking.

I did enjoy some aspects of some races, once I was well into them. I loved the thrill of burning off the opposition, of running alongside or just in front of someone for mile after mile until suddenly I became aware that I was on my own, no other breathing, no other footsteps, only one shadow. I didn't need to look around. I could sense the gap and I knew I was alone. I enjoyed the sense of superiority that came with catching someone up, knowing that with every stride I was that little bit closer and that I was bound to get there in time. If you can catch other runners in a race you rarely fail to pass them, and they rarely come back to you. I enjoyed beating someone in a sprint finish, though I very seldom did so. This was not because I couldn't sprint. It was more to do with my disinclination to run behind anyone unless I absolutely couldn't go any faster. I would never deliberately hang on to another runner's coat tails, running slower than I felt like, waiting for the opportunity to sprint past at the finish. I was by nature what is called a 'front runner'.

Actually the term front runner has very little to do with running at the front. If that were invariably the case then, just like winning, front running would be the reserve of one person at a time in any race. On the contrary, there can be any number of front runners, simultaneously, in a single race. Front runners are those who feel uncomfortable and not vindicated when running closely behind someone else. They only do so when they are hanging on like grim death and can't overtake however hard they try. They would never run slower than they want to in order to be behind other runners. They are happiest running with space around them and, if that means leading, then so be it. I am describing myself of course, but I know I'm not, and never was, by any means unique.

Having said that, and without contradicting myself, I enjoyed running in a group during a race, feeling relaxed, looking about me at the other runners' strained faces, the sweat dripping off their chins, hearing their laborious breathing and heavy feet, saying to myself (though often prematurely) 'I'll finish ahead of you'. I always preferred, however, to run in isolation in a race, imagining that I was on a training run, the only pressure to keep up the pace being self imposed. And, like all runners, I enjoyed the final part of races, approaching the finishing line with an established place, able to relax and contemplate the imminent end of what might have been a gruelling effort.

I enjoyed all these 'races within races', but I didn't enjoy racing as a whole, from hours or even days before the start and then often for the same length of time after the finish. To run badly is depressing and even running well can lead to the depression that comes from physical effort and exhaustion. The public may have thought that it was just the yellow card and with it the prospect of missing the next match that reduced Paul Gascoigne to a cry-baby during the 1990 World Cup in Italy and that losing the 2012 Wimbledon final, by itself, did the same to Andy Murray, but they would only be partly right. Prolonged physical effort alone can bring one to a state of near tearfulness. Add the catalyst of an emotional shock and tears, trembling chin and heaving chest are practically inevitable. I remember myself, during a difficult domestic time in my life, abandoning a race in tears and running into the bushes for a quick sob for absolutely no reason other than I was emotionally stressed at the start of the race and, additionally, after five hard miles of running, considerably physically stressed as well.

Running pundits, coaches, and writers on the subject emphasise, advisedly, the importance of recovery, both from hard training and from races. What they rarely do is distinguish between purely physical recovery and nervous and emotional recovery. My view is that physical recovery is vastly overrated but the other is virtually ignored. I used to find that I could often run better and felt more energetic the day after a hard race than the day before it. The first year I ran in the British Universities Cross Country Championship, at Sheffield in 1970, I did, I thought, pretty well, finishing 24th. The next day we all went for a long training run, about seventeen or eighteen miles over the Yorkshire moors, through misty drizzle and along rough tracks and even rougher paths. I have rarely run so easily at such a good pace. I felt so well; I remember it to this day. Perhaps I didn't run hard enough the day before. I don't think that's true. I think the race cleaned out my system, cleared the tubes and emptied the nooks and crannies and clogged up spaces, which made it more efficient the next day. As for recovery, I didn't need it. I was young. I was fit. I was used to running ten miles quite hard most days of the week. Why would I need to recover?

Indeed, so convinced did I become at one time that a 'blow-out' in the form of a race improved my next day's run that I experimented with deliberately running hard the day before a race. I didn't run far, but I did run very fast. I would do something like a mile flat out, or some 200m sprints, when standard advice might have been to have a rest day or just an easy jog the day before racing. I might even have done what I called a 'suicide run'. This involved, after a warm up, setting out at a very fast pace and keeping it up for as long as I possibly could, the aim being to stop only when I absolutely had to. The thinking behind such runs is explained in the next Chapter. Running hard the day before a race became a habit of mine because it seemed to work. I never found it counterproductive.

As I recount elsewhere (Chapter 10) I was able, the week after my worst ever marathon experience, which was on a Monday, to do a hard ten mile run on Wednesday and a fast 3,000m on the track on Saturday. Almost in my forties I was still able to recover physically remarkably quickly. But mental recovery was not so easy in that case. I was emotionally drained after the marathon, the accumulated effects of months of dedicated training plus a severe disappointment in the race itself, and I had gone into a form of depression, from which I didn't recover for many weeks. No one had warned me about the need for that sort of recovery.

There were a number of things I hated about races. For a start there was everything that is the opposite of the things I enjoyed, and came in equal measure: being caught up, being dropped, being beaten in a sprint finish, running in a group and somehow knowing that I am the sweatiest, the one with the most strained face, the most laboured breathing and heaviest feet, and will be the first to let go. Then there was the pre-race waiting, accompanied by nerves and self doubt, the jostling for a clear place on the start line, eyes fixed to the ground, cold from waiting, maybe wet as well, the ridiculous last minute instructions, made by a representative of the organisers whom no one hears or listens to, the introduction to the token starter, some minor dignitary or celebrity who may even be pompous enough to say a few words himself that also no one hears or listens to.

Then the start itself, a bang, a toot, a blast on a whistle, the drop of a flag, or a click as the gun fails to fire. We break into a shuffle which quickly becomes a jog or a sort of hopping, then finally a slow run and then, the worst bit, a full gallop, much too fast, desperately trying to establish our places in the pecking order. It may entail what is almost a sprint past a slow-coach who shouldn't have been there in the first place. Place found, running becomes free, but all out. It's still much too fast but woe betide anyone with any expectations of a good finishing position who gets left behind at this stage.

I'm talking here about races up to a half marathon, where all out running at the start is permissible, though not always advisable. The problem is that, however well you warm up, you are never really properly warmed up when the field actually gets away. That's partly because you've had plenty of time standing around before the start in which to cool down again (warming up is largely a matter of doing just that, raising the body temperature slightly so that it becomes more efficient). I've sometimes stood at the start line of a race on a cold day in no more than vest and shorts for more than ten minutes waiting for the off. Not being properly warmed up at the start of a race is also partly due to it never being possible, in my experience, to bring yourself to that perfect state, the state sometimes described as 'second wind', by the time of the start. It is the state when the body is at its most efficient. In many years of racing I have never been in that state when the gun goes.

Maybe I never warmed up for long enough. Maybe that was because nervousness or a fear of overdoing it stopped me putting enough effort into warming up. Whatever the reason I could never start a race feeling, as I normally did fifteen minutes into a training run, that nothing was beyond me. Quite the contrary; two minutes into a race I'm wondering how I'll ever keep this up, as waves of oxygen debt hit my legs and I seem to be sprinting, and there are still loads of people ahead of me. Those first few minutes of a race are undoubtedly the worst, as I consolidate my pre-race warm up at what seems to me to be breakneck speed, while merely managing to reach somewhere approaching my eventual finishing position. I'm still usually a few places down on that position after just having run what seems to me to have been a flat out mile. I was never a fast starter, even when I started fast, if you see what I mean.

The marathon, however, as in so many other ways, is very different. Even when I was running the distance quite well I used to line up at the start telling myself that I was just going for a long training run. If the smallest inkling of competitive instinct came to my head I would instantly ignore it. Since I always expected to be running very slowly towards the end of the event, I didn't mind running very slowly at the beginning. The first mile or two always became my warm up. I still consider any warm up for a marathon, by anyone, even if it's just a few stretches or a hundred yard jog, as worse than a waste of time. How many marathon runners, as they approach the last mile of a race, would give anything to have their warm up somehow put into a syringe and injected back into their veins? After all, a mile of warming up is a mile extra, added on to what is already a very long distance to run. I always preferred to run no more than just over 26 miles in one day, not a yard further.

The fast starts and my inability to warm up effectively were the main reasons I grew to hate almost any race shorter than a half marathon. When I was young I could cope with them but now and, really, ever since I turned 43, they have become intolerable. The simple answer would be to start races more easily, but, though I may have lost my ability to cope with a fast start (more correctly an uncomfortable start) I have never lost my impatience, nor my sense of where, by rights, I think I should be placed in any field of runners. Usually my sense of place has been proved right. By attempting to keep up with certain runners over the first mile or so of a race I have almost always finished the race where I feel I should have finished. The odd thing has been the way in which runners who ultimately finished races a little way behind me, managed, not just to keep up with me, but to keep ahead of me for the first mile or so. Perhaps they knew the art of warming up properly.

I owed the ability to recover from an over-hard start to a race simply to training and to being extremely fit. When a runner does stray into anaerobic territory during a race, as is inevitable at times, fitness enables that runner to return to a safe, but still fast pace very quickly. Whatever I felt like five minutes into a race, and sometimes it was pretty grim, I knew I could recover and be running happily and efficiently fairly soon afterwards, just as, at the end of a flat out effort over four hundred metres in training I might sometimes have felt that death was imminent, but I could usually do another equally hard effort a minute later.

It was not always like that. I ran a cross country race at school when I was sixteen or seventeen in a new pair of running shoes. Actually I think they may have been hockey boots. In the sixties there were no specialist running shoes, none that I knew about, anyway. But you still needed a shoe that you could wear for cross country races, that wouldn't slip on wet grass or mud, or snow and ice, and was light enough not to slow you down as a heavy boot would. Some boys did wear rugby boots. Until this race I always wore plimsolls, and slid around like a novice ice skater.

I was so inspired by my new shoes that I started the race ridiculously fast, hammering out a mile across the school playing fields well in the lead. Then I ran into oxygen debt. My shoes began to feel more like the boots that I think they probably were than the running shoes I imagined them to be. My legs wobbled and I slowed to a crawl. Several boys passed me. I began to feel a bit silly in my, by now, rather ridiculous footwear. And I never recovered. I simply wasn't fit. The effects of one mile fast stayed with me for the rest of the distance. Luckily the whole distance of the race was little more than three miles. As I have said before, the acid test of fitness is the ability to recover. Only in later years did I have it in plentiful supply.

I put that down to lots of anaerobic training in addition to the steady aerobic work that is the staple diet of the distance runner. The usual advice regarding the balance in training between aerobic and anaerobic work is to mimic the relative contributions of the two energy producing systems in the event for which you are training. So, for example, since a distance runner relies almost entirely on the aerobic, i.e. the oxygen-derived energy supply system, then the appropriate training regime should be almost entirely aerobic. An 800m runner, on the other hand, should do a fair bit of anaerobic training and a 400m runner even more. A 1,500m man might do a roughly equal amount of each. That is, or has been, the simplistic thinking behind training for distance and middle distance racing. My own experience tells me different.

Where things go wrong in middle and longer distance races is the point when the aerobic system is overloaded and the body goes into oxygen debt. It's easy to say that this shouldn't happen; if it does, it means you're running too fast. The fact is that it happens: a fast start, a sprint to pass someone, a sharp hill, a patch of mud in a cross country race. The runner who is least disadvantaged by these sudden and inevitable anaerobic shocks to the system is the one who recovers quickest. Ironically, recovery from anaerobiosis is an aerobic process. You borrow oxygen and you can only pay it back in kind. So perhaps it does make sense to train aerobically, for example by means of lots of steady running, so as to be able to recover quickly from occasional bursts of oxygen debt. Basing my belief, however, on the principle that you should do in training what you find difficult to do in a race, I always included a decent amount of anaerobic recovery work in my training week. It became my Saturday session, which I described in Chapter 8. I wouldn't have done it if I didn't think, as I still do, that it improved my performances at all distances, even the marathon. It was certainly the secret behind my tolerance, despite my hatred of them, of fast starts, and, I think, the key to my better runs over the country where, because of the unevenness and inconsistency of the ground, a runner is constantly moving into and out of oxygen debt like a yo-yo.

Inevitably in any race, the first mad rush, the enforced second warm up, the two or three minutes of excess and the consequent recovery period come to an end, and if there is any part of a race that's enjoyable, it starts now. It is the middle. It is still hard and there is an acute urge to ease up and drop back into the comfort zone of not running as fast as possible, but at least it is clear where you are and how you are going. It's clear where you're likely to finish, to within a place or two and, physically, it's about as good as you'll feel at any stage of the race. I can remember particular races simply on account of how I felt at the halfway stage. I may not remember exactly what race it was or where I finished but how I felt in it is ingrained in my memory. Feeling good is remembered with pleasure. Feeling bad, I prefer to forget.

For example there was one (I forget the year) Northern Ireland Cross Country Championship race. The course was six laps with a short, steep hill on each lap. At the top of the hill the course turned back on itself, almost a hairpin, to come back down. I think I finished in the first ten but, again, I forget exactly where. What I do remember, vividly, was the feeling. I was never a good hill runner but I had been doing my Saturday hill session for several weeks and I attacked the hill each lap like a sprinter, knowing that the briefest of rests at the top would see me able to continue almost without a pause. Flying up those hills was exhilarating. It reminded me of running as a child. I could also recount examples of feeling bad in the middle of a race, countless examples, but, as I said, I prefer to forget.

As the finish of a distance race approaches, nine times out of ten, for most competitors, the intensity of competition eases. That may seem a strange thing to say. Surely the end of a race is the most competitive, the most exciting and unpredictable part, the essence of the race, the part that everyone has been waiting for? That may be true for spectators and it may be true for the leaders, but for most participants in an average distance race it is not often the case. For me, with a quarter mile to go to the finish of a race it was hardly ever the case. By that stage I had done the ground work and I was rarely in close contact with anyone else. I knew that if I kept running at the same pace I would keep ahead of the nearest man behind me and there was rarely anyone close enough in front and showing signs of weakness suggesting I might catch him. Watch any distance race closely and you will find that I am right. However fierce and exciting the race for first place might be, once it is over the minor places are filled one by one almost like a procession. No runner outside the leading group is ever going to deliberately ease off during any earlier part of a race in order to conserve some energy for the finish.

Doing so might turn twentieth place into nineteenth by means of a prolonged sprint finish, but only at the expense of finishing nineteenth rather than, perhaps, tenth. The luxury of running conservatively and planning for the possibility of winning, belongs to a very select few in any distance race.

In theory, and according to my personal racing ethic, there is only ever one person in any race who can justify running slower than he would have done if the race had been a time trial over the same distance. I don't like to see a leading group still intact with the large part of a race already completed. A massed sprint finish is no way to end an important race. To a serious runner the greatest sight in a race is one of total dominance, someone leading from the gun, steadily getting further and further ahead, never giving the slightest cause for debate as to who will win. That is why Dave Bedford was so loved by fellow runners in the seventies and, before him, Ron Clarke of Australia. They were, like me, front runners, who ran, not as if winning were the sole objective, but like the hundreds of runners who would have finished well behind them in races, all out and unrestrained by a fear of losing.

The sprint finish should be the last resort of the distance runner, reserved either for the runner who knows, absolutely, without the slightest doubt, that he will win with it or for someone who is forced into it because he has already been running at his limit simply to keep up. When Eamon Coughlan of Ireland, for example, won the inaugural World Cup Athletics Championship 5,000m in 1983, he did so with a sprint finish over the last lap, catching the Russian Dmitriy Dmitryev with just over 200 metres to go and rounding him on the last bend before the finishing straight. As he set out in pursuit of Dmitriev, I have no doubt that he was sure he would win. At the bell he was a few yards behind the Russian but must have known what capacity he had in reserve and how inevitable his progress over that last lap was going to be. He had already done the hard bit. He was ahead of the rest of the field and couldn't have been worried about any of them. As I watched that race I almost shared with Coughlan the sense of certainty that he must have had. I could forgive him leaving his moving into the lead until the finishing straight because it really made no difference. He was the man who was going to win on that day.

My one and only sprint finish victory which I recount in chapter 14 was an example of not being able to keep up and having to work as hard as I could to catch the leaders. I didn't deliberately leave it to a sprint at the end. I simply ran to my limit just to be in touch as the finishing line drew near. However hard a well trained runner has run in a race there is always something left for a sprint at the end. It's there to be used should the need arise and it doesn't have to be protected by cautious running earlier in the race.

Only once did I ever deliberately plan for a sprint finish in a distance race and then my anticipated sprint never happened because I went over on my ankle in a patch of mud with about half a mile still to run. It was enough to break the link between me and the runner I had been closely following for almost the entire distance. He gained a ten yard gap and I never closed it. That occasion remains one of the biggest disappointments in my running life. I had been so looking forward to the chance to test my kick finish, a thing I did so rarely, and in the time it took for my foot to stick in the mud and my ankle to bend through a right angle, the chance had gone. The real disappointment was in never knowing if I would have beaten the other runner with a final sprint. I just wish I had been able to find out.

Distance running is not a tactical sport. Perhaps on the track, where bends crop up every hundred metres and space is tight, there is a need for some tactical racing, the more so as the distance shrinks. Middle distance races are often lost through bad tactical decisions though rarely, in my experience, won through good ones. The only true distance event run on the track, the 10,000m, can become tactical but it's a great pity when it does. And even when a race has the appearance of being tactical it's still, more often than not, the best man who wins. In distance running, whether on the road, track or over the country, there's really only one tactic worth anything, and that is to be as good a runner as you can be.

On June 6th 1977, I lined up at the start of the Yeovil ten mile road race as defending champion. Fifty minutes and eight seconds later I had defended my title in a race that I don't think I should have won. The story of that race is worth recounting for two reasons. The first is that it involves one of the few points of tactics, if that's the right word in this case, that does apply to distance races. The second is that, perhaps of all the races I ever ran, it exemplifies the fact that racing involves a lot more than just physical effort. Racing is not even just a combination of physical and mental effort. Racing involves the full commitment of physical and mental powers, both conscious and subconscious, and, just as important, emotional strength.

If the body is weak, the mind, however well attuned, can do nothing to help it. Forget stories of women lifting trucks to save their babies; they're not true. If the body is capable on the other hand, the mind still plays a massive part. Mostly this is a subconscious thing. You can be highly motivated, determined, one hundred per cent committed, 'in the mood', 'focussed', 'in the zone', willing to give your all, intensely competitive, etc. Sports psychologists earn their living by cultivating this sort of mental arousal. I have usually found that a competitive high is already there, as much a part of me as having two legs to run with in the first place. Sometimes, when I'm driving, for example, I wish it would go away. There are such things as being too competitive and being competitive in the wrong context.

To run well, you have to want to do so. In turn this means that your one and only present concern has to be the race, nothing else. All your emotional energy has to be directed at the business in hand; you cannot afford to be distracted or emotionally diminished in any way. The Yeovil ten mile race was a race which, at first, I didn't want to run, because my thoughts and a lot of my emotional energy were directed elsewhere, and, then, when it mattered, something happened that changed my mind. I did want to run. Not only did I want to run, I wanted to win. I wanted to win very much.

That explains how I attained a winning mentality. But it wasn't the reason I won. What enabled me to win the 1977 Yeovil 10, by beating someone whom I estimate, on the basis of performances in other races, was probably the better runner on the day, came from my head, certainly, but not from the emotional part. It was the thinking part. I suppose, therefore, yes, I admit it, I ran the race tactically, though I prefer to call the reason that I won home advantage. If there was a tactic involved it was simply that I exploited the fact that I knew the race route and the man I beat didn't. It's always a good idea, especially when racing on an unknown course, to familiarise yourself with it before the start and, if you can do nothing more, then at least look over the stretch leading to the finish. A universal ritual for cross country runners is to jog a lap of the course as part of their warm up.

The course for the 1977 Yeovil 10 was the same as for the previous year, so I knew it well. I lived no more than fifteen miles away and was very familiar with the whole area, its topography and its landmarks. My main rival was an Essex man, far from home, in unknown territory and probably feeling a bit insecure. Already I had a slight advantage. But I also had my own concerns that were about to affect my running.

The course was in three sections. From the start it climbed for about half a mile, a climb that was barely noticeable at that stage of the race, then continued downhill for nearly three miles to where the road crossed the River Yeo. The second section was mainly flat, meandering along the Yeo valley and back to the road bridge. Then the course retraced itself over the third section, uphill for two and a half miles, and, finally, the half mile descent to the finish line.

He and I ran together, downhill to the Yeo bridge, round the flat section and back towards the bridge. We had done about six miles and were well ahead of the other runners. I got the feeling that he was running with me in order not to get lost and could have gone faster at any stage had he wanted to. You can sense these things when you run alongside another runner. I was also running reasonably easily, but with a degree of reluctance due to my mind not being fully committed. I was running mechanically, using only my innate fitness (I was very fit at the time) and had yet to engage any effort of will. I doubted, on account of my preoccupation with personal matters, whether I would be able to summon up any will power when the time came.

Just before the bridge my premonitions started to come true. I dropped back a few yards. It wasn't that I couldn't keep up. It was more that I didn't want to. I didn't want to do anything hard. I just wasn't in the mood. To reverse a familiar aphorism, my body was willing, but my mind was weak. I more or less settled, there and then, for second place. It was the low point of the race for me.

I saw my wife standing at the bridge. I hadn't expected to see her. She shouted encouragement. The circumstance that was on my mind and taking the heart out of my running concerned her and concerned us, and I was extremely aware that in all of it she was entirely blameless. It was the same thing that had caused me to abandon a race some weeks previously. I may have been physically fit enough to be racing but, emotionally, I was a mess. Just seeing her there, even without her encouragement, was all I needed to restore my sense of purpose and all my will power. Suddenly the heart had been put back into my running and the race had become hugely important to me. I made an effort and caught the leader just as we started the long climb out of the Yeo valley.

One rule of racing is that, however hard you are finding it, never try to show it and never, ever, let on deliberately. About a mile and a half of climbing later, quite steep climbing, where rounding every blind corner disclosed yet more uphill road and every skyline proved a false one, my companion turned to me and said, 'How much more of this is there?' It was a lovely sound, the first sign of weakness on his part. I said nothing, even though I was perfectly well aware of exactly how much more there was. I knew how he felt. Two and a half miles of seemingly endless climbing can be soul destroying.

The road widened. The roadside hedge and trees disappeared and were replaced by the first houses on the outskirts of Yeovil. This, I knew, meant that the top of the hill was no more than three hundred yards away. I suddenly started to run as hard as I could. To him it must have seemed like a finishing sprint. In a way it was. I was aiming for the top of the hill, the exact spot where the tarmac bent downwards towards the last downhill half mile of the course. That was my finishing line. Whatever I felt like when I reached it, even if I was on my knees, I knew I could recover quickly on the downhill stretch.

Did he respond to my injection of pace? I really don't know. I didn't look back and I didn't see him again until after I'd finished. Had he known what I was doing and had he known, as I did, precisely where the hill ended he would certainly have tried to cover my burst. Whatever the case, the tactic (for that's what it was) worked. I owe that win to two things: intimate knowledge of the course, and to my wife supporting me at a time when she really had no reason to do so.

There is one other 'tactic' that applies to all distance races. It is simplicity itself, almost too obvious to mention, but so often disregarded, particularly in track races. It is to run the shortest legitimate route. There is no such thing as a completely straight long distance race. All courses have bends and corners. It follows that the path along which runners are allowed to run, however wide or narrow it might be, will have an inside line, and that line will be the shortest route. Unless a runner has a very good reason for not taking that line in a race he or she might just as well give everyone else a head start.

When I was accused of cutting corners in a race (see Chapter 14) the implication, naturally, was that by so doing I would have gained an advantage. No one would ever think otherwise. Why, then, is it not equally obvious that by running wide around a corner, you are giving yourself a disadvantage?

The extent of the disadvantage is vastly underestimated to the point of being thought by many to be insignificant. Watch any middle or long distance track race and you would conclude that a lot of runners seriously think that they are somehow immune to the laws of geometry and can run wide on bends with impunity. For their benefit and for anyone wishing to run no further than they need to in distance races, here are the facts.

If you run one metre wide all the way around a 180° bend (such as one bend on a track) you run just over three metres more than you need to. It doesn't matter how big or how tight the bend is, the extra distance will still be about three metres. Translating that statistic to a 10,000m track event: the runner who runs the whole race in lane two (I've seen it done), about a metre out from the kerb will cover, not 10,000m, but something like 10,150m. In terms of extra time, for a runner who does 10,000m in 30 minutes, it comes to nearly half a minute. It makes you think.

Even if that runner runs the whole distance one foot out from the kerb, surely a much more realistic scenario, the extra time consumed will be close to ten seconds. What 10,000m runner would not like to reduce his personal best by ten seconds? And what about road races and cross country races? There are fewer bends and they are not so tight, but the same principles apply and the temptation, if anything, is to run wider still. With a thirty yard width of road and a packed field it's easy to find yourself running several yards wide around a right-angle corner. Do the maths yourself.

When, in a road or cross country race, you approach a tight bend and take the inside line, you have to stutter around, almost running on the spot so as not to over-run the corner. You get the impression that you've lost rather than gained time. It seems much more sensible to run wide and maintain your pace, leaning into the bend and sweeping around it like a cyclist. It's an illusion. Not only do you save time and energy rounding a bend as tight as you can possibly get to the inside, but you get a moment's rest into the bargain. While those outside you are running hard just to cover the extra distance, you are carrying out an effortless pirouette; what's more, it's perfectly within the rules.

In January 1981 I travelled to Milan to run in the European Clubs Cross Country Championship, the one and only time I competed in that race. It was bitterly cold, but clear and dry. The course included a 180° hairpin bend that took us around the end of a hedge and back along the other side. On each lap, when you had reversed the direction you were running, the runners behind you could just be made out through gaps in the hedge, coming towards you, as if on a collision course. Every time I approached the turn I got as close to the hedge as I could squeeze, grabbed the very end of the hedge with my right hand, and swung round like a pole-dancer. I probably gained a couple of seconds each lap.

I was so fed up one day with watching track races in which runners ruined their chances by running wide round the bends, often ridiculously wide, that I wrote to Athletics Weekly on the matter. The letter drew quite a response. A number of readers supported what I had said, quoting coaches who had instilled into their charges the sense in running no further than necessary. One described how his own coach had taken him onto a track and shown him the staggered starting points for the 400m, and the distance (something like five or six yards) between the starts in lane one and lane two, to impress on him how much further each lap is when run one lane wide. It was obviously a lesson he hadn't forgotten. I was pleased with the support I got.

There was one letter, however, that dismissed my argument in a rather condescending manner, describing my calculations as 'schoolboy geometry' as if that somehow made them less true. The letter came from Peter Coe, Sebastian Coe's father and coach, whose credentials were, I suppose, much more estimable than mine, especially when it came to the business of winning or aiming to win top class middle distance races on the track. That was the difference between us. I have never been in a good position to be concerned with the winning business, least of all the winning by tactical means business. I would always prefer simply to have done well and to be proud of my performance, whether I had finished first, second, third or 'also ran'. Nor was I writing with reference to the best middle distance runner in the world at the time. I was writing, I had hoped, for the benefit of quite ordinary runners who were making themselves even more ordinary by ignoring a very basic principle.

I wasn't in the least bit deflated by Peter Coe's letter. Although he made some good points, I knew that I was still right and always would be. My geometry may have been 'schoolboy' but it was as good as it gets.

I still see runners running absurdly wide, in all sorts of races. I've just seen it in all distances over four hundred metres during the London Olympics. I recently re-watched the start of the Los Angeles Olympic marathon of 1984 on YouTube. The field did two complete laps of the track before leaving the stadium; it was spread out over the full width of the track. A number of runners must have run in lane three, four or even wider. At the very beginning of a trek of over twenty six miles it might have seemed a matter of no consequence, but the fact remains that some competitors had already run about thirty yards further than others after only half a mile. I see the same thing whenever I watch the London marathon field rounding the Cutty Sark, spread out across the whole width of the road while completing a complete U turn. In a marathon, of all races, I would have thought that minimising the distance run was a matter of the utmost importance. But, no, some competitors seem oblivious to the fact that at the finish of a marathon they will have covered anything up to an extra two or three hundred yards. I saw, at close hand, the same extravagant addition to the distance run in the last half marathon I competed in. There's rarely any need for it. Very few races these days are handicap races.

CHAPTER 13
Hard or what?

'The trick is not minding that it hurts.'

Lawrence of Arabia on putting out a match with his fingers in the film of the same name.

Two words appear with monotonous regularity in any runner's diary. They are 'hard' and 'easy'. Take my own running diary, for example. I've kept a running diary more or less continuously since 1965. For a runner, keeping a record of training, competitions, thoughts and feelings is a sort of proclamation of intent. Recording what you have done becomes almost the same as writing down what you intend to do. A diary keeps you on the straight and narrow.

Excerpts from a running diary:

Thursday 21 November 1968: One lap of golf course easy.

Monday 6 January 1969: Ran round playing fields and golf course; hard but not fast.

Tuesday 7 January 1969: 55 minutes easy running.

Monday 13 December 1976: 11-12 miles steady; last mile hard.

Friday 31 December 1976: 6 mile block, then round bypass and back; 10 miles easy.

Sunday 2 January 1977: With Tony; 20+ miles in 130 minutes; felt quite easy.

Sunday 9 January1977: 20+ miles in 128 minutes; hard work.

Tuesday 6 January 1981: Newtownards Road; brisk, quite hard in parts. 10 miles.

Sunday 11 January 1981: Dixon Park, towpath; 12 miles easy.

Thursday 15 January 1981: Ormeau Park: 7 or 8 miles hard.

Tuesday 20 January 1981: Newtownards Road, hard; going well. 10 miles.

Wednesday 21 January 1981: Newtownards Road; last 2 miles very hard. 10 miles.

Thursday 22 January 1981: Newtownards Road; easy. 10 miles.

Tuesday 17 April 2007: Ran down muddy path - Stranmillis, back up towpath; 55 mins easy.

Sunday 25 April 2010: 13 miles in 104 minutes; quite hard from Drum Bridge - Stranmillis.

I know what those entries mean but no one else can. Hard and easy are both very subjective terms covering a continuum that is only relevant to the individual. My hard and my easy are not necessarily the same as someone else's. Or, at least, I have no way of knowing whether they are. I can't say what it feels like to run hard, any more than a woman can explain to a man what it feels like to give birth. I have heard that childbirth is the greatest pain imaginable. Is it? I shall never know. Is it, for example, worse than one of my own migraine headaches? I hope not, for women's sake, but I shall never find out, and nor will any non-migrainous woman giving birth.

What I do know is that to run as fast as you can, you have to run as hard as you can. The question then becomes one of whether at any point in a race you are, in fact, running as hard as you can. Even that is not a question that is always easy to answer. Only a few times in my life have I been satisfied that I ran to my absolute limit in a race and even then, as I ran, I kept asking myself whether I could go faster or if I could keep up the pace for just a bit longer.

Let's cut straight to one of those races. As a performance it probably represents the best I ever achieved, the absolute pinnacle of my potential as a runner. It is recorded somewhere in the back pages of an old Athletics Weekly (the edition of April 10th 1976) along with countless other titbits of data. It doesn't stand out in any way. No one remembers it now, except me. My performance was well hidden, even when fresh off the press, by nine other better performances on the day. In short, I ran the long leg at the Midland Road Relay at Sutton Park, Birmingham in 26:21, tenth fastest time for the distance on the day. To make that run meaningful requires a bit of explanation.

Sutton Park is the home of road relay running, in England. The National Road Relay is usually held there each year, as is the Midlands Road Relay. As far as possible the course for the road relays remains the same from year to year, so that times are directly comparable. In terms of prestige, for the big running clubs, the annual main area road relays and the National Road Relay, are second only to the corresponding cross country championships. They are large and important events. Consequently the very best runners in Britain are willing and eager to compete for their clubs. There are twelve stages in the senior men's relays, six short (about three miles) and six long (about five and a half miles). It is a lap course, so each runner starts and finishes his leg at the same place. The short and long legs are run alternately. The better runners usually do the longer distance so as to double any advantage they bring to their clubs.

In 1976 I ran the seventh leg, a long one, for my club, Westbury Harriers of Bristol. It was a lovely spring day for running, a vest and shorts day, if ever there was one. Already I was inspired, by the day, and by the beauty of the park. When I took over from our sixth runner and set off along the wide tarmac path, I was alone. This was my first bit of luck. It meant that I could start running at what was, for me, a sensible pace and not burn myself out in the first mile by trying to catch another runner, or keep up with one, or keep ahead of one. Consequently after about a mile I was nicely warmed up, running fast but not too fast and beginning to feel good. At that point the second bit of good fortune struck, the very thing that turned out to be the crucial factor in determining my exceptional performance. I was caught by two of the best runners in the midlands. They came alongside me, engrossed in a battle of their own, intent on passing me as if I had been a traffic cone. They had obviously been running hard already. Their breathing was audible, their faces deeply concentrating, the rapid movement of their limbs almost palpable. I had heard them and felt them before I saw them. I took one glance and knew who they were and why I would have been perfectly sensible to have let them pass me without a murmur of dissent. As to exactly who they were, all I need say is that the one who, at the end of the lap, had run a fraction slower than the other, had a silver medal from the European Championship marathon in his trophy drawer, as well as a number of international cross country awards. Only Dave Bedford in the early seventies had deprived him of some famous victories over the country, including both the English National and the International in 1971.

It was a decision made out of curiosity as much as anything; what would it be like to run at their pace? How long would I last? Could I even begin to run at their pace? It would mean running something like five or ten seconds a mile faster than I would have done by myself. I decided to try. So started my self-examination in the business of running as hard as I could. For a little over three and a half miles I ran like a man carrying a heavy suitcase. He wants to put it down but he decides not to. Then he thinks he really must put it down, but then ... why should he? He doesn't have to let go until he really has to. The only questions left are when will that be, and how will he know?

The time did come. With about three quarters of a mile left to the changeover my two rivals turned pace makers, together, set off towards the finish and I simply couldn't go any faster. I had managed to run for well over a quarter of an hour at a faster pace than I would have thought possible, but I was incapable of speeding up. I was at my absolute limit.

I rate that run as one of my very best performances purely on account of the time that I did. The fastest time run for the long course that day was 25:03 by Tipton Harriers' Ian Stewart, one of Great Britain's best ever middle and long distance runners, winner of the Commonwealth Games 5,000m in 1970 and the World Cross Country Championship in 1975. My two, part-time companions recorded 25:52 and 25:53 respectively. I was half a minute slower. On the basis that Ian Stewart was a 28 minute 10K runner and both my fellow competitors were conservatively worth 29 minutes for 10K at the time, I had just run the equivalent of around 29:30 for 10K, or at the very worst and without the slightest hint of exaggeration, the equivalent of around 30 minutes. My best recorded time for a 10K race is nearly a minute slower.

The lesson I learned from that experience is that the power that lies inside your body, the result of the merger of natural ability and training, can only be fully released by the application of power of the mind, call it will power, sticking power, effort, determination, resolve, or whatever, and that circumstances play a large part in determining whether that mental effort is, itself, fully applied.

That still leaves a question mark hanging over any performance. Could I have applied even more will power? When I eventually failed to keep up during my leg of the Midlands Road Relay in 1976 was it simply that I lacked mental effort or was it, as I believe, due to the limit of my physical capacity? No one, least of all myself, will ever know for sure. Had I not been quite so fit at the time, it would have been an easier question to answer. It is actually more difficult for a well trained runner than for an unfit person to run continuously right at their limit, rather than just below their limit, for two reasons. One is that lots of hard training and racing makes a runner so used to that feeling of giving every ounce of effort during a race that the dividing line between fast enough and too fast becomes blurred. An unfit person, on the other hand, hits that line like a train hitting the buffers. It is therefore easier for a fit runner to think he or she is at the limit when, in fact, a slightly faster pace might be possible. The other reason is that the moment a very fit person over-reaches the limit, given the tiniest respite, recovery happens almost instantaneously. A well trained runner at absolute maximum pace is like a thermostatically controlled oven, theoretically at a constant temperature, but, on closer examination, fluctuating by fractions of a degree at a rate that is so fast as to be hardly noticeable. An unfit runner, by contrast, is like a cooker that switches off completely as soon as it gets too hot.

The near impossibility of running by yourself as fast as you possibly can, for any length of time, is the reason that pacemakers are useful. It's much easier to run at a pace that is dictated to you than to make that pace yourself. The reason has little to do with air resistance or motivation or anything physical. It is more a matter of concentration. Having a pace set for you allows you to maintain that pace without having to think or concentrate or even make a decision, in other words without applying a lot of mental effort. It is the difference between flying on automatic pilot and manually. If you're anything like me you will notice the same effect when driving. On an empty motorway you may be travelling at 70 mph for a minute or so and then you notice that you're only doing 65 so you put your foot down a bit and speed up. A minute later you do the same thing. It's not that you can't, or the car can't maintain the constant higher speed; it's the concentration that goes. On a busy motorway with everyone moving at 70, it's not a problem.

A treadmill is the best pacemaker of the lot. It almost drives your feet without the intervention of the mind at all. On the treadmill you do not control the speed at which you run, the speed controls you. One part of a programme of physiological tests that I underwent in Belfast in the late eighties was a lactate threshold measurement. The test involved running on the treadmill for two minute periods at a fixed speed, the speed gradually increasing for each successive two minutes. After each effort my ear lobe was pierced with a tiny blade and a drop of blood taken for analysis of the lactic acid concentration. Lactic acid, or lactate, is the product of anaerobic muscular activity and starts to accumulate rapidly as soon as you are running faster than your aerobic capacity allows. So the running speed at which my lactate levels suddenly began to rise rapidly represented the limit of my distance running ability, i.e. my ability to keep up that pace for more than about a minute.

My last run was to be at four minute mile pace, i.e. fifteen miles per hour. If I could do that for two minutes I would have run a half mile faster than I had ever done in my life. I almost did it. At one and a half minutes I realised I was not going to make it and gripped the handrails tight before hoisting my protesting feet off the mill. That was another occasion when I ran absolutely as hard as possible at the bidding of an unforgiving pacemaker. As at Sutton Park I was surprised just how far I could go before I cracked.

It was that run on the treadmill in the Queen's University physiological testing centre that gave me the idea for what I called my 'suicide runs', a form of training that I mention elsewhere (Chapter 12). In the manufacturing industry it would be described as 'testing to destruction'. I have never heard such an idea advocated by anyone else, perhaps because, as training, even I never thought these runs were likely to have any special physical effect. But that is not why I did them. They were more a form of discovery, a means to self enlightenment and a path to added confidence. What they did was to mimic that point in a race when you wonder whether you can keep it up any longer, when every part of you is begging to slow down, and the only fuel you have left, if any, is in the mind. So I would start running at a fast pace and just see how long I could keep it up. It had to be a fast enough pace so that I could never keep it up for longer than a few minutes. Otherwise my suicide runs could have lasted all day and might have lived up to their name. Some of these runs were a lot like my one and a half minutes on the treadmill and ended in the same way, an abrupt, enforced stop. Others were more like my Sutton Park relay leg, two or three miles of all out effort.

They may have done me more physical damage than good, but they taught me my limits and gave me an insight into the ability of the mind to rule the body. Above all they removed the fear that all runners have of running too fast at any stage in a race. I learned what too fast really was, and found that it was often faster than I had thought. That was useful information to have. By doing those runs on my own it made me somewhat scornful of the need for pacemakers.

In running, the faster the pace the harder it is to maintain, even when it's still within your physical capabilities, so the more effective a pacemaker becomes. As I ran alongside two much better runners in the Midland relay I concentrated on every single stride. Just one tiny adjustment towards a more comfortable pace became instantly noticeable and had to be corrected. I couldn't afford to wait until a significant gap appeared in front of me before increasing my effort. I was noticing gaps of an inch and correcting them as soon as they appeared, even the ones I only imagined. It's hard to concentrate like that when you're on your own.

Some runners gain a reputation for being hard nuts, for giving everything in competition, for running themselves into the ground, for beating others through sheer guts. To a lot of people, especially those who don't run themselves, that is what running competitions are all about. It's not the best man who wins, it's the hardest. I don't go along with that idea for a moment. For a start it comes back to the question I began this chapter by pondering. How do I know if I am running as hard as the next man? The answer is that I don't and I never will. But my guess is that all highly motivated, serious runners give more or less as much as each other in the pursuit of the best results. We are all about the same hardness. Some exaggerate it and flaunt their hardness and others keep it to themselves. Some show it with grimacing, grunting and groaning and flailing limbs while others disguise it with a smooth and seemingly effortless style. But no serious runner I have ever known has been willing to finish a race without having run as hard as possible.

There was a runner at university with me who appeared in almost every cross country race I ran. Because I always beat him I would usually see him finish. In relay races, as a spectator during the time I wasn't running my own leg of the race, I might watch him running at a number of different parts of the course. He used to froth at the mouth, not small flecks of polite spittle but volumes of sticky foam flying about as he ran, clinging to his cheeks and chin and nose. Together with his ungainly running style and his habit of gasping for breath this gave him the appearance of a man running harder than anyone could be expected to do without immediately collapsing on the spot. Running for him seemed, to an observer, to be a near-death experience. But it was only appearance. I am sure he ran hard, but I doubt if he ran harder than I did, without the froth, without the gasping and with my easier-looking running style.

Emil Zatopek, to some people the greatest distance runner who ever lived, also ran in a manner that suggested he was running harder than was good for him. He perpetuated the myth of success coming from effort, rather than simply from being better, by putting his victories down, in his own words, to being more determined than his opposition. To explain his winning method he is reputed to have said, '*When you think you have nothing left the others have got nothing left at all and, if you can play your last ace, you may have a chance of pulling it off.*' This was a competitive philosophy adopted by a notably hard man of English distance running, Roy Fowler, one of the few British runners ever to have won the international cross country championship, which he did in 1963. In the race he claims to have used the same quote from Zatopek as his mantra for beating the race favourite Gaston Roelants, so adding yet more substance to the idea that the way to beat someone is to out-suffer them. Another influential proponent of the belief in victory through suffering was the Australian coach, Percy Cerutty, mentor to Herb Elliott, the Rome Olympics 1,500m gold medallist. '*If you push through the pain barrier into real agony, you are a champion*', is what he had to say on the matter.

Undoubtedly to 'give everything' in a race, which may or may not be more than the opposition are giving, is going to play a large part in a runner achieving his or her best, but by itself the ability to endure and conquer stress and hardship and then come back for more is never going to turn a tortoise into a hare, however admirable it may be. The irony is that, in most races, in my experience, the winner is the one who has run least hard. All the great long distance running performances that I have witnessed, the memories of which still have the power to thrill and inspire, starting with Abebe Bikila's second Olympic marathon gold in Tokyo in 1964, have impressed not because they have been demonstrations of hardness but, rather, because they have seemed so easy.

Running easily may seem a self explanatory concept. Is it not the opposite of running hard? Not really. It's the same as running hard, but without the feeling that you can't keep it up. It's the holy grail of running, the state that all runners wish to attain. They recognise it when they get there and they never forget it. It is not, by any means, necessarily, the same as running slowly and it certainly doesn't mean running without effort. For me, running easily usually meant running at about six minute per mile pace, though it could have been half a minute faster per mile than that. I have occasionally run easily at close to five minute mile pace, i.e. close to my maximum pace for distances greater than about five miles. I have won races by running easily. I have run faster times over set distances by running easily than by running hard.

If that sounds impossible, I'll give you an example. When I lived in Brighton, during the winter, I would occasionally travel to the Crystal Palace stadium in South London to compete in open track events. The events were not serious races but they gave people like me the opportunity to record a time for a standard distance at a time of year that was outside the normal track and field season. I liked them because I was usually fitter in the winter when it was difficult to find any race over an accurately measured distance, than in the summer, when track races were two a penny.

On the evening of 17th November 1971, I ran 10,000m on the Crystal Palace track in 31:27. For most of the way I ran easily. At 5,000m my time was 15:27 and I know I ran that first half easily. If the half distance had been hard I would have slowed even more. With thoughts of a much quicker 5,000m time to come, I entered the shorter distance at the next open meeting, a month later, on 15th December. It was hard and I ran 15:32.

If I had only one reward for my years of running, for my hours of training in all weathers, my various injuries, pains and discomforts, I would settle for having experienced the joy of fast, easy running. It only comes to those who train sufficiently and it's a fragile thing that can be destroyed by over-indulgence or under-investment. It's like a simmering pot. Turn the heat up and it boils over; remove it from the heat and it cools down. Get it right, with sensible rationing of both training and racing and it's a lasting delight. When I was running at my very best, around 1976, I used to come in from my evening ten mile run, rarely more than an hour, and wonder how something so easy and enjoyable could possibly be called training. At that time running, for me, was almost always easy, even when I called it hard. Running was its own reward.

If I have just given the impression that training could be an endless succession of easy, enjoyable runs, I shall have to disillusion you. Inevitably there would come days when cold rain swept into my face, driven by gale force winds, when the temperature dropped below freezing, or when snow and ice rendered the pavements impossible to run on and turned the edges of the roads into pools of slush melted by salt grit. I was not always well. I could have a cold, or a niggling pain in some crucial part of my running anatomy, or just feel out of sorts for any number of reasons. But nothing stopped the daily training grind. Pleasurable running was ideal, but running, whatever it felt like, came first. The resolve to keep the training going through thick and thin was something all serious runners shared.

To this day I remember some of the races in which I ran easily. On January 8th 1977, for example, I won the Somerset County Cross Country Championship by nearly two minutes. That is not supposed to impress. Somerset is a very small county in running terms. I mention it because it is a race I remember vividly simply on account of how I felt. Having such a lead allowed me to run by myself, as I was so used to doing on my evening training runs. It became an evening training run. I ran fast because I felt even better running fast. At no stage did I run hard, though I probably couldn't have run any faster. I enjoyed every second of that race. I seemed to bounce over the short turf. My body seemed weightless, my legs tireless. It was just the perfect running experience. Isn't that the point? Easy is enjoyable, enjoyable is easy, and hard is neither.

I also remember vividly when I ran and won the Bournemouth midsummer cross country race on 20th June 1976. Traditionally midsummer and cross country go together about as well as strawberries and Christmas. The Bournemouth event could even be unique. But I see no reason why cross country races shouldn't be run in the summer.

With its combination of glorious weather and a course over ground that was a pleasure to run on, the Bournemouth midsummer race became one of my all time favourites. I ran it several times, but only won it once.

Winning on that occasion, of course, made it special but it was memorable for other reasons. Establishing a good lead quite early allowed me to run without pressure, just as I had done in the Somerset Cross Country Championship. Once you are in the lead in a race and have established a gap on your pursuers, provided you still feel strong, suddenly you are free. You run without fear or inhibition. The angst that goes with desperate competition disappears and if, as at Bournemouth, the course is to your liking running becomes nothing except immense pleasure. Being pleasurable makes it easy, even if you can't run even the tiniest bit faster at any stage. I ran through groves of trees on a dry gravelly surface strewn with pine needles, over small humps and protruding tree roots, up gentle slopes and down the other side, nothing steep, no mud, no rough ankle-turning ground, with the sun blazing down and scorching my shoulders. It was, perhaps, the most blissful race I ever ran, appropriately enough for someone born on midsummer's day.

There are some who would dispute the idea that hardness has no place in running well. They are the masochists who get satisfaction from the idea that running should be hard, the harder the better. They are the hair shirt brigade, who raise suffering for their art almost to the level of the purpose itself. They seek out the toughest hill climbs and thickest mud, and wait for the most atrocious weather to run in. They run at six o'clock in the morning when all sensible people are fast asleep and wear just a vest and shorts, whatever the weather. They are not usually very good runners, which is why they seek their satisfaction in battling the elements and being 'HARD'. Perhaps they were brainwashed at school, as I almost was, by house runs (see Chapter 2) and running as punishment.

Unfortunately the cult of glorifying suffering can extend to non participants, those who don't run themselves but merely coach or organise or otherwise control the activities of runners or simply stand and watch. I shall always be grateful that I never had a coach to kick me out of bed in the middle of the night, or force me up one in two sand dunes or over ploughed fields, or to strip to my vest and shorts on a cold day to toughen me up. But I did run on one or two cross country courses that had obviously been designed by an ardent believer in the creed of 'real' cross country. On one occasion I found myself running over extremely rough and wet grazing land where the ground was littered with rocks, like currants in bread dough. On each lap there was a river crossing. As I approached the river for the second time I was already looking for an excuse to drop out. I couldn't really run; it was more like picking my way through a minefield. Someone must have been looking after me because, half way across the river, the plastic plate that held the spikes of one of my shoes dropped off. For all I know it's still there, amongst the rocks and gravel of that stream. I dropped out of that race with a clear conscience and may have saved myself a broken ankle at the same time.

There really is no need to make running any harder than it already is. The only reason that training is sometimes made quite hard is in order that running can become easier in the future. From hard comes easy and, ultimately, the aim of all serious runners is not just to run well but to run well and easily at the same time.

Worse than the adoption of the belief in pain and suffering for sport's sake by those who are themselves involved in the sport is the same belief filtering into the minds of the media and the general public. There is something extremely vicariously attractive about a person overcoming hardship in order to achieve a goal. So completing a marathon, for example, with an obvious disadvantage or after a very painful process, becomes more meritorious than completing it easily, irrespective of the time it takes. Maybe it is more meritorious, but not in running terms. I enjoyed the film 'Run fat boy run', but I was disappointed not to have found out who won the race.

I believe that the London marathon was once completed by a man in a diving suit. Good for him. As an achievement that must rank with climbing Mount Everest or swimming the English Channel. A report of the Great North Run included the fact that *'among those taking part was a man who ran with a fridge on his back.'* Good for him too. But what has either of those feats got to do with running? How can they be reported in the press and on radio and television in the same context as the élite races in the same events? The fact that they are considered newsworthy as a part of what are essentially running events is yet another indication of the way in which the nature of road running races has been distorted beyond recognition.

The process that was described in Chapter 9 as hijacking works like this. The media see all the component aspects of the sport of running and notice that some of them have great potential public appeal. Public appeal is all they are interested in. These may not be the things that are important to serious runners or to the sport itself, but, nevertheless, they may be involved in some way in the pursuit of running. Tolerating and overcoming hardship or disadvantage is a good example. They also notice certain similarities between different forms of what they see as the same thing. So, for example, wheelchair racing is like running in that competitors line up at the start, race over the same course and one person wins. Wheelchair racers, of course, are doubly appealing because they are disadvantaged. No one points out that their disadvantage does not extend to their ability to race in a wheelchair. I am quite sure that if I got in a wheelchair and tried to complete a marathon I would fail miserably. It is actually quicker to travel in a wheelchair than on foot. Wheelchair racers regularly complete the marathon distance over half an hour quicker than the best runners, which is why the wheelchair race gets off first.

Putting the two things together, the appeal of people conquering their personal disadvantages, and the tenuous connection between different ways of covering a distance on the road, a strange chimera is created that maximises public interest. If, at the same time it minimises the relevance of the sport of good, old fashioned running, then so be it. As long as it is good box office. To quote Juvenal, *'The people long eagerly for just two things - bread and circuses.'* The media today, in their coverage of the big events such as the city marathons, and the organisers, in putting them on in the first place, make sure that at least the people get their circuses.

So appealing is the idea of someone achieving an objective that is extremely tough, that it has become the prime emphasis in relation to the presentation of running by the media and, indeed of many other activities, both sporting and non-sporting. This was made very obvious during and immediately after the 2012 London Paralympics, where the theme of overcoming adversity rendered the actual events almost irrelevant. Glorification of the Paralympics may seem to have little to do with the subject of able-bodied running, except that it involves the same contrived reasoning, the greater the hardship the more commendable the performance. In this topsy-turvy world of allotted applause a runner who runs slowly can end up receiving more acclaim than one who runs fast, simply because he or she finds running harder.

The one and only marathon I have ever won was the 1982 Northern Ireland Championship marathon held at Newtownards, county Down. The race was at the beginning of June on a day that lived up to and beyond the epithet, 'flaming June'. In reports of the race the local press nicknamed it the 'Murder Marathon'. *'Yesterday's temperature, which soared into the mid 70s, was just about perfect for everything but marathon running. The drop-out rate in the Newtownards race was catastrophic, as around 100 of the race's competitors were hammered into sun stroke submission.'* said one paper. *'M was for 'murder' for the competitors in Saturday's sun-baked and soul destroying Newtownards Festival marathon.'* said another, and went on, *'Mind-boggling heat, a mountainous circuit and the mystical marathon wall reduced many of the participants to walking zombies.'*

It was certainly a hot day and the tarmac did melt, and it was hilly, but I think the press delighted overmuch in painting a picture of the conditions. One paper even described it as *'unquestionably one of the most arduous and gruelling marathon races ever to be staged in Ireland'.*

They were in their element, creating a story of submission by some and triumph by others in the face of extreme hardship. Even in my case they managed to give the impression of a battle won against all the odds and with suffering on an almost Pyrrhic scale.

I got home from the race at about five o'clock with a migraine headache. Luckily for me it had come on after rather than during the race. I was, therefore, in bed, asleep, when the local reporter rang for something to put in the Sunday paper. The fact that I never spoke to him didn't stop him quoting me. *'I ran the last few miles so slowly I was surprised to find myself still leading.'* Actually that was true, but I never said it. *'Winning made up for all the suffering I endured during the race.'* This time the quote was also invented but, not only untrue, but completely out of character. However bad I may have felt in any running I ever did, I never thought of it as suffering. I **suffered** a migraine headache that same evening and I did get tired and hot and dehydrated during the race, but the two sources of discomfort were incomparable. Nor did winning the race make up for anything. There was nothing to be made up for. But the idea of suffering, and overcoming suffering, and it all being worthwhile in the end, was already well fixed in the reporter's ethos, just as the idea that the Paralympics are somehow more worthy than the able bodied Olympics is now fixed in the general public's minds.

Those who don't actually run love the idea that it involves pain and suffering. Either that or they assume that it is the same for competitors as it would be for themselves, if they were to do it. A report of the 2012 Great North Run, for example, went as follows, *'After 13 gruelling miles and 59 minutes of torture it all came down to the last five yards'.* If racing, however hard, is torture, what does that make me and all the other runners like me in the history of the sport? Contrary to popular mythology we are not masochists; we want to enjoy our running and we usually do so.

Had I been able to speak to the journalist who rang me at home after the Newtownards marathon and had I told the truth, that I didn't mind the heat and I didn't find the race any more distressful than other marathons I'd run, I wonder how I would have been quoted. It would have been a choice between honesty and a good story. I think the story would have won.

For others in that race the heat really did have disastrous effects. One prominent Northern Ireland runner, who had run internationally over the marathon distance, '...*suffering a dizzy spell, almost crashed into a car at 17 miles and sensibly called it a day*'. Another competitor '*imagined the tacky tar-macadam road was rising to face him and bailed out of the race at 22 miles*'. The man who finished second was stretchered off to hospital suffering from heat exhaustion. Interestingly, he had beaten me in that year's Belfast marathon, one month previously, by just over a minute (2:31:44 to 2:32:45), yet here I beat him by 16 minutes (2:33.16 to 2:49.37). Note that I ran only a minute and a half slower than in the Belfast race, on a much hillier course and a much hotter day.

I still find that difficult to believe, that I won by over a quarter of an hour. With about two miles to go someone had shouted at me something about fifteen minutes. I assumed he meant that I had fifteen minutes left to run, though that puzzled me because no one refers to how far is left in a race as a time, always a distance. I dismissed the information as meaningless. At that point I was struggling to keep going myself and running pretty slowly. I was terrified of being caught and passed. It never occurred to me that I might be fifteen minutes ahead of the next competitor!

I have always enjoyed running on a hot day, but never before had I been aware that I was especially good at running in the heat. Heat never affected me like it did some other runners. My mother claimed, as much I think for her and our (mine and my brothers' and sister's) amusement, to have been descended from Spanish gypsies. Gypsies are believed to have come originally from northern India. That would explain my mother's once jet black hair and her fine bones and, if true, perhaps also, my tolerance of the heat.

It goes to show that what is hard for one person is not necessarily hard for everyone. I could never run in thick mud. In 1981 Julian

Goater, another of Great Britain's finest distance runners, won the English National Cross Country Championship by two minutes, an amazing feat given the wealth of running talent in action that day. I can only assume it was because Goater was an especially good mud runner. The championships were held at London's Parliament Hill fields, a course renowned for its sticky clay. That year it was particularly wet and muddy. Then there are the fell runners, to whom a mountain climb and a suicidal descent are of no consequence, and the ultra-distance runners who seem to be able to keep going at the same steady pace however far they run. The sensible runner sticks to what he's good at and avoids things he finds harder than other runners do like the plague. That's why I like firm, dry, flat or gently undulating courses and why I don't complain when the sun comes up and the temperature rises.

Fear of running in the heat, especially marathons, reached a point of near paranoia around the nineteen eighties and left a lasting legacy in the present obsession with 'keeping hydrated' or 'taking water on board'. For many years I ran long distances, including marathons, with not a single drink. I relate what happened to me, for example, in the 1976 Welsh marathon in Chapter 10. I was silly, but not as silly as today's pundits would claim. I sometimes got seriously dehydrated, I slowed down drastically, I probably got overheated at times, but I never had to stop, I never collapsed, and I always recovered by the next morning. There have been some classic examples of heat stress in marathon races, notably Jim Peters in the Vancouver Empire Games marathon of 1954, and the Swiss runner, Gabriela Anderson-Schiess, in the Los Angeles Olympic marathon in 1984. Both runners presented a pitiful sight on the track as they approached the finish line, staggering, wandering from side to side, almost falling. Peters never made it. Anderson-Shiess did, having taken six minutes to cover the last four hundred metres. But both recovered, with no obvious lasting ill effects.

The truth is that more runners have died from over-hydration than from dehydration. It is simply a myth that you need to sip water during the period before a race to make sure you are properly hydrated and only in the longest races on the hottest days do you need to drink (an old term for taking water on board) during a race. Still I see runners out training, carrying their obligatory water bottle, even on cool overcast days. I know they are unlikely to be running further than six or seven miles at a pace that will hardly raise a sweat. Two minutes into the last half marathon I ever ran runners were already stopping for a pee behind the hedge. That's just plain daft.

If hot weather can make running uncomfortable, cold and wet weather is far worse. A word I rarely use in relation to running, one that is a favourite of commentators on the sport, is 'pain'. I don't believe the act of running by itself can ever cause pain. Nor do I believe that the word is a simile for discomfort, or tiredness, or stress, or any of the unpleasant feelings that are the direct result of running. But I have suffered pain while running and quite often it has been the result of cold weather.

When I was teaching I sometimes trained in the evenings with a colleague who worked at the same school. He was a good middle distance runner, not in the highest class but well capable of running a mile in less than 4:10. He would knock on my door at around six thirty, and we'd do about seven miles together. Whatever the weather, he always turned up in shorts. On the coldest nights, there he would be, in white shorts. I felt a bit of a wimp in my track suit bottoms, gloves, anorak and woolly hat but nothing would have persuaded me to dress in less. I had previously learned a very valuable lesson and that was to start a training run feeling comfortable. If the first step outside the door and into the cold night air is the least bit unpleasant it makes training ten times harder and missing training ten times easier.

At the end of our training runs I sometimes wondered whether he was the wise one. I would come back soaked in sweat, knowing that I wouldn't cool down inside the warm house for a long while and that every stitch of clothing would need washing if it wasn't to smell appalling the next day. Still, I preferred my discomfort to come later rather than sooner. For a long time I thought I could always beat the cold as long as I dressed for it. That was until I started extending the distance of my night time runs.

Here things get a bit delicate. I am dealing with something that only another man will understand. In the eighties we had some particularly cold winters. I used to dress as normal for a winter evening run: cotton Y-fronts, two tops, one short sleeved and one long sleeved, tracksters, socks, gloves, windproof jacket and woolly hat. As I left the house I would feel the chill of the air on my face, not an unpleasant feeling, and that was the only indication that it was a cold night. Ten minutes later I would start feeling quite warm and consider removing my gloves. Another ten minutes and I would very obviously be sweating. It takes about half an hour for sweat to soak into the underclothes to the point of saturation, but when that point is reached, suddenly those clothes lose all their insulating properties.

Everyone must have experienced at one time or another the pain of cold finger tips, a pain that first increases as warmth is applied before it eventually diminishes. It feels as if your finger tips have been hit with a hammer. The same pain in another part of the body that sticks out, but only in the male anatomy, is far more disconcerting. I endured it on many hour-long, freezing cold, night time runs, once the downward trickle of sweat, over time, had completely soaked my Y-fronts, both my tops and the mid-region of my tracksters. Once I'd gone through the experience a few times I got used to the idea that there was never any lasting damage, nothing went black and nothing dropped off and I just put up with it. But it never got less painful and I never discovered how to prevent it. If I put on more clothes I sweated more and sooner, which exacerbated the problem. Gloves down the pants or, in extreme cases, gloves and woolly hat down the pants was probably the most effective remedy.

I have also endured severe pain from cold when hail or sleet or just very cold rain has caught me unexpectedly without a hat of any sort. Extremely cold precipitation against the forehead can be mighty painful. It would often happen on what at first appeared to be a pleasant spring day (hence no hat). Then, suddenly, the sky would turn black and a grey blizzard of hail balls would come from nowhere. To have your bare thighs bombarded with ice is uncomfortable enough, but, against the forehead, it's torture. It's torture in reality, and not just in the mind of some imaginative journalist. I find the only remedy is to run with one hand covering my forehead. Luckily those spring showers are usually short-lived.

The 1972 English National Cross Country Championships, held at Sutton Park, Birmingham on March 4th, which, luckily for me as it turned out, I didn't run, saw a particularly nasty instance of a sudden change for the worse in the weather. A lot of runners, quite unprepared at the start of the race for what was to hit them in a few minutes time, and, therefore dressed in no more than singlet and shorts, suffered severe chilling, amounting in many cases to hypothermia.

The day started with bright sunshine but progressively deteriorated. As the races started, it began to rain. Then, as the senior race, the last on the programme progressed, the rain turned to sleet and then to snow and the temperature plummeted. The biting cold was added to by a strong, icy wind blowing into the runners' faces as they headed towards the finish of every lap. The senior race in the National Championships is nine miles in length. That's nearly an hour's running for a lot of runners, a long time to be exposed to such arctic conditions. There's very little shelter on the Sutton Park course; it's almost treeless, open heathland.

Athletics Weekly, reporting the race, described the events of that afternoon under the headline, 'Arctic weather turned 'National' into a grim survival test.' *'The scene in the official's marquee after the race was gruesome, as runners staggered in seeking shelter from the raging snowstorm outside. With icicles in their hair* (this is not journalistic licence – I have often experienced my woolly hat stuck to my hair with ice, or what is actually frozen sweat, in very cold weather) *they shivered uncontrollably and speechless as helpers tried to massage their frozen bodies. These were the lucky ones; others were whisked off to hospital or were left to make their own way back to the changing rooms about a mile and a half away.'* It concluded, *'This wasn't sport ... it was a survival test.'*

To some, mainly non runners, running always was a survival test, but runners, especially serious runners, know better. No one emerged from

Sutton Park with any credit **because** of the weather that day, not in running terms, at any rate. No one would have wished for a day like that, even if they sensed that it might have been to their advantage. The weather made people suffer, and favoured the tough, but spoiled the race and the event.

In a letter from Cambridge and Coleridge Athletic Club to the organising committee, written immediately after the event, some of the runners at the end of the race were described as, *'unable to hold a limb still, sobbing, and even frightened of what was happening to their bodies.'* I didn't see it, but it really was that bad.

There is very little defence against hypothermia. In the opposite case, when the body is overheating, the very activity that is generating the heat becomes impossible. An overheated runner simply cannot continue to run at the same rate. It may not even be possible to continue running at all. Stopping running, either voluntarily or through physical collapse, is the best antidote. If the body is rapidly cooling, however, there is no obvious way for it to reverse the process. Simply stopping will do no good at all. Being exposed to near freezing rain, sleet or snow for a long period of time with vicious squalls adding to the cooling effect, with no protective clothing, as runners were during the 1972 National in Sutton Park, is not a lot different from being immersed in cold water. Life expectancy in near freezing water is measured in minutes. I have, in retrospect rather foolishly perhaps, gone for long training runs on my own over the South Downs or the Belfast hills in the winter, when it has been lashing down with rain or when there was snow or frost on the ground. I have also gone for long runs when the sun beat down from a blue sky and the temperature was Mediterranean, the sweat dripped off me in cupfuls, and I never drank until I got back, sometimes two hours later. I think the winter runs were more dangerous.

Apart from injuries, which can be very painful, and cramp, which is also very painful and has added several minutes to a number of the marathon times I have run, I can think of few running associated pains that I've experienced that are worth calling pains. Blisters and sore nipples and rubbing under the arms or around the groin are mere irritations. As for the common usage of the word pain to describe what a runner goes through during a hard race, in particular a marathon, it just annoys me. A paragraph at the beginning of the chapter 'Hitting the Wall', in John Bryant's 'The London Marathon' starts, *'Marathon runners live with pain. They flirt with pain.'* and goes on, *'...everyone knows the marathon race is painful, that's the whole point of it. If it didn't hurt, no one would do it. If it wasn't agony, it wouldn't be interesting. Pain defines its mythology and its reality.'* I know John Bryant is a runner. He has been through it himself, and he has a better time for a marathon under his belt than I have. But I think that when he wrote that, he was wearing his journalist's hat, and was using a different dictionary from the one I use. In my book, pain is something sharp that makes you cry out, and can sometimes be unbearable, and, when it gets really bad, only then is it called agony. I would have made a very reliable keeper of secrets during the second world war, if all the Gestapo had thrown at me was a simulation of the last few miles of a marathon.

In the summer of 1969 I ran the BUSF 10,000m at Motspur Park in Surrey, finishing fifth in 31:54.6. The track was a cinder track, dry, dusty and uneven, more like the area around the goal mouth of a football pitch after a long period of dry weather than a running track. I didn't know what to wear on my feet so, in a moment of youthful impetuosity I decided to run in bare feet. I finished the race with a number of blisters but none of them had broken, so my feet were still intact, but tender. The next day I put on an extra pair of socks and went for a run as usual. Again my feet were tender but barely painful. If you do a lot of running, with or without shoes, the feet get pretty hard. Blisters are rarely a problem for a serious runner.

I did succumb once in a race to a blister, but it was more a mental than a physical capitulation, and it certainly had nothing to do with the degree of pain. It was the race in which I set my best time for a marathon. At about twenty two miles I was running in the leading group of five and still feeling reasonably strong. I knew, though, that I was hanging on at that stage and that, if anyone was going to be dropped it would be me. I started to feel a sharp pain in the base of my little toe with every stride, as if I was being poked with a sharp stick. I became convinced that I had picked up a small piece of road-stone in my shoe. I debated whether I should just put up with it or whether it would be more sensible to stop and empty it out. I knew that if I stopped I would never get back with the group again. But I could sense I was on the verge of being dropped anyway. I imagined the tiny piece of grit eating into my foot, grinding away at the skin and into the flesh. I thought how easy it would be to stop for a few seconds and how much relief it would bring. In the end I simply gave in to the pressure of hanging on to the group, of keeping up the relentless pace when I'd already been running for two hours, and was getting pretty tired. I stopped, pulled off my shoe and then my sock, only to find that the source of the sharp niggling pain was a small blister. Had I known that was all it was, I wouldn't have stopped. I might have run a few seconds faster but, then again, I might not have done. My only real regret is that I had given in to what amounted to nothing more than mental weakness.

What about the wall, the same 'mystical marathon wall' that was mentioned in the newspaper report of the Newtownards marathon quoted earlier? What is it like to hit the wall and what causes you to do so anyway? And surely there's some truth in descriptions of the suffering that runners go through in the final stages of a marathon? Why did Paula Radcliffe drop out of the Athens Olympic marathon? What makes anyone drop out of a marathon, or any other distance race for that matter? When people talk or write about those last miles of a marathon being so awful are they telling it as it is or are they wildly exaggerating?

I should be able to answer these questions. And I can, up to a point. What I can't do is to share with others the exact feelings that accompany the last miles of a marathon, anymore than I can say what it's like to run as hard as I can, or convey the delights of running freely and easily on a warm day across beautiful countryside. These are things which are known only to those who have experienced them. I can't say why Paula Radcliffe dropped out in Athens, but I find it easy to put myself in her position and know that I would probably have done the same thing and felt the same way, because I have been there myself. I don't mean that literally, of course. I didn't run the Athens women's Olympic marathon. But I have reached the same state of collapse in a marathon and I have seen the promise of the first three quarters of a race turn to dust and disappear like the washing up water when the plug is pulled out.

Any distance race is a tough physical test. The marathon is especially tough on account of its length. Over two hours of even quite easy running leaves the body in a state of exhaustion. If you're lucky it can be quite pleasant exhaustion, the sort that adds extra enjoyment to a quick shower, a bottle of cold beer, a bite to eat, and a comfy chair, but it is exhaustion nevertheless. You may not notice it creep up on you, but every new stride removes a little more stored energy from your muscles, a drop more water from your cells, adds a trace more of waste products to your bloodstream and does a tiny bit more damage to the working tissues. With increasing exhaustion comes decreasing ability to run efficiently. Running becomes harder and when it becomes as hard as it can be it becomes slower. You might expect this process of increasing effort and then slowing down to be gradual and evenly progressive, and so it is for the first two hours or so of a marathon. But then comes the wall!

There is nothing mystical about the wall. It has a very simple explanation. The body can only store a certain amount of readily available energy in the form of glycogen in the muscles. When you start a distance run there is plenty of glycogen to fuel even the hardest running. The glycogen is almost instantaneously converted to the simple sugar glucose which, when combined with oxygen in the muscle cells, provides the energy needed for running. After about two hours of running, shorter if you are running fast, longer if you are running slowly, but inevitably at some point, the stored glycogen runs out. That is what hitting the wall is, quite simply running out of muscle glycogen. You can keep going, using energy derived from blood sugar and fat, but at a very much reduced rate. Within the space of a minute or two you find yourself running much slower, perhaps two minutes per mile slower, and there's nothing you can do about it.

There is a way to delay the arrival of the wall and that is by means of a protocol of training, dieting and 'carbo-loading' in the week prior to a marathon. The method is referred to as the Saltin diet. Does it work? In my experience it almost certainly does, but it's risky, almost unendurable in its initial stage, and, even when it appears to have worked, there's no proof of the fact.

The Saltin diet involves, firstly, draining the muscles of their stored glycogen by means of a long run six days before a marathon race, then making sure every last drop of glycogen is got rid of by means of more running and a carbohydrate fast over the next two or three days, with only protein and fats being eaten, and, lastly, bingeing on all things carbohydrate: cakes and puddings, chips and pasta, bread and jam, anything made of sugar and starch. The two contrasting stages of the diet are referred to as carbohydrate depletion and carbohydrate loading, or carbo-loading, for short. With the modern tendency for short cuts and quick remedies, and the avoidance of anything difficult, the depletion stage is now commonly left out. It is thought that a pasta party the evening before a marathon is enough to boost a runner's glycogen stores. But that is like expecting to get something out of a vending-machine without putting any money in first. The carbohydrate depletion phase, I hate to correct those who don't want to know, is absolutely crucial to the method.

It is this part of the diet that is unbearable. For a day or two, you are trying to live a normal life and run as usual when you don't have an ounce of energy left, added to which you have a permanent craving for the very things that you can't eat. On the day after the energy-sapping long run that starts the whole process, it takes the fortitude of a monk to sit down to a meal of nothing more than a mushroom omelette and salad, when your whole body is like an empty sack crying out to be stuffed with mounds of sweet stodge. You feel weak and trembly. Every effort seems magnified ten times. You hardly have the energy to cross the room. Yet you're supposed to go for a run! The next day is worse still and, as for the third day of depletion, I don't think I ever got to it. Two days was all I could take. The diet is risky because, in its weakened state, your body is very likely to succumb to any cold or flu virus that comes its way.

Three things convince me that the Saltin diet works. The first is that it has the science to back it up. In various studies the muscle glycogen levels of experimental subjects have been shown to be increased by the diet, quite considerably so. The second is that the few times that I ran a marathon without slowing down dramatically towards the end, all took place after my having done the diet. The third is not really a convincing reason, more a very personal form of mental imaging logic. I see the muscles as cupboards full of bags of glycogen. To get more in, first you empty the cupboards bare. Then you stack the bags back neatly and, as if by magic, you find that you have inexplicably made room for a number of extra bags. It's the principle of tidying the garage, or the bookshelves, or the office desk.

I followed the Saltin diet before my most disappointing marathon (see Chapter 10) in which I hit the wall with a crash that must have been heard throughout Belfast. That didn't mean that the diet hadn't work, merely that it has its limits. I ran too fast that day and ate up my stored glycogen at a higher rate than was sensible. Even though my starting supply of muscle glycogen was higher than normal, it was still finite, and it ran out at about twenty two miles.

You don't so much hit the wall as wade into it. Imagine running along a firm sandy beach. Then you start crossing small puddles of water, splashing through them as if they aren't there. Then you hit a longer puddle that is ankle deep and, suddenly, you can feel the resistance of the water as you pull your feet out of it at each stride. The next puddle is even longer and knee deep. You can no longer lift your feet out of the water but have to push through it. From then on the water is continuous and up to your thighs. A short while ago you were running. Now you are wading. That is what the wall is like.

Running after hitting the wall is not painful. It is not hard to keep going, but it is impossible to keep going at anything like the same pace. If anything, once you are resigned to the fact, it is a relief from the physical effort of running at a fast pace. It is, however, accompanied by other unpleasant feelings: slight nausea, fatigue and weakness and, worst of all in my opinion, various forms of mental distress: frustration, disappointment, a sense of inadequacy and of loss. The mental response to hitting the wall is similar to grief.

Running for any length of time in a badly fatigued state is very debilitating, much more so than the apparently effortless running that brought you to that state in the first place. If you hit the wall at 20 miles in a marathon, as I have been known to do, you still have over 6 miles to cover, and you are in a condition that is about to make the first part of the distance seem as nothing. It is a condition that steadily gets worse. It took my two last completed marathons, the 2007 and the 2010 Belfast events, to convince me that my marathon running days were over. In 2007 I was 60 years old and in 2010, 63. Oddly, in the latter event, I ran over 15 minutes faster and finished in 3:41:09, but on both occasions, I reached a point where, having to choose between walking and trying to run, I chose walking because it was quicker. As I started the last mile of the 2007 race I was passed by another 60 year old, a runner I had known well from the time I first came to Belfast. He was a fellow club member, more a miler and half miler than a distance runner. He beat me by ten minutes. I still can't believe he managed to gain that amount of time over me in the space of one mile.

As I covered the same stretch of road in 2010 I may have been going even slower. I had reached the point of simply trying to keep moving forwards about six miles earlier. I could still manage to do it, but I was in a trance-like state, the nearest thing I had ever experienced to going to sleep standing up, but still shuffling towards the finish line at the same time. As people lining the roadside shouted encouragement, 'Well done', 'Keep going', 'You're nearly there', and other kind things, I just longed for someone to stop me, firmly but gently, saying, 'Come on, old man, you've had enough'.

So was I suffering? Was I going through torture and agony? Was I in distress? Was I in danger? Was I straining my heart to bursting point? Was I earning a place in the columns of the popular press by conquering adversity? Not really any of the above. There was discomfort, certainly, but it was tolerable, it was controllable, and it was alleviated by the knowledge that the finish was getting closer all the time. There are many reasons to keep going to the finish when all hopes of doing well have fizzled out long ago. None of them, in my view, is strong enough to overcome the degree of suffering that commentators on the sport would have us believe is involved. As I proceeded along the ultimate mile of my last marathon, for no good reason other than sheer obstinacy and a desire to get it over with, a part of me was still, in a perverse way that perhaps only another runner can understand, sort of enjoying myself.

CHAPTER 14
Sex and drugs and all things controversial

'You know that, if you had a bent tube one arm of which was the size of a pipe stem and the other big enough to hold the ocean, water would stand at the same height in one as in the other. Controversy equalises fools and wise men in the same way.'

Oliver Wendell Holmes.

Running has always been a pretty simple, honest and uncontroversial sport. The worst offences, when I started competing, and for many years after, were the odd false start, the occasional accusation of cutting corners, one or two incidents of barging or impeding, misdirection in races by partisan course marshals, even, in some instances, a total lack of any directions at all, causing runners, usually the leading ones, to go off course. That was about the height of it. For years I ran races with absolutely no thought of the possibility of unfair practices. I never looked at the runner standing next to me on the start line, noticed his prominent leg muscles and spotty cheeks and wondered whether he was on steroids. When someone ahead of me in a race suddenly slipped into the bushes by the side of the road, I assumed it was for a call of nature and not to hide away until the coast was clear and then to take a short cut, or to emerge at sometime during the next lap (though I have seen that happen).

Only once in my whole running life have I been directly involved in any controversy, and then I was never accused to my face. I only heard about it later. I had just moved to Northern Ireland and, although I was fit and running quite well, I hadn't yet adjusted to the move. I was still not up to the standard I felt I should have been. Frankly, I was a shadow of my normal self. They say that, as far as health and wellbeing are concerned, moving home, along with bereavement, divorce and loss of a job, are the most dangerous things anyone can face. I had not only moved home and job, but country as well. It took me another three years to settle down fully and start to run as I knew I could.

Despite this I managed to win the 'Malcolm Cup', a cross country race for 'juniors'. How, you might ask, does a thirty two year old win a junior race? It was possible because the term junior in Northern Ireland athletics includes not only those under a certain age but also anyone who has never won a medal in a senior event. Because I had only just appeared on the Northern Ireland scene, naturally, I hadn't had the chance to win anything. I could have been sixty years old at the time and still run as a 'junior'.

I got dropped by twenty or thirty yards in the middle of the race as two much younger runners, proper age-related juniors, took the lead and stretched away from me. They were both from one club and I was from another. With about a mile to go, dogged pride, and a determination not to have to hate myself afterwards, forced me to summon up a bit of will power, and I gradually closed the gap. With just the finishing straight ahead I drew alongside the leader and sprinted away for the win. I think it was the only time in my life I have won a race with a sprint finish.

Of course I was pleased. I won a track suit and the cup. I wore the track suit for several years until it fell apart at the seams. It was not a quality product. The cup, I think, went straight into my club's trophies cabinet. I certainly never saw it. Or, maybe it existed in name only.

Over a drink afterwards I was told that there had been a protest from the club to which the two young runners I had beaten belonged. I was alleged to have cut corners when catching them up. I was never asked to defend myself, so the complaint can't have been taken very seriously. The incident was quickly forgotten.

I blamed the course. It was over open grassland and marked, as so many cross country courses are, with a series of small flags on sticks, pushed into the ground at wide intervals. I wasn't aware of having deliberately cut corners or even of having run the wrong side of any flag. I simply followed the line of mud that marked where everyone had already run (it was a lap course) and pinned my eyes to the backs of the two runners in front of me, running where they ran. There were too few flags and a number of them were already trodden into the ground by that stage, so it was hard enough to see exactly where the course was supposed to go.

The protest seems to me, looking back, to have been made for the sake of protesting, an example of the less acceptable side of club rivalries. I know I didn't deliberately cover a shorter distance than I should have done and, therefore, was no cheat. Had I been disqualified I would have been resentful, but without an iota of guilt or shame. Several weeks later I was talking to the runner who finished second and he referred to the occasion in a way that might have seemed inimical, except that he had a huge grin on his face and was already, by then, a good friend of mine. I realised that the union of runners is quite separate from the union of officials. It is a true and amicable union, based on mutual respect and shared aims. Another runner is the last person any runner would suspect of underhand actions.

Officials, however, are another kettle of fish. The majority are admirable, decent and reasonable people who give of their time and energy for no monetary reward. Most have been runners themselves at one time. Without them the sport couldn't exist. I take my hat off to them. The trouble is that, unlike the runners, officials have power. Officials organise and control. They make the rules and apply them. Sometimes they over-reach themselves. Unfortunately there are always one or two officials who think that officialism is a sign of strength when, in reality, flexibility and understanding are stronger. Consequently there is a division between those who run the sport and those who just run.

Here is a story about a petty official who, in a situation similar to mine, that is, a case of corner cutting, managed to alienate virtually the whole of Britain's distance running community with one mad act of over-zealous application of the rules. The story has a happy ending. Indeed it could be said to have two happy endings. The first was the more or less satisfactory outcome; the second is the way that runners, *en masse,* some of whom had every motive to side with the official, rallied round and unselfishly condemned what he had done.

The 1974 Polytechnic marathon, organised by Polytechnic Harriers and run on the 22nd June, was the selection race for the European Championships to be held in Rome later in the year. It was, therefore an important race, and attracted the cream of Britain's marathon talent. The race was won by the Japanese runner, Akio Usami in 2:15:16, not a bad time on a very hot and humid day. Second was Bernie Plain of Cardiff Athletic Club and third, the East German Eckhard Lesse (who went on to win the silver medal in the European Games for which this race was the British trial). Fourth, apparently, because he did cross the finishing line in fourth place, was Newport Harriers' Bob Sercombe. But the referee, Arthur Winter, had other ideas. He decided to disqualify both Bob Sercombe and eighth finisher, one of Britain's top marathon runners at the time, Colin Kirkham, for cutting corners.

Winter's account of the incident was that at about the 22 miles mark, on a right hand bend, the two runners refused to obey his instruction to stay on the left hand side of the road. *'They ignored me and were perfectly abusive to me',* he alleged. *'I had to jump out of the way.'* The rule for road races where the course is not traffic free is that runners should stay on the left hand side, between the edge of the road and the mid line. Courses are measured accordingly.

It looked for a while as if Bob Sercombe might lose not only his second Briton place in the AAA marathon and his fourth place in the race as a whole, but also his selection for the European Games. *'He was a picture of dejection as he sat on the grass after the race, exhausted, angry and confused.'* wrote Athletics Weekly.

But then the happy endings. Although the disqualifications were ultimately upheld, Sercombe was selected for Rome. Almost as soon as the disqualifications came to light, fellow competitors in the race, athletics fans and spectators alike, rallied round in a manner that brought a lump to the throat. The blood that flows between runners turned out to be far thicker than the cold water of officialdom. Ron Hill, who finished sixth, refused to accept his prize in protest against the disqualification. Keith Angus, another top British marathon runner of the seventies, who had finished one place behind Sercombe and, therefore, had the most to gain from the disqualification, declared that he would not accept selection for the European Championships over Sercombe. The consensus was that, since practically all the runners had run on the right hand side of the road at times, it was quite unfair to penalise just two of them. The referee's action was to be deplored and could only be explained by the fact that, to quote one runner, *'the poor bloke* (the referee, Arthur Winter) *just freaked out in the heat'*.

A week after the race Athletics Weekly carried a number of letters that confirmed the terrific camaraderie that exists amongst runners, exposing a rich vein of wit into the bargain. First to write to Athletics weekly was Colin Kirkham, one of the disqualified runners, to say that publication of his new book, *'Short cuts to marathon success'*, was delayed but that he was available to advise anyone who might have *'corners to iron out or bends that need straightening.'* Another correspondent referred to Arthur Winter *'successfully promoting the fastest time in the world on the basis of right hand turns from Windsor to Chiswick, year after year.'* Bob Sercombe himself, while adamantly denying he had ever been abusive (though no one would have blamed him if he had been) admitted that he had been running on the right hand side of the road but *'so was every other runner in the race'* and pointed out that, *'in fact two of the feeding stations were on the right hand side of the road!'*

The committee of Polytechnic Harriers met on July 5th to consider the referee's report and a report from the race organiser. The referee's report was more or less the same as the one that had already been submitted to the BAAB (British Amateur Athletic Board). Predictably, the club, with regret that the disqualifications were necessary and with sympathy for the two runners who were disqualified (of course), concluded that the decision of the referee had to be upheld. The disqualifications stood. The BAAB meanwhile had saved the club even more embarrassment by ignoring the fact that Bob Sercombe had been disqualified and had technically, therefore, not been the second British runner in the selection race for the European Championships team, by selecting him after all. What a relief!

What this incident showed clearly was that not only is there a divide, as there is in any organised group, from the very smallest club to the nation and its parliamentary government as a whole, between those who merely participate and those who officiate but that this divide can at times become filled with acrimony. When a difference of opinion between the community of, in this case, athletes and that of officialdom becomes strongly felt, even hostile, officialdom invariably wins. It wins by adopting a tight-knit posture, wielding its power, and sheltering behind the inflexible person's defence - the rule book.

One of the few letters of support for the disqualification of Sercombe and Kirkham (strange how their names rhyme) encapsulated perfectly the arguments used by officialdom everywhere to defend an unreasonable and unpopular decision, namely: 1: these are the rules, 2: rules are necessary and must be obeyed, 3: a rule was broken, 4: the fact that almost everyone broke the same rule is irrelevant and cannot be a mitigating factor, 5: the rule was only applied for the benefit (in this instance the safety on the road) of all participants.

To my mind, this sort of phlegmatic logic (for the argument is undeniably logical), has no place in a sport like road running where the participants, the runners themselves, are of by far the greatest importance. Officials are there for the good of the runners and the sport, not the other way round. Usually this is well recognised and accepted by all and that is one reason why I always loved being a part of the running scene. In all my seriously competitive years there was a general sense of affinity and joint ownership amongst runners and running enthusiasts. Everyone, from the humblest competitor to the highest official, contributed to the good of the sport, supporting each other and creating a wonderfully friendly atmosphere in which to run. Instances of disagreement and argument were extremely uncommon. Only in the last thirty years has there been a noticeable rise in the unwelcome power of officialdom within athletics. I suspect that this rise may be partly to blame for the decline in standards in distance running in this country. Runners and officials are no longer quite so obviously on the same side.

The Daily Telegraph weekend sport section on February 8th 2012 included a report of a row brewing over sponsorship issues prior to the forthcoming London Olympic Games. The sportswear firm Adidas were sponsoring the British Olympic team and the BOA (British Olympic Association), in order to comply with the contractual agreement, were compelling all athletes to wear Adidas kit. *'The rule that athletes had to wear the company's footwear at all times during the Olympic Games, including on the podium, would be strictly enforced,'* said the report.

Just for a moment consider the import of this. A body of officials is telling runners and other athletes and sportsmen and women what they **must** wear, for reasons that have nothing whatsoever to do with the sportsmen and women themselves (no, not even their safety). And on threat of what? Expulsion from the games, fines, forcibly super-glueing shoes to people's feet? Well certainly the first two of these. A week later the Daily Telegraph carried more on the same story, revealing that Olympic organisers *'...will fine or expel British competitors if they fail to uphold a 34-page Team Members' Agreement'*.

Never mind what was in that agreement. Maybe it was all perfectly reasonable. But what was not reasonable is that anyone should have been made to sign it. Nothing could make clearer the relationship that, in 2012, existed or that the officials think existed, between themselves and the athletes, including distance runners. It is not even as generous as that between employer and employee. It is more like slaves and slave owner and just as disrespectful. In Chapter 7 I talked about the loss of respect shown to runners in races. I put this forward as a good reason why the backbone of the sport of distance running has gradually dissolved away since the nineteen eighties, leaving just the hugely long tail and a tiny head, connected by nothing but empty space. Here we have the same attitude. Officialdom thinks it owns the athletes. It does not.

Distance running is and has always been a highly individualistic sport. The history of improvement in standards is filled with introverted, single minded, original, dedicated men and women who, until very recently, never got a penny from any source for their running, least of all from their controlling bodies or government. These people have made the sport what it is. For many years they put Great Britain at the top of the world distance running scene. If athletics has now become a money spinning business, with the Olympics in England again after sixty four years of travelling the world, it is the competitors both past and present who have made it so, not the organisers. In terms of status the athletes outrank the officials like the sun outranks the moon. At one time that was generally recognised. It should still be recognised now.

My fantasy is that I am such a good runner, head and shoulders above anyone else in the world, a practical certainty for the Olympic gold medal in the marathon, and probably the 10,000m as well, a better hope even than Mo Farah and Paula Radcliffe in her day, put together, that my expulsion from the games would cause an outcry from the whole country. Questions would be asked in parliament. Demonstrations and marches would be held throughout the land. Then I could tell the BOA what they could do with their agreement. I would wear whatever I liked during the Olympics, including on the podium, and I wouldn't sign anything unless I agreed with every single word of it, and I probably wouldn't sign it even then, just to show that I refused to be coerced. I wouldn't win, of course, against the massed forces of authority, but I would have made my point; and if my behaviour was a case of 'cutting off my nose to spite my face' I would explain that I would rather have a face without a nose than no face at all.

I have only gone down this side track because the action of the BOA is symptomatic of the controlling behaviour of all official bodies, just as with the example of Polytechnic Harriers' committee handing out disqualifications in 1974. No one questions it. What right has BOA to tell athletes they **must** do anything? What right had Polytechnic Harriers' officials to disqualify anyone who had put their heart and soul and hopes into a race, and into all the preparation for it, and, in the process, had made the race what it was? The sad truth is that rights come from rules and the rules are made by the very people who apply them. In effect, official bodies bestow themselves with the right to do whatever they choose. This is the case in the sport of distance running as much as anywhere else. And, just as elsewhere, control by officials and governing bodies in running has steadily become stricter, more at-a-distance, more subject to outside concerns and more complex as the years have gone by.

One of the most forceful driving factors behind tighter and tighter control and more and more power being wielded by officialdom is, of course, money. The commercialisation of athletics, including running, has been the major phenomenon of my running lifetime. Within the space of a few decades the sport has gone from one where not a penny changed hands, except, perhaps, under the table, or as a legitimate subscription or entry fee, to one worth millions of pounds. In 'The London Marathon' John Bryant states that *'These days the budget* (for the London Marathon) *is £7 million, of which around £2 million goes on assembling and paying for the élite field.'* Mo Farah was reported to have signed a deal worth £450,000 to run half way and drop out in the 2013 London marathon and to run the whole way in the 2014 event. A lot of great runners of the past must have turned in their graves at the news. As late as the nineteen eighties running was, supposedly, a strictly amateur sport. Cash prizes and appearance money were simply not allowed.

I remember when money prizes first appeared, following an international agreement made in 1982, and they did so under the guise of expenses. I turned forty in 1986 and started to win a few veterans' prizes. The most I ever won was £300. After the race I was given a brown envelope (truly) but it didn't bulge with bank notes, nor did it contain a cheque. All it contained was a note to the effect that the Northern Ireland Athletics Board was holding £300 in my trust fund. To get at the money I had to submit a claim for legitimate expenses and, being an honest sort of person, that's what I did. I even waited until I bought some new running kit so that I could supply a receipt. How naive was that? I should have realised that the expenses ploy was simply a way of maintaining the pretence of amateurism within a sport that was quickly becoming as professional as any other.

By the turn of the century there was no pretence. Elite runners had become true professionals. Their trust funds could be massive, as could their expenses. There was no problem accessing the cash under the guise of expenses. To reflect the change and to escape further embarrassment, the word amateur was dropped from the titles of most of the controlling bodies for athletics. The Amateur Athletics Association of England, for example, was wound up in 2005 and a new body, England Athletics was set up to run athletics. It was sad to see the end of the three letters AAA. There was a ring about them. It was an inspiring, romantic sound that had been heard since 1880. In theory the Amateur Athletics Association itself still existed but, to save too many red faces, it was tucked away in a closed draw while the professionals took on the business of running athletics like the multi-million pound global business it had become.

Of all the factors changing the sport of running and the way it is administered, in my opinion, money has been the most corrupting. To reverse a well known saying: 'Where there's money, there's muck'. There was a simple beauty in the middle of the twentieth century in taking part in a distance race. Everything reflected the best that the word amateur implies. No one had been bribed to come to the race and the entry fee was the price of one drink. The most you could expect to win was a set of towels or a few pieces of crockery or, if you were unlucky, a ghastly trophy made of wood, sheet metal and plastic, stuck together with pins and glue. Once, out of curiosity, I had disassembled one of the more garish examples of the trophy makers' art. Then, with it in pieces, I was momentarily struck with the awful thought that maybe it was a perennial trophy and I was only supposed to hold it for one year.

Of course, old fashioned amateurism couldn't last, and there's no way the process of commercialisation can be reversed. Despite recognising the damaging effects of the huge amounts of money now generated by running I wouldn't wish to see a return to a rigidly enforced amateur code of practice.

The story of John Tarrant, the so called 'ghost runner', shows up the less attractive side of strict amateurism. Again it is a story of inflexibility on the part of officialdom, of stubborn sticking to the rules and a total lack of natural sympathy. Tarrant's crime was that, as a very young man, he won a total of £17 in a boxing career that spanned just nine bouts. When he tried to join Salford Harriers running club he made the mistake of declaring his winnings and, as a result of his honesty, found himself banned from all races run under amateur rules. In 1956 he gate-crashed the Liverpool marathon, simply to be noticed, and thereby gained the sobriquet 'the ghost runner'. For two years he ran in races from which he was officially banned until, in 1958, he was reinstated to the amateur ranks, but only for domestic competitions. He would never be allowed to run internationally. Was he good enough to run for Britain? In 1960 he finished second in the AAA Marathon Championship in 2:25:17 and might have expected to gain a British vest, if only in one of the many minor international marathons that were held each year. Only strict adherence to the rules prevented him from representing his country.

Tarrant will be remembered primarily for his exploits over ultra distances, with a world best time for one hundred miles on the track of 12:31:10 in 1967 (imagine that, a whole day running round a track 400 times!). He had several wins in other ultra distance track events and in road races such as, Woodford to Southend (36m), Exeter to Plymouth (44m) and Liverpool to Blackpool (48m). His career was cut short by cancer and he died, aged only 42, in 1975. One of his last races was the 1972 Welsh marathon in which he finished fourth in 2:34:59, the same place and more or less the same time that I managed in 1976. A coincidence like that helps me to identify with this sad and shamefully treated fellow runner.

Most of the disputes arising during the time I ran regularly, were resolved fairly amicably, and can be recounted now with more amusement than rancour. In 1972, on July 15th, for example, there were so many runners entered for the AAA 10,000m Championship that the officials decided to limit the race to thirty runners, the surplus to run in an additional race at the end of the meeting. This decision might have been received by the competitors who found themselves barred from the championship race with a little less indignation had it not been for the fact that it was the selection race for the Munich Olympic team. Just as at Windsor on June 22nd two years later, the hopes of a lot of good runners hinged on a single race.

One runner who found himself demoted to the 'B' race was Dave Holt from Hercules Wimbledon Athletic Club, twin brother of, perhaps, the better known of the pair, Bob Holt. The Holt twins (see Chapter 15) were famous in the South of England in the seventies, regularly finishing well up in distance events. I must have run in dozens of races in which they also ran, usually finishing about two minutes behind them.

Dave Holt had special reason to be aggrieved at his omission from the thirty runners who were about to contest the 'A' race for a coveted Olympic place. He was one of the few there who had already achieved the Olympic 10,000m qualifying standard (28:50). He had also, that year, run 13:50 for 5,000m and 2:16:53 for a marathon. There was no way he should have been seeded outside the top thirty of all the runners there that day. The championship officials had made their first and potentially ruinous mistake, ruinous, that is, to Dave Holt's chance of getting a place at the Olympics.

Holt was not a man to lie down without a protest. So he lined up for the 'A' race anyway, barging into the race just as John Tarrant had done in races before him. I wish I had been there. Did some pompous official try to drag him off the track, or snatch his number from his vest, in the same way that officials had attempted to remove Kathrine Switzer from the 1967 Boston Marathon because women runners weren't allowed? I doubt it. If any official had tried he wouldn't have had any help from the other runners. Athletics Weekly commented on Holt's actions in its report of the championships, *'Good luck to him, and a black mark to the officials responsible who chose to ignore his obvious claims.'* Once again Athletics Weekly, the community sheet for runners throughout the land, showed solidarity where it was properly due.

The story, of course, has a fairytale ending. Dave Holt finished fourth in 28:42 and was selected for Munich. The three G.B. 10,000m runners who went to the Olympics in 1972 were Dave Bedford, Lachie Stewart (who had won the Commonwealth Games 10,000m in Edinburgh two years previously) and Dave Holt.

About this time there was one issue being continuously discussed in running circles that, unlike other debates, could not be said to have united the distance running community against the officials. If anything it split it right down the middle. It was an issue on which the controllers of athletics did have the last word, but one where as many runners agreed with the officials as disagreed. Besides, the governing body itself kept wavering. For many years there was no consistency of either opinion or action. The issue was that of selection, specifically pre-selection and in particular selection for the marathon for the Great Britain team for major games. The twin problems associated with selection of marathon runners for major games are the infrequency with which the distance can be run and the inadvisability of having a trial race too close to the event itself. Current form and the relative merits of different runners are often a bit of a mystery.

The debate came to a head with the non-selection of Ian Thompson for the marathon at the Montreal Olympics of 1976. Thompson's record up to that point had been, run five marathons, won five marathons. Following his dramatic first marathon win in 1973, the story of which was recounted in Chapter 5, his second win was at the Christchurch Commonwealth Games of 1974, where he set a British best time for the distance of 2:09:12. Then he won the 1974 Marathon to Athens classic. His last win of any significance had been the European championships of 1974, though he also won a low key race in Korso, Finland, in October 1975. The irony associated with his European win was that he **had** been selected for that race without trial. As I've already recounted, the selection race for the European championships in 1974 was the same Polytechnic marathon that threw up the disqualification for cutting corners controversy, and which Thompson had not been required to run.

With the 1976 Olympics approaching and no other British runner even close to Ian Thompson's recent record it might have seemed a foregone conclusion that he would occupy one of the berths to Montreal. I, for one, thought he would surely be selected without undergoing a trial. Not so, said the selectors. Three marathon wins in a row might have been good enough for pre-selection in 1974 but, in the incomprehensible thinking of selectors, five in a row was not good enough in 1976. Thompson had to run the trial race, the AAA marathon at Rotherham on May 8th. The first three home in that race would be picked for the Olympics, and they were: Barry Watson, Jeff Norman and Keith Angus. Thompson had a bad run and came in seventh. The selectors had made their bed the day they forced Thompson to take part in the trial and, perhaps to their credit, now they lay on it. Thompson missed out on the games.

I still think he should have been selected, well before the trial race, but I don't intend to argue the case here. All the arguments, both for and against, came out immediately after the race, in the pages of Athletics Weekly and elsewhere. And they were all good arguments. The debate went on and on and never really reached a conclusion, except that the selector's lot is not an easy one. In fact it's a pretty well impossible one.

I have seen the problem of selection from all angles: as a runner who may or may not have been selected for a team, as a runner who would have benefited from a pre-selection policy and as one who definitely wouldn't have done and, when I was teaching and having to select the school cross country team, as a selector myself. I would rather be the selectee than a selector. There are no decisions to make and no repercussions, just pleasure or disappointment, mixed at times with resentment or even a degree of anger.

A selector is caught between trying to be fair to the athletes and, indeed, to the public who follow athletics, and trying, by a process of assessing evidence and a bit of crystal-ball gazing, to pick the best prospects. The rather unacceptable truth is that, in the first place, fairness is a concept of mirage-like consistency which really has no place within a sport where the whole point is for one runner to be better than another, and, secondly, no one can ever predict how someone will run on a specific day in several weeks time. Whatever a selection panel opts for, whether solidarity with the runners in general or individual runners in particular, or forecasting the best team, it will almost always be wrong. The more important the event for which runners are being selected, the more wrong the selectors are likely to be.

When I decided which boys would make up the school cross country team I took the view that it was more important to reward what I considered the qualities I wanted to encourage in the boys than to assemble the best possible team. So I might pick a boy who trained regularly, who helped out whenever possible, who was enthusiastic and tried hard, who never gave up, who, in short, deserved to be picked, over a faster runner who lacked these qualities. But this was not the Olympics. It was just a school team.

If I were asked to help select runners for the British Olympic team I would have to discard all thoughts of who deserved or didn't deserve a place, of what was fair to the runners, of how selection or non-selection might affect individuals, and of what anyone might think of me and my selections. My sole consideration would be to pick those who, in my opinion, and according to the evidence, were, potentially able to perform to the highest standard at the games. I have to qualify that sentence with the word potentially because there is a world of difference between runners who may be the best around at the time of selection but who are unlikely to be any better at the time that matters and runners who may be in poor form at the time of selection but who have already shown themselves to be capable of superior, maybe even medal winning performances, in the past.

For that reason I believe Ian Thompson should have been picked for the marathon at the Montreal Olympic Games and, for the same reason,

Sebastian Coe should have been picked for both the 800 and 1500m at the Seoul Olympics in 1988. Sometimes it is not simply a question of how well someone is likely to perform in a forthcoming event but more a matter of how good that person is at his or her very best. The possibility, if it exists at all, that someone can reach as high a level as previously has to be allowed for. There was no reason to suppose that Ian Thompson in 1976 and Sebastion Coe in 1988 could not have performed to their own very highest standards at the respective forthcoming Olympic Games. In Thompson's case it was absolutely clear that none of the runners who were picked at his expense had ever reached nearly the same heights, nor seemed likely to be about to make an almost unimaginable leap towards his known standard. Though I hate to say it, fairness sometimes has to give way to established class in the matter of selection.

In making my selections for Olympic places I would be as objective and unemotional about my job as Star Trek's Mr. Spock. Then, as quickly as possible, I would develop a skin as thick as a rhinoceros'. I would like to believe that the selectors of our major games athletics teams act in the same way. But I suspect that they still retain ideas of fairness and of rewarding previous service or speculative promise. I even suspect that sometimes, and I shudder at the mere thought, selectors may see non-selection as a suitable punishment for some transgression or non-compliance on the part of an athlete. I am certain that they adopt protectionist practices. Selection by trial is the perfect example. If you state in advance that a trial race will be held and that the first three home will be selected, you rid yourself of any difficult decisions and you protect yourself from scrutiny. In one way it is the fairest method. It stimulates the least controversy and is favoured by many athletes. But it is basically an abdication of responsibility. As someone once said in reaction to an extreme example of selection by trial, 'They're the selectors. Why don't they select?'

Sebastian Coe talks very wisely and surprisingly calmly about his own non-selection for either the 800m or 1500m for the 1988 Olympics in his autobiography 'Running My Life', painting a very uncomplimentary picture of the work, not of the selectors themselves, but of the General Council, which would normally be expected to rubber stamp the selectors' decisions. If you want to know what goes on behind the scenes in the selection of runners for Great Britain teams for the major games it is essential reading.

For me, as a runner, selection by trial worked well on some occasions and not so well on others. Three times I made the Northern Ireland team for the World Cross Country Championship on the basis of my position in the Northern Ireland Championship. Each year the selectors stuck pretty rigidly to a policy of selecting the first eight eligible runners finishing in the championship race. That suited me for a number of reasons. The trial race came at the beginning of March, a time when I was usually approaching a peak in anticipation of a half marathon in April and a marathon in May. The course that hosted the Northern Ireland Championships at that time was very much to my liking, mostly dry and not too hilly. Finally, I was always able to rise to the occasion. The more important a race, the better I ran. Other runners responded to pressure by cracking up and I beat a lot of people in those trial races whom I really shouldn't have beaten.

I remember sitting in a cold changing room one December at an impromptu meeting of runners like myself, along with a few Northern Ireland athletics officials, discussing the merits of pre-selection for the World Cross Country Championships. I knew exactly what had prompted the meeting. One of the officials, who happened to be the driving force within my own club, was excited about a young runner who, he believed, was going to be Northern Ireland's next star athlete, and he was determined to do all he could to encourage the youngster. One thing he thought he could do was to make sure his protégé would be picked for the Northern Ireland team for the WCCC, hence the talk of pre-selection. I sat and fumed quietly. I was nearing forty and I knew that if anyone were to be pre-selected for the most prestigious event in the cross country calendar, it wouldn't be me. I also knew that my only chance of selection was through a trial race and a strict policy of places counting. I used the argument that I had heard or read so many times before, not aloud, but in my head, to myself, 'If anyone is good enough to deserve pre-selection, then they're good enough to win a place in a trial'.

The meeting came to nought. Come the Northern Ireland Championship the selectors stuck to a trial system. I ran well enough to be selected for the WCCC team that year and in the process finished ahead of the young man who had been the implied subject of the changing room discussion regarding pre-selection.

A trial system for selection may have served me well in the case of the WCCC but it could also go against me. I only ran in the European Clubs Cross Country Championship once, despite having been a member of my club's winning team in the Northern Ireland Championship on several occasions. In fact I was the only member of the club who had been one of the scoring six on every single occasion that we had won the Northern Ireland event. The European Clubs Cross Country Championship is for a team from the best club in each of Europe's nations, that is, the club that wins its particular National Cross Country Championship. In the eighties my club, Annadale Striders A.C. was, more often than not, the top club in Northern Ireland and was usually, therefore, invited to send a team to the European event.

The problem for me was that almost a year separated the race that made us the best team in Northern Ireland and the date of the European race. In 1981, for example, when I did make the team for the European Clubs Championship (in a bitterly cold Milan that year) the date of the event was 31st January and the Northern Ireland Championship, the result of which had decided which club sent a team to Milan, had been 16th February 1980. Because of this long gap between booking our place and the event itself, my club always used a race at the beginning of January, more than ten months after the Northern Ireland Championship, to select the team for Europe. I always thought this was very unfair. I believed that those who had done the donkey work in earning a place in Europe by winning the Northern Ireland Championship, including me, barring injury, should get their reward by having a European trip, even if it was almost a year later, with no trial race.

I was rarely in top condition at the beginning of January. Invariably I had just got back from a Christmas break in England. I hadn't started peak training for the important races in the spring. I was generally run down and unenthusiastic about competing. The course used for the January selection race was not to my liking. It was around football pitches and was always very soft going with long stretches of wet mud. I never ran well in that race and, as a result, when people I had beaten in the Northern Ireland Championship enjoyed themselves in the Algarve, or some such exotic venue, I stayed at home. Should I have been pre-selected for the European Clubs Championship? If I could answer that question I would have solved the fundamental selectors' dilemma once and for all.

Two mammoth sources of controversy remain to be discussed. They are seemingly of much greater importance than any of the issues that have preceded them though I would argue that from a runner's point of view they are barely of any importance at all. They are the two things that head the title of this chapter, namely sex and drugs. I'll consider them in reverse order.

In over fifty years of competitive distance running I have had no experience of drugs whatsoever. I have never known a single runner who was even suspected of having taken banned, performance enhancing drugs. To my mind there simply never was a drug problem in the sport. Yet, today, one could be forgiven for thinking that drug use is the most important factor that troubles the sport of athletics, regardless of the event. Mandatory, out of competition-season drug testing is applied to élite athletes as a matter of course. If a test is missed it can lead to big trouble for the athlete concerned, a case, if ever there was one, of 'guilty until proven innocent.' Prior to the London Olympics, in the spring of 2012, it was reported that, *'All 900 British Olympic and Paralympic athletes would be drug-tested at least once in the build up to the games.'* This policy of testing was not new, but it was, or would be, *'on an unprecedented scale.'*

Very large amounts of money have been spent on drug testing in the last few decades. All the effort and all the cost have been justified with an amazing lack of embarrassment and with the implied consent of the majority of athletes and non participants alike. Putting the present situation, as it is popularly viewed, in a nutshell: drugs are evil; those who use them are cheats of the worst sort and anything that can be done to catch the cheats, to prevent them profiting from their crimes, to stop others cheating, and to clean up the sport, irrespective of the effects on the vast majority of completely drug free participants, is wholly justified.

That is not my opinion. From the point of view of ninety nine percent of runners such as myself it is of no importance at all whether others have or have not taken banned drugs. The so called problem of drug use is not our problem. It is only a problem for the user and for those at the periphery of the sport, the hangers-on who stand to gain in some way from the efforts of the competitors. If I became aware that a drug user had beaten me in a race I wouldn't be too bothered about it, since my performance would not have been affected. Of course there is the one percent of competitors for whom this is not the case. They are the absolute élite, for whom to be beaten by a 'drugs cheat' may mean losing an Olympic medal, the glory that goes with it and a very large amount of money into the bargain. But is the sport itself comprised only of this one percent, or is the ninety nine percent more important? My answer to that question does not comply with that of the public at large, the media and the official bodies who run athletics, which is why I see the use of performance-enhancing substances as a matter of little concern, whereas a large majority see it as a crime worthy of the highest condemnation and the most Draconian measures to deal with it.

One of the most impressive and most memorable events I have ever witnessed in athletics, albeit only via the TV screen, was Ben Johnson 'winning' the Olympic 100m in 1988. When it later came out that Johnson had been a drug user my opinion remained unchanged. His performance was still something I felt privileged to have seen. It was still wonderful, admirable, exciting, inspiring and, also, in my book, still winning. I just wish he hadn't been found out.

The idea that Johnson had benefited from using banned substances was never questioned. It was, despite being untested and untestable, simply taken for granted. Aren't such drugs referred to as performance-enhancing? The possibility exists, however, that he still might have won the Olympic 100m if he had never taken a drug in his life. That is, to me, perhaps the saddest part of the whole affair. No one can prove he needed drugs to perform as he did, anymore than it can be proved that he didn't. That is the nature of any controversy. It can never be resolved. There are no clear cut answers, only rigid rules and brutal treatment of breakers of the rules. Regarding the present situation; the policy of indiscriminate and compulsory testing of athletes for the presence of drugs is, in my view, indefensible and serves only to cast the blanket of suspicion over everyone, rather than only over the tiny proportion of athletes who break the rules. It also demonstrates unequivocally who is in control of the sport. If the price paid for athletes' rights, freedom and independence is a few cheats, in my view it's one worth paying.

And what of this concept of cheating? Why have some types of drugs been singled out as the most invidious form of cheating in athletics? Consider what is presently allowable: drugs that are not banned (painkillers, caffeine, over the counter remedies, prescription medicines, antibiotics, etc.), corrective and therapeutic surgery, massage and physiotherapy, professionalism, energy gels and sports and recovery drinks, special diets and supplements, compression wear, nose strips, training machines, altitude training, reduced partial pressure apparatus (oxygen tents), vaccinations and all modern medical advances, strips of springy carbon fibre attached to the legs - the list goes on.

I may be a minority of one but in my opinion the world of present day running, indeed athletics in general, has to accept and tolerate drug taking as yet one more inevitable consequence of the sport or, more accurately, the adjuncts of the sport, having become grossly over-important. Drug use and drug control are not the bad and the good side of the drugs question. They are both bad. They are two symptoms of the same disease. And the disease is not the use of drugs; it is the transfer of importance from what is at the heart of a sport to what emanates from it. At the peak period of competitive distance running in the UK, the three decades following the middle of the twentieth century, the things that were important were the competitors, their performances, the races they ran, the running community, all the things that are at the heart of a sport. Since then importance has shifted to other things and in the process it has grown to an absurd degree: things like control and management issues, public image (drug control is defended on the grounds of 'public confidence'), media coverage and media stories, celebrities, advertising and sponsorship, charities, commercial links, politics and jingoism and, underlying everything else, money, money, money.

I try to understand why so called drug cheats are so loathed and reviled. I don't believe it has much to do with the obvious complaint that they are trying to improve their performance with chemical assistance. To me that is no more than an unsavoury show of human weakness. The real crime is that, if indeed drugs do work, using them becomes a massive fraud against the system and against fellow competitors, involving vast sums of money, fame and prestige, both for the individual and for the country for which he or she competes, all compounded by the need for denial and dishonesty. We will find the real significance of the crime of drug cheating, not in those who are found to have used drugs, but in the circumstances that brought the sport to a place where drugs have become worth using. As I have said elsewhere the very simple sport of running is now one in which the wrong things have become of overwhelming importance. None of the good club runners of the sixties and seventies would have contemplated taking performance enhancing drugs because, in the first place it wasn't worth it and, in the second place, we all knew instinctively what was fair and what was not, what mattered and what didn't.

Throughout my time as a competitive runner, running was an immensely important part of my life. It was an essential component of everything that made me what I was. It gave me status, confidence and self respect. I devoted hours of effort to it, both physical and mental. Hundreds of others, like me, could say the same thing. Yet I never lost the ability to step outside myself and see running as a disinterested observer might. I was always able, and still am, to see running as a slightly ridiculous, trivial and ultimately irrelevant appendage to life, as for that matter is every sport. Most things are like that, simultaneously both hugely important and of absolutely no importance whatsoever.

It is a pity that so many people, especially those who are empowered to influence the sport of running, are unable or unwilling to see it from different viewpoints. Of course it is of tremendous interest, especially to those directly involved, who wins the gold medal in the Olympics and who doesn't, but does it really matter? And if, from one point of view, it's unimportant, then it's also unimportant that the winner might have taken drugs. I wish the political and media machine that controls athletics would lighten up. It's just a sport after all. Once upon a time we all simply enjoyed it and no one had any reason to look to drugs or any other form of cheating.

Ottavio Missoni, the Italian fashion designer who represented his country in the 400m hurdles at the 1948 London Olympics, also recognised the change in athletics since the war and decried the loss of innocence that made the sport what it was when he was competing. So closely do his words reflect my own views that I'll quote them again (you will already find them at the head of Chapter 5). I first read them in his 2013 obituary. Recalling the Olympics, he remarked, *'beautiful, natural and spontaneous, not like now, when everything is inflated, blown out of proportion.'*

Now, turning to sex, another issue that has generated more controversy during the time I have been running than it ever should have done. There are two sources of debate (and I'm not talking about whether you should have sex before an important race). The first and longest running is whether or not women can do and whether they should be allowed to do what men can. The first Olympic Games to include a women's marathon was, believe it or not, Los Angeles in 1984. In 1972 the Boston marathon allowed women entrants for the first time, and, in that same year, I ran the Isle of Wight marathon alongside a woman who had had to join in unofficially as, to quote the local newspaper *'women are not allowed to compete in a marathon'*. Since then, of course, women have proved, not only that they are perfectly capable of running any distance that men can but that they may well be relatively better than men over the longer distances. In the year that Paula Radcliffe set a world's best time for the marathon in London (2:15:25) it ranked her top British runner, irrespective of sex. I mention that not as evidence that women are better than men over the marathon distance but merely as a reminder that women are perfectly capable of coping with the distance and, incidentally, to highlight the appalling drop in standards in men's distance running since the late nineteen hundreds. It took a woman to show up the men.

The puzzling thing is why it took so long for the penny to drop that the Victorian view of women as fragile flowers who would faint at the slightest degree of over-exertion, was a figment of male imagination. Women are as tough as the toughest men, and the world of athletics should have realised this at the time of the first Olympics, let alone the twenty first.

The other and less easily resolved problem relating to sex is the matter of gender determination. To put it crudely - is she or isn't she? There have been a few cases that may have been blatant cheating, where a man has posed as a woman and competed in athletics events, though never, to my knowledge, in running races. The German high jumper Dora Ratjen, who was fourth in her event at the 1936 'Hitler' Olympic Games in Berlin, was a case in point. Her deep voice, refusal to share the shower room and five o'clock shadow were pretty good clues to the fraud. Britain's Dorothy Tyler who won the silver medal claimed she *'knew he was a man'*. Soon after the Olympics a doctor examined Ratjen and declared him to be a man. In 1938 he was banned from further competition.

At least there is something plain and honest about a blatant deception. Most cases of gender dispute involve the very complex issue of gender definition and gender determination. It could even be that Dora Ratjen herself (or himself) was not such a clear case of misrepresentation after all. The matter of whether someone is male or female, although it may be crystal clear in the vast majority of cases, can, in rare instances, be extremely difficult to decide. The distinction between the two genders is, itself, hard to define. There are those who are born to be neither clearly male nor clearly female and it is such unlucky people who present the sport with an insoluble dilemma. Distance and middle distance running has had its share of examples, there being no suspicion, however, that any of them were clear-cut men masquerading as women.

When I was a teenager in the early 1960s it was the Korean runner Sin Kim Dan, holder of world records for 400m and 800m. Other female runners refused to compete against her because she looked like a man. When compulsory chromosomal sex testing for international athletes was introduced in 1966 Sin Kim Dan disappeared from the sport. In this implied admission of guilt, she behaved like the Russian Press sisters, who also left the scene when gender verification was introduced. I remember the publicity surrounding Irina and Tamara Press well. Winners of five track and field Olympic gold medals and holders of 26 world records, they were the source, for me and my friends, of much adolescent humour. Humour may be a despicable reaction to what is undoubtedly a personally traumatic situation for the subject of the jokes, but sometimes all you can do is laugh. There is no satisfactory way of resolving the issue where gender is in doubt. There simply isn't.

Gender uncertainty is only a problem at all because men are better than women at every single athletic event and, in order to be fair to women and allow them to excel on their own terms, there have to be separate male and female competitions. One way to eliminate any disputes over gender would be to amalgamate women's and men's events and make no further distinction between the sexes. No one, least of all any woman, would want that.

So the officials are left with an insoluble problem. How do they stop individuals in women's competition taking advantage of the fact that they are not women at all or are not quite women or have some beneficial male characteristics? And, remember, the rule-makers need to find an answer that is not unfair or hurtful to the individuals who pose a problem, nor offensive to the various countries concerned, is not financially embarrassing, does not provoke legal reprisals, and is fair and acceptable to the body of competitors directly involved. It cannot be done.

Most recently a classic case of gender uncertainty has arisen and has been resolved with a wonderful example of Alice-in-Wonderland compromise. The case involves the South African middle distance runner, Caster Semenya, who came to prominence when she won the World Athletics Championship 800m in Berlin in 2009. Following her win she underwent gender verification tests, the outcome of which seems to have been that she is hermaphrodite or intersex, with both male and female characteristics. I say 'seems to have been' because the results and nature of the tests are now confidential. A cloak of legally guarded secrecy has been cast over all information regarding the specifics of her case. Between the time that her femininity was first questioned, however, and the resolution of the case, it was generally agreed, and much publicised, that there was a problem, that it was a genuine one, and that it meant that Semenya could not be described as one hundred percent female.

For a period she was banned from competition but, at the end of 2009, was cleared to race again and finished second in the 2011 World Athletics Championships 800m. She was also second in the same event in the London Olympics. She now seems set to continue her career without fear of any future impedance due to questions about her gender. The key to rehabilitating the luckless Semenya seems to have been (again, that word 'seems' must be applied) the proviso that she have treatment for her condition, or what might be described as a sort of feminising programme. Who knows, a situation could one day arise in which a female runner undergoing treatment is banned for not taking her drugs!

Why am I amused by this compromise? Because it demonstrates the devious ways in which officialdom wriggles out of embarrassing situations. It makes new rules and breaks old ones. It allows itself to be bribed and bullied and influenced by irrelevancies. In trying to solve one problem it throws up many more. Most of all, it turns what amounts to an unfortunate anomaly of very little ultimate importance into a matter of worldwide gravity.

There is only one logical, if hard-hearted solution to women of questionable gender. That is to ban them from women's competition. As to my previous point, one that has been much better made by much more expert people than myself, that it is not always easy to draw firm conclusions on gender matters, then the policy has to be an unforgiving one. At the first sign that everything is not quite right remove the suspect from the competitive arena. That is not my solution but it is the only sensible one.

I would prefer to stretch the rules in the opposite direction, a case not so much of, 'if in doubt then chuck her out', rather, 'if in doubt then let her compete as a woman, with no questions asked'. I say that, not because I am a kind-hearted liberal, but because I recognise that the best solution to an insoluble problem is the one that is easiest to apply, much along the same lines as cutting the Gordian knot. And, speaking as someone who has already declared that I would rather be involved in a sport in which there was a small amount of drug abuse than one in which the runners are controlled as in a totalitarian state, I am always willing to accept a certain amount of unfairness.

Two other examples of illogical decision making over controversial issues on the running scene have happened within the last few years. Both further demonstrate the dilemmas facing officials and the extent to which the importance of such matters has been inflated. I'll start with the less dramatically newsworthy. It is about when a world record is a world record and when it's just a world's best time (or, perhaps, it's neither).

You would think that if anyone were to run an accurately measured distance quicker than anyone else had ever done before, the time would constitute a world record. But that would be just too simple. Take the marathon distance, for example. No two marathons, though they may be as accurately measured as is humanly possible, are identical. Some marathons are renowned as fast courses. Some are notoriously slow. The Road Runners Club, a club that thrived when I started to run seriously, awarded standard certificates, first, second and third class, to any member who had completed a marathon under a certain time. But the time was not the same for every marathon. The Isle of Wight marathon, for example, was given a four minute allowance because it was so hilly. The Boston (USA) marathon, by contrast, is notably fast because it starts at a higher altitude than the finish. Very sensibly, therefore, for a while at least, there was no such thing as an official world record for the marathon, only (as if there is any difference) a world's best time.

The arguments don't stop there. In 2003, in the London marathon, Paula Radcliffe set a time for the distance of 2:15:25 which, to this day, no other woman has bettered. It became recognised as the world record since, by then, it had been decided that there could, after all, be a world record for the marathon. But, in September 2011 the IAAF decided that Paula's record was no longer valid; it could only be a world's best time. The reason given was that the time had been set in a mixed race, with the aid of two male pace-makers. From now on there would be separate records for women, those set in women only races, and those set in mixed races.

Paula Radcliffe appealed and two months later was allowed to keep her world record. The absurdity of the situation and the time consuming seriousness of the whole business defies belief. Not only the IAAF, the definitive governing body for world athletics, was involved, but also the World Marathon Majors (WMM) and the Association of International Marathons (AIMS). Did they have nothing better to do than to decide on a trivial matter of semantics? Outside their cloistered zone of finance, administration, rules and red tape, the sane world of running could see that there really was nothing to get bothered about.

At the core of the discussion regarding the validity of Paula Radcliffe's world's best was the benefit she might have gained from running with male pacemakers. The arguments, therefore, were not really about mixed versus women only racing but about pacemaking (would Paula's time have been acceptable if she had been paced for part of the distance by two women rather than two men?). Pacemaking was a bone of contention in races decades before the advent of mixed road races. Sir Roger Bannister broke four minutes for the mile for the first time in 1954 and in the process set an undisputed world record for the distance with the overt help of friendly pacemakers. For many years after the nineteen fifties, however, any hint of organised pacemaking in races became taboo. But nowadays it seems to be completely acceptable. It has become so routine as to be extremely boring and, in my view, detracts considerably from the interest value of races. I get the impression that pacemaking is very like professionalism in athletics. Is it legal, or isn't it? No one seems to know.

The other source of much public argument that recently resulted in a botched decision being made about permitted participation in international running competitions, including the World Athletics Championships and the Olympic Games, was the case of the South African 400m paralympic runner Oscar Pistorius. I call it a botched decision because it must vie for the prize for the most hare-brained and illogical decision ever made in any sport. Oscar Pistorius is a double amputee, having lost both legs below the knee at the age of eleven months. He runs by means of strips of carbon fibre attached to his legs, which has given rise to endless debate as to whether these Flex-Foot carbon fibre transtibial prostheses, to give them their full name, give him an advantage over able-bodied runners. In that this debate is not only largely irrelevant but can never be finally resolved, it is simply a waste of time.

Nevertheless it became the basis for the IAAF's decision in 2008 to rule Pistorius ineligible for competitions held under its rules. Within four months of Pistorius having been banned from able bodied competition the decision was overruled by the Court of Arbitration for Sport. Is there no end to the organisations that have their fingers in the athletics pie? Pistorius subsequently ran for South Africa in the 2011 World Championships and the 2012 London Olympics (able bodied events) in both the individual 400m event and the 4 x 400m relay. It was a triumph for the man himself, for legal argument, for public opinion and for politically correct lobbying, but in terms of the sport of running it simply made no sense. Perhaps the ultimate irony was that when Pistorius was beaten into second place by the Brazilian, Alan Oliveira, in the 200m at the 2012 Paralympics, immediately following the Olympics themselves, he complained vociferously about the length of Oliveira's blades. He obviously considered that someone else's blades gave an unfair advantage, having previously argued long and hard that his own didn't.

This has been the longest chapter in this book. I think that is because controversy, and the sort of things that give rise to it, reflect very well what is seen to be important in a sport at a particular era in its evolution. From the early days of my introduction to competitive running, when most disputes were either to be laughed at or settled in a friendly and low-key manner, we have come to a stage where controversial matters can seem almost of a magnitude to start wars. Purely as a long overdue reminder to anyone reading this; none of them are ever that important.

I think there is a connection between the immense amount of time, money and effort, argument and counter-argument, newspaper column inches, TV coverage and legal wrangling that goes into dealing with individual problems, whether relating to drugs, gender issues, nationality disputes, politics, when a world record is not a world record but just a world's best time or whether a man with no legs gains an advantage by using springs instead of feet and all such essentially unimportant matters and the decline in interest in athletics at the grass roots. In 1970 I knew where my interest in the sport lay. I still know where it lies and it is still in the same place but the public, the media and the sport's controlling bodies are looking elsewhere.

CHAPTER 15
Nature or nurture?

'A good big one will always beat a good little one.'

Old sporting saying.

In Chapter 1 I looked for the reasons I became a runner. I concluded that there were three: I enjoyed running, I was quite good at it, and it satisfied my somewhat inflated need for achievement. Now, looking back on a lifetime of competitive distance running, I can see that there was really only one reason. The other two stemmed from it. That reason was the middle one; I was quite good at it. I was born that way. I had the skin and bones, the heart, the lungs, the nervous system, the muscles and the physiology of a long distance runner. If I hadn't been inherently quite good at it I wouldn't have enjoyed it, I wouldn't have achieved anything through doing it, and I wouldn't have been prepared to put any effort into it. In summary, therefore, this chapter is a declaration of my deterministic conviction that, ultimately, how good a runner someone becomes is written indelibly and unalterably in the genes.

Hence the quote at the beginning of this chapter. It's not to be taken literally, of course. Originally, I think, it applied to combatants in the boxing ring, where pure size probably does give some advantage. But the sport of running has had a large enough number of superlative exponents of diminutive size to make it seem that the opposite might be the case. Anyone who watched the closing stages of the 2010 London marathon would have looked foolish putting their money on the eventual winner, the Ethiopian runner Tsegaye Kebede, against the Kenyan Emmanual Mutai, who came second. As they ran side by side in the last stages of the race they looked like a father and his young son out for a jog together. Mutai had at least six inches to spare over Kebede.

But the smaller man won, in the very fast time of 2:05:19. No one should be surprised by the ability of tiny runners to compete on equal terms with bigger ones. I have two English Springer Spaniel bitches, a quarter my size, both of whom can outrun me over any distance. But, then, I suppose a giraffe would outrun me with ease, as would an elephant. In running, size is practically irrelevant.

It is what is implied in the quote that is significant. There are two things. One is the fact that size is something that you cannot change; it is inborn. The other, the suggestion that God-given gifts may not be enough. It is still necessary to be a good big one to beat a good little one, and there are ways to become good that are not pre-determined. In distance running of course it is largely training that liberates the full capacity of the genes.

If I take two watering cans, a large one and a small one, I can see at a glance which one will hold more water. But it could well be that, at a particular time, the small one actually contains more than the bigger one. To guarantee that the large one contains more water than the small one ever could, I need to fill it up. Runners are like that. They fill up their metaphorical watering cans by training. That's why, sometimes, a poorer runner will beat a potentially better one but also why, in the end, the inherently better runners always come out on top.

To some people the idea that even the smallest component of our abilities is pre-determined is terrifying. It negates any politically correct notion of equality. It seems to make the act of trying hard a little bit pointless. And it is a form of judgement from which we have no escape. On the other hand the suggestion that anyone can become a great runner by working hard enough is a wonderfully attractive one, but it is a myth. The same idea is often expressed in relation to almost any activity, usually in the form, 'you can do anything you want to, if you put your mind to it'. It is a sort of anthem for the people, an egalitarian canon. It is a great stimulant for those who would like to achieve what others achieve and it has undoubtedly done a large amount of good to a lot of people who followed its message. The sad thing is that it is a lie.

I wanted to be a great runner. I put my mind to it. For years, having got so far but no further, I wondered whether I had put my mind to it enough. Now, after almost a life time of putting my mind to it, I have reached the conclusion that, as I keep mentioning, I probably got about as far as I ever could have done. I filled my watering can, so to speak, if not right to the top, then to within a few millimetres of the top. After years of hoping and trying, I eventually had to accept that my watering can was not an extra large one, but just medium sized.

I base my view that good runners are born rather than made, i.e. nature rather than nurture, on four main sources of argument. First there is *a priori* reasoning. An *a priori* argument is one that the British philosopher Galen Strawson described as one that, *'you can see is true just lying on your couch'*. It is also defined as, 'relating to or derived by reasoning from self evident propositions' . I prefer Strawson's way of putting it. Secondly there is my own observation of the plateau effect that I described elsewhere, the fact that all runners sooner or later reach a peak or plateau that no increased amount of training will get them beyond. Thirdly there are filial, sibling and, of especial value, twin studies. This third source of evidence inevitably has to include the sensitive topic of human races, since it involves the same discussion of shared genes. Lastly there are the phenomena of running, the super-runners, the geniuses of distance running who seem simply to override the principle that to be a great runner you need a background of years of lots of training.

In addition I have my own experience to draw from, and the feelings and hunches that come from it . As a scientist I should know better than to rely on such things for evidence, but it is impossible not to listen to them. Anyone who has trained and competed for years will have a feel for the limits to performance and a sense of the body's ultimate capability. I know, from pure instinct, for example, that, although I might have been capable of running a marathon a few minutes faster than I actually did, I could never have run 2:10 or anywhere near it. You may call that defeatism, or a form of sour grapes. I call it realism.

When you watch the start of a world class distance race what do you see? A line of runners of remarkably similar build. They may vary in height. Some may be slightly more muscular than others, but, without exception, they will be lean and lightweight for their size. Their limbs will seem relatively long, but only because they are slim. They will move in an easy, fluid manner. Everything is symmetrical. Their joints flex in parallel as they jog lightly about waiting for the call to their marks. As well as being the start of a race it is it is also the starting point for my *a priori* reasoning.

If I say that a good runner has to be built for running I don't need to prove it. It stands to reason. As soon as you see a top class runner performing it is obvious that their running is, first and foremost, efficient. No runner can afford to expend more energy than is absolutely necessary, any more than a car can go fast with the brakes on. This is especially true for the longer distances, where energy conservation is paramount. I am thinking of some of the great marathon runners who ran almost as if running required no energy at all: Abebe Bikila, two time Olympic marathon winner, Bill Adcocks, most famous for his 2:11:07 record breaking performance on the tough Athens course in 1969, Ian Thompson, Tsegaye Kebede, Waldemar Cierpinski, the second man to win the Olympic marathon twice, in Montreal in 1976 and in Moscow, in 1980, Josia Thugwani, the South African who won the 1996 Atlanta Olympic marathon gold medal, and Joan Benoit, winner of the first Olympic women's marathon, to name but a few of my favourites. Their movement was like the sweep of a second hand on a precision made watch, continuous, unvarying and effortless.

No amount of training, coaching, dieting, bending or stretching, will change a person's basic build or their running style. None of the runners who look like runners owe their characteristics to nurture in any form. When I left school at the age of nineteen I weighed nine stone twelve pounds (62.7kg, if you insist). I was as tall as I ever would be at just under five feet nine inches. The most I ever weighed subsequently was ten and a half stone (67kg), at a time when I was middle-aged and not training very much. I never dieted or even watched what I ate. I had inherited the lean gene, just one more piece in my running armoury. It was the same gene, or genes, that prevented me ever having the body that I craved as a teenager. However much I exercised, did press ups, sit ups, pull ups, back presses, and lifted weights, my muscles stayed the same size. It frustrated me then, but later I learned to be grateful for it.

What you don't see at the start of a top class distance race are runners built like weight lifters or sprinters, with shoulders you could stuff a pillow into and not notice any difference, or runners with legs that are wide at the ankle and the knee, or with joints that don't bend smoothly or in the right direction. I hope I'm not being rude, but there are such people, and they are not like that as a result of injury, illness or self-abuse. They do not make good distance runners. Why not? Isn't it obvious? For *a priori* reasons, of course.

I could be accused here of contradicting myself. In Chapter 6 I talked about all the good club runners who owed their success to training but who had ugly, inefficient-looking styles or atypical physiques. Here I seem to be saying that to be a good runner you have to look like a good runner. It's a matter of degree. None of those somewhat inelegant club runners were ever beyond the pale when it came to build or efficiency. They just weren't ideal. Nor were they top class. You will hardly find a world class distance runner of today who is not a paragon of running physique and style. If some of the great runners of the past do not pass comparison with those of the present (I mentioned Zatopek, for example, as winning no prizes for style) it is because they were at the top of a relatively small pile. The pile today is much bigger and much higher and is, therefore, quite unforgiving of the smallest weakness if anyone is to climb to the top. Would I be guilty of an unforgivable heresy if I suggested that Zatopek, for example, might not have been such a great runner after all? Is he such a famous figure in the history of distance running simply because he reached his potential as a runner in the years that he did? In asking this I am very much aware that, had I been running in the nineteen forties as well as I did in the seventies and eighties, I would now be a familiar name in the history of British athletics. A huge number of runners of my era could say the same. Many of them, complete unknowns today, had they been born just twenty years earlier and reached their same lifetime best, would have been more famous than Zatopek himself.

Michael Winner made a film about the marathon called 'The Games', released in 1970. It served to make the point that to be a convincing runner an actor has to look at least a little bit like one. Michael Crawford played the British entrant, the favourite for the gold medal, whose coach, a caricature of a bullying, disciplinarian taskmaster, played by Stanley Baker, set his protégé the target of a two hour marathon. This at least was almost believable as Michael Crawford did look a little bit like a runner. Apparently he had trained for the role and had run a mile in a respectable time prior to acting in the film. Despite being the only faintly credible runner in the marathon field, he didn't win. In perhaps the only other plausible feature of the film, he set off far too fast and blew up. I'm afraid I laughed out loud when the winner came in sight, a very stocky and unfit-looking Charles Aznavour! I'm sure I wasn't the only one who thought that the casting for the film, with the possible exception of Michael Crawford, bore absolutely no relationship to reality. It doesn't take any knowledge or personal experience of running to spot a non-runner.

In Chapter 7 I mentioned what I called the plateau effect. I took as my case studies myself and Brendan Foster. Foster ran 5,000m a minute and a half faster than I did and 10,000m three minutes faster, but we could both ask the same question, 'could we have done still better?' Although no one can be absolutely sure, I suspect that the answer is no. We both reached, as every runner does, a plateau of performance that was determined by what we were born with. The more someone runs the more obvious the plateau is, and the more ingrained the ultimate performance level becomes. I ran a lot of ten mile races between the late 1960s and the late 80s. Almost all of them took me between 50 and 52 minutes. It even got a bit boring. I could churn out a 51 minute ten miler almost to order, just as I could produce a 2:30 - 2:40 marathon without really trying.

Occasionally I raised myself off my plateau, but only by a small amount. I take that to mean that every runner's plateau is actually slightly higher than it appears. In other words we rarely perform to our ultimate limit. An especially good run is not a sign of genuine improvement, just a good day. Of course we improve continuously on our way to reaching our own personal plateau, sometimes at an amazing rate, but once we get there the plateau is real and fixed.

If it is real and fixed for me and others like me, then it is also fixed for the very best runners in the world. As each new genius of distance running appears it may seem that he or she has no limits. In 1960, for example, when the world record for 10,000m, stood at 28:18.2, to the Russian Pyotr Bolotnikov, along came Ron Clarke of Australia to knock a total of nearly 39 seconds off that time. He also shattered the two mile, three mile, six mile and 5,000m records and set a total of seventeen world records during his career. In the 1990s Haile Gebrselassie did something similar, followed by Kenenisa Bekele in the first decade of the twenty first century. No doubt there will be another world beater in the near future who appears to defy the concept of limits and has no plateau of his own. But it will be an illusion. Every runner has a plateau. My belief is that at least ninety percent of the world's best runners of the last fifty years reached their plateau. If I could prove it, then the case for inherited ability, for nature rather than nurture, would be pretty solid.

Consider, for example, how Ron Clarke might run today if he could somehow be rejuvenated to the condition he was in at the time of his peak, around the mid 60s. Two scenarios are possible. Either he would rise to the occasion, by dint of more or better training, increased knowledge, better support, more time and sponsorship and greater motivation, and run considerably faster than he did at his best. Or he would reach the same sort of standard as he did in his day and turn what used to be phenomenal performances into merely good ones. The same would apply to any of the great runners of the past. Would a rejuvenated Roger Bannister run a lot further under four minutes for a mile today? Would Jim Peters be running marathons in single figures of minutes over two hours? Would Dave Bedford be running under 27 minutes for 10,000m, just as he ran under 28 minutes in his heyday? I suspect that, in most such cases, the answer is no, though exceptions would be those runners who clearly, for whatever reason, didn't train sufficiently. If we go back far enough in the history of distance running, of course, lack of training becomes the norm, so I'm not suggesting that before, say, 1950 the best runners in the world could not have been any better. But the nearer the present we get, the more likely it is to be the case.

I would argue, firstly, that if any of the past world beaters could have run faster, then they probably would have done. If your response to that is to point out that they didn't need to run any faster than they did in order to be the best, I would reply that they didn't need to run as fast as they did. Ron Clarke didn't need to knock thirty nine seconds off the 10,000m world record. Two or three seconds would have done. I don't believe for a moment that he didn't always run as hard and as fast as he could. He wasn't like the Russian pole vaulter Sergei Bubka who raised the world record a centimetre at a time in order to earn a good living from a succession of generous bonuses at different athletics events (an extremely shrewd, professional strategy, I should add). Besides, needing to run a certain time doesn't mean that you can do it. All my life I have needed to run much faster than I did in order to be the best. I just couldn't do it. And being born thirty, forty or fifty years later wouldn't have helped me one bit. Secondly, I would iterate that all the top runners of the past, in common with the Toms, Dicks and Harrys of the running community, if they had any length of a career, attained a plateau of performance that they were unable to raise when, subsequently, standards were raised by others.

The only argument I would accept concerning the artificiality of a runner's personal plateau, after lack of training, is the psychological one. At a time when world standards are poor compared to what is to come, it is difficult for any runner to accept the advances that are going to be made. Had someone told Christopher Chataway when he set a 5,000m world record of 13:56 in 1954, that fifty years later several athletes would be running a whole minute quicker he would have had trouble taking it in, let alone believing it. Had he known it to be true or actually seen it done, he might have run better times himself. To a degree we all do only that which we believe to be possible. But Chataway was a good example of a runner who probably could have trained a lot more than he did to good effect, and I don't think the same argument applies to more recent world beating runners or to any runners who have, in the light of what is known about distance running today, done everything by way of training and preparation that a man or woman could possibly do.

There is a tendency to see the latest phenomenon of the world running scene as the yardstick by which all others are to be judged. He or she has got to the top of the pile by doing something that the others haven't done or, if they have, by doing it differently or better. In the past this was quite likely to be true but not today. Dave Bedford probably became the best distance runner in Britain and the 10,000m world record holder during the 1970s because he covered more miles in training than almost anyone else had previously contemplated. Someone else might have been the best because they trained faster than everyone else or more often or with some novel approach. There are a number of ways in which runners can apply themselves differently to the job of becoming the best but we are gradually running out of these different ways to use as reasons for one person's supremacy.

By about the time that Lasse Viren became the top distance runner in the world in the mid 1970s, followed by Miruts Yifter, then Haile Gebrselassie and Kenenisa Bekele leading to the present day when a number of predominantly African runners could claim at any one time to be the best, the well of distinguishing causes had run dry. The superiority of one or more runners can never again be explained on the basis of any differences in what each one does, either in training or in any other aspect of daily life. There's nothing new. It's all been done by someone before. All that remains is inborn difference.

My mother ran the 800m for Manchester University in the 1920s. She once showed me the shorts she wore. They were Burgundy coloured and immense by comparison with what women wear today for running, more like a small tent than a pair of shorts. (I have never understood, incidentally, why men, when running, still need to cover their midriffs and the tops of their thighs, while women dress as if for the beach, wearing little more than a bikini. I think they look ridiculous. I am grateful to African women and Asian women, who retain their dignity with traditional vest and shorts and show that they don't have to flaunt their belly buttons and bum cheeks in order to win races). Both my brothers were quite good at running. The younger of them (but still older than me) trained for a while when he was at university and reached a reasonably high standard. The eldest of the three of us never trained at all to my knowledge, and made no progress in his running beyond being promising at school and running for his section while doing national service. I don't think my father was a distance runner, but he was a sportsman. He played football and cricket, and was generally athletically gifted.

The point I am making, if it isn't obvious, is that running ability, like any number of human characteristics, runs in families. It is, therefore, to my mind at any rate, clearly a genetic trait. Kenenisa Bekele, the outstanding distance runner of the early years of the twenty first century, has a brother, Tariku Bekele. Tariku is not just a good distance runner. He is world class. In the London Olympics he finished third in the 10,000m final. I don't believe that the degree of similarity shown by the Bekele brothers can be explained purely on background and upbringing. It has to be genetically determined.

The traditional and most convincing test of the relative contributions of inherited factors and background environment to any human aptitude is twin studies. It is known that identical twins share precisely the same genes, so any very obvious differences between them must be due to plasticity of development, usually as a result of different upbringings. Twins who have been separated at a very early age, for example by being adopted into different families soon after birth, provide perfect material for the scientific study of the genes versus environment debate. I think it is fair to say that the results of most such studies come down heavily on the side of genetic determination of most human characteristics and abilities. In some cases similarities between twins who have been brought up separately, often in complete ignorance of the other's existence, have been so extraordinary as to resemble stories from the twilight zone.

It so happens that, at the time I was running well, there were at least five pairs of identical twins who ran long distance at international level and who provide me with material for my own somewhat impromptu twin study. They were, in no particular order: Bob and Dave Holt of Hercules Wimbledon Athletic Club, both of whom I must have run against on many occasions; Grenville and Graham Tuck of Cambridge and Coleridge Athletic Club, both regular members of the English cross country team in the seventies; Paula and Ann Yeoman who became better known after marriage as Paula Fudge and Ann Ford, under which names they represented England and Great Britain on many occasions; Angela and Susan Tooby of Wales, who ran for Great Britain at the Seoul Olympic Games of 1988, Angela in the 10,000m and Susan in the marathon; finally, from Japan, the Soh twins, Shigeru and Takeshi, who regularly featured at the front of marathons during the seventies.

I made no proper study of any of these twins. My observations are confined to records of their performances in races. The thing that stands out for me, and convinces me that how good they were as runners was determined the moment they were conceived, is how similar their best performances were. It wasn't just that each one of the pairs was a good runner, but that their respective levels of attainment as runners were almost as alike as all the other features they shared. I know, of course, that since they grew up together and presumably often ran together and raced together, they shared a lot that was not inherited. But is it likely that the background they shared was exactly as similar as their performances? Did they do exactly the same training, eat exactly the same things, become ill or injured in tandem, live entirely parallel lives? I would find that hard to believe.

Consider, for example, the Soh twins, about whom I know least of all. Their marathon performances are uncannily similar. Both twins were prolific marathon runners, usually completing the distance in well under 2:20. In 1975 Takeshi ran 2:12:52 and two years later Shigeru managed 2:11:42. In 1978 Shigeru set his personal best time for the marathon, 2:09:06 and Takeshi ran his best, 2:08:55 in 1983, making them the worlds fastest ever pair of twins. Notice that Takeshi was a mere eleven seconds faster than his brother. But it was at Fukuoka in Japan in 1979 that their twin-ship was most accurately reflected in their performances. Shigeru finished second in that race in 2:10:37, precisely one second ahead of his brother Takeshi in third place. Had the marathon times for a pair of male twins been thirty minutes slower than that, it wouldn't have signified much, but for both Shigeru and Takeshi to have run so fast, within very little more than two minutes of the then world's best time, and to within one second of each other, is about as much evidence as one would need to prove the genetic origin of peak performance.

Women are no different. After running extremely successfully at cross country and on the road and track over medium length distances both Paula Fudge and her twin sister Ann Ford moved up to the marathon and achieved very similar personal bests, perhaps not to the same degree of correspondence as in the case of the Soh twins but to within not much more than half a percent of each other, 2:29:47 for Paula and 2:30:38 for Ann.

The Holt brothers provide me with most information about the performances of running twins because they ran in the same general area in the South of England as I did. I often ran in the same races. They were also, like the Soh twins prolific racers, and ran some race or other almost every week, on road, track or cross country. You may remember from Chapter 14 that Dave Holt was the one who unexpectedly made the British Olympic team for the 10,000m in 1972. I say unexpectedly for two reasons. One is that, of all the 10,000m hopefuls for the Olympic team that year, neither of the Holt brothers would have been on the list of favourites for a place; secondly, because Bob Holt was generally regarded as the slightly better runner of the two. In close run races it was more often than not Bob who came in ahead of his brother, but usually by no more than a few seconds. So often did the Holt brothers compete together in the same races that it became evident to everyone who had eyes to see that not only did they reach a performance plateau and travel along it together for a number of years, but that they both reached exactly the same height on their respective plateaus. In 1972 they each set a personal best for 10,000m, 28:39.8 for Bob and 28:41.8 for Dave. How much closer can you get?

Grenville and Graham Tuck were like the Holt twins in that one was usually slightly ahead of the other. It was Grenville who achieved more, but I don't think that means much as far as my reasoning is concerned. There are any number of reasons why one twin might be more successful than another. Training is one obvious one. I have never denied that training is not only important but absolutely essential to the full development of running talent. In fact I have tried to hammer home this very point time and time again. Other factors also affect the degree to which an individual approaches his or her potential. If anything is surprising about identical running twins it is not that one of a pair might achieve slightly more than the other but that there is often so little to choose between them. In the men's English National Cross Country Championship of 1973 Grenville Tuck finished eighth and Graham sixteenth. Anyone who is familiar with that particular event will know that there is very little distance between those two positions. They will also know that any place inside the top twenty in 'The National' during that era represented running of the highest order. In that same race Dave Holt finished thirty first and Bob Holt fortieth.

We now come to what most people would consider a sensitive issue, namely the matter of running and race (as in races of man rather than running races). Specifically I am talking about the reason or reasons that a few African racial groups have come to dominate the distance running scene. I don't consider it a sensitive issue at all. I consider it no more controversial to suggest, or in my case to state with conviction, that Kenyans and Ethiopians are better runners than white Europeans, than to say that Brendan Foster or Dave Bedford or Mo Farah, or any number of other star runners are or were better than I ever was. To me the two statements are equally neutral and equally obvious. To make it absolutely clear where I stand on this issue I'll lay it down as emphatically as I can:

The sole reason why the world of distance running today is dominated by East Africans is that they are genetically better endowed than other racial groups in the running department.

A statement like that must surely need to be backed up with evidence, especially as some would consider it verging on a prosecutable offence. I'm sorry I don't have any. I only have argument and circumstance, some of which I've already been through in different but related contexts. But to me the statement is as undeniable as that 'the emperor has no clothes'.

The puzzle to me is why, even now, so many people are in denial when it comes to racially related differences in running ability. The running magazines are full of articles titled, 'Train like the Kenyans', 'Eat like the Kenyans', 'Live like the Kenyans', 'How can we compete with the Kenyans?' and so on, the implication being that it may still be possible to be as good as they are, if only we were to do what they do. The issue of race as an explanation for superior running ability is usually absolutely the last possibility suggested in any discussion and then in an apologetic manner as if the very idea could only come from someone of highly suspect character. I'm still waiting for an article, 'Genetic engineering - the only way to beat the Kenyans'. Yes, I'm being facetious, but that might be my best weapon against what seems to be communal blindness within the world of athletics and athletic commentary. What's wrong with one racial group being better than others at something? It doesn't bother me. And denial of the facts certainly won't change anything.

Denial extends as far as racial denial itself. Sometime in the late twentieth century a movement grew up to counteract racism with scientific or, as it turned out, pseudo-scientific argument. It was a direct response to the recruitment of the modern science of genetics in support of racist theories. In particular, it was a reaction to the publication in 1994 of the book 'The Bell Curve,' by Richard Herrnstein and Charles Murray which, amongst other things, discussed the relationship between race and intelligence. Seeing the potential damage that might be done if the traditional racist position of white supremacy gathered even a whiff of scientific support, the left wing mobilised quickly. Of course, it over-reacted. It set out to show that race, as a genetic phenomenon didn't exist. Even as eminent a scientist as Steve Jones, professor of genetics, author and broadcaster (not to be confused with Steve Jones the British marathon record holder), a man whose authority can hardly be doubted, once wrote, *'If genetics shows us one thing it's that race is a social construct.'* Similarly he wrote, *'In the end really there is only one race, to which we all belong, the human race.'* These are lovely, saccharine sentiments and, if true, would do a lot to eliminate racial problems. They might also encourage runners to get training with a view to becoming as good as the Kenyans. Unfortunately, neither is true.

It so happens I'm a bit of a geneticist myself, having lectured on the subject for many years, and I can assure you that the biological concept of race is not only real, with a firm base in genetics, but it is also well able to explain why the East Africans have taken over the running world. Attempts to pretend, either that race itself is not real, or that racial differences are merely skin deep, are well intentioned, but are politically rather than scientifically motivated.

Thankfully, athletics, including middle and long distance running, is one sport where the ugly side of racial difference does not exist. In my view if we admit to the truth of race and accept that the races are different in a number of ways we make more progress towards racial harmony than if we continue to make out that differences don't exist and, bottom line, that separate human races themselves are a figment of our imagination.

One of the main arguments put forward by those who wish to deny the concept of race in order to pull the carpet from under the feet of anyone and any thing that might arouse racial disharmony (not a bad thing to do, but quite misguided) is that the genetic evidence shows more variation within different races than between different races. A lot of work, for example, has been done on human blood groups, showing that, though there is variation between individuals, there is no correlation between blood group variation and racial groups. So what? Separate races do not have to differ in every way, only in a tiny proportion of their shared genes. Could we conclude that there was no difference between the male and female sexes if we could show as much genetic variation within the genders as between them? I don't think so.

Mentioning the two different genders reminds me of another piece of evidence favouring the genetic basis of running talent. Would anyone argue that there is no truth in the statement that men are better runners than women? Does anyone really believe that if women trained as much and as hard as men (which some of them undoubtedly do anyway) they would reach the same levels? And what is the basis of the difference between the sexes? It is genetic. Gender is decided at conception, on the throw of a dice as to whether we inherit an X or a Y chromosome from our father and, once decided, it very rarely changes as we develop. We are not like some fish species which can change sex almost at will.

I must remember that I'm writing a book on running, not on genetics or racial matters, but I'll continue in this vein for a while longer because it is immensely relevant to the modern athletic scene. The whole world of distance running has to come to terms with the fact that certain African nations have risen to a totally dominant position in all distance running events and, as far as I can see, will remain in that place for as long as running remains a global sport. To be constantly looking for reasons for this other than the self evident is not really very helpful.

About this definition of race; Steve Jones, in a lecture on the subject, described the term race as indefinable. He used this assertion as a reason why race could not be studied scientifically. What he should have said is that the human races are impossible to delineate. They merge one into another. To say, as he implies, that there is no such thing as race is the same as saying that there is no such thing as the colour orange because it is impossible to say where orange turns to red on one side and to yellow on the other in a rainbow. Much the same argument applies to specific racial differences. If I say that East Africans are better distance runners than white Europeans, or, for that matter, that people of West African origin, who gave rise to the black populations of the USA and the West Indies, are better sprinters, I do not mean that every single one of them is better than every single European. I mean it as a generalisation. Being a generalisation doesn't make it false.

The scientific definition of a race is 'a human population with a shared gene pool, more or less genetically isolated (i.e. breeding within itself rather than freely with other populations) and showing some distinction between itself and other races'. That is my definition, but I think it would satisfy most students of evolutionary genetics. Within the subject of evolution the existence of races is absolutely crucial. Races are as it were, as Darwin himself recognised, an intermediate stage on the long road to new species. Without the process of evolution there would be no races and without the existence of races there would be no evolution.

Take the inhabitants of the area we now call Kenya, more specifically the Rift Valley region of Kenya, where most of the good Kenyan runners seem to come from. Before the advent of modern civilisation and the shrinkage and interconnection of the world through modern means of travel, it is very unlikely that there was much, if any, interbreeding between the population of the region and other outlying populations. In other words the local population was just one big family, made up of fathers and mothers, brothers and sisters, grandparents and grandchildren, uncles and aunts, cousins and second cousins and cousins once, twice, three and four times removed. Given some genetic differences between this population and neighbouring populations and what exists is a separate race or, at the very least, a separate race in the making.

The main cause of dispute regarding race is the mistake almost universally made of lumping people together into crudely amalgamated major groups that have no proper biological basis. So we have Black and White and Oriental, and maybe a few others: Australian Aboriginal, Polynesian and Native American, rather than a subtle mix of a large number of distinct races. Is it not obvious, for example, that the race to which most Kenyan runners belong is quite different from the race to which the Ethiopians belong? We cannot simply call them both black. That would not only be wholly inaccurate but would be insulting to both types. It would reflect the same obtuseness of thinking that allows President Barack Obama to be referred to as the first black president of the USA, when everyone knows that he is no more black than he is white, having a white European mother and, coincidentally in the context of this chapter, a native Kenyan father. I wonder whether, if every president of the USA up to Obama's presidency had been a true full-blooded African American, Obama would have been referred to as the first white president of America.

If the Kenyan and Ethiopian cross country teams walked together into a room, no one present would have much difficulty sorting them into their correct teams. Ethiopians, or at least those who appear regularly in running competitions, are several shades lighter than Kenyans. They are not quite so tall, nor quite so lean. Some of them are even a little bit chunky. Kenyan runners are uniformly stick-like. As representatives of two quite distinct races they are classic examples of racial difference. I don't see why that should be regarded as anything but a source of celebration. *Vive la différence!*

The nearest the issue of racialism came to spoiling the calm of the running world was when anti-apartheid activists targeted Zola Budd, the South African girl who was fast-tracked to British nationality in 1984, just in time for her to compete for Great Britain in the Los Angeles Olympics. Almost as soon as she entered Britain demonstrators hovered around her like wasps to a jam pot. In February 1985, she was forced out of the English National Cross Country Championship race, when anti-apartheid demonstrators rushed onto the course in front of the leading group of runners and in July of that year television coverage of an athletics meeting in Edinburgh was cancelled at the last minute on account of anti apartheid banners, allegedly put up by officials of the local municipal authority. During her mile win in the same meeting Budd again had to endure the sight of a demonstrator running onto the track to interfere with the race. It all became too much for her, and in 1988 she flew back to South Africa saying that the pressure from anti apartheid activists was pushing her towards a nervous breakdown. It was a shameful period in British athletics.

I had a soft spot for Zola Budd. I watched her win the World Cross Country Championships in Neuchatel, Switzerland. She ran through the mud in bare feet as if it was the most natural thing in the world (which I suppose it was). She was a totally innocent, if somewhat unworldly-wise young girl, who became unwittingly involved in matters that had nothing to do with running. Some extremists, by their reaction to her being given a British passport, made it seem that she, personally, was the architect of the South African policy of apartheid. It was especially sad because all she seemed to want to do was to run, a thing that she happened to be extremely good at. When I watched her at Neuchatel I saw nothing but a girl running, and winning, and seeming to enjoy herself. Was she British or South African, black or white? Frankly, I couldn't have cared less.

Before leaving the topic of race I have to remark on the irony surrounding the rise and Olympic triumph of Great Britain's own Mo Farah, winner of both the 5,000m and 10,000m gold medals at the 2012 Olympics. I often read, both before and after the Games, words to the effect that Farah was trying to show, was about to show or had shown that a European runner could compete on level terms with, and even beat the Africans. Never have race and nationality been so confused. Mo Farah is from Somalia. That makes him East African by origin and, therefore, of an East African race. Being British cannot change his genes.

The case of Mo Farah is doubly ironical when compared to that of Zola Budd. Zola Budd was British by descent; her grandfather was British. Mo Farah is British through residence and through his father's previous residence (his father moved to England as a young man and Mo moved to England as an eight year old). Neither Mo Farah nor Zola Budd is any more or less British than the other. Yet Farah's running for Britain is universally welcomed (quite rightly so) whereas Zola Budd was vilified by a large minority, both in this country and internationally and was never really accepted as a British runner. It's sad when within the sport of running the running itself becomes of virtually no importance compared to what, to my mind at least, are completely irrelevant issues.

The last thing I put forward as evidence for a genetic basis for running ability was the appearance every so often of what I called super-runners. I am thinking, for example, of Sammy Wanjiru, the Kenyan winner of the 2000 Sydney Olympic marathon. Wanjiru set a world's best time for the half marathon of 59:16 when he was still only eighteen. At the same age he set a world junior record for 10,000m of 26:41:75. When he was a year younger he ran 5,000m in 13:12. How do you explain such a prodigy? It can hardly be years of hard training. I stated earlier that I estimated that, starting from scratch an average runner needs something like three years of consistent training to reach his or her plateau. I still think that's about right. Ron Hill, as quoted in Chapter 7, puts the decline in standards in British distance running down to a lack of patience, adding that he had reached his peak in the marathon only after something like ten years of consistent training and racing. Of course Wanjiru must have trained hard and long, but it can't have been for many years. He was barely fully grown when he began setting world records. To me that points very clearly to a man who was born to break records and win gold medals rather than being predominantly the product of environment and upbringing. Sadly Sammy Wanjiru was killed in a fall in 2011 so we will never know if he had reached a peak or whether he might have gone on to even more amazing feats. He had said himself in 2008, *'In five years time I feel capable of clocking a sub 2 hour time for the marathon.'* I would have liked to have seen that.

So much for the genetic basis of running ability. What about nurture? Mo Farah, by a strange stroke of luck as far as this discussion is concerned, has a twin brother. When Mo came to Britain in 1991 his twin, Hassan, stayed in Somalia. Apparently, as children they were equals when it came to running. If anything Hassan had the edge. Since then Mo Farah has become, for 2012 at least, arguably the best runner in the world at distances up to 10,000m and, who knows, possibly beyond 10,000m as well. Hassan, meanwhile, has never taken to the sport with any serious intent. What a wonderful subject he would make for a twin study. At the age of just around thirty years he is certainly not too old to release his full potential as a runner, given a bit of training under his belt.

But isn't Hassan Farah, compared with his twin brother, perfect evidence for the crucial importance of environment, upbringing and, in the case of runners, specific training in producing the goods? Of course he is. Isn't he, therefore, the antidote to the determinist argument? Not at all. I have pointed out, many times by now, that training and a suitable upbringing are essential if a runner is to succeed. But these things are controllable. A person's genetic make up is fixed and unalterable. My conviction is that Hassan Farah could have been just as good a runner as Mo Farah had he been the one to have moved to Britain and had become as committed to running as his brother. When Piers Morgan wrote in the 'Mail Online' column for August 12th 2012, *'...if someone like Mo Farah can come over here, penniless and helpless, from war-torn Somalia as an eight year old boy and turn himself into the greatest athlete we've ever had, then so can they* (the British kids of today)', he was merely expressing the self-same equality principle that I tried to put to rest before. Once again it is false. But I would agree that had Hassan Farah been one of those kids, the statement would have been true for him.

I would love to know how fast Hassan Farrah, in his presumably average state of fitness, assuming he is well and uninjured, could run

10,000m. That might answer the question as to how much improvement proper training can bring about in a runner. When I was a teenager at school, doing very little training, I could run a mile in just under five minutes. At my very best, after a few years of what could be called proper, running-specific training I managed to reduce that time to about 4:20. That's an improvement of something like thirteen per cent. As the distance run increases, the contribution of training to performance also increases. I would guess, and that is all I'm doing, just guessing, that someone's time for 10K would be reduced by nearer twenty to thirty per cent by proper training, starting from average but untrained fitness. If I'm right then Hassan Farah, if he is at all active in his non running life but in an untrained state, should be able to cover 10,000m in well under forty minutes, which is quite a respectable time on the roads of Britain today.

But this is all extremely hypothetical conjecture. What remains is a very rough figure for the improvement that training can bring about. It's a large figure. My guess of up to thirty percent is by any standards a large one, but whatever the figure is, it must have a limit. What that means is that the end point for any runner depends on, and is limited by the starting point. I'm afraid that puts paid to the idea that if you do enough training you can beat the world. A good trained runner was always, at one time, a good untrained runner. I recognised that fact as a ten year old, which is why I was always keen enough to engage in the long and arduous process of working for that thirty percent or so improvement.

In my view training is about the only part of nurture that makes a significant difference to running performance. To read the running magazines you would begin to believe that the key to success lies in what you eat, or drink, or don't eat or drink, where you live, what you wear, how you breathe, how you plant your feet, when and how you sleep; anything other than plain, simple training, allied to natural ability.

When I was at my second university and starting to see myself as a full time runner with serious intent, I burnt a lot of calories. To replace them I ate what I would now consider huge amounts. For convenience, and to save myself the bother of cooking, washing up and keeping the kitchen clean in the house I shared with three other students, I usually ate my two main meals of the day in the university refectory. A typical days intake would be an average sized or light breakfast, maybe just some toast or a couple of eggs, then, for elevenses, a cup of coffee and a cheese or ham roll, a full two course meal of student catering proportions for lunch, a cup of tea and a scone or something similar at tea time and then my main meal of the day at about six o'clock after my daily run, another two or three course meal in traditional British meat and two veg. and pudding and custard style and, finally, some sort of supper, often a ploughman's lunch in the local pub with a couple of pints of beer. There may have been snacks as well in between meals. It was a lot of food, and the remarkable thing is that I never ate unless I was hungry. Nor did I ever put on weight.

The real point I'm making is that I didn't care what I ate as long as I enjoyed it and there was enough of it. To read about running and diet today is like studying for a university degree. It's yet another example of turning something that is essentially very simple into a matter of such complexity and debate that it can addle the brain.

There are only two things worth knowing about diet if you are a runner. The first is that in a modern, civilised and affluent country like ours you will never be short of any essential dietary requirements, provided you eat enough. Having said that I did hear rumours when I was at my first university about a student who tried to get by on a diet of nothing but fish and chips and ended up with scurvy but I suspect that was more a joke than a true story. You may, in this same affluent country of ours, as so many people do, eat more of some things than is good for you but you won't, at any time, be lacking in proteins, carbohydrates, vitamins, essential amino acids, fatty acids and minerals or anything else you may need for healthy living, unless you are extremely self-abusive in your eating habits. So my advice to any serious runner is to eat and drink away, being guided solely by appetite and what you feel like. It's what I and many others have done all our lives without our running suffering.

The second thing worth remembering is that there is no such thing as a super-food. It is true that some foods contain more per gram of a particular nutrient than other foods, but that doesn't make them special. You won't suffer by not eating them. More to the point there is no food on earth nor any combination of foods that can, by itself, improve anyone's performance as a runner. The secret of the sudden emergence of the Chinese women long distance runners, with Wang Junksia setting a world record for 10,000m in 1993, was said to be due to their consumption of turtle blood. At least part of the success of the present day Kenyan runners has been attributed to their native corn meal paste called ugali. All sorts of foodstuffs have been put forward as especially beneficial to runners: pasta, blueberries, beetroot, oily fish, oatmeal, kale or broccoli, coconut milk; the list is added to almost every day. But it is not worth remembering. All food contains something that is good for us. As long as we have sufficient of what we need an excess will not do us any more good. An apocryphal story, which may even be true, concerns a man who drank so much carrot juice for its vitamin A content and reputed health giving properties that he turned orange and died. Yet all around him people lived on with a perfect sufficiency of vitamin A. The finer study of diet is all, if not quite nonsense, then, at least, pretty much worthless baggage. As with training theory, dietary theory has expanded to the point of meaninglessness, simply to fill the space available and to give researchers something to do.

The one and only recipe for running success starts with the genes you were born with and comprises the training that you do, nature on the one hand plus the only form of nurture that makes any difference on the other.

CHAPTER 16
Ageing

'You don't see ninety year olds running for the bus.'

Diana Oxlade.

As a ten year old I don't remember ever getting stiff or tired; sleepy tired, of course, but not tired in the limbs and the muscles, like a car engine running on one cylinder. Now that I am well into my sixties and still running, I feel tired at different times in one or other of so many kinds of ways. Just as the Inuit have many words for snow, so runners need many words for tiredness. When I was ten I only needed one. Now I need at least a dozen. As Samuel Butler wrote, *'Life is one long process of getting tired.'* How right he was.

I ran well, and when I say well, I mean as well as I ever did, until I was just over forty. I have to qualify that. I ran as fast as I ever did until I was past my fortieth birthday, but not as easily. In the same way that an old and rickety ladder may reach as high as when it was new, but climbing it is more difficult, more uncomfortable, more uncertain, and distinctly more risky, I could run as effectively; that was all. If running well is judged solely by performance then there was nothing to choose between me as a forty year old and me at any previous age. But I knew there was a difference. I felt it in training and in races and, more than ever, I experienced it after training and racing. I learned new meanings for the word tired. I found new parts of my body that could feel the strain, and stiffen up, and ache, and, sometimes, give way altogether. During my second running peak, around 1976, I used to descend the stairs in the morning one at a time, placing my feet sideways and holding on to the banister. Good Lord, I was only thirty!

In 1987, my first full year as a veteran (over 40) runner, I was competing in a cross country race at Mallusk playing fields on the outskirts of Belfast and got talking to Jim Alder, the Scottish athlete who won the Commonwealth Games marathon at Kingston, Jamaica, in 1966. He is a few years older than me so I saw him as an expert on the subject of running into veteran years. He told me that I would begin to decline as a runner at 43 years old. He was quite specific, not 42 or 44 nor even about 43, but 43 to the year. The remarkable thing is that he was right. Of course I had to wait more than two years to find out, but when the time came I discovered I could no longer stay on my running plateau, however much I wanted to and however hard I tried.

I can almost date the time that I first noticed the start of my decline to the day. I was just 43. I had joined up with some of my club mates for a training run that was to include a number of faster efforts of about three or four minutes each. It was over a course I used regularly so I knew, or thought I knew, what to expect. I knew where the hills were and where it was likely to be especially tough running. I knew the points that three or four minutes hard running would bring me to. It was the sort of session I'd done countless times before. I knew, or thought I knew, that I was in good shape. I was running with people, most of whom I would have expected to beat in a race and none of whom were a whole lot better than me. In short, I felt in control. It was just another training session. I would run hard but not especially hard and I would always be ready for the next three or four minute effort. One thing I had always previously been good at was recovering quickly from hard running.

I think it was during the second effort that I realised something was wrong. I obviously hadn't recovered from the first one. I started to drop back from the group and having lost a few yards I started to lose ground even quicker. By the time the others had slowed to a jog and I had caught them up, having run hard for five minutes to their four, I barely had time to rest before they were off again. This time I let them go and completed the course by myself at a steady pace.

That was my last season as the runner I had been for the previous twenty years. I had managed to run a half marathon in 72:10 three days before my forty third birthday. The race was run over the same course on which I had set my personal best time for a half marathon, six years earlier, and six minutes quicker. The difference in the two performances should have told me that I was not just at the beginning of my decline but that my decline was already well underway. If I wanted to identify the real starting point I needed to look about a year earlier, when I was forty two. It must have originated then, though I hadn't really noticed a big change in my running until a year later. It's very easy to dismiss poor performances, increasing tiredness, loss of enthusiasm, decreasing energy levels, and so on, like symptoms of a serious illness, even if these things persist for long periods, as nothing more than 'going through a bad patch'. That's what I did for nearly a year. The last thing I wanted to admit was that it was a real and irreversible decline and that it was due to my age. I was in denial. If I accepted the truth, I would lose everything.

The training session I have just described, the one that forced me to face the realities of the ageing process, plus an increasing number of similar experiences, had a profound effect on me, reminiscent of the effect that my failure in the 1984 Belfast marathon had had. I went into mourning. I lost my motivation. In all my previous years up to the age of 43 I had responded to low points in my running in the certain knowledge that I could always bounce back as good as ever at some time in the near future. I had coped with periods of unfitness, dereliction of commitment, injuries, illness, bad performances and staleness by determining to train more and harder in the future and, always, it had worked. Once health and motivation returned, so did the performances. But this was different. For a start I simply wasn't able to train more or harder. I was already beyond my training limit. What my body was telling me, in a very loud voice, was that I had to train less, not more.

If I had been a sensible person I would have accepted that I had reached the turning point in my running life and made the necessary adjustments: less hard running, more rest days, a gradual moderation of all aspects of my training and, most difficult of all for me, an admission that from then on I was always going to perform slightly worse than before. But I couldn't do it. It would have been too much of a change of attitude, a total transformation of the code by which I had lived and run for the past twenty years. So I took the easier and much less admirable way out. I effectively gave up running seriously altogether.

My running diary, which had been continuous from some time in the late nineteen sixties, peters out on December 1st 1989 with the brief entry, *'short run, calf stiff, 3 or so,'* and doesn't resume until 14th August 1990. The entry for that day is highly informative, *'ran round Belvoir Park without stopping'.* In the space of a little over eight months I had been reduced to a state of unfitness in which it had become surprising to me that I could run for thirty minutes without stopping! I went on to write: *'not too unfit - much better than when I started back in June'.* So I had done some running between June and August but, presumably, none between December and June. I had had over six months off. That was the degree to which my failure to come to terms with what I saw as the loss of my serious running career had affected me. Looking back, I can see that it was one of the most significant times of my whole life; much more than a minor adjustment to changing circumstances. It was my response to the loss of a major part of what I lived for and what defined me. Although I had always known that my prime motivation as a serious runner was the quest for success and the ever-present dream of doing better than before, it took the loss of the dream to make the fact brutally clear to me. Without the prospect of ever being better, or even staying as good as I had been, there really seemed no point continuing as a competitive runner. I could see my three reasons for running seriously disappearing one by one. I was no longer so good at it and I could no longer achieve what I needed to. Potentially I still enjoyed it, but it was hard to hang on to even that one remaining reason after the loss of the other two.

The idea for veterans athletics or masters athletics as it's now universally called stems from the recognition of the very thing I went through as I started to lose my running ability and which I obviously shared with every runner before me. It was an attempt to address the innate unfairness of the process of getting older, and to return some motivation to competitive runners like myself who had realised that they would never be as good again. If we couldn't achieve what we were used to achieving in open competition we could at least compete on equal terms against people our own age. In this respect the veteran or masters running movement is the exact equivalent of the separation of men's and women's events. How could any woman runner have been in the least bit motivated to compete without that distinction between the sexes?

The idea itself for age class competition is at least eighty years old but the origin of formal masters competitions on a countrywide scale is credited to a lawyer from San Diego called David Pain who, with others, initiated the U.S. National Masters Athletics Championships in 1968. In 1975 the first World Masters Championships were held in Toronto. With remarkable perceptiveness the age at which a male athlete became a master athlete was first set at forty. And with further insight, ten year age groups were introduced for all events. A fifty year old cannot compete fairly with a forty year old, nor a sixty year old with a fifty year old, and a means had to be found for athletes, as they got older, still to be able to make a profit in a falling market. Age groupings became the running equivalent of 'shorting' on the stock market, giving athletes an incentive to compete even though they were deteriorating rapidly year by year. The span of each age group is now five years rather than ten, in recognition of the very obvious fact that a forty year old has a distinct advantage over a forty nine year old.

In Britain the Veterans Athletics Club, said to be the oldest of its kind, was founded in 1931. Since then and throughout my running lifetime veterans competitions have always been enthusiastically supported. The British Masters Athletics Federation, the umbrella organisation for all masters athletics competitions, currently (2013) has 7,000 active members. I would guess that more than half of them are distance runners, running being by far the most popular athletic discipline amongst competitors of all ages, and especially amongst older ones. As physical proficiency declines, the ability to progress on two legs is probably the last thing to go. When my wife said to me, when I complained about not being able to run like I used to, 'You don't see ninety year olds running for the bus', she might have added that an even rarer sight would be a ninety year old doing the pole vault.

There is absolutely no doubt that the establishment of age-class related competition has been a colossal stimulant to a very large number of runners of qualifying age. On June 24th 1986 I became a veteran runner. We were still called veterans at that time and the qualifying age was still forty rather than thirty five. The change to thirty five as the qualifying age for a male master runner was made in 2003 in order, I think, to bring it in line with the rule for women. It didn't make a lot of sense in the light of very clear evidence that thirty five year old distance runners were often still at their very best. Hadn't Carlos Lopes won the Olympic marathon in 1984, aged thirty seven? It would have been more sensible to have raised the qualifying age for women to forty.

Becoming a veteran was the start of a brief but extremely satisfying period in my career, during which I was competitively more successful than at any time previously. I became intensely motivated due to being elevated from having been a good runner in open competition to one of the best and often **the** best in veterans' races. It proved to me once again that achievement and approbation were what drove me on.

In a way I cheated the system. I was still running as well as I ever had. I shouldn't have needed a new and lesser class in which to compete. But then I hadn't made the rules, nor broken them. They were there to be taken advantage of, which is what I intended to do. Besides, my experience of being able to run as well as ever into my forties and a couple of years beyond is by no means unusual.

The history of distance running is full of examples of runners, both men and women, who achieved world class feats when in their late thirties and occasionally as forty and forty plus year olds. Carlos Lopes was just one of many. When Ian Thompson won the 1974

Commonwealth Games marathon in Christchurch, New Zealand, he was followed home in second place, by the forty one year old New Zealander Jack Foster. Foster ran 2:11:18.6 in that race which, at the time, was within less than three minutes of the world's best time; not bad for a man who had already, for over a year, earned the right to be called a veteran. Mamo Wolde of Ethiopia, who won the Olympic Games marathon in Mexico in 1968, went on four years later to win the bronze medal in Munich at the age of forty. The world's best time for a marathon by an over forty year old is now 2:08:46 by Andres Espinosa of Mexico, a truly élite performance for a man of any age. One is bound to wonder what sort of time he might have run when he was ten or fifteen years younger. My guess would be about 2:08:46.

I had two, nearly three glorious years as a veteran runner, reaping the combined benefits of being at the younger end of the forty to forty five year class, and of not yet slowing down appreciably. I won several first vet prizes, broke the Northern Ireland veterans' marathon record (2:25:58) in May 1987 and, on the basis of that performance, wangled an all expenses paid trip to the Boston marathon in April 1988. For that I had to thank the newly appointed Northern Ireland endurance coach who did all the negotiating without my so much as suggesting it in the first place. This was my introduction to the human trading of the road running market, the bargaining system that grew from small beginnings, such as here, putting together a half decent international veterans' representation in a prestigious marathon, to become the multi-million pound business that it is today. I may not have felt like it but I was one of the goods being traded. Because it was the Boston marathon, of course, the Irish connection raised my profile considerably; odd for an Englishman.

The outcome of that trip became another of the great disappointments of my running life. I shared a room with the Swedish veteran Kjell-Eric Stahl, who had already caught some sort of bug, which he passed on to me. He didn't even start the race the next day. I ran steadily until halfway, feeling a bit sluggish but keeping up a reasonably good pace nevertheless, but from then on I grew weaker and weaker. I stopped at about seventeen miles and was violently sick. I took the stragglers' and invalids' bus back home, half lying on the back seat, shivering and retching and feeling miserable. It was the consequence of the risky business of travelling and staying in strange places, sharing with strange people.

Also, about this time, I embarked on the veteran runners' gravy train, combining a trip to see my uncle and his family in Nova Scotia, Canada, with a couple of what I hoped would be money spinning races on the eastern seaboard of the USA. I had entered the Asbury Park 10K in New Jersey and the Falmouth road race in Massachusetts a week later. I was staying in a flat in New York and it was unbearably hot. When I arrived in Asbury Park I discovered that I wasn't the only just-turned 40 runner who had seen the money to be made from road racing in the USA (commonly at that time about $1,000 for the first vet.). I took one look at the opposition (I knew two of them well) and immediately deflated my hopes from hundreds of dollars to double figures of dollars, if I was lucky. If I hadn't beaten the best American vet in the field (Barry Brown), the man who had been picking up practically all the money in the previous months simply due to home advantage, I would have won nothing, but, by doing so and thus finishing fourth vet, I managed to leave with a hundred dollars in my pocket. My one and only deliberate attempt to turn running into a profession had not been very successful, even less so after handing twenty percent of my earnings, two ten dollar bills, to my agent. My calf muscles were so stiff after the Asbury Park race (maybe it was the humid heat or the endless walking around New York) and because I couldn't bear the thought of spending several more days on my own in the city, I never did go to Falmouth. I took an early flight to Montreal instead. I was wise to do so. The pain in my calf muscles didn't fully ease until two weeks later.

I was very aware as I passed forty years old that I would only have a very short time to take full advantage of my entry into the veterans' ranks. The best year in any age class is always going to be the first. So I ran a lot of races. Very soon after turning forty I came third in the 10K road race that was part of a gathering of veteran British Commonwealth athletes held in Edinburgh in July 1986. Perhaps that was the highlight of a very gratifying period. Above all I found a new and quite extraordinary enthusiasm for running.

But, of course it couldn't last. Although, as I have described, I very evidently started to go downhill at the age of forty three, the warning signs of my imminent and irreversible decline were there to be seen even before the rot actually set in, almost as soon as I turned forty. In my first season as a veteran runner, in November 1986, I travelled with my club mates to Gateshead for the annual cross country festival, held over the same ground, if not exactly the same course, as had been used for the 1983 World Cross Country Championships. I ran quite well, finishing third in a race won by the Welsh runner whom I had beaten in the New York WCCC and mention in Chapter 11 (who was also the winner of the 10K at the British Commonwealth veterans' event). I didn't notice that I was running especially hard during the race, only that there were some severe hills and that because the distance for veterans was only about three miles rather than the more usual five or six miles for cross country races I was always that little bit closer to my racing limit. Even so, when I finished I was unaware that I had had an especially fatiguing run.

We were spending two nights in a local motel and, being serious runners, the first thing we did the next morning was to put on our kit and head out for an easy training run or, as it might be called today, a recovery run. I kept up with the group for about four hundred yards, at which point I realised I was about as physically drained as it was possible to be. I jogged on for a mile or so, watching my companions disappear ahead of me, turned round and jogged even more slowly back to the motel. I realised that the term recovery run had become, for me at my age, a contradiction in terms of an almost frightening order. I thought back to similar days, ten or fifteen years before, when I had laughed at the very idea of needing to recover from hard efforts and had sometimes run a long brisk run less than twenty four hours after a big race. In Chapter 12, for example, I mentioned the long run that I did over the Yorkshire moors the day after the BUSF Cross Country Championships at Sheffield. I was exhilarated that morning, both mentally and physically, despite an all-out effort the previous day. That run bore as much resemblance to any form of recovery as it did to my attempts to do the same thing at Gateshead fifteen years later.

After Waldemar Cierpinski won the Olympic marathon for the first time in Montreal in 1976, that same night, as he relates, he couldn't sleep. What did he do? He got up and went for a run round the streets of Montreal to quench his excitement. At one time I could identify with that, but now, having turned the big four zero, I could no longer empathise to anything like the same degree.

The growing need for recovery and the power of hard efforts to exhaust the whole body to a level not previously experienced is, perhaps, the most significant first sign of ageing for a runner. And by recovery I don't mean some meaningless concept of running easily, with a view to calling it recovery running rather than training, I mean enforced, flat on the back or sitting in a chair type recovery, preferably with the eyes closed. The facts as far as I can see concerning recovery are that if you can run at all after a race or a hard training run, then you don't need to recover and, if you do need to recover, then you can't run at all.

Inevitably the need for more recovery time as you get older means that you can't do as much training. This becomes a very vicious circle leading ultimately, I suppose, to an end-point when the slightest exertion requires so much recovery that you never get to exert yourself again. I haven't reached that point yet but there are times when I get a glimpse of it poking around the corner. When I started a serious comeback at the age of 58, having run only very casually during the previous fifteen years, I thought that I would be able to do more or less the same training as at my peak. I wasn't stupid enough to suppose that I would run as fast but I saw no reason not to run as often or as far. I still aimed to work up to about seventy miles a week with a long run each week of about twenty miles. I vastly underestimated the debilitating effects that the sort of training I had envisaged would have on me, and the amount of recovery time I would need. Consequently I soon had to abandon the idea and adjust to a more realistic training régime.

I think it was after my experience at Gateshead that I invented the term 'whole body tiredness' to add to my list of variations on a theme. It was a feeling I had never fully experienced before but was to get very familiar with in years to come. The tiredness seemed to come from within and radiate outwards, so that the last place I felt it was where I would previously have expected to notice it first, that is, in the leg muscles. This new and slightly frightening sort of tiredness was, quite literally, in the heart of me. My heart kept on beating as normal, but very much more reluctantly. It was obviously crying out for a rest, but stuck to its task because it had to. At the same time it refused to beat any harder than absolutely necessary, and every part of me slowed down and suffered as a direct consequence. The tiredness permeated every nook and cranny of my body and my senses. It was an eerie feeling.

It was only hard, fast running that caused me this degree of bodily shutdown. I was still able in my later years to recover from running long distances in training, and even marathon races, very quickly. In May 1988, for example, I retained my vet's title for the Belfast marathon by finishing tenth in 2:29:00, just two weeks after my Boston marathon run (which proved to me that my retirement in the Boston race was caused by illness rather than by the run alone). Between the Boston run and the Belfast marathon I had a total of five days free of any running at all, but otherwise I trained normally, over ninety miles in eight days. In the week after the Belfast marathon I didn't have a single day off running, not even the very next day, and managed a total of sixty two miles on top of the twenty six miles of the race itself. Surely I was tired? Well, yes, but not unusually so and nothing like to the same extent, nor in the same way as the day after a three mile sprint over the country at Gateshead - a perfect example of my need for different words for two quite separate types of tiredness.

I don't regard stiffness as a symptom of age in a runner, nor the onset of minor aches and pains and overuse injuries. Undoubtedly these things become more commonplace as time goes by, but they happen to twenty year olds as well as to sixty year olds. Only children never get stiff, and, if they get injured at all, it is by means of an accident rather than through normal physical activity. The worst case of stiffness I have suffered was at the age of thirty, worse than anything I've ever experienced since. I was running a lot at the time and rarely got more than averagely stiff as a result of that, but I made the mistake of volunteering to play hockey for the college staff against the girls' team. The worst thing about muscular stiffness is that it is an after-effect. You cannot feel it coming on as the damage is done. Like drinking alcohol, the deed itself is painless, but the result can be agony. I was barely able to move the next day and, worse, the stiffness extended to every muscle in my body. Even now, past the pensionable age, I never get as stiff as I was after that hockey game.

Disregarding stiffness and minor injuries, therefore, the second noticeable sign of ageing for a runner, after the need for recovery, is the need for an ever-increasing length of time for warming up. I have always been amazed how all four of the dogs that I have owned, until they got very old, could move from deep sleep to hyperactivity with no apparent transitional state. One moment they are flat on their backs, legs in the air, eyes tightly closed or half open but showing only the white part, their only movement a slight quivering of the cheeks; the next they are standing up, fully alert and, more than likely, seconds later, in hot pursuit of whatever has woken them. I was once like that. I could move straight into running, without a warm up and without a pause for my body to adapt to a change in tempo. Then slowly, over the years, I began to need longer and longer periods for getting used to the move from inactivity to full exertion.

For a while, when I was in my late thirties, I trained once a week with a friend who was at least ten years younger than me. He would come to my house in the evening and we would do about ten miles together. The problem for me was that I needed a long and gradual warm up and he didn't. Moreover he was primarily a 1,500m and 3,000m runner and, therefore, much quicker than me. As soon as we left the house he took off down the road at a pace I could barely keep up with and the first mile or so of those training runs became so difficult for me I was quite glad when the arrangement came to an end.

Twenty five years later I was experiencing exactly the same phenomenon but without the need for the presence of a faster and younger training partner to have to keep up with. I would leave the house by myself and, however slowly I ran, after no more than half a mile, I would feel that if I didn't stop by choice I would be forced to do so through necessity. Often I did stop, or slow to a walk, knowing that the feeling of complete unfitness was only temporary and that if I kept going, as slowly as necessary, for another ten minutes or so I would start to run more easily. I learned this after a period of time during which the drastic effects of those initial two or three minutes of running on my unprepared body came as an unpleasant shock. I couldn't believe I could be so unfit. Not since my school days had such a small amount of running had such a ghastly effect on me.

If I eventually give up running all together it will be for one of a number of reasons. One would be that I need so long to warm up that I don't have any time left for the run itself. You can't enjoy running until you are properly warmed up. Even now when I go for a forty minute run I get only perhaps ten minutes pleasure from it. Soon I won't be able to run for as long as forty minutes and, even if I still can, it will be the pleasurable part that is reduced, not the warm up. One day there'll be no pleasure left at all.

The most obvious sign of getting older, the measurable slowing down, is in many ways the oddest of all. Why, when I ran a marathon at the age of 63, did I run consistently at a pace that was over two minutes per mile slower than it would have been in my prime? Often in the last few years, both in training and in the very few races I still enter, I have run, at least for short periods, in a way that seems no different to what I remember with a disquieting fondness: the same rhythm, the same lack of effort, the same ease of movement, the same enjoyment; only the watch says there is a difference.

One Wednesday evening in the summer of 2010 I was running along the River Lagan towpath with a group of my younger training companions at what seemed to me to be a brisk, steady pace. I had already run two miles to join the group and we were a mile into our shared training session, so I was nicely warmed up. So easily was I running and so free and mobile did I feel that, for a moment, I drifted into a previous time. I was still in my twenties or thirties. I was in peak condition. I was running at six minutes per mile pace and I was going to keep it going for another seven or eight miles. I would return home refreshed and with energy remaining. My dream lasted a few seconds, but was no less real for that. When I came to I still felt wonderful. I asked a friend running alongside me how fast we were running, knowing that he was equipped with the watch that sees everything. 'The last mile was just under eight minutes', he said. I wished I hadn't asked. I can only infer that I now run with a shorter stride length. It is the only explanation. Perhaps it's time to throw away the measuring stick and the clock, and forget competition, and look only for the feeling that makes running, at any age, and at any speed, worthwhile.

If I had any doubt at all about the extent to which my running prowess had faded away since the start of my decline, it was wholly dispelled by reality in one brief moment on 13th March 2011. That was the day I ran my last twenty mile road race. I had quite a good day really. I finished in 2:36:52 and only started to feel my age on the last of the four laps. With no more than two miles to go I clipped a raised paving slab with my toe because my feet were hardly leaving the ground at that stage and went flying onto my hands and knees in an undignified sprawl. But it wasn't the episode that brought me face to face with the full revelation of my aged state. That happened a mile earlier; it was when I was lapped by the eventual winner. Had I sat down before the race and calculated my likely finishing time, and compared it with the likely winning time, I would have seen that, for certain, I was going to be lapped. Still it came as a shock. It was just something I had never contemplated. And when it happened it was so emphatic. Suddenly he was there and then he was gone. It was as if I was on a bicycle and he was in a fast car.

The fact that, at this point of the course, this apparent paragon of modern day road running had run seventeen miles to my twelve, and had five miles less still to complete, could not have made me feel any more inferior. What it didn't show immediately and unequivocally, however, was the extent of my decline. I had to work that out later. It turned out that the winner, when he subsequently crossed the finish line, recorded a time that was no faster than I once ran for the same course. In fact it was nearly a minute slower. That was the real revelation. It was as if the man who lapped me was my younger self, caught in some time warp, brought back to the same place and time for the sole purpose of wrenching me back to the real world. Never again would I have any illusions about my present running ability. Instead I would just have questions to wonder about. Did I really run like that, years ago? Did I once seem, to some old man of the past, just as superior? Had my decline been quite so great? What had happened to me in the space of thirty years, and how and why? These were all very bitter-sweet conundrums.

It took me the twenty years between the age at which I started to deteriorate as a competitive runner and the middle of my sixties to be able to ask questions like that. It took me almost that length of time to come to terms with the psychology of decline and to resume running as a day to day habit, which I did approaching my sixtieth birthday. Two years later I was running as much as I ever did, in terms of time, if not distance. Still I couldn't fully escape the clutches of competitive instinct. My whole purpose in returning to proper training was to see how well I could run in a new veteran 60 - 65 age group. Call it curiosity if you will, but it was also my indefatigable quest for running success. I believed I could be a good sixty year old. That's really what drove me on. If the training I did also saw me recapture the joy of running easily, that was a bonus. But the main purpose of my running was the same as it ever was.

All serious runners with a successful running career behind them and nothing but inevitable age-related decline to look forward to must go through the same process of adjustment as I did. Each of them tackles the change in his or her own way but I imagine that there are shared emotions, shared questions, shared rationalisations, shared indecision, and throughout it all, continual oscillation between wanting running to continue as before (with a heavy sustaining dose of wishful thinking) and wanting to throw in the towel and never think of running again.

Some runners, usually those who have been highly successful, pre-empt the critical time and retire from competition prematurely. Herb Elliott, for example, won the Olympic 1500m in 1960 at the age of 22, went to Cambridge University and, later the same year, finished second equal alongside Mike Turner and behind the winner, Tim Briault, in the varsity cross country race. To my knowledge, he never competed seriously again. Sebastian Coe also won the Olympic 1,500m, in his case twice, and retired well before his thirty fifth birthday. Countless other runners, many of note, others of a whole range of standards, have chosen to give up running seriously long before they have reached the point of physical decline. I could never have done that. But then I never won an Olympic medal.

At the other extreme I know many runners who have ridden over the high point of their careers and onto the downward slope as if it were all level ground. I am thinking in particular of two runners whom I met when I moved to Northern Ireland. I ran against them and trained with them over many years, until I became the first to break the link by taking my running much less seriously in about 1990. They stand out because they are both good friends of mine and were only ever that little bit better than I was, so that in any race we ran I was never sure whether I would beat them or they would beat me. Neither of them paused for thought as their decline with age started. They became two of the best forty year olds in the UK, forty five year olds, fifty year olds and fifty five year olds. I am sure that, if it is physically possible, they will continue their progress still further through the veteran ranks. What they shared and I didn't was a commitment to the running habit that was independent of absolute performance. Unlike me they seemed to be equally well motivated through their time of declining performance levels as through their earlier days of improving or sustainable standards.

The veteran's running scene is populated by such people. They breeze through the age groups regardless of waning performance. They become the stars of their generation through longevity rather than original brilliance. It is a strange anomaly that very few of the best veteran runners, now or at any time in the past, in this country or in any other, have been the best runners when at their peak. The further up the age groupings you go the truer this becomes. For a while I was arguably the best over forty year old runner in Northern Ireland, and one of the best in Britain. That could only be explained on the basis of default by the majority of the better runners of previous years. You can't go from being at the bottom of the top one hundred to somewhere in the top ten without a lot of other runners retiring. My time at the top of the veteran's ranks, however, was very short. I became yet another one to give up. When I tried years later to become the best sixty year old and then the best sixty five year old, I failed comprehensively.

That, I discovered, is one of the most depressing things about running and the ageing process. Different runners decline at different rates. In my first year as a sixty year old, and again in my first year as a sixty five year old, I ran one or two cross country races. I was soundly beaten by runners whom I used to beat easily thirty years previously. Clearly my decline had been more rapid than theirs. It was something I found hard to understand and hard to accept.

Forty is not old but, I think, sixty is. What was it like as I embarked on a running comeback as an old man? I started my comeback thinking that if I wanted to be a good 60 year old it might not be a bad idea first to be a good 59 year old. So I spent a year building up my training gradually, starting from a very low base of nothing other than my natural reserves of fitness, not expecting rapid progress and without trying to be too ambitious. I hoped that a year of progressive training, mostly in the form of steady running, would bring me to a degree of fitness that would enable me to cope with what I thought of as 'proper training'. I might even consider a race or two.

To a degree the plan worked. In the six months before my fifty ninth birthday I ran conservatively but consistently, averaging twenty three miles per week, with my longest run at just under nine miles. And I did gradually improve. But I didn't do it easily. On Wednesday 12th January 2005, for example, as I recorded in my diary, I ran the same six mile block that twenty years previously, whenever I wanted an easy run, I used to cover in around 36 minutes. It took me 46 minutes and I commented *'Very hard going; couldn't run easily. I seem to have lost the bounce in my legs.'* Three weeks later, having just run my longest run of the period, I noted, *'It's still hard. Afterwards I felt relaxed but tired. My only problem is my right knee, which is stiff and weak.'* I was discovering more of the irreversible signs of ageing.

My knees gave me a lot of trouble during my return to what I called serious running. It is said that any runner who doesn't, at some time or another, experience problems with the knees, never really trained enough. I don't like to think of the force that is transmitted through the knee at every running stride. It is a force that manifests itself first as a colossal shock when the foot hits the ground and the whole weight of the body plus its forward momentum rams into the knee joint. Only the muscles pulling on the tendons and the ligaments that hold the bones together stop the knee buckling as if it belonged to a puppet with no strings. Then, milliseconds later, the force is reversed as the muscles pull the knee tight and straight, ready to absorb the impulse that propels the body off the ground. It is like the action of a piston in the cylinder of a car engine, the knee being the equivalent of the small end, the joint that joins the piston to the connecting rod. Sometimes, when I am driving at speed, with the rev-counter telling me the engine is doing 4,000 revs per minute I get frightened for those small ends and wonder how they can possibly survive. It is the same with the knees. How can you run mile upon mile at a good pace without the knees giving way?

The sad truth is that they often do give way, not catastrophically so, but with minor indications of weakness, a slight niggling but sharp pain, sometimes just above the knee cap but, more often, just below it, or an ache in the cable-like tendons that run at the back and either side of the knee joint, or, as I recorded in my diary, stiffness and a vague feeling that the knee is not responding quite as easily and as quickly as it should. A second sad truth is that these numerous manifestations of degeneration of the knees occur far more commonly with increasing age.

The same could be said of most running injuries. One of the main reasons that my comeback to serious training was much slower than I had intended was a series of injuries. Some of them were typical runner's overuse injuries: the knees, the lower back, the feet, the ankles. Others were the results of accidents. I dropped a sheet of thick plywood onto my big toe. Weeks later the toenail came off; I found it in my sock. Then I fell backwards in my front room and cracked my back so hard I couldn't move. When I had recovered from that injury I jumped off a step ladder onto a tiled floor and bruised my heel; it still hurts now, well over a year later. Next I slipped on a wet grassy slope and bent my trailing leg underneath my body to the point that I thought it was going to snap. All these things interfered with my running. In some cases I couldn't run at all for days on end. Although none of them were things that couldn't have happened to a twenty year old my greater age not only made me more accident prone but, and this is the worst part of ageing and injuries, injuries are much slower to mend. Even bruises and scratches take weeks rather than days to clear when you are older. It's a double whammy for the aged runner; injuries are more likely in the first place and more persistent when you get them. At times, when I was running as a sixty year old, I wondered whether it was worth it. No sooner had I made some progress, it seemed, than along came yet another painful reason for my not being able to run. And, if I worried unnecessarily about days off when I was thirty, now I worried even more, quite justifiably this time, about days off at twice that age.

The mid nineteen eighties saw the beginning of an aberration in the results of distance races that seems to have lasted right up to the present. It was the consequence of two factors. One was the deterioration in standards in distance running in general in this country. The other was the graduation into the veterans' ranks of the baby boomers who had become serious runners; those such as myself, born in the period immediately following the second world war, who populated the glory days of British distance running. The aberration in question was that older runners proceeded to dominate practically all distance races. I learned recently, for example, that every one of the six scorers in my own club's winning team in the Northern Ireland cross country championship that year was a master runner. Admittedly the term master now includes runners who are over thirty five as well as those over forty but, nevertheless, it is a measure of the loss of quality amongst runners who, according to their young age, should be at some sort of peak. A far more revealing statistic comes from the last big race that I watched, the 2013 Belfast marathon. Of the top fifty male finishers, very nearly half, twenty four to be precise, were over forty.

In the early seventies, any veteran runner who featured at the top of the field in any distance race was considered a bit of a phenomenon. There were very few such people and everyone knew them simply because they were rare and atypical. I felt ashamed if I was beaten by them, which I occasionally was. I would have felt worse if I had regularly been beaten by lots of veterans as so many young runners are today. By the time I became a veteran myself, fifteen years later, I became like those exceptional older runners of my early competitive days but without quite the same rarity value. I was in the leading part of the tidal wave of good older runners, the demographic bulge, twenty years long, that swept through the running population and is only just losing its momentum now.

Ageing is not a pleasant experience for anyone, least of all a sportsperson, to whom, after all, physical performance is of vital importance. The ageing process will ultimately destroy anyone's running ability but, in my experience, it doesn't seem to be able to dampen the runner's spirit. Some very old people still run or, if they simply cannot do so, I am quite sure they dream of running. The shared ethos of runners of my generation and those close to it became so ingrained that no change in circumstance could shift it. Once a runner always a runner. I don't see quite the same character in the body of runners today. I would go so far as to say that it is largely the lack of such spirit that has changed the overall complexion of the sport of distance running in this country for ever.

POSTSCRIPT
What now?

In the introduction I claimed that my running career had mirrored that of British distance running as a whole. If it is to continue to do so then there is no future for the sport of distance running in this country. Will it come to that? For me there is no hope. But could the sport of distance running in Britain ever return to the days when there was a continuum of talent, from the average club runner to the true élite, all mucking in together, in training and in races, all prepared to commit fully to the pursuit of improvement, when the best in Britain were among the best in the world, when the media paid due respect to the sport and those who made it what it was and when it wasn't necessary to import runners for races on domestic roads, nor to look to other parts of the world for interest and excellence? My view is that the sport has already been forced too far down the sensationalist road to popular appeal for the process to be reversed. But there might still be a chance for an independent national revival. The key would be to give back to the British runners of today the same incentives and respect that constituted the driving force behind my generation. It is a disgrace, for example, that there are no national road running championships, other than relays, that are independent of any other event. There has to be, at the very least, an annual national marathon championship that is not integrated into a big city affair. It would be for serious runners only. It could be used as the main trial race for international representation. There would be no invited runners, no appearance money, no expenses paid, no money prizes, no pacemakers, no women in the men's version and no men in the women's, no association with charities, no wheelchairs, no novelty runners: in short just a plain old fashioned marathon race. It would not need to compete for attention with anything else, and the entrants would be running only for those simple rewards that motivated runners in the past. They were sufficient then and should be sufficient now. All it would take would be to resurrect them.